WORKERS AT RISK

WORKERS AT RISK

The Failed Promise of the Occupational Safety and Health Administration

Thomas O. McGarity
& Sidney A. Shapiro

Westport, Connecticut
London

Library of Congress Cataloging-in-Publication Data

McGarity, Thomas O.
    Workers at risk : the failed promise of the Occupational Safety
and Health Administration / Thomas O. McGarity and Sidney A.
Shapiro.
        p.   cm.
    Includes bibliographical references and index.
    ISBN 0–275–94281–3 (alk. paper)
    1. United States. Occupational Safety and Health Administration.
2. Industrial hygiene—United States.   3. Industrial safety—United
States.   I. Shapiro, Sidney A., 1947– .   II. Title.
HD7654.M39   1993
363.11′7′0973—dc20   92–1753

British Library Cataloguing in Publication Data is available.

Library of Congress Catalog Card Number: 92–1753
ISBN: 0–275–94281–3

First published in 1993

Praeger Publishers, 88 Post Road West, Westport, Connecticut 06881
An imprint of Greenwood Publishing Group, Inc.

Printed in the United States of America

(∞)™

The paper used in this book complies with the Permanent
Paper Standard issued by the National Information Standards
Organization (Z39.48—1984).

10 9 8 7 6 5 4 3 2 1

Contents

Preface

In 1986, the authors were asked by the Administrative Conference of the United States (ACUS) to evaluate rulemaking at the Occupational Safety and Health Administration (OSHA) and make recommendations for improving that process. We soon realized that, by almost any measure, OSHA had failed to fulfill its mandate to protect American workers. Thousands of men and woman are victims of preventable workplace accidents and occupational disease. We resolved that it was imperative to find the reasons for OSHA's failure.

The goal of this book is to analyze why OSHA has failed, and to suggest what can be done to set it back on track. Our plan of attack is twofold. The first two parts of the book present an evaluation of the current status of the protection of workers and a history of OSHA regulation. Based on the prior analysis, the next two parts analyze how the protection of workers can best be improved without changing OSHA's basic mandate.

We draw three general conclusions from the first two parts. First, as noted, workplaces are still dangerous for many workers. Prior to working for ACUS, we were largely unaware that workers are in such peril, and we believe that our ignorance is not uncommon. The reason may be that a declining number of Americans are employed in blue-collar occupations, where most dangerous work occurs. In the case of workplace accidents and occupational disease, out of sight is out of mind. We strongly believe that the American public supports OSHA's basic mandate to provide safe and healthful workplaces for all workers. Yet, without general public awareness of the current plight of workers in America, labor unions and worker advocates are little more than voices crying in the wilderness.

Second, much of the progress that OSHA made during its first decade was dissipated during the first five years of the Reagan administration. The president's appointment of administrators who were extremely hostile to the agency's mission during this period rendered OSHA impotent. Yet, unlike the deregulatory failures underlying the EPA scandals and the savings and loan debacle, OSHA's equally catastrophic attempts to deregulate worker safety and health have attracted comparatively little public attention.

Third, even when under the leadership of professionals committed to occupational safety and health, OSHA has not risen to its potential. The public policy literature long ago came to the conclusion that government agencies face almost insurmountable obstacles to implementing their programs. OSHA's story does not refute that conclusion. Indeed, OSHA operates in a more complex bureaucratic, political, and legal thicket than most other health and safety agencies. We reject the suggestion of some political economists that the solution is for OSHA to lower its sights and promulgate "lite" rules that effect very little change in employer and employee behavior. We recognize, however, that OSHA is unlikely to accomplish significant change if it cannot find ways around the roadblocks that currently stand in the way of effective standard-setting.

This diagnosis of OSHA's problems leads us to two additional general conclusions. First, the implementation of the "patch and repair" solutions discussed in parts III and IV can help OSHA surmount some of the difficult roadblocks it faces. Second, "patch and repair" solutions will still fall short of protecting workers adequately. Although ways can be found around some of the roadblocks OSHA faces, they are too numerous and difficult to be avoided entirely under the current statutory regime. To achieve genuine progress toward worker health and safety, it is necessary to examine new solutions to the perennial problems. In parts V and VI, we consider some possibilities. What these solutions have in common is that they give workers more power to protect themselves. Worker empowerment is crucial, because if OSHA's history proves anything, it establishes that there are finite limits to the agency's capacity, operating alone, to protect workers.

Our research has led us to one more general conclusion. The country has failed to make the same commitment to protecting workers that we have made to protecting the environment. When EPA has faced similar roadblocks to effective rulemaking, Congress has acted to remove them. It has also established higher penalties for violating the EPA's regulations than employers face for violating OSHA's rules. No doubt these differences reflect the greater political support for environmental protection than worker protection. After all, the environment affects all of us. But these differences cannot be defended as a matter either of public policy or of common decency. The workers who build our homes, provide our food, assemble our appliances, nurse our illnesses, and dig our graves are part of our shared environment and are deserving of protection.

In closing, we would like to note that this book would not have been possible without support from several sources. Professor McGarity thanks the University of Texas School of Law. Professor Shapiro thanks the University of Kansas School of Law, the University of Kansas General Research Fund, and the University of North Carolina School of Law. We both thank the Administrative Conference of the United States for setting us out on our journey; the research assistants, too numerous to mention, for digging through thousands of pages of congressional hearings and *Federal Register* notices for the critical historical facts; and Krissi Wielunski-Bell, who had to adapt to the nomenclature of two authors as she worked her way through too many drafts of the manuscript. Finally, we are, as always, deeply appreciative of the support and forbearance of Cathy and Joyce, whose patience through the last six years bespeaks their commitment to worker health and safety.

Part I

OSHA'S FAILED PROMISE

1

The Plight of America's Workers

I begin to work in the carding room soon after, and the fluff got into my lungs and poisoned me. . . . Little bits, as fly off fro' the cotton when they are carding it, and fill the air till it looks all fine white dust. They say it winds round the lungs, and tightens them up. Anyhow, there's many a one as works in a carding room, that falls into a wate, coughing and spitting blood, because they're just poisoned by the fluff. . . . Some folk have a great wheel at one end o' their carding rooms to make a draught, and carry off the dust; but that wheel costs a deal of money . . . and bring in no profit, so its but a few of the master as will put 'em up.[1]

This inarticulate description of an early-nineteenth-century workplace provided by Bessy Higgens, a character in the 1854 novel *North and South*, portrays the plight of workers in an unregulated industrial economy more starkly than any modern academic treatise. Popular culture and current economic theory both recognize that employers will not protect the safety and health of their employees without the spur of governmental regulation. When injured or ill workers can easily be replaced, safety precautions are not in an employer's self-interest because, as Bessy observed, precautions cost money and "bring in no profit."

In a world where workers cannot sue employers to recover compensation for work-related injuries and where no regulatory agency exists to order employers to protect their workers, the industrial workplace can become a killing ground. During the early twentieth century, a period in which the United States economy closely approximated a laissez-faire labor market, working conditions were appalling by any civilized measure. In 1913, there were approximately 25,000 industrial fatalities and 700,000 injuries involving a disability of more than four weeks among the 38 million employed men and women. Between 1907 and 1912, industrial accidents caused nearly one out of every ten deaths among male Americans. Occupational fatalities accounted for an even higher percentage of all male deaths among miners (23 percent), powder makers (72 percent), and electrical linemen (49 percent).[2]

The modern industrial workplace, while not as hazardous as at the turn of the century, is still very dangerous. Although statistics on workplace injuries and fatalities are appallingly poor, estimates of annual work-related fatalities range from 4,650 to 12,000 persons, or 13 to 50 occupational deaths each working day.[3] Viewed from a slightly different perspective, more than twice as many Americans died between 1964 and 1975 from work-related causes (123,600) as were killed in the entire Vietnam conflict (58,000).[4] Estimates of nonfatal injuries range from 2 million to 11 million, which, assuming a total of only 2.5 million injuries, translates into about 10,000 serious injuries each working day.[5] At this rate, about one worker in nine employed in the private sector experiences an occupational injury each year.[6] Moreover, as explained below, these estimates may seriously understate the actual occurrence of illness and injury.

The economic consequences for the country of this toll are staggering. Two prominent economists estimate that the value of each life lost in a workplace accident is between $5.4 million and $6.8 million, which means that 7,000 annual fatalities cost society between $37.8 and $47.6 billion dollars each year.[7] A study sponsored by the Rand Institute estimated that workplace accidents cost society $83 billion each year.[8] And the National Safe Workplace Institute estimates that when both accidents and diseases are taken into account, the annual cost to the economy exceeds $200 billion each year.[9] Even assuming dramatic improvements in workplace safety and health, the costs of past practices will extend far into the future. A 1983 study predicted that between 1979 and 2027 the costs (exclusive of medical care) associated with asbestos-related illnesses alone will exceed $300 billion.[10]

The human consequences are, of course, incalculable. Thousands of American families have suffered the devastating personal loss of a working family member. Because many of the workers who are killed on the job are young (46 percent of all occupational fatalities occur in workers under 35 years of age),[11] the tragedies often deprive young children of a parent.

American workplaces are far more dangerous than those in many other countries. The International Labour Office found that the United States had the worst safety record for construction fatalities among the seven nations that were studied. Based on the international data, Table 1–1 indicates that between 2,000 and 7,000 lives would be saved annually if the United States had the same occupational fatality rate as other industrialized countries. For example, while fatalities involving scaffolding accidents are quite common in the United States, they are comparatively infrequent occurrences in the rest of the industrialized world. Japan did not have a single scaffold-related death from 1977 to 1987. During the same 10-year period, about 2,200 Americans died in scaffold-related accidents.[12]

The dangerous nature of the modern American workplace is not due to a lack of regulatory programs. Every state has workers' compensation laws that provide

Table 1–1
Lives Saved if the United States Had Foreign Fatality Rates, 1986

Country	Fatality Rate[1]	Percentage of U.S. Rate	Comparative Lives Lost[2]
United States	.105	100.0	10,700
France	.074	70.4	7,541
West Germany	.080	76.2	8,152
Greece[3]	.053	50.4	5,401
United Kingdom	.034	32.4	3,465
Sweden	.018	17.1	1,834
Japan	.030	28.5	3,050

Notes:
1. Per 1 million man-hours worked.
2. Number of lives lost if the United States would have had the same job fatality rate as the country compared.
3. For 1984.
Source: National Safe Workplace Institute, *Unmet Needs: Making American Work Safe for the 1990s* (Chicago: The Institute, 1989), 6.

some compensation to employees on a no-fault basis if they are injured or become ill because of work. The federal Occupational Safety and Health Administration (OSHA) has promulgated hundreds of regulations requiring employers to maintain safe and healthful workplaces. Yet, the statistics still reveal that workers remain at substantial risk. In a decade in which the efficacy of governmental regulation has become an increasingly important social issue, it is appropriate to ask whether OSHA has achieved the degree of workplace health and safety that a modern industrial society is capable of providing.

MEASURING THE EFFICACY OF REGULATION

Obtaining an accurate measurement of the efficacy of existing regulatory programs is no easy task. Reliable statistics on the incidence and trends of industrial accidents and illnesses are difficult to find. Nevertheless, it is evident that existing statistics likely understate the extent of work-related injuries and illnesses and that if the incidence of workplace injuries and illnesses is declining, it is doing so at a very slow rate.

The most authoritative sources of statistical information about work-related injuries are the annual surveys of injuries and illnesses compiled by the Bureau of Labor Statistics (BLS), a federal agency located in the Department of Labor. BLS obtains its data by surveying 280,000 representative workplaces, each of which is required to keep a log of all injuries and deaths. The BLS survey, however, excludes independent mining contractors and a large number of farms, construction companies, and other high-hazard employers. BLS data are further compromised by the agency's dependence on voluntary compliance. Employers have an incentive not to report, because they recognize that OSHA uses BLS data to determine inspection priorities and that some insurance companies use the data to set their workers' compensation rates.[13] A 1988 Congressional Office of Technology Assessment (OTA) review of record-keeping accuracy found "possibly significant injury and illness underreporting and subsequent underreporting to the BLS."[14] A 1987 study by the National Research Council of the National Academy of Sciences (NAS) found that employers may be failing to report as many as 30 to 45 percent of worker fatalities. Moreover, because identifying work-related deaths is more clear-cut than attributing nonfatal injuries to the workplace, some authors of the NAS study concluded that nonfatal injuries may be even more seriously underreported than fatalities. The panel concluded, however, that although underreporting unquestionably exists, its exact magnitude is impossible to estimate from existing data sources.[15]

The reporting of occupational diseases is particularly understated. Because very little is known about the complex relationships between exposure to toxic chemicals and the onset of particular occupational diseases, these illnesses are often difficult to identify, diagnose, and link to specific workplace causes. In addition, by the time employees become ill from a work-related disease such as cancer, which can be as long as 20 to 30 years after exposure to a dangerous chemical, many of them have changed jobs or are no longer in the work force. Employers, therefore, often fail to report occupational illness to the BLS. Two BLS researchers found that "the procedures normally followed by employers . . . in [answering the BLS inquiries] result in a gross understatement of occupational disease in the United States,"[16] and the NAS study described above concluded that there is "little doubt that serious underreporting exists for occupational diseases."[17]

Some additional information about the extent of occupational disease is available from "epidemiological studies" in which researchers calculate the incidence of a disease among workers exposed to some substance by interviewing the workers or their families or by studying public records such as death certificates, life insurance applications, or Social Security records. The prevalence of a disease among the exposed workers is then compared with the prevalence of the disease among persons of similar ages and backgrounds who were not exposed to the substance. The greater the comparative occurrence of the disease in the worker group, the more likely it is that the exposure caused the disease. In other words, if workers exposed to vinyl chloride have a rate of liver cancer 200 times that of comparable persons who were not exposed to that chemical, it is highly probable that vinyl chloride was the cause of their illness.

On the basis of existing epidemiological studies, government researchers have estimated that a total of over 2 million persons will die from exposure to asbestos,

Table 1–2
Estimates of U.S. Occupational Disease Deaths for 1987

Cause of Death	Total Deaths	Percentage Realted To Work Exposure	Low Range	High Range
Cancer	483,497	5-10%	24,175	48,350
Neurological Disease	34,100	3-5%	1,012	1,705
Cardiovascular Disease	963,611	1-3%	9,636	28,908
Pneumoconioses	8,670	100%	8,670	8,670
Other Pulmonary Disease	164,164	2-4%	3,283	6,567
Renal Disease	22,052	1-3%	220	662
Congenital Anomalies	12,333	3-5%	370	617
Total Deaths	1,688,427		47,377	95,479

Source: National Safe Workplace Institute, ''Beyond Neglect: The Problem of Occupational Disease in the United States—Labor Day '90 Report,'' (Chicago: The Institute, 1990), 8.

and other chemicals and dusts will cause thousands of additional illnesses per substance per year.[18] (See Table 1–2). The accuracy of these estimates, however, is in doubt, because the long latency period for many occupational diseases renders research based on interviews unreliable. If researchers undertake a study only a few years after workers are exposed to a substance, the disease will not have manifested itself in many workers. If they undertake a study 15 or 20 years after exposure, they are often unable to locate all of the exposed workers. Research is further hindered by incomplete or incorrect records, which often do not accurately list occupational disease as the cause of death or illness.

Besides their unreliability, epidemiological studies are not a good replacement for the BLS data, because studies have been conducted for only a few substances. For example, epidemiological studies have been completed for only 14 percent of the nearly 450 chemicals and industrial processes that the International Agency for Research on Cancer considers to be hazardous on the basis of animal studies.[19] Moreover, the limited amount of current testing has focused on potential carcinogens. A 1990 OTA report warned that risks posed by neurotoxins could be as severe as those posed by carcinogenic substances, but that no reliable studies exist concerning the extent of this risk.[20] Donald Miller, director of the National

Institute of Occupational Safety and Health (NIOSH), a government agency charged with studying occupational safety and health issues, summed up the recent state of knowledge about occupational disease as being "70 years behind . . . [surveillance] of communicable diseases."[21]

The absence of definitive data results in widely varying estimates of the total incidence of occupational diseases. Government scientists have estimated that occupational exposures may account for 20 to 38 percent of all cancers, but some academic researchers have calculated the incidence to be somewhere between 1 and 15 percent of all cancers.[22] These estimates differ so dramatically because each group employed different assumptions. Academic researchers conservatively assumed that the total incidence of occupational disease is no worse than the average incidence for those few chemicals that have already been studied. The government estimate assumed that some of the unstudied substances produce occupational illnesses in the magnitude of the worst results revealed by existing research.[23]

A similar controversy surrounds another government estimate that 390,000 cases of occupational diseases and 100,000 deaths from those diseases occur annually.[24] This estimate was derived from 1951 British mortality data comparing deaths of persons in various occupations with the average number of deaths of persons with similar characteristics in the country as a whole. These outdated British data were used because no comparable sources of American data were available. Another study by a prominent occupational medicine physician estimated that 50,000 to 70,000 deaths annually result from occupational disease.[25] Other estimates place the number of deaths at 10,000 to 210,000.[26]

Although the actual number of work-related accidents, injuries, and diseases cannot be determined precisely, there can be little doubt that thousands of American workers are killed or injured or suffer from serious occupational diseases each year. Although this toll is probably lower than at the turn of the century, the trends in the accident and illness rate are difficult to determine. Even more difficult to estimate is the effect that OSHA has had on accident trends. Most observers believe, however, that OSHA has, at best, had only a modern impact.

Statistics published by the National Safety Council indicate that occupational injury rates have fallen,[27] but the difficulty of collecting accurate information precludes heavy reliance on those data. Nevertheless, injury rates today do not appear to be as high as the appalling rates that were common at the turn of the century. Because even less is known about comparative occupational disease rates, it is not possible to make even a gross estimate of whether those rates have declined.

Some recent trends indicate that workplaces have become safer, but other data raise serious doubts about the conclusion. Figure 1–1 indicates the number of workplace fatalities has declined from 1974 to 1990 by approximately 42 percent. The BLS has warned, however, that its data "seriously understates [sic] the work-related fatalities . . . because fatalities are difficult to measure through employer surveys."[28] NIOSH has confirmed the BLS warning. It identified almost

Figure 1–1
Workplace Fatalities

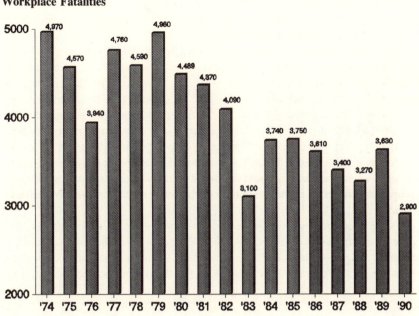

Source: U.S. Department of Labor, Bureau of Labor Statistics.

7,000 work-related deaths in each of the six years from 1980 through 1985.[29] Moreover, as Figure 1–1 shows, the rate at which fatalities were dropping slowed in the 1980s, as compared with the 1970s. A worker advocacy institute estimated that nearly 6,000 workers who died in the first half of the 1980s would still be alive if the fatality trends of the late 1970s had continued.[30]

The number of injuries has also declined. Figure 1–2 indicates about an 18 percent decrease in the injury rate (number of cases of injury and illness). Yet, Figure 1–3 demonstrates that the number of workdays lost because of work-related illnesses, a measure of the seriousness of the injuries, has been rising since 1983 and was at an all-time high in 1990. Sadly, an earlier downward trend in the injury rate has been reversed. Figure 1–2 indicates that the injury rate declined from 1974 to 1983 (10.4 to 7.6), but it has increased since that time, reaching 8.8 by 1990. As a result, the 6.4 million total occupational injuries in 1988 were 300,000 more than in 1987 and 700,000 more than in 1986.[31] The increases from 1983 to 1984 and from 1986 to 1987 were the largest increases of any year measured by the BLS. According to the BLS, some of the increases may be accounted for by its ongoing efforts to improve employer understanding of record-keeping requirements in conjunction with OSHA's increased monitoring of employer records. An AFL-CIO spokesperson responds that whatever

Figure 1–2
Workplace Injury Rate (per 100 full-time workers)

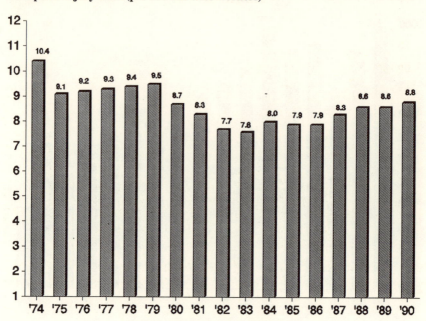

Source: U.S. Department of Labor, Bureau of Labor Statistics.

the reason for the increase, the data point to the conclusion that "too many workers are being killed or injured and getting sick on the job, and that problem is more significant than previously reported."[32]

OSHA AND THE ACCIDENT RATE

Not only is it difficult to determine whether workplaces are becoming safer, but the reasons for changes in the rates of injuries and illnesses are difficult to pinpoint. Nevertheless, there are good reasons to believe that OSHA has had only a limited effect on the number of industrial accidents and illnesses. Several economists have suggested that OSHA may not be responsible for even the decrease in accidents that has occurred. Worse, there are some indications that workplaces are actually less safe today than they were a few years ago. In any event, the rate of injury and disease is still unacceptably high, despite OSHA's efforts.

Economists studying OSHA's impact have adopted three different approaches. Some economists have used the injury rates before OSHA existed to project the injury rates after it was established. If the actual rates are below those predicted, OSHA may have been the cause. Studies using this methodology have had mixed

Figure 1–3
Workdays Lost (per 100 full-time workers)

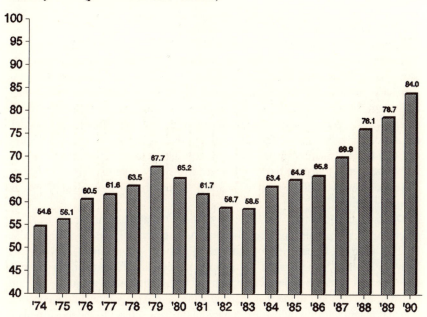

Source: U.S. Department of Labor, Bureau of Labor Statistics.

results. Smith found no statistically significant declines in injury rates in several high-hazard industries targeted by OSHA for its enforcement efforts.[33] Mendeloff did find significant decreases in California in several types of injuries he judged likely to be preventable by OSHA activity, but he also found that OSHA has had no effect on aggregate injury rate data for California and for the nation.[34] A second type of study uses a statistical model to explain changes in the injury rate. Using a variable that measures OSHA's activity, such as the number of inspections per year, this approach analyzes whether changes in injury rates correlate with OSHA activity. These studies have found no significant correlation between the number of OSHA inspections and injury rates.[35] The third type of study compares the injury rate experiences of plants that have been inspected with those that have not. Most of these studies have found that OSHA inspections have had no effect,[36] but one study of workplace injuries in Maine found a statistically significant reduction in the number of lost workdays per worker in the inspected plants.[37]

All three types of studies point to an overall conclusion that OSHA has had at best a modest effect on the rate of workplace injuries. This would suggest that other factors overwhelm OSHA's impact. Besides OSHA regulatory efforts, injury and fatality rates are affected by the effects of the business cycle, various changes in the administration of workers' compensation programs, the practice of occupational medicine, and other sociological factors. The OTA, the research arm of Congress, concluded that "national injury rates since 1972 have been largely related to the level of business activity."[38]

Some commentators believe that OSHA's relatively insignificant impact on the accident rate stems from the fact that most industrial accidents are of the type that OSHA cannot easily prevent. Bartel and Thomas, for example, argue that most industrial accidents are caused by "complex epidemiological inter-actions of labor, equipment and workplace environment," such as workers' carelessness, inattentiveness, or lack of training. They note that OSHA's safety regulations mostly concern the safety of equipment, not the workers' activities, and that OSHA's safety inspections are more likely to detect unsafe work conditions than the transient hazards that lead to many injuries.[39] Bacow agrees, and concludes that OSHA may be incapable of preventing more than 25 percent of all accidents.[40]

These conclusions may be overly pessimistic for at least three reasons. First, other studies suggest different conclusions. A retrospective evaluation undertaken by the California Department of Industrial Relations, for example, reported that between 30 and 50 percent of the injuries in several different industries could have been prevented by compliance with safety regulations. In addition, Leviton, Carlson, and Shapiro found that reduced injury and fatality rates in the construction and manufacturing industries, the two industries subject to the most frequent OSHA inspections, dropped significantly from 1973 to 1984.[41]

Second, the Bartel and Thomas study and similar studies contain significant methodological flaws that cast doubt on their conclusions. For example, Bartel and Thomas reached their conclusion that full compliance with OSHA's regulations would reduce the injury rate by only 10 percent by examining the extent to which the number of lost workdays attributable to occupational accidents is statistically related to the number of dollars in OSHA-collected penalties per employee. They posited that if OSHA regulates efficiently, the number of dollars in penalties will vary inversely with the level of compliance. Since they found low penalties in industries with a high injury rate, Bartel and Thomas concluded that OSHA has had little or no effect on the rate of injuries. Kelman, however, correctly cautions that "[i]t is quite doubtful . . . that the authors' surrogate variable to measure compliance, penalties (in dollars) per employee, actually captures the degree to which an industry in fact complies with OSHA's regulations." Kelman explains that the penalties were low in the industries studied because of several factors having nothing to do with the extent to which the industry complied with OSHA's regulations. These factors include the fact that the level of penalties set by OSHA does not correspond proportionately to the danger imposed by an infraction, the fact that the vast bulk of the penalties assessed by OSHA (95 percent) for the year that Bartel and Thomas studied were for non-serious violations, and the fact that OSHA usually reduces its penalties by as much as 80 percent as a result of factors that have nothing to do with the risk posed to workers, such as administrative convenience for the agency.[42]

Finally, Bacow and others fail to recognize that changes in equipment and workplace design can prevent workers from injuring themselves even when they are careless or inattentive. To the extent that accidents are attributable to worker inattentiveness to the dangers posed by equipment and other physical hazards, they can be partially prevented by redesigning machinery. New regulations addressed to the design and installation of equipment might increase the proportion of injuries that OSHA can prevent. Finally, even if Bacow is correct, it merely suggests that OSHA could have a more significant impact on workplace accidents by encouraging, or even requiring, safety training programs that address the problems of worker inattention and carelessness.

OSHA AND THE ILLNESS RATE

Those who doubt whether OSHA can significantly decrease the workplace accident rate have fewer doubts about OSHA's ability to prevent occupational diseases.[43] The incidence of such diseases is directly related to the extent that workers are exposed to dangerous chemicals and dusts. Worker inattention, carelessness, and lack of training are generally unimportant factors. Moreover, studies of existing OSHA regulations indicate that they have been successful in reducing workers' exposure to dangerous substances. A 1985 OTA report concluded that new OSHA standards for cotton dust, lead, and vinyl chloride "have clearly reduced workplace exposures."[44] Nevertheless, information about the prevalence of occupational disease is so limited that no reliable conclusions can be drawn about trends in the incidences of such diseases and OSHA's impact on those trends.

It is clear, however, that OSHA has not promulgated adequate regulations to address many dangerous health hazards. The paucity of OSHA's regulatory efforts to combat occupational disease is suggested by the National Cancer Institute's (NCI) Annual Report on Carcinogens. Congress requires NCI, a research arm of the Department of Health and Human Services (HHS), to provide annual lists of known or suspected carcinogens to which a significant number of persons residing in the United States are exposed. The 1985 report identified 145 known or suspected carcinogens. In 1987, OTA found that 110 of those carcinogen were produced or used in the United States in 1986 and were subject to regulations by OSHA. It also found that OSHA had no worker protection regulations addressing the carcinogenic hazards of 93 of the 110 chemicals.[45] Indeed, the OTA numbers may be overly optimistic. HHS reports that scientists have identified toxic effects for 45,000 to 50,000 chemicals that may appear in the workplace and that over 2,000 of these are suspected human carcinogens (a conclusion based on experiments with laboratory animals).[46] Yet fewer than 20 are addressed in full-fledged OSHA standards. As we shall see in Chapter 9,

OSHA has promulgated a single generic standard that partially addresses the risks posed by almost 400 of these chemicals,[47] but much more regulation is necessary even for those compounds.

OSHA AND THE PLIGHT OF WORKERS

When Congress originally gave OSHA the mandate to make every American workplace safe and healthful, its supporters were confident that the agency would have a significant impact on worker safety and health.[48] This optimism is no longer warranted. The continuing high rate of injuries and fatalities indicates that American workplaces are still dangerous places. OSHA's past failures raise serious questions about whether OSHA can be reoriented in ways that offer more workers greater protection from the ravages of workplace accidents and disease. The remainder of this book is devoted to examining the causes of OSHA's failures and to suggesting administrative and statutory changes that can provide affirmative answers to those questions.

NOTES

1. Elizabeth Cleghorn Gaskell, *North and South*, vol. 1 (London: Chapman and Hill, 1855), 155–56.

2. Anthony Bale, "America's First Compensation Crisis: Conflict over the Value and Meaning of Workplace Injuries Under the Employer Liability System," in *Dying for Work: Workers' Safety and Health in Twentieth-Century America*, ed. David Rosner and Gerald Markowitz (Bloomington: Indiana University Press, 1987), 37.

3. U.S. Congress, Office of Technology Assessment, *Preventing Illnesses and Injury in the Workplace* (Washington, DC: United States Government Printing Office, 1985), 30.

4. National Safe Workplace Institute, *The Rising Wave: Death and Injury Among High Risk Workers in the 1980s* (Chicago: The Institute, 1987), 5.

5. Office of Technology Assessment, *Preventing Illnesses*, 30.

6. Department of Health and Human Services, *Promoting Health/Preventing Disease: Objectives for the Nation* (Washington, D.C.: United States Government Printing Office, 1980), 40.

7. Michael Moore and W. Kip Viscusi, *Compensation Mechanisms for Job Risks— Wages, Workers Compensation, and Product Liability* (Princeton: Princeton University Press, 1990), 80.

8. Deborah Hensler et al., *Compensation for Accidental Injuries in the United States* (Santa Monica, Calif.: Rand Institute, 1991), 104.

9. National Safe Workplace Institute, *Basic Information on Workplace Safety & Health in the United States* (Chicago: The Institute, n.d.), 1.

10. William Johnson and Edward Heler, "The Costs of Asbestos Associated Disease and Death," *Milbank Memorial Fund Quarterly, Health and Society* 2 (1983): 185.

11. National Safe Workplace Institute, *Rising Wave*, 9.

12. Ibid., 12.

13. Bryan Burrough and Seth Lubove, "Some Concerns Fudge Their Safety Record to Cut Insurance Costs." *Wall Street Journal*, 2 Dec. 1986, 1.

14. U.S. Congress, Office of Technology Assessment, *Occupational Safety and Health: Assuring Accuracy in Employer Injury and Illness Records* (Washington, D.C.: United States Government Printing Office, 1988), 3.

15. National Academy of Sciences, National Research Council, *Counting Illnesses and Injuries in the Workplace: Proposals for a Better System* (Washington, D.C.: National Academy of Sciences Press, 1987), 59–60.

16. Harvey Hilaski and Chao Ling Wang, "How Valid Are Estimates of Occupational Illnesses?" *Monthly Labor Review* 25, no. 8 (1982): 27.

17. National Academy of Sciences, *Counting Illnesses*, 2.

18. National Cancer Institute, National Institute of Environmental Health Sciences, and National Institute for Occupational Safety and Health, *Estimates of the Fraction of Cancer in the United States Related to Occupational Factors* (Washington, D.C.: United States Government Printing Office, 1978), 9.

19. Ralph Althouse et al., "An Evaluation of Chemicals and Industrial Processes Associated with Cancer in Humans Based on Human and Animal Data: IARC Monographs Volumes 1 to 20," *Cancer Research* 40 (1980): 1.

20. *BNA Occupational Safety and Health Reporter* 19 (23 May 1990): 2240.

21. U.S. Congress, House Committee on Government Operations, Subcommittee on Manpower and Housing, *Occupational Illness Data Collection: Fragmented, Unreliable, and Seventy Years Behind: Communicable Disease Surveillance*, 98th Cong., 2d sess., 1984, H. Rep. no. 98–1144, 1–2.

22. National Cancer Institute, *Estimates of the Fraction of Cancer*, 24; Richard Doll and Richard Petro, "The Causes of Cancer: Quantitative Estimates of Avoidable Risks of Cancer in the United States Today," *Journal of the National Cancer Institute* 66 (1981): 1212–13; Phillip Cole, "Cancer and Occupation: Status and Needs for Epidemiological Research," *Cancer* 39 (1977): 1790; Ernst Wynder and Gio Gori, "Contribution of the Environment to Cancer Incidence: An Epidemiologic Exercise," *Journal of the National Cancer Institute* 58 (1977): 830.

23. Elinor Schroeder and Sidney Shapiro, "Responses to Occupational Disease: The Role of Markets, Regulation, and Information," *Georgetown Law Journal* 72 (1984): 1235.

24. *The President's Report on Occupational Safety and Health* (Washington, D.C.: United States Government Printing Office, 1980), 111.

25. Phillip Landrigan, "The Recognition and Control of Occupational Disease," 266 *Journal of the American Medical Society* 25 (Aug. 1991): 676.

26. Peter Barth, *Workers Compensation and Work-Related Injuries* (Cambridge, Mass.: MIT Press, 1980), 15–19.

27. National Safety Council, *Accident Facts* (Washington, D.C.: The Council, 1991), 43.

28. *BNA Occupational Safety and Health Reporter* 19 (22 Nov. 1989): 1147.

29. Ibid., 1160.

30. National Safe Workplace Institute, *Rising Wave*, 5.

31. *BNA Corporate Counsel Weekly*, 4 (22 Nov. 1989): 7.

32. *BNA Occupational Safety and Health Reporter* 19 (22 Nov. 1989): 1147.

33. Robert Smith, *The Occupational Safety and Health Act: Its Goals and Achievements* (Washington, D.C.: American Enterprise Institute, 1970), 70.

34. John Mendeloff, *Regulating Safety: An Economic and Political Analysis of Occupational Safety and Health Policy* (Cambridge, Mass.: MIT Press, 1979), 164.

35. W. Kip Viscusi, "The Impact of Occupational Safety and Health Regulation," *Bell Journal on Economics* 10 (1979): 136; Ann Bartel and Lacy Thomas, "Direct and Indirect Effects of Regulation: A New Look at OSHA's Impact," *Journal of Law and Economics* 28 (1985): 1.

36. David McCaffery, "An Assessment of OSHA's Recent Effects on Injury Rates," *Journal of Human Resources* 18 (1983): 144; Robert Smith, "The Impact of OSHA Inspections on Manufacturing Injury Rates," *Journal of Human Resources* 14 (1979): 145.

37. William Cook and Frederick Gautschi III, "OSHA Plant Safety Programs and Injury Reductions," *Industrial Relations* 20 (1981): 253.

38. Office of Technology Assessment, *Preventing Illnesses*, 36.

39. Bartel and Thomas, "Direct and Indirect Effects," 24–25.

40. Lawrence Bacow, *Bargaining for Job Safety and Health* (Cambridge, Mass.: MIT Press, 1980), 35–50; John Mendeloff, "The Role of OSHA Violations in Serious Workplace Accidents," *Journal of Occupational Medicine* 26 (1984): 353.

41. Sar Levitan, Peter Carlson, and Isaac Shapiro, *Protecting American Workers: An Assessment of Government Programs* (Washington, D.C.: Bureau of National Affairs, 1986), 121; Office of Technology Assessment, *Preventing Illnesses*, 267.

42. Mark Kelman, "On Democracy Bashing: A Skeptical Look at the Theoretical and 'Empirical' Practice of Public Choice Movement," *Virginia Law Review* 74 (1988): 251–55.

43. Smith, *Occupational Safety*, 84–85; Richard Zeckhauser and Albert Nichols, "The Occupational Safety and Health Administration—An Overview," in U.S. Congress, Senate Committee on Government Affairs, *Study on Federal Regulation*, 96th Cong., 1st sess., 1978, S. Doc. 96–14, app. to vol. VI, 169.

44. U.S. Congress, Office of Technology Assessment, *Preventing Illnesses*, 268.

45. U.S. Congress, Office of Technology Assessment, *Identifying and Regulating Carcinogens* (Washington, D.C.: United States Government Printing Office, 1987), 182–83.

46. Department of Health and Human Services, *Promoting Health/Preventing Disease*, 40.

47. "Air Contaminants Standard," 54 *Fed. Reg.* 2332 (1989).

48. U.S. Congress, Senate Committee on Labor and Human Resources, *Hearings on Oversight on the Administration of the Occupational Safety and Health Act*, pt. 1, 96th Cong., 2d sess., 1980, 1 (statement of Sen. Harrison A. Williams, Jr.).

2

Regulatory Failure and Reform

The founder of the Chicago School of Economics, Professor Frank Knight, once observed that the distinction between laborers and the owners of companies is that laborers have freely elected to risk their health and safety, whereas owners have chosen instead to risk their capital.[1] Modern-day economists share Knight's belief that workers freely accept risky employment in return for additional compensation. As if to underscore the point, a prominent OSHA analyst, W. Kip Viscusi, titled his widely read book *Risk by Choice.*[2] Those who actually encounter workplace risks on a day-to-day basis rarely share this sanguine view. Indeed, the history of occupational safety and health regulation is as much a story about workers seeking government help in adjusting the balance of power in the employer-employee relationship as it is a chronology of scientific discoveries concerning the cause and prevention of workplace injuries and diseases.[3] State legislatures enacted workers' compensation statutes at the turn of the century in response to the extraordinary dangers to which the industrial revolution subjected powerless workers, many of whom were recent immigrants or former slaves and hardly in a position to strike hard bargains with the industrial tycoons of the day. The Occupational Safety and Health Act of 1971, which created OSHA, represented a reaction at the federal level to the failure of workers' compensation and state regulation to ensure reasonably safe and healthy workplaces.

Since its inception, OSHA "has been at the forefront of a growing debate over the costs, benefits, and proper thrust of government regulation."[4] Echoing Knight's views, OSHA's modern-day critics call for greater reliance on unregulated labor markets to address health and safety problems. Where those markets fail, they maintain, cost-benefit analysis should determine the level of workplace risk reduction, because it replicates the balance between risk and risk-reduction technology that private markets would produce. Worker organizations, by contrast, reject cost-benefit analysis, advocate reforms that would strengthen OSHA, and lobby for legislation to establish even more substantial health and safety protection.

This book aims to sort out the arguments over the appropriate future for OSHA and thereby to contribute to an agenda for government regulation for the twenty-first century. Our strategy for this undertaking adopts Komesar's suggestion that "legal analysis and law reform must be based upon careful consideration of the behavior of the social institutions assigned the task of making and implementing law." To set the stage for this analysis, this chapter evaluates several alternatives to OSHA for addressing workplace risks, some of which have been tried in other historical and governmental contexts. We recognize with Komesar that "[i]n a society of millions of people, with ever-changing technology, selecting the best means of preventing injury means carefully considering and comparing highly imperfect alternatives."[5] Unlike many of OSHA's critics, however, we conclude that OSHA's role in protecting workers should be enhanced, not diminished. We find that a strong OSHA is a critical element in any strategy for achieving the degree of workplace health and safety that a civilized society rightly demands.

WAGE PREMIUMS

According to economic theory, workers will demand a "wage premium" to compensate them for additional workplace risks. In response, employers will reduce those risks up to the point at which it is less expensive to pay workers additional compensation than to take additional health or safety precautions. In this manner, labor markets result in the abatement of some health and safety risks while compensating workers for the risks that remain.

The economists' faith in unimpeded labor markets is based on empirical studies that purport to show a positive correlation between the level of safety risks in an industry and its wage rates. For example, one analyst believes that the findings

on compensating differentials indicate that labor markets are operating as they should. Although they do not exist in the paradigm labor market, workers are being rewarded for risk bearing and there are wage benefit tradeoffs. There are workers who are risk adverse, have information about job risk, and collect for bearing risk.[6]

The best evidence of this sort suggests a positive association between fatal accident rates and wages. The relationship between nonfatal accident rates and wages is less well established: a relationship appears to exist in some studies but not in others.[7] Most wage studies, however, have been limited to safety risks rather than the risk of disease.[8] Viscusi found evidence of modest premiums for known health risks.[9] More recently, Moore and Viscusi found stronger evidence of wage-risk trade-offs.[10] By comparison, Selikoff found a "virtual absence of a significant wage premium" for asbestos insulation workers, even though powerful construction unions and the workers themselves knew of the virulent health hazard presented by asbestos.[11] Robinson noted a "clustering of undesirable . . . characteristics" in jobs at the low end of the wage scale, and concluded that "[w]hile modest wage premiums are paid to workers exposed to hazards within particular occupations and industries, the general pattern of wages and working conditions reveals that hazardous employments pay wages 20–30 percent less than safe employments."[12]

Another problem with the voluminous economic literature on the existence of wage premiums is that economists cannot evaluate whether workers are *fully* compensated for the risks they face. As Robert Smith observed, "because so many injury-related losses are of a psychic nature ('pain and suffering'), we cannot begin to tell if the wage premiums are in fact fully compensating."[13] More fundamentally, the adequacy of wage premiums cannot be determined without first resolving the fundamental issue of whether employees have an enforceable right to a reasonably safe workplace. We may legitimately conclude that an employee has "voluntarily" accepted a workplace risk in return for higher compensation only if he or she otherwise had a right to force the employer to reduce or eliminate the risk. Since employees presently lack this power, no firm conclusions about the adequacy of existing wage premiums are valid. It might be argued that an employee always has the "right" to eliminate a risk by quitting the job, but (as we shall see in Chapter 18) this response is necessarily ideological and dependent on the analyst's view of the adequacy of the status quo power relationships in the workplace.[14]

The conditions in many current labor markets suggest that workers do not freely accept the health and safety risks to which they are exposed. The outcome of any negotiation depends on the relative economic power of employees and their employer. Since the Progressive era, realistic observers of the sociology of the workplace have recognized that a worker who can be fired at the whim of an employer cannot be very insistent in demanding safer working conditions.[15] This is especially true in jobs in which employees can easily be replaced and for which alternative jobs with marginally fewer risks at marginally lower wage rates are not freely available. Further, the costs associated with switching jobs, such as loss of health benefits, pension rights, and seniority, the necessity of becoming familiar with a new employer, and the expense and personal disruption of relocation, may be too high for many employees.[16]

The emergence of unions as a market force has assisted employees in confronting employer market power. Indeed, wage premiums may exist only in the unionized work sector.[17] Even so, the capacity of unionized employees to obtain fully compensating wage premiums is questionable. Union power diminished in the 1980s to the point where workers in many important industries were forced to accept wage concessions.[18] In other industries, prominent companies have been able to replace unionized workers with nonunion ones.[19] At the same time, the percentage of the American work force that is unionized declined from 29.5 percent in 1964 to 21.9 percent in 1982.[20]

The ability of both unionized and nonunionized workers to obtain adequate wage premiums is affected by their knowledge about workplace dangers. Workers cannot demand appropriate risk premiums if they are unaware of workplace risks or underestimate their severity.[21] The knowledge disadvantage of employees is especially acute in the case of health risks posed by toxic materials.[22] Chapter 1 demonstrated that little information is available about which chemicals cause occupational disease and that obtaining additional information is very expensive. Even armed with the limited information available from epidemiology and animal toxicity studies, workers will have difficulty predicting the precise effects of health risks on longevity and the quality of life once a disease has manifested itself.[23] Although safety risks are more easily identifiable, it is not enough that "people know that working in a steel mill is more dangerous than working for an insurance company."[24] To bargain for appropriate wage premiums, workers must be able to discern marginal differences in risks between jobs within the same firm or between two firms in the same industry.

Market forces undoubtedly play some role in reducing workplace risks, but the extent to which they yield real protection is impossible to determine. Two apparently unavoidable features of many labor markets—employer market power and lack of risk information—suggest that whatever risk premiums exist are unlikely to compensate workers fully for the risks to which they are exposed. It is therefore not at all surprising that workers have looked beyond labor markets to state, and later federal, regulation to protect them from workplace hazards.

TORT LAW

When the inability of markets to reduce risks first became apparent in the middle of the nineteenth century, workers first turned to the courts for redress. Lawrence Friedman explains:

The explosion of tort law, and negligence in particular, must be entirely attributed to the age of engines and machines. In pre-industrial society, there are few personal injuries, except for assault and battery. The machines and tools of modern man, however, blindly cripple and maim their servants.[25]

Victims of the industrial revolution, however, found little relief in the courts. In the tort system, a plaintiff must prove that the defendant's negligence caused his or her injuries. For a worker, this required a showing that the employer's conduct was not that of a reasonable employer in the same or similar circumstances.[26] Generally, expert testimony was required to establish that employers failed to take "reasonable care" with respect to machinery, chemicals, or other hazards. Because industry hired most of the professionals with the relevant expertise, workers were unable to prove their cases. In addition, the worker had the burden of proving that the employer's conduct "probably" caused specific damage to the employee. Although the cause-effect relationship between the workplace and accident-induced injuries was usually easily established, even the most highly trained experts were unwilling to testify that exposures probably caused a particular employee's disease.

Even if the worker could sustain the foregoing burden of proof, the employer had available an "unholy trinity" of defenses that virtually guaranteed victory in every case.[27] Under the "fellow servant" rule, the employer could escape liability if it could show that the negligence of another employee played a role in the injured employee's accident.[28] The doctrine of contributory negligence allowed negligent employers to evade claims by showing that the complaining employee was also negligent. Perhaps the most unfair doctrine of all was captured in the Latin phrase *volenti non fit injuria* (to he who is willing, no harm is done), also called assumption of risk, under which the employer could evade liability merely by demonstrating that the employee knew of the workplace hazard and willingly encountered it. In the blinkered view of the nineteenth-century courts, the choice to face the risk was a willing one, even if a choice not to accept it led to unemployment.[29] The net result was that during the later half of the nineteenth century and the first two decades of the twentieth century, the tort system provided very little incentive for employers to invest in health and safety.[30] Comfortable employers convinced themselves that industrial accidents and diseases were either the fault of clumsy employees or otherwise "inevitable."[31]

WORKERS' COMPENSATION

The abject failure of the common law tort system did not go unnoticed for long. In the 1920s and 1930s, prominent muckrakers brought the plight of the industrial worker to the attention of an outraged public.[32] Progressive state legislatures seized the initiative and began to enact quasi-administrative schemes for awarding compensation for workplace accidents that discarded most of the discredited common law doctrines. The causation hurdle was reduced by allowing compensation for any disease or injury "arising out of" the employment, and some diseases were established by statute or regulation as work-related, thereby effectively shifting the burden to the employer to establish that a particular disease associated with its industry did not arise out of employment. The "arising out of" language also eliminated the necessity of proving that the employer was negligent or otherwise at fault. All of the unholy trinity of defenses were abolished. Finally, compensation was awarded by a court or commission soon after the injury, when the employee needed the money most, not after a long and expensive trial.[33]

Workers' compensation is a remedy for inadequate risk reduction in labor markets because it creates a financial incentive for employers to abate health and safety risks. In order to save money, an employer will invest in abatement up to the point where it is less expensive to pay workers' compensation than to engage in further efforts to reduce health or safety hazards. Thus, an employer might not prevent all diseases or injuries, but workers should be compensated for those that are not prevented.

The capacity of workers' compensation to reduce risks, however, was severely curtailed by its fundamental underlying policy: it was designed to keep an employee from starving, not to compensate the person for medical expenses, lost wages, and other pain and suffering. States limited compensation rates to levels that often were below the employee's salary. For example, 42 states currently have a cap of $450 per week or less in compensation for employees who temporarily cannot work.[34] Almost identical caps exist for permanent disabilities.[35] Moreover, some states do not meet the minimal goal of preventing disabled employees from starving. The maximum compensation rate in eight states for workers who temporarily cannot work is below the poverty level for a family of four. Compensation in another nine states is within $50 of the poverty level.[36]

For workplace fatalities, compensation can amount to less than the cost of burial. For example, Larry Hensinger, age 29, was killed as he attempted to rescue another worker who had been cleaning sludge from a zinc cyanide tank when a reaction with muriatic acid produced deadly hydrogen cyanide gas. Four other workers also died, including the worker Hensinger attempted to rescue. Because Hensinger was single, the only workers' compensation award was for burial expenses, and even that was insufficient. "It wasn't enough to bury him," said his father. "Is this all a man's life is worth?"[37] Clearly it is not, but this experience is typical. Maximum burial allowances in every state are below the national funeral cost of $6,500.[38] If the only incentive for employers to eliminate risks that kill workers is avoiding the cost of cheap funerals, very few health and safety improvements are likely to be forthcoming.

Further improvements in the level of benefits are likely to be slow in coming. Although benefits levels have gradually improved since the 1970s, the political power of employers in most states has usually been sufficient to derail most legislative reform efforts.[39] One expert suggests that increases in the cost of workers' compensation insurance for employers in states that have increased benefits "make[s] further improvements in state laws difficult and [has] generated pressures in several jurisdictions to reduce costs, often by cutting back on benefits." He predicts that "In a number of states, there will be a continuing struggle to achieve or maintain adequate benefits, with the likely outcome that, in a significant minority, benefits will remain below [adequate levels]."[40] Some economists seriously suggest that increasing workers' compensation benefits may be a bad idea, because it will encourage employees to have more accidents. Moore and Viscusi posit: "As the degree of coverage of their income loss from job injuries is increased, workers have less of a financial incentive to avoid the injury since the size of the loss has been reduced."[41] Workers in the real world marvel at such muddleheaded pronouncements from comfortably situated academics.

One serious obstacle to workers' compensation reform is that low compensation benefits in some states drive down benefits in other states. A former assistant attorney general for the Maryland Division of Labor and Industry explained this process as follows:

Workers compensation benefits are generally higher in Maryland than in other parts of the country, particularly when compared to our neighbor, Virginia. So, insurance companies urge their customers (who complain about high workers' compensation premiums) to leave Maryland. Some companies resettle in Virginia. To avoid this, Maryland reduces the workers' compensation benefits, and premiums will then be reduced in industry. But the insurance companies are not satisfied. Insurance companies then move to Virginia, using the same argument but comparing Virginia, for example, with Alabama. Virginia then lowers benefits and the spiral downward of benefits continues from state to state. Unfortunately, state legislators have been falling for this scheme and benefits are lowered to the lowest common denominator.[42]

Several other aspects of the workers' compensation insurance system sap employer incentive to abate workplace hazards. Perhaps most important, worker compensation premiums are not "experience rated." The premiums for all but the largest employers are based primarily on the historical experience of the industry as a whole rather than on the firm's own safety record.[43] Even experience rating, however, would not create an adequate incentive for employers to undertake adequate health precautions. An employer's decision about how much to spend to prevent disease is not based on current workers' compensation expenses, which result from past actions, but on the likelihood that such expenditures will prevent future diseases. Most occupational diseases have long latency periods, usually between 20 and 40 years. Since the present value of a liability 30 years from now is small, employers may be disinclined to risk today's profits to reduce tomorrow's losses.[44]

In a few industries, the problem with workers' compensation is much more fundamental than low benefit levels—it is not available at all. For example, powerful farming lobbies have persuaded state legislatures to exclude field workers, who can be harmed in accidents with farm implements and through exposure to agricultural chemicals, from the compensation schemes in all but a few states.[45] In Texas, farm workers were brought under the workers' compensation regime in 1985 only after the Texas courts held that to exclude them violated the state's equal protection clause.[46]

TORT LAW REDUX

Worker advocates at the turn of the twentieth century had to make an important concession as a quid pro quo for securing the enactment of workers' compensation statutes. In return for guaranteed limited compensation for medical expenses and disability and the elimination of the unholy trinity of defenses, workers gave up their right at common law to sue employers for full medical expenses, disability, pain and suffering, and punitive damages. The tort system is generally available only to employees who can identify a negligent third party who caused their injury. This has been a costly concession for workers. While the statutory law of workers' compensation stagnated in state legislatures, the common law of torts was undergoing a profound reformation in the state courts. By the 1980s, state courts were much more congenial to those injured by the march of technological progress.

The shift in tort laws away from protecting employers was influenced by a change in the way lawyers thought about the purposes of law. In the 1800s, lawyers believed that they could deduce the "correct" result in a case through formal reasoning from prior legal principles. This approach abetted the "tradition-bound, moralistic brand of tort law—secretly tailored to the interest of early capitalism, and symbolized by the complex notions of fault" that were discussed earlier.[47] In the early 1900s, critics attacked the idea that universal legal propositions could be derived through the application of conceptualistic logic. They suggested that the legal system, informed by social research, could be an instrument for improving social conditions.[48] Influenced by these critics, judges began to change tort law to address the absence of risk reduction in markets. The increasing availability of liability insurance accelerated this trend. Once insurance spread the costs of compensating plaintiffs across society, "[a] tort suit was no longer a two-party affair, whose costs were imposed on one party or the other, but a 'three-party affair,' in which the third party was American society at large." Consequently, judges decided that "more injured persons could be compensated and the "blameworthiness' requirements of tort law could be liberalized."[49]

In hindsight, it is apparent that workers as a class might have been better advised to have waited for the reformation of tort law. Consider a recent tort suit brought by Tammye May, age 25, against the manufacturer of boltmaking machines. May was cleaning the six-bladed machine with a rag when it caught and pulled her arm into the blades. After a jury found that the machine had been designed in a negligent manner, she was awarded $3.5 million in damages against its manufacturer.[50] By contrast, May was eligible for a maximum of only $34,600 in workers' compensation from her Oklahoma employer.[51] Even if her award is reduced by an appellate court, the fate of many large tort awards, the result demonstrates that the tort system enables plaintiffs to seek damages that more closely approximate complete compensation for their injuries. Moreover, the expansion of tort law has been relatively effective in promoting risk reduction. Outside of the employer-employee context, a firm's insurance premiums are more likely to be correlated with its safety record, thereby providing an incentive to reduce accidents in order to avoid higher premiums.

Nevertheless, the impact of tort law on risk reduction has been minimal for several reasons. First, most injured or ill employees cannot identify a third party to sue and are therefore stuck with their workers' compensation remedies. Second, workers must still overcome substantial legal hurdles, particularly in cases involving toxic chemicals. For example, workers in some states may not sue if they discover their illness after the statute of limitations has run.[52] More important, plaintiffs still encounter difficulties in proving the existence of a cause-effect relationship between workplace exposures and particular diseases. Unless the disease is very rare (such as angiosarcoma) or clearly associated with a particular substance (such as asbestosis), the tort system's requirement that the plaintiff establish that the defendant's conduct probably caused the plaintiff's individual harm means that chemical manufacturers seldom pay for occupational diseases.[53] Third, the expansion of tort liability during the 1970s and 1980s provoked a lobbying campaign by risk producers to limit their liability. In the 1980s, states enacted tort reform legislation limiting the damages available in some types of tort cases and making it more difficult for plaintiffs to sue in other types.[54]

REGULATORY REFORM

Despite the foregoing deficiencies in markets, workers' compensation, and common law tort actions in regulating workplace risks, OSHA's critics have called for deemphasizing, if not eliminating, the role of that agency in enhancing workplace health and safety. To the extent that OSHA's role is retained, the critics would subject OSHA rules to a cost-benefit test that replicates the degree of risk reduction that would occur in private labor markets as the result of bargaining between workers and employers.

Two early studies of OSHA recommended that its jurisdiction over *safety* risks be eliminated. Economist Robert Smith, in a study published by a conservative think tank, concluded in 1976 that OSHA safety standards should be replaced by a federal "injury tax" set at the level required to induce "optimal" employer expenditures on worker safety.[55] This proposal was echoed in 1978 by Richard Zeckhauser and Albert Nichols, both policy analysts at the Kennedy School of Government, who concluded that "[r]ather than continue on the course of its first 7 years . . . OSHA should be disbanded."[56] They proposed that workers' compensation be reformed by tying each firm's cost more closely to its safety record and that an injury tax receive "careful consideration."[57] Like Smith, they favored a tax because it is easy to administer and creates significant financial incentives for employers to reduce injuries.[58] Zeckhauser and Nichols, however, were willing to retain OSHA if it was limited to serving as a "complement" to markets and to workers' compensation in the reduction of injuries.[59]

Both the Smith and Zeckhauser and Nichols studies concluded that because markets and compensatory regulation did not do a good job of reducing *health* risks, OSHA regulation had to be retained for that purpose. While Smith opposed any health standard for which costs exceed predicted benefits,[60] Zeckhauser and Nichols proposed only that OSHA estimate the cost of alternative methods of compliance for a health standard and choose the least expensive. They opposed the use of cost-benefit analysis because of the "difficulties, both analytical and political, of valuing lives and health."[61]

More recent analysts have not shared Zeckhauser and Nichols's hesitation about cost-benefit analysis. In a 1979 book, John Mendeloff endorsed the "injury tax," but he concluded that Congress was unlikely to adopt it.[62] He therefore called on OSHA to start comparing the costs and benefits of safety standards and to do a better job of enforcement.[63] Kip Viscusi, a professor of business administration, also argued that the cost-benefit analysis was central to OSHA reform.[64] In a 1988 book, Mendeloff renewed his call for a cost-benefit test, this time for regulating health hazards.[65]

Economists favor cost-benefit analysis because they believe it identifies the amount of risk reduction that would result in unimpeded markets from wage bargaining between workers and their employers. As Chapter 18 will explain in more detail, economists believe it is a waste of scarce resources to eliminate risks that workers would voluntarily accept if they had adequate information and bargaining power equal to that of their employers. Mendeloff's 1988 book further argues that using cost-benefit analysis will speed up the pace of OSHA decision making by decreasing industry opposition. Convinced that regulatees would be less likely to contest standards whose costs and benefits were equated, Mendeloff concludes that OSHA could promulgate more standards with the same resources and thereby benefit a larger number of workers.[66] Mendeloff's argument is an important one, because it suggests that worker advocates who previously opposed cost-benefit analysis on the ground that it led to less worker protection are deceiving themselves. Some liberal commentators have relied upon the Mendeloff study to advocate that agencies like OSHA make greater use of cost-benefit analysis.[67]

This book provides a substantially different account of OSHA's failures and regulatory reform. The analysis presented here of OSHA's standard-setting in its historical context suggests that OSHA has too little legal authority to regulate, not too much. We agree with many of OSHA's critics that its failure to make a significant dent in its enormous regulatory agenda invites a reexamination of its original charter. But we argue that if agencies are ill-equipped to overcome existing impediments to regulation, Congress must give them new powers that specifically address the constraints they face. In addition, congresss must empower the workers themselves to induce appropriate changes in the workplace. Congress has, to some extent, recognized this lesson in the context of environmental law, and over time it has reduced constraints to rule making in the Environmental Protection Agency. It has also empowered the victims of pollution to participate in the standard-setting process and to enforce environmental laws without governmental participation or approval. Congress's failure to address OSHA regulation in a similar fashion severely limits its potential to protect American workers from crippling or fatal accidents and diseases.

We do not subscribe to the theory that subjecting OSHA rules to a cost-benefit test best serves the interests of workers. As we shall explain, this test inappropriately assumes that the existing distribution of wealth in this country should define the limits of preventive regulation. Cost-benefit proponents appear to be indifferent to the choice between compensating the victims of accidents and occupational disease and preventing accidents and illnesses in the first place. We regard prevention as ethically preferable to compensation. Contrary to Mendeloff's assertion, we shall show that cost-benefit analysis does not lead to greater protection of workers. Finally, we object to cost-benefit analysis because its proponents assume that workers will receive compensation for injuries and illnesses that are not prevented. In fact, as we have seen, workers usually receive woefully inadequate compensation for injuries or illnesses.

In addition to our preference for preventing injuries over compensating victims, we are skeptical of arguments that increased reliance on markets or compensatory regulation will significantly reduce health and safety risks. We support efforts to give workers more information about workplace dangers, but doubt that this alone will sufficiently empower workers to protect themselves. Compensatory regulation is unlikely to lead to further reductions in risk unless it is reformed, and reform is unlikely. Current trends in tort reform in state legislatures are in precisely the opposite direction: toward retrenchment from existing protective doctrines. Finally, we agree with Mendeloff that Congress is unlikely to abolish OSHA and enact an injury tax or, for that matter, any other radical reform of the existing regulatory approach.

Nevertheless, we believe that more modest reforms of the Occupational Safety and Health Act are politically and institutionally feasible, though it will not be an easy task. Moreover, OSHA can achieve some modest reforms without legislative action. Similarly, workers have some options within existing arrangements that have not been fully exploited.

Our preference for making OSHA the centerpiece of attempts to reduce workplace health and safety risks, however, does not mean that we do not support efforts to make markets and compensatory regulation more effective. In the best of circumstances—which is to say when it has been under committed and talented leaders—OSHA has had a disappointingly low output. It has accomplished even less when, as was true during most of the Reagan administration, administrators were committed to deregulation. Although workers have the ability to force OSHA to regulate in extreme cases, alternative approaches to risk reduction take on special importance when OSHA is lackadaisical. More important, no matter how productive OSHA might become, there will always be limitations on how much risk reduction it can accomplish. Workers will always benefit, therefore, from a multifaceted approach to risk reduction. Although this book will focus primarily upon ways to make OSHA more effective, it will examine as well the inevitable links among OSHA reform, workers' compensation revisions, and more fundamental changes in the nature of the employer-employee relationship.

When Congress created OSHA, it adopted the worthy goal of protecting every American worker from dangerous and disabling workplace conditions. The agency has not lived up to this noble aspiration. Although the goal may never be fully achieved, it should not be abandoned. The goals that we set for our least advantaged citizens say much about the kind of people we are. The lessons of the 1970s and 1980s should provide the impetus for OSHA to reform itself and for Congress to reform OSHA.

NOTES

1. Frank H. Knight, *Risk, Uncertainty and Profit* (Boston: Houghton Mifflin, 1921), 301.

2. W. Kip Viscusi, *Risk by Choice: Regulating Health and Safety in the Workplace* (Cambridge, Mass.: Harvard University Press, 1983).

3. David Rosen and Gerald Markowitz, eds., *Dying for Work: Workers Safety and Health in Twentieth Century America* (Bloomington: Indiana University Press, 1987); Bennett Judkins, *We Offer Ourselves as Evidence: Toward Workers' Control of Occupational Health* (Westport, Conn.: Greenwood Press, 1986).

4. Michael Levin, "Politics and Polarity: The Limits of OSHA Reform," 3 *Regulation* (Nov./Dec. 1979): 33.

5. Neil Komesar, "Injuries and Institutions: Tort Reform, Tort Theory, and Beyond," *New York University Law Review* 65 (1990): 24–25.

6. John Worrall, "Compensation Costs, Injury Rates, and the Labor Market," in *Safety and the Workforce: Incentives and Disincentives in Workers Compensation*, ed. John Worrall (Ithaca, N.Y.: ILR Press, 1985), 13. See also W. Kip Viscusi, *Employment Hazards: An Investigation of Market Performance* (Cambridge, Mass.: Harvard University Press, 1979), 271.

7. Ronald Ehrenberg, "Workers' Compensation, Wages, and the Risk of Injury," in *New Perspectives in Workers Compensation*, ed. John Burton, Jr. (Ithaca, N.Y.: ILR Press, 1988), 80–81.

8. Elinor Schroeder and Sidney Shapiro, "Responses to Occupational Disease: The Role of Markets, Regulation, and Information," *Georgetown Law Journal* 72 (1984): 1240.

9. Viscusi, *Risk by Choice*, 43–45; Viscusi, *Employment Hazards*, 269.

10. Michael J. Moore and W. Kip Viscusi, *Compensation Mechanisms for Job Risks: Wages, Workers' Compensation, and Product Liability* (Princeton: Princeton University Press, 1990).

11. Irving J. Selikoff, *Disability Compensation for Asbestos-Associated Diseases in the United States* (New York: New Environmental Sciences Laboratory, Mount Sinai School of Medicine of the City University of New York [available from National Technical Information Service], 1981), 570–71, 577.

12. James C. Robinson, *Toil and Toxics: Workplace Struggles and Political Strategies for Occupational Health* (Berkeley: University of California Press, 1991), 93.

13. Robert Smith, *The Occupational Safety and Health Act: Its Goals and Its Achievements* (Washington, D.C.: American Enterprise Institute, 1976), 30.

14. Thomas O. McGarity, "Media Quality, Technology and Cost-Benefit Balancing Strategies for Health and Environmental Regulation," *Law and Contemporary Problems* 46 (1983): 173.

15. Charles Noble, *Liberalism at Work: The Rise and Fall of OSHA* (Philadelphia: Temple University Press, 1986), 8.

16. Schroeder and Shapiro, "Response," 1241.

17. Julie Graham, Don Shakow, and Christopher Cyr, "Risk Compensation in Theory and Practice," *Environment* 25 (1983): 14, 17; William Dickens, "Differences Between Risk Premiums in Union and Nonunion Wages and the Case for Occupational Safety Regulations," *American Economic Review* 74 (1984): 320.

18. Charles Graver, "Financial Crises and Collective Bargaining," *George Washington Law Review* 56 (1988): 468.

19. Ibid., 469.

20. Bureau of the Census, *Statistical Abstract of the United States* (Washington, D.C.: United States Government Printing Office, 1988), 401, Table 666; ibid. (1979), 427, Table 705.

21. Peter Asch, *Consumer Safety Regulation: Putting a Price on Life and Limb* (New York: Oxford University Press, 1988), 49; Mary Lyndon, "Information Economics and Chemical Toxicity: Designing Laws to Produce and Use Data," *Michigan Law Review* 87 (1989): 1796.

22. Schroeder and Shapiro, "Responses," 1231–36; W. Kip Viscusi, "Structuring an Effective Occupational Disease Policy: Victim Compensation and Risk Regulation," *Yale Journal on Regulation* 2 (1984): 57–58.

23. Viscusi, "Structuring," 58–59.

24. Dickens, "Differences," 323.

25. Lawrence Friedman, *A History of American Law* (New York: Simon and Schuster, 1973), 262.

26. Joseph O. Page and Mary-Win O'Brien, *Bitter Wages: Ralph Nader's Study Group Report on Disease and Injury on the Job* (New York: Grossman, 1973), 49–50; Schroeder and Shapiro, "Responses," 1253.

27. See William J. Maakestad and Charles Helm, "Promoting Workplace Safety and Health in the Post-Regulatory Era: A Primer on Non-OSHA Legal Incentives That Influence Employer Decisions to Control Occupational Hazards," *Northern Kentucky Law Review* 17 (1989): 9.

28. William Prosser, *Handbook of the Law of Torts* (St. Paul, Minn.: West, 1941), 528.

29. Judith Thompson, "Imposing Risks," in *Rights, Restitution, and Risks: Essays in Moral Theory*, ed. William Parent (Cambridge, Mass.: Harvard University Press, 1986), 191.

30. Page and O'Brien, *Bitter Wages*, 51.

31. Ibid.

32. Daniel M. Berman, *Death on the Job: Occupational Health and Safety Struggles in the United States* (New York: Monthly Review Press, 1978), 18–20; Noble, *Liberalism at Work*, 41–43.

33. Maakstad and Helm, "Primer," 17–21.

34. U.S. Department of Labor, Employment Standards Administration, Office of Workers Compensation Programs, *State Workers' Compensation Laws* (Washington, D.C.: United States Government Printing Office, 1990), Table 6.

35. Ibid., Table 7.

36. Ibid., Table 6; U.S. Bureau of the Census, *Current Population Reports: Poverty in the United States* (Washington, D.C.: United States Government Printing Office, 1987), 157.

37. William Robbins, "Grieving Relatives Gird for Federal Hearings on New Rule for Job Safety," *New York Times*, 30 Jan. 1990, A17, col. 1.

38. U.S. Department of Labor, *Workers' Compensation Laws*, Table 13; Joseph Kinney, director, National Safe Workplace Institute, telephone interview, 13 Jan. 1990.

39. Schroeder and Shapiro, "Responses," 1250.

40. John Burton, Jr., "Introduction," in *New Perspectives in Workers Compensation*, ed. John Burton, Jr. (Ithaca, N.Y.: ILR Press, 1988), 3.

41. Moore and Viscusi, *Compensation Mechanisms*, 67.

42. *National Safe Workplace Institute Newsletter* 3 (May 1990): 3.

43. John Mendeloff, *Regulating Safety: An Economic and Political Analysis of Occupational Safety and Health Policy* (Cambridge, Mass.: MIT Press, 1979), 153; Berman, *Death*, 70–76; Schroeder and Shapiro, "Responses," 1246 n. 113; Maakestad and Helm, "Primer," 21–25.

44. Schroeder and Shapiro, "Responses," 1245; Jerry Mashaw, "A Comment on Causation, Law Reform, and Guerrilla Warfare," *Georgetown Law Review* 73 (1989): 1393; Maakestad and Helm, "Primer," 25–28.

45. Noble, *Liberalism*, 55; Page and O'Brien, *Bitter Wages*, 70.

46. *Vernon's Texas Stat. Ann.*, art. 8306–26.

47. G. Edward White, *Tort Law in America: An Intellectual History* (New York: Oxford University Press, 1980), 68.

48. Richard H. Gaskins, *Environmental Accidents: Personal Injury and Public Responsibility* (Philadelphia: Temple University Press, 1989), 27, 32.

49. White, *Tort Law*, 148–49.

50. *Kansas City Star*, 15 May 1990, B2, col. 1.

51. U.S. Department of Labor, *Workers' Compensation Laws*, Table 9a.

52. Viscusi, *Risk by Choice*, 67; Schroeder and Shapiro, "Responses," 1252–53.

53. Viscusi, *Risk by Choice*, 67; Schroeder and Shapiro, "Responses," 1253.

54. Schroeder and Shapiro, "Responses," 1255.

55. Smith, *Goals and Achievements*, 75–78.

56. Richard Zeckhauser and Albert Nichols, "The Occupational Safety and Health Administration—An Overview," in U.S. Senate, Committee on Government Affairs, *Study on Federal Regulation*, 96th Cong., 1st sess., 1978, S. Doc. 96–14, app. to vol. IV, 165–67, 236–37.

57. Ibid., 223.

58. Ibid., 187; Smith, *Goals and Achievements*, 79.

59. Zeckhauser and Nichols, "An Overview," 165.

60. Smith, *Goals and Achievements*, 39, 57, 84.

61. Zeckhauser and Nichols, "An Overview," 226; Albert Nichols and Richard Zeckhauser, "Government Comes to the Workplace: An Assessment of OSHA," *The Public Interest* 49 (Fall 1977): 39.

62. Mendeloff, *Regulating Safety*, 28–31; 155–56, 168.

63. Ibid., 148–49, 162.

64. Viscusi, *Risk by Choice*, 118–20, 162.

65. John Mendeloff, *The Dilemma of Toxic Substance Regulation: How Overregulation Causes Underregulation* (Cambridge, Mass.: MIT Press, 1988).

66. Ibid., 8–16.

67. Cass Sunstein, "Interpreting Statutes in the Regulatory State," *Harvard Law Review* 103 (1989): 405; Susan Rose-Ackerman, "Comment: Progressive Law and Economics—and the New Administrative Law," *Yale Law Review* 98 (1988): 363.

Part II

OSHA'S HISTORY

3

The Nixon/Ford Years:
Inauspicious Beginnings

When Congress delivered the Occupational Safety and Health Act (OSH Act) to the Nixon administration in 1971, the federal government had limited experience with protecting the health and safety of employees. To make matters worse, Nixon's appointment of weak administrators had an immediate debilitating effect on the agency. As a result, OSHA both needlessly antagonized the business community and clumsily failed to establish significant health and safety protection for workers. A more inauspicious beginning is hard to imagine.

WORKPLACE SAFETY AT THE FEDERAL LEVEL

Because Congress regarded worker protection as primarily a matter for state attention, the federal government was only sporadically involved in implementing occupational safety and health programs prior to the 1960s. The Federal Employer's Liability Act was an early attempt to federalize a workers' compensation regime for railway workers.[1] Congress also undertook a few somewhat feeble efforts to protect federal workers. For the most part, however, the federal government adopted a hands-off posture.[2]

As time passed, it became increasingly apparent that most states were unwilling to write laws that would protect workers at the expense of local employers. Even so, the federal initiatives were tentative and gradual.[3] The largest federal regulatory presence was the program established in the Department of Labor under the Walsh-Healey Act of 1936, a piece of New Deal legislation designed to regulate private employment relationships through the administration of government contracts. Under this chronically underfunded program, the Bureau of Labor Standards promulgated health and safety standards for federal contractors. Since the Bureau had no independent research arm, these standards were normally

based on recommendations by private and quasi-public standard-setting organizations, such as the American National Standards Institute and the American
Council of Governmental Industrial Hygienists. Even these relatively weak standards were seldom enforced. For example, during 1969 only 2,929 of more than
75,000 covered establishments were inspected. Although a total of 33,378 health
and safety violations were discovered, only 34 formal complaints were filed and
only 2 firms were blacklisted for a period of time.[4] Consequently, government
contractors did not take the Walsh-Healey program very seriously.

THE OCCUPATIONAL SAFETY AND HEALTH ACT OF 1970

By the late 1960s, occupational safety and health had become a national
problem. In the generally activist climate of that period, frequent reports of
mining catastrophes and the discovery of new occupational diseases like "brown
lung" precipitated strong demands for federal legislation.[5] More important, the
unions finally decided to assign occupational safety and health a high priority
on their legislative agendas. In 1968, the Johnson administration drafted a bill
that would have empowered the Labor Department to establish and enforce
occupational safety and health standards for workplaces not already regulated
by other federal agencies.[6] It also established an inspectorate and empowered
the department to secure an injunction shutting down any plant or machinery
that posed an imminent hazard to workers.[7] The bill was intensely resisted by
industry, which argued that most industrial accidents were attributable to human
error.[8] "States rights" became a rallying cry of businesses that were content
with existing arrangements at the state level. They also painted distressing pictures of a post-OSHA America in which everything from local building codes
to professional football would fall in the wake of a power-hungry bureaucracy.[9]
Lacking strong union support, the administration's initiative died aborning.

The issue did not go away. Seeking to lure blue-collar support away from the
Democrats, the Nixon administration launched a new occupational safety and
health initiative. A mine disaster in Farmington, West Virginia, which had killed
88 miners, provided an initial stimulus.[10] With both Democrats and Republicans
in the opposite corner, industry shifted strategies and attempted to cut its losses
by producing a bill that it could "live with." It decided grudgingly to support
a Nixon administration bill that would have placed regulatory power in an independent board appointed by the president. The unions wanted to house regulatory authority in the Department of Labor, over which they thought they held
greater influence,[11] and they argued that no bill at all was preferable to the
"abomination" concocted by the Nixon administration.[12] After some highly
partisan battles, the final statute struck a compromise between warring Republicans and Democrats by lodging the Department of Labor standard-setting authority in OSHA but creating another agency, the Occupational Safety and Health
Review Commission, to adjudicate whether the act had been violated.[13] This
compromise has plagued the act's administration ever since.

The act also created the National Institute for Occupational Safety and Health (NIOSH), within the Department of Health, Education and Welfare (now the Department of Health and Human Services) to conduct the research and analysis upon which OSHA would base its occupational safety and health standards.[14] Finally, Congress allowed OSHA to establish two kinds of advisory committees to aid it in promulgating standards. The National Advisory Committee on Occupational Safety and Health could make general recommendations "on matters relating to the administration of the Act,"[15] and OSHA could create separate advisory committees for individual rulemaking initiatives to provide needed outside technical expertise.

One issue that came to a head in the conference committee was the question of formal versus informal rulemaking for standard-setting. The Senate bill allowed the secretary of labor to set standards through informal rulemaking. The House bill forced the board to use formal rulemaking, a triallike process that had long bogged down the Food and Drug Administration.[16] In another major compromise, Congress adopted informal rulemaking with a "substantial evidence" scope of review by the federal courts of appeal, which is the scope of review normally associated with formal rulemaking.[17] This compromise, too, has had long-lasting effects.

There was surprisingly little debate in Congress about the appropriate criteria for setting occupational health and safety standards. For example, the question of the role that cost considerations should play in standard-setting received virtually no direct attention. The question of costs surfaced most prominently in the phrase "to the extent feasible," which served as a limitation on standards for toxic substances and harmful physical agents. Yet there was virtually no discussion in the legislative debates about the meaning of the word "feasible."[18] This legislative failure to address the role of costs made the Supreme Court's job much more difficult later when industry argued that OSHA was required to balance benefits against costs in setting occupational health standards. Mendeloff plausibly suggests that the failure to focus on costs was a necessary part of the employers' strategy of focusing upon "human error" as the cause of most workplace accidents.[19]

As federal statutes go, the OSH Act is not especially complicated. Its purpose is "to assure so far as possible every working man and woman in the Nation safe and healthful working conditions."[20] The "general duty clause" requires every employer "to furnish to each of his employees employment and a place of employment which are free from recognized hazards that are causing or are likely to cause death or serious physical harm to his employees."[21] In addition, employers must comply with OSHA-promulgated occupational safety and health standards[22] that are supposed to require conditions and practices "reasonably necessary or appropriate" to provide safe or healthful employment.[23] An occupational health standard dealing with toxic materials or harmful physical agents must be established in a way that "most adequately assures, to the extent feasible, on the basis of the best available evidence, that no employee will suffer material impairment of health or functional capacity even if such employee has regular exposure to the hazard dealt with in such standards for the period of his working life."[24] Occupational safety and health standards must prescribe the use of labels, emergency treatments, and "proper conditions and precautions of safe use and exposure." Where appropriate, standards should in addition prescribe suitable protective equipment, control or technological procedures, monitoring requirements, and time and frequency of medical examinations.[25] Finally, OSHA may promulgate an immediately effective "emergency temporary standard" if the agency determines that employees are exposed to a "grave danger" from toxic substances. An emergency temporary standard lasts for six months, during which time OSHA must promulgate a permanent standard.[26]

Recognizing that it would take some time before OSHA could write its own occupational safety and health standards from scratch, Congress established a one-time abbreviated procedure by which OSHA was, within two years, to promulgate as an occupational safety or health standard any "national consensus standard" and any established federal standard under the Walsh-Healey Act, unless the agency determined that such standard would not result in increased safety or health. With the help of this "jump start," Congress hoped to send OSHA rapidly on its way toward providing American workers safer and more healthful workplaces.

Prominent members of Congress were exuberant about the bill they had just passed. Senator Jacob Javits, who played a significant role in formulating the legislation, predicted that it "will mark the greatest single contribution to the health and welfare of American workers that has yet been made by Congress."[27] A Democrat active in the bill's passage, Senator Ralph Yarborough, concluded that based on passage of the OSH Act alone, 1970 "will surely be recorded as one of the most productive legislative sessions in the history of the country."[28] Not to be outdone, another Democrat, Congressman William Steiger, characterized the legislation as an "unprecedented response by Congress to the need to help save the lives and protect the health of the working men and women throughout the nation."[29]

FROM DREAM TO REALITY

Even with allowances for the usual political hyperbole, these congressional statements indicate an unusual enthusiasm for a piece of legislation. This optimism was soon dashed by the disappointing reality of OSHA's first few years.

George Guenther

Rather than searching for dynamic new leaders for the infant agency, the Nixon administration drew heavily upon the officials in the Department of Labor and the Department of Health, Education and Welfare who had been administering the programs that the OSH Act was designed to change. The first assistant secretary of labor for OSHA was George Guenther, a former president of a small hosiery company who had been serving as the head of the Bureau of Labor Statistics. He was appointed with the strong support of the steel industry.[30] Assistant Secretary Guenther is perhaps best remembered for the "Guenther Memo" that came to light during the Senate Watergate investigations. The memo appeared to suggest to companies regulated by OSHA that in return for contributions to the Committee to Re-Elect the President, Guenther would slow the agency's output of proposed standards such as the one for exposure to cotton dust.[31] Labor unions quickly seized upon this memo as proof that the agency under Guenther was attempting "to get business support for the President by going easy on business."[32]

OSHA's first job was to promulgate the national consensus standards that Congress had mandated. In only four months the agency rushed to the *Federal Register* 400 pages of standards from the old Walsh-Healey program, the American National Standards Institute (ANSI), and the National Fire Protection Association (NFPA). Although the statute gave OSHA discretion not to promulgate consensus standards that would not result in improved health and safety, OSHA did not attempt to sort through the existing standards to weed out those that were obviously silly and outdated. Consequently, the standards contained ridiculous and petty requirements, such as an injunction against stepping in slippery cow manure, that later subjected OSHA to unfair ridicule.[33] Worse, as will be discussed below, it took OSHA years to extract itself from the political hot water that resulted from its attempts to enforce the consensus standards. Congress may have been laboring under the misapprehension that those standards were generally followed in the real world. In reality, they were often mere aspirations that could be freely ignored because they were "flexibly" enforced.[34] A Nader Report issued in 1971 criticized OSHA for mixing the reasonable Walsh-Healey standards with the otherwise nonbinding standards from ANSI and NFPA.[35]

In addition to the consensus standards, the Guenther administration proposed eight new safety standards and finalized six of them. It also started and finished one health standard for asbestos.[36] The completed safety standards, which covered subjects like load indicators for cranes and derricks, rollover bars for construction machinery, and scaffolding, went into effect without legal challenge. The asbestos standard suffered a different fate.

In 1971, OSHA adopted as part of the national consensus standards a permissible exposure limit (PEL) for asbestos of 12 fibers per cubic centimeter of air. It soon became evident, however, that the consensus standard, based on a Walsh-Healey PEL, was inadequate to protect the 3.5 million workers who were then exposed to asbestos fibers.[37] In December 1971, OSHA promulgated an emergency temporary standard (ETS) restricting exposure over eight hours to a weighted average of five fibers per cubic centimeter of air.[38] In June 1972, OSHA followed with a permanent standard of two fibers per cubic centimeter of air, but it delayed its effective date for four years, applying the five-fiber PEL in the interim. It said the delay was necessary because of the difficulty of industry compliance.[39]

The AFL-CIO, outraged over the delay, sued OSHA in the District of Columbia Circuit. Judge McGowan's opinion first attempted to determine what Congress meant in the compromise that subjected OSHA to a "substantial evidence" scope of review. Sympathetic to the agency's plight, he noted that OSHA faced questions "on the frontiers of scientific knowledge" and that judicial review should be calculated only "to negate the dangers of arbitrariness and irrationality." Under this scope of review, OSHA's choice of a two-fiber limit was "doubtlessly sound." The court, however, rejected OSHA's delay because the agency did not have any proof why it was necessary to impose an across-the-board delay in the protection that workers badly needed. The standard was remanded to OSHA to develop evidence on which industries required a delay.[40]

Consistent with the Nixon administration's policy favoring federalism, Assistant Secretary Guenther quickly delegated much of OSHA's power to the states. The OSH Act authorizes a state to regulate its employers if OSHA accepts its enforcement plan as being "at least as effective" as the federal program in providing safe and healthful employment conditions.[41] Soon after the act was passed, the secretary of labor invited the governors to create their own programs. Although 44 states submitted plans for OSHA's approval by the end of 1972, it was apparent that, as submitted, the plans did not meet the statutory criteria for approval. When OSHA approved them anyway, the AFL-CIO and steel workers unions sued. After a federal district court held the approval to be beyond its statutory authority, OSHA abandoned its attempts to approve state plans in violation of the act. By the end of 1972, only three state plans had been approved.[42]

John Stender

When Guenther resigned in January 1973, at the end of Nixon's first term, he was replaced by John H. Stender, a former union official and Republican legislator from the state of Washington. Carefully avoiding controversy, Stender served through the Watergate years until near the end of the Ford administration. One analyst sums up his contribution this way: "The best that those who remember his reign will say about him is that his heart was in the right place, for both union and management lobbyists agreed that Stender was hopelessly out of his depth in running OSHA. Stender served his purpose by being there, thus providing an argument that the Nixon administration was no enemy of unions."[43]

During Stender's tenure, OSHA promulgated 7 safety standards (including 2 started during the Guenther administration) and initiated another 5 standards. Even fewer health standards were promulgated. OSHA finalized 2 health standards (14 carcinogens and vinyl chloride) and proposed 4 additional ones (coke oven emissions, arsenic, lead, and noise).[44] As before, the safety standards were relatively uncontroversial, and only 3 were challenged.[45] By comparison, industry fought both health standards in court.

The standard for 14 carcinogens began as an ETS issued in June 1973.[46] The Third Circuit vacated the ETS for two of the carcinogens—dichlorobenzidine (DCB) and ethyleneimine (EI)—because it had "doubts—more serious as to EI than to DCB" as to whether the substances were carcinogenic.[47] After a permanent standard was promulgated in January 1974,[48] OSHA convinced the Third Circuit to uphold most of the regulation.[49] As in the asbestos case, the court interpreted OSHA's obligations to establish the necessity for regulation with "substantial evidence" in a manner favorable to the agency. In rejecting industry's argument that OSHA could not determine carcinogencity on the basis of animal data alone, the court treated the validity of the agency's scientific conclusion as a "legal" question that was not subject to "substantial evidence" scope of review. It affirmed the agency's reliance on animal studies because it was "consistent" with the "statutory language and purposes" of the OSH Act.

In April 1974, OSHA promulgated an ETS for vinyl chloride, and a final standard followed in October of that year.[50] The permanent standard initially proposed by OSHA called for a "no detectable" exposure level. Faced with intense industry opposition, however, OSHA backed down and adopted a 1 ppm PEL. OSHA prevailed in the legal challenge that followed.[51] The court held that OSHA's adoption of the lowest exposure level feasible was appropriate when no dose-response curve could be calculated. It regarded OSHA's decision to seek minimal exposures as a policy judgment to be affirmed as long as it was not arbitrary and capricious. In light of scientific evidence that no safe exposure level was known for this human carcinogen, the court concluded that OSHA's decision reasonably served the protective policies of the act.

These two health standards provided important protection to hundreds of workers. In fact, OSHA regulated more chemicals more comprehensively with the 14 carcinogens standard than it regulated for the next 15 years through individual standard-setting initiatives. Moreover, the early judicial precedents suggested that OSHA had much discretion to set protective standards and little excuse for delay. Still, by the end of 1974, OSHA had a backlog of 20 recommendations from NIOSH for potential rulemaking initiatives.[52]

Part of the reason for the backlog was the strained relationship between OSHA and NIOSH. While the OSH Act envisioned that NIOSH would do much of the technical work supporting OSHA's regulations, the two agencies were unable to agree upon priorities. NIOSH sent OSHA criteria documents for workplace hazards that, in the minds of OSHA staffers, were of little or no consequence, while OSHA initiatives on other, more dangerous chemicals were hampered by lack of scientific support. Although OSHA was required by its statute to take economic and technological feasibility considerations into account, NIOSH looked solely to a chemical's health effects. It was therefore not the case, as many members of the public believed, that OSHA could simply "tear the covers off'' a NIOSH criteria document and use it as the technical support for its standard. Even the health effects discussion in NIOSH criteria documents were not sufficient to support OSHA rules. OSHA scientists increasingly undertook their own literature searches and health effects assessments, often hiring outside contractors for needed technical support.

In late 1974, OSHA launched two major programs designed to speed up the standard-setting process. The first, dubbed the Standards Completion Project, was an attempt to promulgate complete health standards for 400 toxic substances for which PELs existed under the consensus standards (sometimes called the Table Z standards). Although the Table Z PELs were legally enforceable, they merely prescribed maximum concentrations for chemicals in indoor workplaces. They lacked many of the other elements of adequate health standards, such as exposure monitoring requirements, medical surveillance, removal of employees to other areas as a medical precaution, employee training, and warning labels. The agency estimated that the ambitious process of converting the PELs to full-fledged standards would take three years.[53] Although the Standards Completion Project was never completed, OSHA did attempt to update the PELs in 1988 in a single generic standard. The second major project was aimed at writing standards for the 20 hazards that were the subjects of NIOSH recommendations.[54] Both of these initiatives were abject failures. In the next two years, OSHA promulgated only one occupational health standard (for coke oven emissions).

Like his predecessor, Assistant Secretary Stender chose to lower the quality of state programs. The OSH Act requires that a state plan contain ''satisfactory assurances'' that the state will have ''qualified personnel necessary for the enforcement'' of the state's health and safety standards.[55] OSHA interpreted this requirement to mean that states were required to provide staffing and funding levels at least as effective as those that would be provided if OSHA itself were in charge of enforcement. Stender decided, however, that since OSHA, because of budget restrictions, had only limited resources, staffing requirements for the states would be based on OSHA's emasculated budget rather than on the number of inspectors that would be necessary for effective enforcement.[56]

The AFL-CIO sued, claiming that the OSH Act required the states to provide sufficient funds and staffing ''to ensure that normative standards are in fact enforced,'' and that OSHA therefore had to make a judgment whether a state had the ''necessary'' staff.[57] The District of Columbia Court of Appeals agreed, rejecting the agency's argument that ''at least as effective'' meant ''at least as ineffective'' as OSHA's own efforts, and held that OSHA had to come up with ''a coherent program to realize a fully effective enforcement effort at some time in the future.'' The court remanded the case to OSHA to come up with new criteria for state funding and staff.[58] OSHA's attempts to meet the court's order are taken up in Chapter 4.

Morton Corn

In late 1975, in anticipation of the 1976 elections, President Ford with great fanfare appointed an occupational health specialist to head OSHA. Morton Corn, formerly a professor of occupational health and chemical engineering at the University of Pittsburgh, promised to build OSHA into a more professional agency that was at the same time more open to public input, especially from small businesses.[59] Corn also made a concerted effort to improve the qualifications and training of OSHA compliance officers.[60]

Like his predecessors, however, Corn was unable to accomplish very much in the area of standard-setting. During his brief tenure, OSHA completed two safety standards started during Stender's tenure (ground-fault protection[61] and farm machinery safeguards[62]) and issued an ETS for commercial diving.[63] The ETS, however, was stayed by the Fifth Circuit,[64] and the standard for ground-fault protection was vacated by the District of Columbia Circuit because of a procedural error.[65] No new safety standards were proposed. Corn promised to devote more attention to occupational health standards and to set such standards primarily on the basis of health considerations. More personnel were hired to work in the health area, and Corn placed the Health Standards Directorate in the hands of an aggressive young administrator, Grover Wrenn. Following this shake-up, Corn hoped that the agency could reduce the time necessary to develop a health standard to 14 months.[66] Yet, Corn completed only one standard (coke oven emissions) and proposed only one more (cotton dust). With some justification, Corn blamed the slow pace for setting health standards upon OSHA's lack of technical expertise.[67]

The coke oven emissions standard dated back to 1971, when the United Steel Workers had petitioned OSHA for rulemaking based on strong epidemiological evidence that coke oven emissions were carcinogenic. In November 1974, a standards advisory committee, chaired by Dr. Eula Bingham, who would become the next administrator of OSHA, supported the petition. OSHA proposed a standard in July 1975 and promulgated a final standard in October 1976.[68] When the industry sued to block the regulation's implementation, the Third Circuit affirmed OSHA's PEL, but it rejected the agency's requirements mandating new health research and qualitative fit tests for respirators.[69]

ENFORCEMENT

Although OSHA's standard-setting problems were cause enough for alarm, its reputation for mismanagement during the Nixon and Ford years stems more from misguided enforcement policies that created political difficulties for years to come. From its inception, OSHA recognized that a sustained enforcement effort would have to accompany its standard-setting initiatives and that this would in turn require a well-trained professional inspectorate. The agency also realized that with millions of workplaces subject to OSHA standards, it would never have enough inspectors to devote a significant amount of attention to any single site. OSHA therefore accepted the fact that it would have to rely heavily upon voluntary compliance and conserve its limited enforcement resources for investigating genuine complaints, following up on investigations of serious accidents, and spot-checking remaining workplaces in accordance with some general inspection policy. In 1972, OSHA established two inspection targeting programs, one for high hazard industries and the other for selected health hazards. It added additional programs for trenching in 1973 and for foundries in 1975.[70]

These early efforts were largely wasted. First, OSHA failed to train and supervise its inspectors adequately. Most compliance officers lacked formal safety and health education, and they received only a four-week training course from OSHA before they were sent into the field. Further, OSHA managers failed to insist that these inexperienced inspectors identify the most serious hazards. The agency provided no preinspection information concerning which equipment, operations, or processes were most likely to pose serious dangers to workers, and it had no formal evaluation system to monitor the quality of the inspections. Worse, OSHA's reward structure under Assistant Secretary Stender emphasized the quantity of violations detected, rather than their seriousness, by establishing quotas for each inspector.[71]

Second, most of OSHA's early enforcement actions focused on violations of the "national consensus standards," many of which were hopelessly vague and some of which were plainly ridiculous. Since OSHA had not screened those standards prior to making them legally binding, overly enthusiastic inspectors could issue citations for nonserious violations of silly standards. Moreover, because many of the consensus standards had originally been written as non-binding recommendations, compliance officers had difficulty determining the exact duties of the employers being inspected.[72]

Third, the OSH Act required OSHA to conduct an investigation in response to an employee complaint if there were "reasonable grounds" to believe a violation that threatened "physical harm or an imminent danger" had occurred.[73] OSHA's interpretation of this statutory obligation seriously constrained its enforcement discretion and caused OSHA inspectors to investigate many nonserious complaints. In 1976, for example, OSHA discovered that an area office had ignored a complaint by an employee of the Life Sciences Products Company that he had been exposed to the particularly dangerous pesticide Kepone, and that several employees consequently suffered nervous system damage. (The discharges into the James River also prevented commercial fishing in much of Chesapeake Bay.) OSHA reacted by establishing a new policy that complaints would be investigated according to strict deadlines if they contained "any" information indicating that any safety or health hazard existed at a workplace. The dramatic increase in complaint inspections that resulted from the new policy had the effect of shifting resources away from the inspection of high-hazard employers and toward businesses that usually did not have any serious hazards.[74]

OSHA's early inspection efforts also created serious political problems for the agency. Labor unions and other worker representatives were angered by the fact that 91 percent of the citations that OSHA issued between 1970 and 1977 were for nonserious violations.[75] Business groups decried the enforcement of "Mickey Mouse standards" that imposed silly burdens without noticeably improving safety or health.[76] One employer complained, "A few years ago this type of harassment by the mobsters was considered illegal. Today the U.S. government does it and it is legal.''[77] The net result was a serious deterioration of the early political support for OSHA. Testifying in 1980, Lloyd McBride, president of the United Steel Workers of America, told Congress, ''Because of the hue and cry over these 'nitpicking' aspects of the program, the more serious and important goals of the OSHA program became lost in a morass of largely unintelligible debate and political animosity.''[78]

CONCLUSIONS

Although industry reluctantly acquiesced in the enactment of the OSH Act at the end of the politically turbulent 1960s, employers were never very enthusiastic about the prospect of oversight by a centralized bureaucracy. The predictable attacks on OSHA began not long after it started promulgating and enforcing standards. In 1972, for example, Senator Carl Curtis proposed amendments to the OSH Act that would have excluded small businesses from OSHA inspections. Small businessmen flooded the hearings on the bill with horror stories about ''overly aggressive'' OSHA inspectors.[79] In 1973, several bills were introduced to require OSHA to pay explicit attention to costs in setting occupational safety and health standards.[80] The force of these efforts was blunted somewhat by the District of Columbia Circuit opinion in OSHA's first really important standards case (asbestos) that instructed OSHA to consider costs without conducting a finely tuned cost-benefit analysis.[81] In 1976, Congress did limit OSHA's jurisdiction by exempting small farms (with 10 or fewer employees) from OSHA enforcement. The legislation was a reaction to OSHA's proposal to regulate field sanitation and to what some legislators considered to be a patronizing OSHA education pamphlet on farm safety.[82] An irritated farm state congressman explained: ''Believe me, my colleagues, I do not want to 'castrate OSHA' because if I do it might grow more rapidly. . . . But if castration is the only solution I would sooner castrate the zealots who are drawing up regulations at OSHA than let them destroy the smaller farmers of America.''[83]

Feeling election-year pressure from sentiments such as these, President Ford appointed a special task force on ''regulatory reform'' in July 1976 and told it to begin with an examination of OSHA.[84] OSHA got the message. After completing the coke oven emissions standard, OSHA did not promulgate any new health standards during the Ford administration. Upon leaving the agency with the change of administrations in 1977, Assistant Secretary Corn expressed disappointment with the slow pace of the chemical-by-chemical approach to setting occupational health standards and urged the agency to adopt ''generic'' approaches to regulating chemicals, such as the carcinogen policy that the agency had recently begun to formulate. In a memorandum to the new secretary of labor, he candidly assessed the agency's problems as including the incompetence of top administrative officials at the time he took over, the ''minimal'' attention paid to health (as opposed to safety) standards, the small size of the staff who worked on health standards (only 26 persons), and the fact that the Washington staff lacked sufficient expertise to command the respect of the field staff.[85] In addition, he proposed that Congress transfer NIOSH to the Department of Labor, so that the two agencies could coordinate their priority-setting processes under a single administrator.[86] These sentiments were echoed in a timely GAO report that chronicled OSHA's progress from its inception until the fall of 1976.[87]

As President Ford left office, OSHA was an agency cast adrift. Lacking its earlier enthusiasm for protecting workers, the agency's staff seemed content to steer a middle course, thereby avoiding criticism from either end of the political spectrum. As a result, it had accomplished very little either by way of shielding employers from "nitpicking" consensus standards or by way of protecting workers from the very real occupational health hazards posed by toxic chemicals in the workplace. The election in 1976 of a Democratic president with a strongly expressed commitment to occupational and environmental health promised to set OSHA back on the course that Congress plotted for it in 1970.

NOTES

1. 45 U.S.C. §§ 51–60 (1988).

2. Joseph O. Page and Mary-Win O'Brien, *Bitter Wages: Ralph Nader's Study Group Report on Disease and Injury on the Job* (New York: Grossman, 1973).

3. Ibid., 87.

4. Ibid., 100.

5. Lloyd Meeds, "A Legislative History of OSHA," *Gonzaga Law Review* 9 (1974): 327.

6. Steven Kelman, "Occupational Safety and Health Administration," in *The Politics of Regulation*, ed. James Q. Wilson (New York: Basic Books, 1980), 239.

7. Page and O'Brien, *Bitter Wages*, 39–40.

8. Kelman, "Occupational Safety," 240.

9. Page and O'Brien, *Bitter Wages*, 142–43.

10. Kelman, "Occupational Safety," 239.

11. Meeds. "Legislative History," 332.

12. Page and O'Brien, *Bitter Wages*, 144.

13. 29 U.S.C. § 661 (1988).

14. 29 U.S.C. § 671 (1988).

15. 29 U.S.C. § 656(a)(2) (1988).

16. Meeds, "Legislative History," 336–37.

17. 29 U.S.C. § 555(f) (1988).

18. *Industrial Union Dept., AFL-CIO v. American Petroleum Institute*, 448 U.S. 607, 681–82 (Rehnquist, J., concurring); John Mendeloff, *Regulating Safety: An Economic and Political Analysis of Occupational Safety and Health Policy* (Cambridge, Mass.: MIT Press, 1979), 20–24.

19. Mendeloff, *Regulating Safety*, 21.

20. 29 U.S.C. § 651 (1988).

21. 29 U.S.C. § 654(a)(1) (1988).

22. 29 U.S.C. § 654(a)(2) (1988).

23. 29 U.S.C. § 652(8) (1988).
24. 29 U.S.C. § 655(b)(5) (1988).
25. 29 U.S.C. § 655(b)(7) (1988).
26. 29 U.S.C. § 655(c) (1988).
27. *Congressional Record*, 91st Cong., 2d sess., 1970, 116: 41,764.
28. Ibid., 41,763.
29. Ibid., 42,206.
30. Mendeloff, *Regulating Safety*, 38.
31. Nicholas Ashford, *Crisis in the Workplace* (Cambridge, Mass.: MIT Press, 1976), 543.
32. Linda E. Demkovich, "OSHA Launches Dual Effort to Reduce Job Health Hazards," *National Journal Reports* 6 (7 Dec. 1974): 1834.
33. Kelman, "Occupational Safety," 259.
34. Mendeloff, *Regulating Safety*, 36–41.
35. Page and O'Brien, *Bitter Wages*, 201–02.
36. U.S. Congress, Office of Technology Assessment, *Preventing Illnesses and Injury in the Workplace* (Washington, D.C.: United States Government Printing Office, 1985) 363–64.
37. Benjamin W. Mintz, "Occupational Safety and Health: The Federal Regulatory Program—A History," in *Fundamentals of Industrial Hygiene*, 3d ed., ed. Barbara A. Plog (Washington, D.C.: National Safety Council, 1988), 695.
38. 36 *Fed. Reg.* 23,207 (1971).
39. 37 *Fed. Reg.* 11,320 (1972).
40. *Industrial Union Department* v. *Hodgson*, 499 F.2d 467 (D.C. Cir. 1974).
41. 29 U.S.C. § 667 (1988).
42. Mintz, "A History," 696.
43. Graham K. Wilson, *The Politics of Safety and Health: Occupational Safety and Health in the United States and Britain* (Oxford: Clarendon Press, 1985), 60–61.
44. Office of Technology Assessment, *Preventing Illnesses*.
45. *AFL-CIO* v. *Brennan*, 530 F.2d 109 (3rd Cir. 1975) (mechanical power presses); *Bethlehem Steel Corp.* v. *Dunlop*, 540 F.2d 679 (3rd Cir. 1976) (industrial slings); *Associated Industries* v. *Department of Labor*, 487 F.2d 342 (2nd Cir. 1973) (lavatories).
46. 38 *Fed. Reg.* 10,929 (1973).
47. *Dry Color Mfrs. Ass'n.* v. *Department of Labor*, 486 F.2d 98 (3rd Cir. 1973).
48. 39 *Fed. Reg.* 3756 (1974).
49. *Synthetic Org. Chem. Mfrs. Ass'n.* v. *Brennan*, 506 F.2d 384 (3rd Cir. 1974); *Synthetic Org. Chem. Mfrs. Ass'n.* v. *Brennan*, 503 F.2d 1155 (3rd Cir. 1974).
50. 39 *Fed. Reg.* 35,890 (1974); 39 *Fed. Reg.* 12,342 (1974).
51. *Soc. of Plastics Ind.* v. *OSHA*, 509 F.2d 1301 (2nd Cir. 1975), *cert. denied* 421 U.S. 992 (1975).
52. "Criteria Developed for 22 Hazards," *National Journal Reports* 6 (7 Dec. 1974): 1832.
53. Ibid., 1835; Mintz, "A History," 704.
54. Demkovich, "OSHA Launches Dual Effort," 1835.
55. 29 U.S.C. § 667(e) (1988).
56. Mintz, "A History," 701–02.
57. *AFL-CIO* v. *Marshall*, 570 F.2d 1030, 1034 (D.C. Cir. 1978).
58. *AFL-CIO* v. *Marshall*, 570 F.2d 1030 (D.C. Cir. 1978).

59. Morton Corn, "Report on OSHA Prepared by Outgoing Secretary Morton Corn and Submitted to Labor Secretary W. J. Usery," repr in *BNA Occupational Safety and Health Reporter* 6 (20 Jan. 1977): 1094; James W. Singer, "New OSHA Head May Signal Change in Agency's Approach," *National Journal* 7 (27 Dec. 1975): 1725.

60. Corn, "Report on OSHA," 1095.

61. 41 *Fed. Reg.* 55,695 (1976).

62. 41 *Fed. Reg.* 10,190 (1976).

63. 41 *Fed. Reg.* 24,272 (1976).

64. *Taylor Driving and Salvage Co, Inc.* v. *Department of Labor*, 537 F.2d 819 (5th Cir. 1976).

65. *National Constructors Assoc.* v. *Marshall*, 581 F.2d 960 (D.C. Cir. 1978).

66. Corn, "Report on OSHA," 1094; Singer, "New OSHA Head," 1731.

67. Corn, "Report on OSHA," 1095.

68. 41 *Fed. Reg.* 46,742 (1976).

69. *Iron and Steel Inst.* v. *OSHA*, 577 F.2d 825 (3rd Cir. 1978).

70. Occupational Safety and Health Administration, *Report of the President to the Congress on Occupational Safety and Health for Calendar Year 1987* (Washington, D.C.: United States Government Printing Office, 1988), 47.

71. General Accounting Office, *Workplace Inspection Program Weak in Detecting and Correcting Hazards* (Washington, D.C.: 1978), 9–10, 24–25; Mark Rothstein, "OSHA After Ten Years: A Review and Some Proposed Reforms," *Vanderbilt Law Review* 34 (1981): 94; Mintz, "A History," 698.

72. Kelman, "Occupational Safety," 258–59.

73. 29 U.S.C. § 658(f) (1988).

74. General Accounting Office, *How Effective Are OSHA's Complaint Procedures* (Washington, D.C.: 1979), 9; Benjamin Mintz, *OSHA: History, Law, and Policy* (Washington, D.C.: Bureau of National Affairs, 1984), 411–22; Mintz, "A History," 698.

75. General Accounting Office, *Workplace Inspection Program*, 10.

76. Kelman, "Occupational Safety," 258.

77. U.S. Congress, House Committee on Education and Labor, Select Subcommittee on Labor, *Hearings on Occupational Safety and Health Act of 1970, Oversight and Proposed Amendments*, 93rd Cong., 2d Sess., 1974, 44.

78. U.S. Congress, Senate Committee on Labor and Human Resources, *Hearings on Oversight on the Administration of the Occupational Safety and Health Act*, pt. 1, 96th Cong., 2d sess., 1980, 731.

79. Page and O'Brien, *Bitter Wages*, 237.

80. Mendeloff, *Regulating Safety*, 50.

81. *Industrial Union, AFL-CIO* v. *Hodgson*, 499 F.2d 467 (D.C. Cir. 1974).

82. Mintz, "A History," 701.

83. *Congressional Record*, 94th cong., 2d sess., 1976, 122: 20,366–72.

84. James W. Singer, "New OSHA Task Force—Political Payoff or False Alarm?" *National Journal* 8 (10 July 1976): 973.

85. Wilson, *Politics of Safety*, 62.

86. James W. Singer, "A Farewell to OSHA," *National Journal* 9 (29 Jan. 1977): 179.

87. General Accounting Office, *Delays in Setting Workplace Standards for Cancer-Causing and Other Dangerous Substances* (Washington, D.C.: United States Government Printing Office, 1977), 12–13.

4

The Carter Years:
OSHA on the Move

At the outset of the Carter administration, OSHA promised to adopt health standards much more aggressively[1] while adopting a low-key approach to enforcement that stressed its service and educational functions.[2] The new secretary of labor, Ray Marshall, appointed a respected expert in industrial hygiene, Dr. Eula Bingham, of the University of Cincinnati Medical School, to head OSHA. An unpretentious Washington outsider who ate lunch at her desk and interacted freely and informally with low-level staff, Bingham sought to convey the image of a down-to-earth "common sense" administrator.[3] At the outset, she declared: "We will not be an apologetic, defensive agency, but we will be an aggressive agency that does things."[4] True to her promise, Bingham moved quickly to address OSHA's political difficulties by responding to business and labor complaints about its enforcement policies. She also acted to increase the agency's output of health regulations. While the changes in the agency's enforcement policy were effective, efforts to increase OSHA's regulatory productivity were largely unavailing. Although OSHA was on the move during the Carter administration, it did not travel as far as Bingham hoped it would.

CHANGES IN ENFORCEMENT PRIORITIES

Bingham rapidly shifted the agency's enforcement policies. The agency established more comprehensive training programs, provided better supervision for compliance officers, devised a new policy for addressing complaints, and developed a more effective inspection targeting policy.[5] By the end of the Bingham administration, the number of compliance officers had almost doubled from about 750 to nearly 1,400. As a result of these efforts, OSHA's inspection program became more effective and less controversial.

The centerpiece of the new approach was a three-tiered policy for responding to complaints. OSHA's area offices were required to investigate immediately any "formal" complaint that alleged an "imminent hazard." All other formal complaints were ranked according to the "gravity of the hazards" involved and were investigated either within three days, if they were "serious," or within 20 days, if they were not. OSHA responded to any other complaints by notifying the employer and allowing it 15 days to correct the alleged violation. If the employer failed to respond to OSHA's letter, or it was otherwise indicated that the hazard had not been corrected, an inspection was conducted.[6] As a result of this change in policy, the percentage of complaint inspections dropped from 37.6 percent in 1978 to 23.4 percent in 1981.

OSHA devoted the resources thereby saved to "targeted" inspections that were conducted "primarily" in "high hazard industries."[7] An industry was designated as a high hazard either on the basis of injury data supplied by the Bureau of Labor Statistics or on the basis of the quantity of chemicals it used, the toxicity of those chemicals, and the number of exposed workers.[8] The agency also eliminated its inspection quota system under which compliance officers were evaluated according to the numbers of inspections conducted and violations cited.[9] Finally, by eliminating almost 1000 of the "nit-picking" consensus safety standards, OSHA ensured that the compliance officers would not waste their time enforcing unnecessary regulations.[10]

These dramatic efforts paid off for OSHA. Although the Bingham administration performed about 20,000 fewer inspections each year than OSHA had undertaken between 1974 and 1976, the agency found many more serious violations. In 1975, the year before Bingham took over, OSHA reported 7,800 serious violations. In 1976, OSHA found nearly three times as many serious violations (21,000); in 1977, four times as many (33,200); and in 1980, almost six times as many (44,700).[11] OSHA also began to demand stiffer penalties, and it referred many more cases to the Justice Department for criminal prosecution.[12] The amounts of proposed penalties for serious, willful, repeated, and failure-to-abate violations rose from around $6 million in fiscal 1977 to more than $11 million in fiscal 1980.[13] Since the forum for OSHA's enforcement efforts was the independent Occupational Safety and Health Review Commission (OSHRC), however, the agency could not be sure that its efforts would have any real impact on employers. As Chapter 16 details, large backlogs at OSHRC and several instances of substantially reduced fines took some of the punch out of OSHA's stepped-up enforcement efforts.

As it became clear to industry groups that OSHA meant business, they began to mount potent political challenges.[14] Sensing that the country was shifting to the right politically, Senator Richard Schweiker introduced a bill that would have completely revamped OSHA inspection priorities by reducing random safety inspections in workplaces that had above-average safety records.[15] Assistant Secretary Bingham testified vigorously in opposition to the Schweiker bill asking, "Is an air carrier not inspected for safety because it had no accidents the prior year?''[16] Organized labor joined OSHA's efforts to defeat the bill, and it was never reported out of committee. In 1979, however, Senator Schweiker secured the enactment of an appropriations rider that served a similar purpose by limiting OSHA inspections of ''safe'' employers with ten or fewer employees. The rider remains in effect.[17]

THE NEW DIRECTIONS PROGRAM

Toward the end of Bingham's tenure, OSHA launched an experimental New Directions program, the goal of which was ''to utilize labor unions, trade associations, educational institutions, and nonprofit organizations to provide to employers and employees job safety and health education and training, including assistance in hazard recognition and control, and training in employer and worker rights.''[18] In August 1980, OSHA gave $3.5 million to 66 private organizations for training in hazard abatement. Because the program's funding was drastically reduced during the Reagan administration, it is difficult to evaluate the extent to which it succeeded in enhancing the ability of private organizations to educate employees about health and safety. Had it been given a chance to succeed, it might have given employees the intellectual wherewithal to bargain for health and safety in collective bargaining negotiations.[19]

CRACKING DOWN ON THE STATES

OSHA also got tough with the states. As discussed in Chapter 3, OSHA had attempted to delegate its regulatory responsibilities to the states by accepting state plans that did not meet statutory requirements. Under Bingham, OSHA acknowledged its responsibility to monitor closely the effectiveness of state programs.[20] For the first time, OSHA started a proceeding to withdraw prior approval of a state plan and threatened the same action with respect to other plans.[21] These actions predictably created an uproar in the states. State representatives charged that OSHA was ''insensitive to the states' needs,'' that its requirements were ''prohibitive'' and ''self-serving,'' and that it wished to ''preserve complete federal jurisdiction'' contrary to statutory policy.[22] Bingham replied that OSHA had a ''leadership role which does not lend itself to a traditional partnership of equality as I believe a number of States desire.''[23]

SAFETY AND HEALTH STANDARDS

In addition to improving OSHA's enforcement policies, Bingham made a concerted effort to increase the agency's production of full-fledged health standards. Soon after she came into office, she told a congressional committee of her intentions: ''Quite honestly, I plan to stretch the resources of the agency in putting out health standards, and I intend to use the Emergency Temporary Standard authority whenever employees are exposed to grave dangers.'' She

added, "All I can say is watch the *Federal Register*."[24] With additional resources
provided by a sympathetic White House and Congress,[25] Bingham quickly hired
a number of highly qualified professionals to increase the agency's health standards output.[26] In addition, OSHA and NIOSH promised a new cooperative
attitude to facilitate a more efficient use of both agencies' technical resources.[27]

New Initiatives

The first evidence of OSHA's more aggressive posture was not long in coming.
Two months after Bingham took office, OSHA issued an Emergency Temporary
Standard (ETS) for benzene, a very heavily used and economically important
industrial chemical that posed a variety of health dangers, including cancer.[28]
Shortly thereafter, OSHA issued a second ETS for the pesticide DBCP (1,2
dibromo-3-chloropropane), based on research indicating it is a carcinogen and
causes sterility.[29] An ETS for acrylonitrile, a carcinogen that is the feedstock
for making acrylic plastics, was promulgated in January 1978.[30]

Two of the three initiatives were successful. The ETS for DBCP was not
challenged, and it was replaced by a permanent standard in March 1978.[31] The
Sixth Circuit refused to stay the acrylonitrile ETS,[32] and it was replaced by a
permanent standard in November 1978.[33] These are the only health standards in
OSHA's history that have not been appealed. OSHA's experience with benzene
was much less successful. The ETS was stayed for five months by litigation
concerning which federal circuit court would review its legality. Since an ETS
remains in effect no longer than six months, OSHA decided that it would not
be productive to pursue the litigation any further, and the order expired without
ever becoming effective.[34] OSHA's experience with a permanent benzene standard was no happier. As described later in this chapter, the standard was not
only reversed by the Supreme Court but the Court's opinion established a substantial new barrier to promulgating health and safety standards.

The permanent standards for DBCP, acrylonitrile, and benzene were three of
the nine health standards promulgated during the Bingham administration. OSHA
also promulgated standards for arsenic, cotton dust, lead, employee access to
exposure and medical records, occupational noise, and cancer policy. During
this time period, OSHA proposed two new standards (hazard communication
and ethylene oxide) that were not completed until long after the 1980 election.[35]
OSHA's record for safety standards was similar to that of the Stender administration. It proposed five new safety standards and completed six standards
(including one started under Morton Corn).[36]

Completing Old Projects

Four of the standards finalized during Bingham's tenure had been proposed
during previous administrations. OSHA received a National Institute for Occupational Safety and Health (NIOSH) criteria document for arsenic in 1971,

but it did not propose a new standard until 1975.[37] The final standard, adopted in May 1978, lowered the PEL from 500 μg/m^3 to 10μg/m^3.[38] After a prolonged judicial battle, the standard was affirmed in 1985 by the Sixth Circuit Court of Appeals.[39]

The lead standard, which was the subject of a 1973 criteria document, was proposed in November 1975, during the Corn administration.[40] Lead has been an easily available and useful metal for thousands of years, and its health effects at high doses are well known. Much lower concentrations can cause anemia and birth defects.[41] Workers in at least 120 occupations, including lead smelting, battery manufacturing, solder manufacturing, shipbuilding, auto manufacturing, and printing, are regularly exposed to airborne lead.[42] The 1971 national consensus standards for lead established a permissible exposure limit (PEL) of 200 μg/m^3 in the air.[43] After holding extensive hearings, OSHA promulgated a final standard in November 1978 that established a PEL of 50 μg/m^3.[44] The standard also introduced a "medical removal" protection provision that required employers to transfer workers who were at excess risk from lead exposure to lower exposure jobs and to maintain their wage levels and seniority for a period of up to 18 months while the employees were on the other jobs or were laid off. The District of Columbia Circuit Court of Appeals upheld the lead standard in most respects, but found that OSHA had failed adequately to justify the feasibility of the standard for certain industries. The court stayed the provision that required engineering controls and work practices for those industries, but it allowed OSHA to require employers to meet the PEL by providing respirators. The court gave OSHA six months to reassess the feasibility of engineering controls for those industries.[45] OSHA reopened the proceedings to address this narrow question and issued a "Supplemental Statement of Reasons" in late January 1981, concluding that the standard was feasible for most of the 46 affected industries. For many of the remaining industries, it proposed to extend the compliance deadlines slightly, and for a very few industries OSHA concluded that respirators might be the only feasible way to meet the standard.[46] Despite these successes, however, OSHA was not done with the lead standard, as Chapter 5 discusses.

At the time Bingham took over, OSHA's attempts to regulate workplace exposure to cotton dust had a long and somewhat sordid history. Cotton dust is a generic name for airborne particles of cotton that result from ginning and textile manufacturing. It causes byssinosis, or "brown lung," a debilitating disease that afflicts hundreds of textile workers. Even though brown lung was one of the clearly recognized workplace diseases that led to the enactment of the OSH Act,[47] OSHA was very slow to take action. After receiving a petition from the Textile Workers Union and a Ralph Nader organization demanding that the agency promulgate a PEL of 100 μg/m^3, OSHA in late 1976 issued a notice of proposed rulemaking suggesting a 200 μg/m^3 PEL.[48]

This major regulatory initiative resulted in a pitched battle between OSHA and President Carter's "inflation fighters" in the Regulatory Analysis Review Group, a group of economists in the Executive Office of the President. When

Charles Schultze, the chairman of the Council of Economic Advisers, "ordered" OSHA to change the standard just prior to the issuance of the final rule,[49] Bingham and Secretary of Labor Marshall took the issue to President Jimmy Carter.[50] With some minor exceptions, Carter backed OSHA,[51] and a comprehensive cotton dust standard was issued in mid-1978.[52] President Carter's favorable resolution of this confrontation effectively broke the back of the campaign by Carter administration economists to harness OSHA, but major interagency skirmishes continued to erupt throughout the Carter years.[53] The ultimate fate of the cotton dust standard is taken up in Chapter 5.

On the last day of her term, Bingham issued a final health standard regulating occupational noise,[54] which had been proposed in 1974, during Stender's tenure.[55] The final standard continued an exposure level of 90 decibels (dBA) for eight hours that was implemented by a 1971 consensus standard. The new standard, however, required employers to use engineering controls to reduce noise rather than personal protective devices such as earplugs. Under industry pressure, OSHA decided not to adopt a recommendation by NIOSH for an 85 dBA level because it would have increased the cost of compliance from $1000 per worker to comply with the 90 dBA level to $1,800 per worker.[56] But the agency refused to back down on the engineering controls requirement, even though personal protective devices were substantially less expensive. The fate of the standard, which was immediately withdrawn by the Reagan administration in response to industry complaints, will be taken up in Chapter 5.

Attempting a Generic Approach

Despite its strong emphasis on standard-setting, OSHA's administrators soon realized that proceeding case by case could have only a limited impact on worker health. Secretary of Labor Ray Marshall compared OSHA's case-by-case approach to putting out a forest fire one tree at a time.[57] The agency therefore initiated a number of innovative "generic" rulemaking proceedings in which it attempted to regulate more than one subject or problem in the same proceeding.

One of OSHA's generic rules was its standard for employee access to exposure and medical records, which was promulgated in 1980.[58] When OSHA had mandated that employers maintain exposure and medical records as one of the requirements of previous health standards, it had also required employers to give their employees access to those records.[59] The new generic standard required employers to give employees access to voluntarily maintained exposure and medical records as well. OSHA also proposed, but did not finalize, a generic rule requiring employers to communicate known work hazards to employees.[60] OSHA anticipated that when workers were armed with the information covered by these two standards, they could do a better job of protecting themselves from health hazards.

The Generic Carcinogen Policy

By far the most innovative and far-reaching OSHA generic initiative was its attempt to promulgate a cancer policy. The Generic Carcinogen Policy (GCP) was one of the most ambitious generic rulemaking efforts undertaken by *any* agency, and OSHA predicted that it could be "the most important single proceeding OSHA has ever had or will ever conduct in the future in this area."[61] A rudimentary GCP had been floating around OSHA when Bingham arrived. The GCP's substantive principles closely resembled a statement entitled "Evaluation of Chemical Carcinogens," prepared in 1970 by a panel of scientists from government and academia assembled by a National Cancer Institute scientist, Dr. Umberto Saffiotti. The panel's report noted that the existing scientific evidence indicated that many human cancers had environmental origins and that once a person is exposed to a carcinogen, damaged cells will retain their potential to develop into fully developed cancer for most or all of that person's lifetime. This irreversibility means that humans exposed to a carcinogen generally remain at increased risk of developing cancer even after the exposure is eliminated. Given this risk, the report concluded that "it is urgent that every effort be made to detect and control sources of carcinogenic contamination of the environment well before damaging effects become evident in man."[62] To that end, the report articulated a conservative, risk-adverse approach to interpreting scientific evidence of cancer risks. These principles included a presumption that the results of testing chemicals in laboratory animals were generally applicable to humans, that a chemical should be regarded as risky whether it caused malignant or benign tumors in animals, and that there was no safe level of exposure for carcinogens.

The proposed GCP, which came out in late 1977, consisted of a four-part scheme for categorizing workplace chemicals and a set of model regulations to match that scheme.[63] Only Category I had any immediate regulatory consequences. Substances that caused an increase in benign or malignant tumors in (1) humans, (2) two mammalian test species, (3) a single mammalian species in more than one experiment, or (4) a single mammalian species if supported by short-term tests were presumed to fall into this Category I. The presumption could be rebutted with one of five specified showings designed to demonstrate that the chemical was not likely to be hazardous. Any person would be allowed to petition to place a substance in Category I, and the agency was required to respond within a specified time period.

A Category I listing would have had four regulatory consequences. First, the agency was required immediately to issue an ETS. Second, OSHA was obliged to issue a notice of proposed rulemaking within 60 days in accordance with a model standard that specified labeling, monitoring, surveillance and housekeeping requirements. Third, the permanent standard would require employers to reduce employee exposure to the lowest feasible level, unless there were less hazardous substitutes for the chemical, in which case no exposure would be allowed. Fourth, at the rulemaking hearing that followed, debatable issues would be limited to (1) whether the substance was correctly placed into Category I; (2) whether the classification had been rebutted; (3) whether the determination of the lowest feasible level was correct; (4) whether the substance possessed unique properties that would make specific protections inappropriate or infeasible; and (5) the environmental impact of the regulation.[64]

The aim of the GCP was to speed up decision making for health standards. Not everyone in the government, however, agreed with OSHA's solution. EPA had recently adopted a "weight of the evidence" approach to regulating carcinogenic pesticides that stressed the need for discretionary judgments in individual proceeding.[65] An EPA official described OSHA's less discretionary approach as a "meat axe."[66] The President's Office of Science and Technology Policy also weighed in with a "framework" for federal decision making concerning carcinogens that stressed the need for individual scientific judgment, questioned the relevance of some animal tests for humans, and pressed the use of "best estimates" rather than conservative estimates of carcinogenic risks.[67] The economists in the Regulatory Analysis Review Group complained that the generic policy would cost from $1 billion to 20 billion, lacked sufficient flexibility, and was generally not "cost-effective."[68] In addition to these competing governmental initiatives, the chemical industry created the American Industrial Health Council for the express purpose of challenging the GCP.[69]

OSHA envisioned that the hearings on the GCP would be a massive "shoot-out" on the content of federal carcinogen policy.[70] The chemical industry launched a massive campaign to defeat the new policy. A vice president of Monsanto declared, "For the chemical industry, it's the most important regulatory issue that has ever come down the pike."[71] According to another industry spokesperson, "It's the domino theory. . . . If OSHA goes, so goes [sic] EPA, CPSC and others."[72] The lengthy hearings were followed closely in the press,[73] and they attracted widespread public participation. Before it was over, the record exceeded 250,000 pages.[74]

The bulky preamble to the final rule, which was issued on January 22, 1980, was a virtual encyclopedia of scientific and economic information relevant to chemicals in the workplace.[75] The document reaffirmed OSHA's generally conservative approach toward regulating carcinogens, but the final rule made several changes in the proposed regulatory approach. Significantly, it eliminated the automatic trigger for OSHA action. Rather than requiring OSHA to respond within ten days to any petition to regulate a chemical, the final GCP established a priority-setting schedule under which the agency could choose from a list of ten items. The final GCP otherwise retained the presumption-rebuttal format with some significant refinements. For example, the broad rebuttal criteria were replaced with stringent threshold requirements specifying in great detail the kinds of rebuttal evidence that the agency would be willing to consider.

Although the final rule in some ways represented a step backward from the proposal, it was still very ambitious and innovative. By making generic presumptions, the rule effectively put the burden of persuasion for most of the difficult issues on industry. In addition, the fill-in-the-blank generic approach to much of the content of individual rules had the potential of speeding up future rule development. Indeed, Assistant Secretary Bingham confidently predicted that the new rule would more than double the agency's output.[76] If this prediction had become a reality, the four-year, multimillion-dollar effort might have been worth the time and expense. Unfortunately, the GCP died aborning. It was immediately stayed by the Fifth Circuit Court of Appeals. Before the rule went into effect, the Supreme Court decided the *Benzene* case, and OSHA's life has never been the same.

THE *BENZENE* DECISION

The fate of OSHA's GCP was decided by the Supreme Court when it ruled on the agency's health standard for benzene. Benzene is a familiar substance used in producing motor fuels, solvents, detergents, pesticides, and a host of other organic chemicals. Although virtually the entire population is exposed to small amounts of benzene, over 1 million workers are exposed on a daily basis in service stations, petroleum refineries, coking operations at steel mills, chemical processing, benzene transportation, rubber manufacturing and laboratory operations. High exposures to benzene (250–500 parts per million [ppm]) can cause vertigo, nausea, and other symptoms. Persistent exposures at much lower levels (25–40 ppm) can cause blood deficiencies and aplastic anemia. Long-term exposure to even lower levels can cause leukemia. Because so little is known about the mechanism of carcinogenesis, it is not clear how much exposure will lead to leukemia in any individual, although it is undoubtedly true that the incidence decreases as exposure decreases.

After OSHA's failure to implement an ETS for benzene, it immediately went to work on a permanent standard, which it published in early 1978.[77] Once again, the petroleum industry appealed to the Fifth Circuit. That court held that OSHA had misinterpreted the OSH Act, because it had failed to subject the final rule to a cost-benefit test. The court focused on the definition of "occupational safety and health standard" in section 3(8) of the OSH Act, which Congress said was "a standard which requires conditions, or the adoption or use of one or more practices, means, methods, operations, or processes *reasonably necessary or appropriate* to provide safe or healthful employment and places of employment."[78] The court held that the word "reasonably" connoted a cost-benefit balancing test. The court was unmoved by the agency's argument that section 6(b)(5) of the OSH Act, which addressed "toxic materials and harmful physical agents" in particular, required the agency to "set the standard which most adequately assures, to the extent feasible, that no employee will suffer material impairment of health or functional capacity even if such employee has regular exposure to the hazard dealt with by such standard for the period of his working life."[79] OSHA believed that in the particular case of carcinogens, where a "no-effect" level could not be determined, section 6(b)(5) required the standard to be set at the lowest "feasible" level, whether or not it posed a high risk at that level and regardless of whether the "value" of the risks eliminated exceeded the "cost" of eliminating them. The court disagreed, holding that section 3(8) "trumped" section 6(b)(5).

A deeply divided Supreme Court accepted neither the OSHA nor the Fifth Circuit view of the statute.[80] Writing for a plurality of only three judges, Justice Sevens wrote that the agency had skipped an analytical step when it determined that exposure to carcinogens in the workplace should automatically be reduced to the lowest feasible level. Implicit in the word "safe" in section 3(8) was a requirement that the agency make a threshold determination that the current workplace exposures to a chemical give rise to a "significant risk" of harm. Significantly, the plurality found that the agency had the burden of making the significant risk showing. Since OSHA had not made such a showing for benzene, the court remanded so that OSHA could determine whether existing exposure levels gave rise to a significant risk of harm. The Court thereby neatly avoided the difficult question of whether the agency, after making this showing, was obliged to balance costs against benefits. But it did so only by adding a test that was not at all explicit in the words of the act.

Having ordered OSHA to apply a "significant risk" threshold test, the court gave very little indication of how the agency should go about meeting its burden, and the one example that the plurality opinion provided, demonstrated rather clearly that the author of the opinion did not understand the concept of environmental risk assessment. Justice Stevens, by way of explanation, offered the following example:

Some risks are plainly acceptable and others are plainly unacceptable. If, for example, the odds are one in 1 billion that a person will die from cancer by taking a drink of chlorinated water, the risk clearly could not be considered significant. On the other hand, if the odds are one in a thousand that regular inhalation of gasoline vapors that are two percent benzene will be fatal, a reasonable person might well consider the risk significant and take appropriate steps to decrease or eliminate it.[81]

The example is an ideal illustration of a confused approach to risk assessment in the public health context. Drinking chlorinated water is an activity engaged in by practically everyone in American society. If 250 million Americans drink 4 glasses of water a day and are exposed to a 1 in 1 billion risk each time, then an average of 1 cancer per day will result. This amounts to about 365 cancers per year, a number that reasonable people might find "significant." Justice Stevens's example of a significant risk is harder to address from a public health perspective, because he neglected to provide two important pieces of information: the length of exposure that would result in a cancer and the number of persons who regularly breath gasoline vapors. If we assume that exposure for a year presents the 1 in 1,000 risk and that 2 employees in each of the approximately 200,000 service stations in America are regularly exposed to benzene (an estimate that is, by the way, on the high side), then a 1 in 1,000 risk would yield 400 cancers per year, a number that is not meaningfully different from the 365 cancers per year that Justice Stevens found to be clearly insignificant.

CONCLUSION

Not surprisingly, OSHA was mystified by the Supreme Court's *Benzene* opinion. The agency reluctantly concluded that it was now required to employ quantitative risk assessment techniques in determining whether workplace carcinogens posed a ''significant risk,'' but it was not quite sure what degree of risk was in fact ''significant.'' At the very least, OSHA staffers knew that they would have to amend the GCP in response to the decision. As one of the ''midnight'' regulations issued in the waning hours of the Carter administration, OSHA published a final GCP that deleted all references to the requirement that exposure levels for carcinogens be set at the lowest feasible level, thereby signaling its willingness to apply risk assessment models in individual rulemaking initiatives.[82] At the same time, OSHA issued a proposed rule suggesting additional language that would require the agency to set exposure levels in individual proceedings at ''the lowest feasible level which is necessary to eliminate significant risk.''[83] Hence, as a practical matter, the *Benzene* case deprived the GCP effort of much of its bite. If the agency was required to determine the significance of exposure to every regulated chemical in each regulated workplace and to consider feasibility arguments in individual proceedings, the resulting rulemaking initiatives would vary little from the ponderous proceedings of the past.

OSHA had hoped that once the GCP became law, the dam would burst, and OSHA would promulgate at least ten major standards per year into the indefinite future. Unfortunately, OSHA had broken through the industry's defenses, only to be tackled from the sidelines by the Supreme Court. To make matters worse for worker safety advocates, the activist Bingham management was about to be replaced by a new regime committed to reducing the burdens of OSHA regulation under a president who was willing to give anti-interventionist government economists a much larger role in setting federal health and environmental standards.

NOTES

1. James W. Singer, ''A New OSHA Tries to Put Its Pieces Back Together Again,'' *National Journal* 9 (2 July 1977): 1046.
2. Joan Claybrook, *Retreat from Safety: Reagan's Attack on America's Health* (New York: Pantheon, 1984), 77.
3. Helen Dewar, ''An Rx for Ailing OSHA,'' *Washington Post*, 12 Sept. 1977, A1, col. 5.
4. Singer, ''New OSHA,'' 1046.
5. Ibid., 1046–49; ''OSHA to Revoke Nit Picking Rules,'' *National Journal* 9 (10 Dec. 1977): 1936.
6. Benjamin W. Mintz, ''Occupational Safety and Health: The Federal Regulatory

Program—A History," in *Fundamentals of Industrial Hygiene*, 3d ed., ed. Barbara A. Plog (Washington, D.C.: National Safety Council, 1988), 710.

7. Ibid.

8. U.S. Congress, Senate Committee on Labor and Human Resources, *Hearings on Oversight on the Administration of the Occupational Safety and Health Act*, pt. 1, 96th Cong., 2d sess., 1980, 273, 276–77 (testimony of Basil Whiting, deputy assistant secretary, OSHA) (hereafter cited as Senate, *Oversight Hearings of 1980*, pt. 1).

9. Ibid., 260 (testimony of Basil Whiting, deputy assistant secretary, OSHA); Basil Whiting, "OSHA's Enforcement Policy," *Labor Law Journal* 31 (1980): 261–62.

10. Timothy B. Clark, "What's All the Uproar over OSHA's Nit-Picking Rules," *National Journal* 10 (7 Oct. 1978): 1594; *National Journal* 10 (28 Oct. 1978): 1743.

11. Mark Rothstein, "OSHA After Ten Years: A Review and Some Proposed Reforms," *Vanderbilt Law Review* 34 (1981): 71, 98.

12. Claybrook, *Retreat from Safety*, 77.

13. Mintz, "A History," 710.

14. James W. Singer, "Labor Lobbyists Go on the Defensive as Political Environment Turns Hostile," *National Journal* 12 (15 Mar. 1980): 441.

15. Mintz, "A History," 712; "OSHA Is Target of Antiregulatory Bill," *National Journal* 12 (5 Jan. 1980): 31.

16. U.S. Congress, Senate Committee on Labor and Human Resources, *Hearings on Occupational Safety and Health Improvements Act of 1980, S.2153*, 96th Cong., 2d sess., 1980, 33–36.

17. Mintz, "A History," 713.

18. Ibid., 711.

19. See David Bollier and Joan Claybrook, *Freedom from Harm: The Civilizing Influence of Health, Safety, and Environmental Regulation* (Washington, D.C.: Public Citizen, 1986), 158.

20. Mintz, "A History," 714.

21. U.S. Congress, House Committee on Education and Labor, Subcommittee on Health and Safety, *Oversight Hearings on OSHA—Occupational Safety and Health for Federal Employees, Part 4: State Plans*, 96th Cong., 2d sess., 1980, 478 (testimony of Eula Bingham, assistant secretary of labor for occupational safety and health).

22. Ibid., 515.

23. Ibid., 497.

24. U.S. Congress, House Committee on Government Relations, Subcommittee on Manpower and Housing, *Hearings on Performance of the Occupational Safety and Health Administration*, 95th Cong., 1st sess. 1977, 77–78 (hereafter cited as House *Oversight Hearings of 1977*).

25. During the Carter administration, OSHA's budget increased in constant dollars from $117 to $137 million.

26. James W. Singer, "OSHA in the Spotlight," *National Journal* 12 (15 Nov. 1980): 1946.

27. House, *Oversight Hearings of 1977*, 99 (testimony of Dr. Eula Bingham, assistant secretary for occupational safety and health); ibid., 60 (testimony of Dr. Jack Finklea, director of NIOSH); *BNA Occupational Safety and Health Reporter* 9 (13 Dec. 1979): 661 (reporting changes undertaken by NIOSH to make its output more useful to OSHA); ibid. 8 (19 Apr. 1979): 1673 (reporting on interagency agreement between OSHA and NIOSH to promote joint consultation).

28. 42 *Fed. Reg.* 22,516 (1977).
29. 42 *Fed. Reg.* 45,536 (1977).
30. See 43 *Fed. Reg.* 45,764 (1978).
31. 43 *Fed. Reg.* 11,514 (1978).
32. *Viston Corp.* v. *OSHA*, 6 O.S.H. Cases (BNA) 1483 (6th Cir. 1978).
33. 43 *Fed. Reg.* 45,762 (1978).
34. Mintz, "A History," 707.
35. U.S. Congress, Office of Technology Assessment, *Preventing Illnesses and Injury in the Workplace* (Washington, D.C.: United States Government Printing Office, 1985), 364.
36. Ibid.
37. 40 *Fed. Reg.* 3392 (1975).
38. 43 *Fed. Reg.* 19,584 (1978).
39. *ASARCO* v. *OSHA*, 746 F.2d 483 (9th Cir. 1984).
40. 40 *Fed. Reg.* 45,934 (1975).
41. See *Ethyl Corp.* v. *EPA*, 541 F.2d 1, 8 (D.C. Cir. 1976).
42. Occupational Safety and Health Administration, "Final Standard for Occupational Exposure to Lead," 43 *Fed. Reg.* 52,952 (1978).
43. Ibid.
44. Ibid.
45. *United Steel Workers* v. *Marshall*, 647 F.2d 1189 (D.C. Cir. 1980), *cert. denied* 453 U.S. 913 (1981).
46. Occupational Safety and Health Administration, "Occupational Exposure to Lead; Supplemental Statement of Reasons; and Amendment of Standard," 46 *Fed. Reg.* 6134 (1981).
47. See *American Textile Manufacturers Inst., Inc.* v. *Donovan*, 452 U.S. 490 (1981).
48. 42 *Fed. Reg.* 56,498 (1976).
49. *BNA Occupational Safety and Health Reporter* 8 (8 June 1978): 27.
50. "Memorandum for the President from Secretary of Labor Roy Marshall re: OSHA's Cotton Dust Standard," dated May 24, 1978, repr. in *BNA Occupational Safety and Health Reporter* 8 (8 June 1978): 54.
51. *BNA Occupational Safety and Health Reporter* 8 (15 June 1978): 59.
52. 43 *Fed. Reg.* 27,350 (1978).
53. Timothy B. Clark, "Carter's Assault on the Costs of Regulations," *National Journal* 10 (12 Aug. 1978): 1281.
54. 46 *Fed. Reg.* 4078 (1981).
55. 30 *Fed. Reg.* 37,773 (1974).
56. See Robert D. Bruce, "The Economic Impact of Noise Control," *The Otolaryngologic Clinics of North America* 12 (1979): 601–5.
57. Tom Alexander, "OSHA's Ill-Conceived Crusade Against Cancer," *Fortune*, 3 July 1978.
58. 45 *Fed. Reg.* 35,212 (1980).
59. Elinor Schroeder and Sidney Shapiro, "Responses to Occupational Disease: The Role of Markets, Regulation, and Information," *Georgetown Law Journal* 72 (1984): 1265–66.
60. 46 *Fed. Reg.* 4412 (1981).
61. See generally Thomas O. McGarity, "OSHA's Generic Carcinogen Policy: Rulemaking Under Scientific and Legal Uncertainty," in *Law and Science in Collaboration*,

ed. Milton M. Carrow and J. Daniel Nyhart (Lexington, Mass.: Lexington Books, 1983); Occupational Safety and Health Administration, "Identification, Classification and Regulation of Potential Occupational Carcinogens," 45 *Fed. Reg.* 5001 (1980); General Accounting Office, *Delays in Setting Workplace Standards for Cancer-Causing and Other Dangerous Substances* (Washington, D.C.: United States Government Printing Office, 1977).

62. Ad Hoc Committee on the Evaluation of Low Levels of Environmental Chemical Carcinogens, "Report to the Surgeon General" (22 April 1979), repr. in Samuel S. Epstein, *The Politics of Cancer* (San Francisco: Sierra Club Books, 1978), 523.

63. 42 *Fed. Reg.* 54,148 (1977).

64. "Identification, Classification and Regulation of Toxic Substances Posing a Potential Occupational Carcinogenic Risk," 41 *Fed. Reg.* 54,147 (1977).

65. "Interim Procedures and Guidelines for Health Risk and Economic Impact Assessments of Suspected Carcinogens," 41 *Fed. Reg.* 21,402 (1977).

66. Alexander, "Ill-Conceived Crusade," 88.

67. Office of Science and Technology Policy, *Identification and Control of Potential Human Carcinogens: A Framework for Federal Decisionmaking* (Washington, D.C.: United States Government Printing Office, 1979).

68. *BNA Occupational Safety and Health Reporter* 8 (2 Nov. 1978): 706.

69. Timothy B. Clark, "At Last, a Battle Plan for the Regulatory War on Cancer," *National Journal* 11 (27 Oct. 1979): 1808.

70. See McGarity, "Generic Carcinogen Policy," 79–80.

71. Alexander, "Ill-Conceived Crusade," 86.

72. Ann Pelham, "Government Tackles Tricky Questions of How to Regulate Carcinogens," *Congressional Quarterly Weekly Report*, 22 April 1978, 961.

73. "OSHA's Action Plan on Cancer," *Wall Street Journal*, 11 Oct. 1978, A18, col. 3; Alexander, "Ill-Conceived Crusade," 86.

74. See Rothstein, "OSHA After Ten Years," 79, n. 50.

75. Occupational Safety and Health Administration, "Identification, Classification, and Regulation of Potential Occupational Carcinogens," 45 *Fed. Reg.* 5002 (1980).

76. See Rothstein, "OSHA After Ten Years," 79, n. 52.

77. 45 *Fed. Reg.* 5001 (1978).

78. 28 U.S.C. § 652(8) (1988) (emphasis added).

79. 29 U.S.C. § 655(B)(5).

80. *Industrial Union Department, AFL-CIO* v. *American Petroleum Institute*, 448 U.S. 607 (1980).

81. 448 U.S. 607 at 655 (1980).

82. Occupational Safety and Health Administration, "Identification, Classification and Regulation of Potential Occupational Carcinogens: Conforming Deletions," 46 *Fed. Reg.* 4889 (1981).

83. Occupational Safety and Health Administration, "Identification, Classification and Regulation of Potential Occupational Carcinogens: Proposed Amendments," 46 *Fed. Reg.* 7402 (1981).

5

The Reagan Years: Going Backward

The *Benzene* case was a significant brake on OSHA's momentum under Eula Bingham. Although the flow of OSHA regulations had never been more than a trickle even before that case, the Reagan administration was not content merely to slow the pace of regulation. OSHA's rulemaking efforts in the early years of the Reagan administration consisted almost entirely of fruitless attempts to weaken existing regulations. These deregulatory initiatives, together with significant budget cuts and new management procedures, left OSHA with little time or money to pursue new health and safety standards.

When President Reagan assumed office in January 1981, he believed that his landslide electoral victory represented a mandate to get the government "off the backs" of American business. Since he had frequently invoked OSHA as a symbol of intrusive and inefficient bureaucracy, few were surprised when he chose an assistant secretary for OSHA who was committed to "stemming the flow" of health and safety standards. Thorne Auchter, a thirty-six-year old executive vice president of a family-run construction company with a degree in business from Jacksonville University, had managed special events for President Reagan's Florida campaign.[1] He came to the job with a penchant for fine hotels, a contempt for officious bureaucrats, and virtually no experience with occupational safety and health issues. Auchter's credentials included an OSHA fine for maintaining unsafe working conditions and service on a state committee to evaluate the advantages of state, as opposed to federal, safety and health programs.[2] After his appointment, Auchter announced, "We're here to do what the President was elected to do—provide regulatory relief."[3]

The administration chose another deregulator, Timothy Ryan, to be solicitor of labor, OSHA's chief attorney. Soon after his appointment, Ryan, a former private practitioner with a specialty in labor law, told a conference that Congress had "run amok" in the occupational safety and health area, and the resulting "overregulation" had thrown the labor-management relationship out of balance. Ryan assured skeptical labor unions that the department's plans to reduce federal regulation of occupational health and safety would benefit labor by increasing the frequency of union organizing victories.[4] Ryan apparently based this curious prediction on the unassailable assumption that diseased and maimed workers would be more likely to vote to unionize.

In late 1982, Auchter hired another like-minded deregulator, R. Leonard Vance, to head the Health Standards Directorate. Vance outraged many of his employees when he referred to some staffers as "communistic." Upon reading in a proposed preamble for a rule "federal regulation is necessary because of imperfections and failings in the capacity of the free market to internalize costs to the public of excess occupational exposure to [chemicals]," Vance announced that the language sounded as if the author had been "trained in Moscow."[5] In reality, the language, which articulated the traditional economic rationale for federal regulation, would more likely have been drafted at the University of Chicago Department of Economics.

Although the White House was confident that appointees like Auchter, Ryan, and Vance would try their best to steer the agencies in a new deregulatory direction, it nevertheless feared that even the staunchest anti-interventionists would eventually become "captured" by their bureaucracies. Two actions were taken to protect Auchter from this fate. One step was to initiate a centralized review process under the Office of Management and Budget (OMB). Executive Order 12,291, signed by President Reagan on February 17, 1981, required all federal agencies to prepare Regulatory Impact Analyses (RIAs) detailing the costs and benefits of all "major" rules.[6] The executive order further provided that, to the extent allowed by law, agencies were not to undertake regulatory initiatives unless "the potential benefits to society for the regulations outweigh[ed] the costs." Finally, the executive order mandated that no regulation could be proposed or finalized until OMB had approved its RIA. The executive order added to OSHA's already considerable burden to justify its rules and gave OMB a powerful role in the promulgation of OSHA standards.

President Reagan also established a new high-level entity, the Presidential Task Force on Regulatory Relief, to resolve any disputes between OMB and the agencies, and he appointed incoming Vice President George Bush to be its chairman. As its name implied, the task force had a strong mandate to bring about a dramatic shift in the direction of federal regulation.

Immediately upon assuming office, President Reagan directed the executive agencies to suspend for 60 days almost 200 "midnight regulations" issued during the waning moments of the Carter administration, in order to give the new administration an opportunity "to ensure that they comported with the President's regulatory principles."[7] On March 27, 1981, the task force announced a "hit list" of 27 existing regulations, including OSHA's noise standard and carcinogen policy, that were to be "reassessed and possibly modified" in accordance with the executive order. The vice president also wrote a letter to business groups, asking each of them for a list of ten regulations to be placed on the "hit list" and specific recommendations for "the ways you wish these changed."[8] A strong industry response resulted in the addition of almost one-hundred more existing rules, including many OSHA standards, to the "hit list."

As further insurance against overaggressive regulation, the Reagan administration attempted to force steep budget reductions upon the agency. Assistant Secretary Auchter told the House Appropriations Subcommittee that the agency's shift in focus away from the "prevailing adversary spirit" and toward training and consultation would drastically reduce OSHA's staffing needs. He therefore proposed to cut 298 staff persons for standards enforcement and eliminate 52 positions in health and safety standards development in fiscal 1981.[9] By fiscal 1983, Auchter proposed to reduce the number of field inspectors to 983 from the 1,967 inspectors that OSHA had employed in fiscal 1980.[10] The threat of such draconian cuts induced Dr. Eula Bingham, the former OSHA head, to form a political action committee to challenge budget cuts and staff reductions in OSHA.[11] Although Congress resisted the administration's proposals, it did cut deeply into the agency's budget to meet the Gramm-Rudman-Hollings deficit targets during the years that followed. OSHA's appropriation was reduced by $11 million (from $206 to $195 million) in 1982. OSHA's 1983 appropriation of $209 million was still less in real dollars than its 1981 appropriation.[12] The budget reductions forced significant cutbacks in agency staff and outside technical support. The agency did, however, manage to summon sufficient resources to ghostwrite speeches for sympathetic congressmen when OSHA's deregulation activities were attacked.[13]

MANAGING THE RULEMAKING PROCESS

When Thorne Auchter first assumed office, he assured skeptical observers that what he lacked in technical expertise he more than offset with managerial savvy. According to Auchter:

The problem [with OSHA] has not been incompetence but an almost total lack of management. The system they had [in the Bingham administration] was very weak, if you could even call it a system. The ideas and answers to problems were never allowed to percolate upward. We are changing that.[14]

In its early years, OSHA had in fact been a very loosely run organization. Rulemaking initiatives were generated internally in an ad hoc fashion. The heads of the Health and Safety Directorates had traditionally controlled standard-setting within their functional bailiwicks, with sporadic input from the assistant secretary. Loose internal work groups were assembled to draft rulemaking documents with substantial technical help from outside consultants. It was not uncommon for the head of a directorate to work directly on the rule, even to the point of

typing the final version of the rule at 4 A.M. on the morning it was due.[15] The
entire agency tended to gear up for a single rulemaking effort, putting aside
most other initiatives until they assumed front burner status.[16]

Auchter quickly set about reorganizing the agency to give him more personal
control over the policy-making apparatus. With the help of a management consultant, Auchter prepared a lengthy and extremely complicated procedural directive that specified intricate internal rulemaking procedures with a heavy
emphasis on documentation.[17] Elaborate organization charts soon papered his
office walls. The directive established a Regulation Review Committee composed
of high-level OSHA officials and charged it with "coordinating issues among
the directorates and reviewing documents and issues resulting from the standards
development process prior to the Assistant Secretary's review."[18] If the assistant
secretary decided to go forward with a rulemaking effort, a preliminary team
was supposed to prepare a concise summary of the nature of the proposed action,
the justification for that action, alternatives to the action, and groups with an
interest in it. If the assistant secretary wished to pursue the effort further, the
Regulation Review Committee would assemble a new regulation team composed
of representatives from each of the agency's relevant directorates and an attorney
from the solicitor's office.

The team's first task was to prepare a workplan, containing a schedule and
an estimate of required resources, and an additional summary for the Regulation
Review Committee and assistant secretary. The team was next supposed to
prepare a risk analysis, an alternatives analysis, an action recommendation, and
an options memorandum.[19] Following approval of the action recommendation,
the team was to draft a notice of proposed rulemaking and its associated preliminary regulatory impact analysis. Finally, the team had to assemble a rulemaking
package and draft a second options memorandum for review by the Regulation
Review Committee, the assistant secretary, the Labor Department's Policy Review Board, and OMB. After the public hearing for those rules that survived
this multiple review, the team reconvened to analyze the public comments and
make any necessary revisions in the standard and supporting documents. The
regulatory package for the final rule was supposed to follow the same internal
path through the Regulation Review Committee, the assistant secretary, the
Policy Review Board, and OMB.

As the above description suggests, Auchter's new standard-setting procedures
did not facilitate rapid decision-making. In the opinions of several long-time
OSHA staffers, the procedural quagmire that predictably resulted from the new
management regime reflected an undisguised desire of upper-level management
to slow down the agency's already ponderous internal rulemaking process.[20] The
excessive documentation requirements and repetitive review procedures provided
almost insuperable barriers to the production of rules; thus, as Chapter 6 reveals,
only a handful of health and safety standards emerged during Auchter's almost
four-year tenure.

The intricate rules were after a time observed mostly in their breach.[21] The staff often effectively bypassed the Regulation Review Committee, and high-level input was secured through informal meetings between staff and the assistant secretary. Most of the detailed status reports and formal papers were replaced by traditional briefing documents. Although Auchter proclaimed to the world that his management innovations were his greatest contribution to OSHA's legacy,[22] they never really worked as planned, and they were abandoned altogether soon after he left the agency in late 1984.

REWRITING OLD STANDARDS

With the strong encouragement of the Task Force on Regulatory Relief and OMB, OSHA devoted its first years under Auchter to an ambitious program of reviewing the few regulations it had already promulgated.[23] At the task force's insistence, OSHA immediately withdrew the Bingham administration's proposed changes to the carcinogen policy that were intended to square it with the *Benzene* decision.[24] Although OSHA promised to reconsider the policy in the future, it "languishe[d] in ignominious neglect" and ultimately vanished from the scene.[25] Other existing regulations that rapidly found their way to the top of OSHA's regulatory reform agenda included its commercial diving safety standard and its health standards for cotton dust and lead.

Commercial Diving

Commercial divers work in an inherently dangerous underwater environment. They are continually exposed to risks posed by high pressure, temperature extremes, unpredictable seas, and necessary tools such as oxy-arc cutting instruments, electric arc welders, and various explosive devices. Tolerances for error in a deep-water environment are not large, and the consequences of any accident are enhanced by the hostile environment. Workers can protect themselves against these hazards by following prescribed procedures, using the right equipment, and (perhaps most important) undergoing training.[26] OSHA's commercial diving standard originated during Morton Corn's tenure as a result of a union petition and a report from an interagency federal task force on commercial diving risks. After conducting an unusual set of joint public hearings with the U.S. Coast Guard and soliciting technical advice from the U.S. Navy, NIOSH, the Smithsonian Institution, and the agency's Advisory Committee on Construction Safety and Health, OSHA published a final standard on July 22, 1977.[27] The standard was not especially controversial or demanding. To a large extent, it merely codified existing industry practices.[28] Only one relatively minor aspect of the standard was challenged in court.[29] OSHA later reported that it had received "virtually no complaints" about the diving standard.

On August 12, 1981, Vice President Bush announced that the OSHA diving standards had made the presidential task force "hit list," although the task force could not later document his claim that a large number of businesses had requested that OSHA reexamine the standard.[30] The impetus behind the reexamination was apparently the staffs of OMB and the task force, many members of which worked for the Council on Wage and Price Stability when it filed harshly critical comments on the proposed rule during the Carter administration.[31] James C. Miller III, who was a staffer on the council and a vigorous opponent of the diving standard, was a charter member of the task force and later became the head of OMB.[32] A House subcommittee investigation revealed that task force members and staff had met privately with parties interested in the diving standard.[33]

The pressure to reform the commercial diving standard died shortly after the machinations of OMB and the task force were exposed to the sunlight of the subcommittee's investigation. After issuing a halfhearted advance notice of proposed rulemaking, OSHA quietly let this early regulatory reform initiative fade away.

Cotton Dust

The cotton dust standard was a far more significant target of OSHA's deregulatory intentions. When the standard was promulgated in 1978, the District of Columbia Circuit Court of Appeals had affirmed it in all important regards. Because the assistant secretary, by sheer coincidence, had determined that cotton dust posed a "significant health hazard," the *Benzene* holding was not dispositive, and the Supreme Court agreed to use the *Cotton Dust* appeal as a vehicle for deciding whether the OSH Act required OSHA to use cost-benefit balancing in setting occupational health standards.

One of the first official acts of the Auchter OSHA was to ask the Supreme Court to remand the case to OSHA for reconsideration in light of President Reagan's executive order requiring cost-benefit balancing.[34] In announcing his intent to reopen the rulemaking,[35] Auchter maintained: "It's time to reexamine [OSHA's] traditional resistance to cost-benefit analysis."[36] At the same time, Auchter recalled 50,000 educational booklets on "brown lung," because he felt that the cover photograph portraying a "brown lung" victim was "too sympathetic."[37] The unions vigorously objected, arguing that OSHA was switching positions solely for political reasons.[38] The Supreme Court rebuffed OSHA's last-minute overture,[39] and it ultimately rejected the textile industry's argument that OSHA was required to use cost-benefit analysis.[40]

Auchter did not, however, accept the Supreme Court's ruling as a defeat. Against the advice of agency scientists, he decided to reexamine the scientific basis for the 200 $\mu g/m^3$ standard.[41] Skeptical unions worried that Auchter's hidden agenda was to gut the standard by making it more performance-oriented. A performance-oriented standard is a rule that requires an employer to reduce a health or safety hazard by a specified amount but gives the employer flexibility to choose the methods it will use to comply with the rule. Under a performance standard, for example, an employer could place greater reliance on respirators, instead of engineering controls, to reduce employee exposure to cotton dust.[42]

On May 5, 1981, 300 textile workers demonstrated at the Labor Department Building in Washington, D.C., against the proposed changes.[43] Although four union officials were allowed to meet with Vice President Bush and the head of OMB's Regulatory Review Office, they left with the impression that they had received "no really substantive response" to their grievances.[44] Auchter, on the other hand, assured labor leaders that "we have done no damage to the standard nor do we intend to."[45]

On February 9, 1982, OSHA published an advance notice of proposal rule-making (ANPR) requesting comments and information on whether the new standard was cost-effective. In addition, the agency reopened the question of whether cotton dust exposure posed a "significant" risk in several industries in light of two reports from the National Academy of Sciences (NAS) and the textile industry that were expected in the near future.[46] The NAS report, which was financed by a $100,000 grant from the Department of Agriculture (a longtime supporter of cotton growers), concluded that the relationship between cotton dust exposure and chronic respiratory disease "has yet to be resolved."[47] This conclusion drew a stinging dissent from committee member Kaye H. Kilburn, director of pulmonary and environmental medicine at the University of Southern California. Several other prominent epidemiologists agreed with Kilburn that the report was "a misleading representation of the current state of knowledge of byssinosis."[48] The director of the National Institute of Occupational Safety and Health (NIOSH) wrote to the head of the NAS that the report was "depressing in its narrowness of viewpoint, in the superficiality of its review of the literature and in the glibness of its tone," and "most distressing from the point of view of public health and preventative medicine."[49] Eric Frumin, safety and health director of the Amalgamated Clothing and Textile Workers Union, complained that the committee was "stacked" in favor of the textile industry. For example, the only other epidemiologist on the committee was Dr. Hans Weill, whose research on byssinosis had been funded by the textile industry's chief lobbying group. Two other committee members were associated with North Carolina State University's School of Textiles, an institution with little expertise in pulmonary disease that received heavy support from the textile industry. Still another committee member had testified on behalf of the textile industry at OSHA's hearings on the cotton dust standard.[50]

The second report was an industry-sponsored study by Harold Imbus, a former medical director of Burlington Industries, that concluded that "brown lung" disease was not as prevalent in textile industry workers as previously reported.[51] NIOSH scientists were critical of the study, which because of the rush to meet the deadline for responding to OSHA's ANPR had not been circulated for peer review, and they concluded that OSHA should disregard it entirely.[52]

At a September 1982 House subcommittee hearing on research into "brown lung,"[53] Congressman Albert Gore charged that the textile industry, "having lost on economic grounds in the Supreme Court," was now fighting the ruling on scientific grounds "even though the weight of scientific analysis clearly supports the current standard."[54] The testimony at the hearing tended to bear him out. The subcommittee concluded that the "new data" alluded to in the ANPR "did not justify OSHA's initial decision to utilize its limited scientific resources to reopen the record on the [standard]."[55]

OMB took a very different view. In September 1982, Christopher DeMuth, the head of OMB's Regulatory Review Office, wrote to the Labor Department, urging OSHA to pick up the pace on its review of several allegedly "cost ineffective" rules, including the cotton dust standard.[56] When the secretary of labor four months later approved a proposal for a new standard that did not revise the 200 μg/m^3 permissible exposure limit and did not depart from the existing rule's emphasis on engineering controls over the use of respirators, OMB was incensed. DeMuth complained that he "had thought that a much more fundamental reassessment of the 1978 standard was in store." In particular, DeMuth criticized the continued emphasis on engineering controls. Citing the NAS report, he asserted that "there has been a much more significant shift in scientific thinking on this subject since 1978 than OSHA acknowledges."[57]

OSHA responded that respirators did not provide as much protection against cotton dust as engineering and work practice controls, a position that the agency had steadfastly maintained since its inception. The agency further warned that "[i]f OSHA appears to be giving only superficial attention to important health or technical evidence because of policy preferences that are not factually well-supported, we believe that it will damage the agency's scientific credibility."[58] This strong protective stance indicates either that the agency's scientists had convinced Auchter that cotton dust posed very real risks that could not be adequately addressed with respirators or that Auchter's political advisers convinced him that gutting the cotton dust standard would have serious political repercussions. Whatever the reason, Auchter forcefully defended the agency's position in the interagency debate.

OMB elevated the dispute to the Task Force on Regulatory Relief. DeMuth argued that OSHA should leave the choice between engineering controls and respirators up to individual employers. OMB opined that engineering controls would actually *increase* the incidence of byssinosis and that workers would rather wear dust masks. Finally, DeMuth maintained that the standard would put American textile manufacturers at a competitive disadvantage against foreign companies.[59] The task force met in May 1983, but it failed to resolve the dispute. It appeared that the only way to break the impasse was to take the matter to the president himself.[60] At this point Congressman Albert Gore entered the fray, criticizing OMB for "pressuring" OSHA and calling on Vice President Bush and OMB Director David Stockman to halt OMB's interference with OSHA's evaluation.[61] The textile worker's union complained to Vice President Bush that OMB was claiming expertise in health-related areas far beyond its institutional competence while ignoring strong evidence that many companies had already installed engineering controls as part of a major modernization effort aimed at recapturing lost markets.[62]

A key turning point in the OMB-OSHA dispute was a letter from Harold Imbus, written at Auchter's request, stating that "[n]o conclusion can be made from my study regarding the effectiveness of respirators in protecting cotton textile workers from cotton dust."[63] In May 1983, OSHA presented the Imbus letter to C. Boyden Gray, head of the task force staff, and Gray took up the matter with Dr. George Keyworth, the White House science adviser. Keyworth agreed with Imbus that the study did not support allowing the use of respirators. A task force aide later referred to OMB's reliance on the Imbus study a "goof." Since DeMuth was out of the country, Gray next brought the matter up with OMB head Stockman, who called a halt to OMB's resistance. A White House official said that OMB "was only interested in raising the issue on the general principle of performance standards."[64] As a face-saving concession to OMB, OSHA inserted new language in the rule's preamble confirming OSHA's continued commitment to performance-oriented standards.[65]

OSHA held hearings on the proposed rule on September 13, 1983. The unions expressed pleasure that OSHA had rejected OMB suggestions for replacing engineering controls with respirators, but they were still disappointed with the proposal. The American Textile Manufacturers Institute gave the proposal a qualified endorsement but argued that "medical surveillance and proper work practices, coupled with a less stringent exposure limit to dust, would be adequate to provide employees with health protection."[66]

The agency staff then began an internal deliberation process that lasted for almost two years. During this period, however, most aspects of the 1978 standard remained in effect. In May 1984, Dan River, Inc., Virginia's largest textile firm, requested a variance from the existing federal and state cotton dust standards so that it could perform an "experiment" to determine the exact cause of "brown lung" disease. Dan River reasoned that since so many companies already complied with the standard, it was becoming increasingly difficult to find a group of workers exposed to sufficient quantities of cotton dust to contract serious forms of the disease. Fortunately, the Dan River plant, which was nowhere close to complying with the new standard, afforded a unique opportunity to observe the effects of cotton dust on workers, if only it could be relieved of its obligation to comply while the experiment was being conducted. Auchter specifically requested the Virginia agency to grant the "variance."[67] Outraged worker groups, however, accurately characterized the novel exemption as "human experimentation."[68] Margaret Seminario, a health specialist for the AFL-CIO, charged that it was "outrageous" that OSHA would allow a "variance" that "amounts to an exemption from the standard."[69] The Director of NIOSH stated emphatically that the study could not be conducted without exposing the employees to "unnecessary hazards."[70] In response to the public outcry, the study was quickly terminated.

On December 10, 1985, OSHA promulgated the final cotton dust standard.[71] To meet OMB's objections, OSHA relaxed the medical surveillance and exposure monitoring requirements of the rules, but to satisfy union objections, it restored the wage retention protection for workers who had to be removed from cotton dust exposure. Although the unions were dissatisfied with the agency's capitulation to OMB,[72] they did not appeal. The industry likewise grudgingly accepted the new standard, which, after years of effort and expense, did not vary significantly from the 1978 standard that the Supreme Court had approved in 1981.

Lead

The cotton dust and diving standards were not the only instances of OSHA's wheel-spinning. The agency also went around and around on the lead standard, only to end up about where it originally started. OSHA issued a supplemental lead standard the day before the Carter administration left office. The supplemental standard never went into effect, however, because it was one of the "midnight regulations" that President Reagan suspended.[73] Soon thereafter, three industry attorneys, one of whom was on the Reagan administration's OSHA transition team, persuaded OSHA's lawyers to join the Lead Industry Association in asking the Supreme Court to vacate the District of Columbia opinion upholding the other aspects of the standard and to remand the entire standard.[74] Not surprisingly, the unions were outraged. George Taylor, AFL-CIO director for occupational safety and health, charged that the Reagan administration was making a "grim mockery" out of the OSH Act, and promised that union members would hold the administration accountable.[75] The Supreme Court, however, declined to review the lead standard.[76]

The Supreme Court's failure to review the lead standard did not stop OSHA from attempting to revise it informally. According to a subsequently issued General Accounting Office report, the leader of the agency working group for lead was threatened with a letter charging her with insubordination if she did not write a new provision that would relax the exposure level for lead in the battery manufacturing industry. The report also concluded that high-level managers on several occasions told lower-level staffers to reduce the stringency of the standard with changes that were, in the staff's opinion, unsupported by the scientific evidence.[77]

On July 21, 1981, OSHA promulgated a new final rule that provided a new timetable for gradually meeting the 50 $\mu g/m^3$ standard.[78] The three largest primary lead smelters, however, remained under interim exemptions, and many workers therefore were not covered by the standard. A year later, the agency gave smelters and battery manufacturing plants several months to install required engineering controls.[79] A progress report from the Task Force on Regulatory Relief boasted that OSHA's implementation delays and other changes in the lead standard had saved industry $50 million. Since employees were still presumably wearing their respirators, this savings allegedly came at no cost to worker health.[80] On December 3, 1982, OSHA stayed the engineering controls once again.[81]

By the middle of 1983, with the newspapers filled with stories of the Environmental Protection Agency's attempts to provide scandalous deregulatory benefits to polluters, OSHA adopted the somewhat more forceful approach of seeking negotiated agreements between employers and labor on a plant-by-plant basis concerning the introduction of engineering controls.[82] When OSHA successfully tried out the new approach at an ASARCO smelter early in 1984,[83] OMB almost completely undermined the informal negotiations by insisting that OSHA place greater emphasis on personal protective devices. OMB ultimately relented after both industry and labor vigorously objected.[84]

In April 1984, the District of Columbia Circuit reentered the picture and ordered OSHA to vacate the previously issued stays.[85] Responding to the court order, OSHA lifted its stays and set an effective date of December 1, 1984, for all companies to meet the 1980 standard. After virtually all affected companies said that it would be impossible for them to meet the new deadline,[86] OSHA announced that it would not issue citations for failure to meet the deadline. The union agreed that the enforcement directive would adequately dispose of any "legitimate" industry complaints.[87] Finally, in March 1986, OSHA announced a final cooperative program to allow secondary lead smelters and battery manufacturers and their unions to develop engineering compliance plans.[88]

Thus, what started out as a dramatic last-ditch effort to rework the Carter administration's lead standard resulted four years later in a cooperative program for implementing that standard on a case-by-case basis in individual plants. Most of the affected companies received at best a three-to-four-year grace period. It is highly unlikely that this turn of events saved industry $50 million, but it is clear that the effort did cost the agency significant time and resources. Whether it came at a cost to worker health depends on the answer to the extremely controversial question of whether respirators are adequate substitutes for engineering controls.

Noise

OSHA's occupational noise standard was another victim of President Reagan's order suspending the last-minute regulations of the Carter administration.[89] After the president's order expired, Assistant Secretary Auchter suspended the standard a second time in order to consider industry complaints that OSHA should have relied to a greater extent on personal protective devices (e.g., earplugs).[90] This act prompted a lawsuit by the AFL-CIO claiming that OSHA had violated the Administrative Procedure Act by failing to permit the union to comment on the advisability of a second stay.[91] Before the lawsuit was resolved, OSHA proposed an interim revised standard in August 1981 and a final revised standard in March 1983.[92]

According to Auchter, the revised standard allowed employers "the flexibility they need to find the most cost-effective means of providing . . . protection."[93] The revisions deleted or relaxed previous requirements for monitoring, audiometric testing, and training. Despite these concessions, industry was not pleased, because the rule still emphasized engineering controls over personal ear protection devices. The U.S. Chamber of Commerce noted that while the revised rule was a step in the right direction, it fell short of the "reform" that industry had demanded.[94] The Forging Industry Association agreed, and it sued OSHA to prevent the revised standard from going into effect.

In a remarkable decision, a panel of the Fourth Circuit vacated the standard in its entirety.[95] Two of the three members of the panel held that OSHA had exceeded its statutory authority when it required employers to protect the hearing of employees with preexisting hearing damage that was partially attributable to nonwork sources. As the dissent observed, this conclusion would have prevented OSHA from regulating any hazard the health effects of which could be aggravated by other factors. Faced with this disastrous decision, OSHA persuaded the entire Fourth Circuit to review the case, and the full court unanimously reversed the panel decision.[96]

The Fourth Circuit's *en banc* decision upholding OSHA's standard was, however, a Pyrrhic victory for workers. In 1983, OSHA issued an administrative directive that permitted employers to use personal protective devices instead of engineering controls to comply with the standard, even in situations where engineering controls were feasible.[97] The directive was issued in response to the OSH Review Commission decision, affirmed by the Ninth Circuit, that OSHA could not cite an employer for violation of the noise standard if the costs of implementing engineering controls exceeded the benefits of those controls.[98] Although the commission abandoned this wholly unwarranted cost-benefit defense to OSHA citations after the Supreme Court's *Cotton Dust* decision,[99] the administrative directive remains in effect.

Personal Protective Devices

OSHA's acquiescence in the use of personal protective devices for compliance with the hearing standard was part of a more general plan by Assistant Secretary Auchter to decrease the agency's reliance on engineering controls. OSHA's preference for engineering controls was based on the strong belief of its industrial hygienists that personal protective devices are never as effective as engineering controls in the real world, where jobs have deadlines, technologies fail, and workplace conditions make wearing personal protective devices extremely uncomfortable. According to Morton Corn, an industrial hygienist and former head of OSHA, virtually all health professionals agree that engineering controls are the "preferred solution" compared with personal protective devices.[100] By the 1980s, however, OSHA's insistence on the use of engineering controls to abate health hazards was the most widely criticized element of its efforts to reduce occupational disease. Industry vigorously supported the argument of many economists that OSHA could adequately protect workers at far less cost by relying on personal protection devices, such as earplugs and respirators.

OSHA's last major deregulatory initiative was an attempt to change the policy favoring engineering controls to allow greater use of personal protective devices. In March 1981, the Bush task force unveiled plans to induce a major policy shift at OSHA in this direction.[101] Alluding to OSHA's "unpublished," but "consistently adopted," policy of favoring engineering controls over personal protective equipment,[102] the task force concluded that "[a] policy that simply set performance standards, allowing employers the option of using personal protective devices where they are as effective as engineering controls, might be more cost-effective and ultimately more beneficial to workers in society."[103] Vice President Bush explained that the administration was keeping its promise "to achieve the regulatory relief our economy desperately needs—to reduce costs, to reduce inflation, to increase productivity and to provide for more jobs."[104]

The unions vigorously objected to the plan, arguing that enforcement of personal protective requirements was virtually impossible. One union official pointed out that "[y]ou can hang a respirator around a worker's neck and be in compliance ... ," even though the respirator never gets used.[105] Another union official maintained that "[p]ersonal protective gear is in no way a substitute for engineering controls—the only people who argue that are economists."[106] To the unions, the issue was a "moral question of who will bear the burden" of protecting workers.[107] In addition, the unions argued that, at the very least, respirator use had to be combined with a program of worker surveillance to ensure that the respirators were in fact working. Qualitative fit testing, which had been used for many years to check how well the respirator fits the worker's face, relied on the subjective ability of the wearer to detect an odor or irritation from airborne chemicals introduced into the air near the respirator. The unions maintained that only quantitative fit testing, which was quite expensive, could adequately ensure that respirators were working as intended. The unions' contention was supported by a panel of experts who found that although NIOSH had a program to certify respirators, it "[did] not ensure the users that devices produced under the program had a sufficiently high assurance of safety."[108]

Industry representatives disputed the proposition that personal protective devices were insufficiently protective, and they stressed the expense of engineering controls relative to personal protective technologies. According to some industry hygienists, however, it was not clear that personal protective devices were necessarily less expensive than engineering controls when administered properly. Lawrence Birkner, an industrial hygienist for Celanese Corp., observed that: "With regular maintenance, changing cartridges and filters, keeping a supply on hand, rotating equipment for cleaning, plus training and medical surveillance, a respiratory program in terms of operating cost may far exceed any capital cost."[109] In addition, quantitative fit testing requirements, which even industry scientists recognized were the best way to ensure that respirators really worked, were quite expensive, and could well be beyond the means of small employers.[110] One highly regarded industrial hygienist from the Los Alamos National Laboratories opined that "a respirator program is not cheap if it is to provide adequate protection."[111] Personal protective equipment also had hidden costs in reduced productivity caused by worker discomfort and resistance.[112]

Auchter nevertheless believed personal protective equipment should be used selectively in "stemming the tide of overregulation and inflation."[113] James Miller, head of OMB's regulatory review office and later head of OMB, pointedly remarked, "[i]t's not the Occupational Safety, Health and *Comfort* Administration."[114] On February 22, 1983, OSHA issued an ANPR asking for public comment on its plan to review its long-standing policy in favor of engineering controls. In the face of significant criticism from labor representatives and from occupational health professionals, however, OSHA gradually retreated from its suggested changes. Indeed, OSHA became a rather forceful advocate of engineering controls in numerous battles with OMB over individual standards during the ensuing years. Whether or not Auchter became captured by the agency staff, as some OMB officials contended, OSHA soon lost interest in the personal protective device initiative, and it did not surface again until George Bush became president. We will resume the story in Chapter 11.

CONCLUSIONS

During his first two years in office, Auchter kept OSHA busy redoing standards already on the books. These efforts fulfilled President Reagan's campaign promise of deregulation, and the White House, led by Vice President Bush's Task Force on Regulatory Relief, played a major role. Whatever the merits of these attempted reversals, they did not amount to much. The initiative to weaken the commercial diving standard was abandoned, and the cotton dust standard did not vary significantly from the 1978 version. Employers were permitted some additional flexibility in using personal protective devices to comply with the lead and noise standards, but the agency did not abandon its overall preference for engineering controls. Whether intended or not, a more important consequence of these efforts was the impact that they had on the agency's ability to develop new standards.

NOTES

1. "OSHA Is Now Trying to Help You," *Nation's Business*, Aug. 1981, 20.

2. Graham K. Wilson, *The Politics of Safety and Health: Occupational Safety and Health in the United States and Britain* (Oxford: Clarendon Press, 1985), 65.

3. Joann S. Lublin, "New OSHA Chief Tries to Please Business and Labor, but Rule Cutback Riles Unions," *Wall Street Journal*, 23 Nov. 1981, 25, col. 4.

4. *BNA Occupational Safety and Health Reporter* 11 (25 June 1981): 80.

5. Kenneth B. Noble, "Panel Is Told of Poor Morale in Job Safety Administration," *New York Times*, 10 May 1985, D22, col. 1; Peter Perl, "OSHA Office Clouded by Threats, House Told; Top Officials Said to Intimidate Agency Staff," *Washington Post*, 10 May 1985, A4.

6. Executive Order 12,291, 3 C.F.R. 127 (1982), repr. in 5 U.S.C. § 601 (1988).

7. Staff of the Office of Management and Budget, *The President's 60-Day Regulatory Postponement: A Report to the Presidential Task Force on Regulatory Relief* (Washington, D.C.: The Office, 1981), 2.

8. Letter from George Bush to Small Business Groups, dated 25 March 1981.

9. *BNA Occupational Safety and Health Reporter* 10 (14 May 1981): 1537.

10. Ibid., 11 (8 Oct. 1981): 368.

11. Caroline E. Mayer, "Led by Ex-Chairman, Group to Hit OSHA Cuts," *Washington Post*, 12 Dec. 1981, F11, col. 1.

12. Office of Management and Budget, *Budget of the United States* (Washington, D.C.: The Office, 1985), app. I–O16; ibid. (1984), app. I–O17; ibid. (1983), app. I–O16.

13. "OSHA Drafted Counterattack to Critic's Hill Colleagues," *Washington Post*, 7 Sept. 1984, A15, col. 3.

14. "OSHA Is Now Trying," 20.

15. Grover Wrenn, president, Environ Corp., telephone interview, 23 Oct. 1986.

16. Ibid. Charles Gordon, Department of Labor, Office of Solicitor, telephone interview, 23 Oct. 1986.

17. OSHA Instruction RUL.1, 1 Mar. 1982.

18. Ibid.

19. Gary Strobel, special assistant to the assistant secretary for regulatory affairs, OSHA, telephone interview, 23 July 1984.

20. Edward Stein, Directorate of Health Standards, OSHA, telephone interview, 21 Oct. 1986; Jennifer Silk, Directorate of Health Standards, OSHA, telephone interview, 24 Oct. 1986; Barry White, director of safety standards programs, OSHA, interview, Washington, D.C., 26 Sept. 1986.

21. Gordon interview; White interview.

22. Kathy Sawyer, "Leaving OSHA March 30; Job Safety Chief Says He Has Finished His Work," *Washington Post*, 7 March 1984, A21.

23. U.S. Congress, Senate Committee on Labor and Human Resources, Subcommittee on Investigations and General Oversight and Subcommittee on Labor, *Joint Hearing on Oversight of the Administration of the Occupational Safety and Health Act*, 97th Cong., 1st sess., 1981, 81–82; Fred Barbash, "OSHA to Review Work-Exposure Rules," *Washington Post*, 21 March 1987, A1, col. 4.

24. *BNA Occupational Safety and Health Reporter* 10 (2 Apr. 1981): 1387.

25. James C. Robinson and Dalton G. Paxman, "OSHA's Four Inconsistent Carcinogen Policies," *American Journal of Public Health* 81 (June 1991): 775.

26. 41 *Fed. Reg.* 24,272 (1976).

27. 42 *Fed. Reg.* 27,650 (1977).

28. U.S. Congress, House Committee on Government Operations, Subcommittee on Manpower and Housing, *Office of Management and Budget Control of OSHA Rulemaking: Hearings*, 97th Cong., 2d sess., 1982, 289 (hereafter cited as House, *OMB Control of OSHA Rulemaking Hearings of 1982*).

29. *Taylor Diving and Salvage* v. *U.S. Dept. of Labor*, 599 F.2d 622 (5th Cir. 1979).

30. House, *OMB Control of OSHA Rulemaking Hearings of 1982*, 203.

31. Ibid., app. at 377, 381.

32. U.S. Congress, House Committee on Government Operations, *OMB Interference with OSHA Rulemaking*, 98th Cong., 1st sess., 1983, H. Rpt. 98–583, 10.

33. Ibid., 8.

34. Fred Barbash, "OSHA Will Seek to Relax Rules on Cotton Dust," *Washington Post*, 27 March 1981, A1, col. 4; *BNA Occupational Safety and Health Reporter* 10 (2 Apr. 1981): 1385.
35. 46 *Fed. Reg.* 19,501 (1981).
36. *BNA Occupational Safety and Health Reporter* 10 (2 Apr. 1981): 1385.
37. "OSHA Official Has Cotton Dust Booklets Destroyed," *Washington Post*, 27 March 1981, A8, col. 1.
38. Barbash, "OSHA to Review."
39. *American Textile Mfrs. Inc.* v. *Donovan*, 452 U.S. 409, 505 n. 25 (1978).
40. 452 U.S. 490 (1978).
41. U.S. Congress, House Committee on Science and Technology, *Review of the Scientific and Technological Issues in the Regulation of Cotton Dust in Primary Cotton Textile Industry*, 98th Cong., 1st sess., 1983, H. Rpt. 98–215, 24 (hereafter cited as House, *Issues in the Regulation of Cotton Dust Report of 1983*).
42. *BNA Occupational Safety and Health Reporter* 10 (16 Apr. 1981): 1427.
43. Warren Brown, "Textile Workers Protest Against Reagan Review," *Washington Post*, 5 May 1981, E1, col. 1.
44. *BNA Occupational Safety and Health Reporter* 10 (7 May 1981): 1521.
45. Ibid., 1522.
46. 47 *Fed. Reg.* 5906 (1982); Marjorie Sun, "OSHA Reviewing Cotton Dust Standards," *Science* 217 (2 Sept. 1982): 1232.
47. Sun, "OSHA Reviewing."
48. Ibid.
49. Ibid.; House Committee on Science and Technology, Subcommittee on Investigations and Oversight, *Hearings on Byssinosis: Evaluation of Scientific and Technological Issues*, 97th Cong., 2d sess., 1982, 104–05 (hereafter cited as House, *Byssinosis Hearings*).
50. Sun, "OSHA Reviewing."
51. Ibid.
52. House, *Byssinosis Hearings*, 17.
53. Ibid.
54. *BNA Occupational Safety and Health Reporter* 12 (30 Sept. 1982): 355.
55. House, *Issues in the Regulation of Cotton Dust Report of 1983*, vi.
56. *BNA Occupational Safety and Health Reporter* 12 (7 Sept. 1982): 323.
57. Letter to T. Timothy Ryan from Christopher DeMuth, dated 27 January 1983, in House Judiciary Committee, Subcommittee on Administrative Law and Government Relations, *Hearings on the Regulatory Reform Act*, H.R. 2327, 98th Cong., 1st sess., 1983, serial no. 98–25, 383 (hereafter cited as House, *Regulatory Reform Act Hearings of 1983*).
58. *BNA Occupational Safety and Health Reporter* 12 (19 May 1983): 1075.
59. Memorandum to the Presidential Task Force on Regulatory Relief from Christopher DeMuth, dated 3 May 1983, in House, *Regulatory Reform Act Hearings of 1983*, 386.
60. *BNA Occupational Safety and Health Reporter* 12 (12 May 1983): 1059.
61. Ibid., 1075.
62. Ibid. (26 May 1983): 1099.
63. Ibid.
64. Ibid., 1100.

65. Ibid., 1099.

66. Ibid. 13 (16 June 1983): 43.

67. Ibid. (17 May 1984): 1326.

68. Sandra Sugawara, "Labor Protests Brown Lung Study; Va. Backs Firm's Research, Lets It Exceed Dust Standard," *Washington Post*, 13 May 1984, A1, col. 5.

69. *BNA Occupational Safety and Health Reporter* 13 (17 May 1984): 1326; ibid. (31 May 1984): 1356.

70. Sandra Sugawara, "Va. Criticized for Permitting Dust Exposure at Dan River," *Washington Post*, 19 June 1984, A1, col. 1; *BNA Occupational Safety and Health Reporter* 14 (21 June 1984): 38.

71. 50 *Fed. Reg.* 51,120 (1985).

72. *BNA Occupational Safety and Health Reporter* 15 (12 Dec. 1985): 587–88.

73. Staff of Office of Management and Budget, *President's 60-Day Regulatory Postponement*, B–7.

74. Peter Behr, "OSHA Switches Sides in War over Lead," *Washington Post*, 18 Apr. 1981, A1, col. 2; *BNA Occupational Safety and Health Reporter* 10 (30 Apr. 1981): 1498.

75. *BNA Occupational Safety and Health Reporter* 10 (30 Apr. 1981): 1498.

76. 453 U.S. 913 (1981).

77. *BNA Occupational Safety and Health Reporter* 16 (11 March 1987): 1064.

78. 46 *Fed. Reg.* 33,516 (1981).

79. 47 *Fed. Reg.* 26,557 (1982).

80. *BNA Occupational Safety and Health Reporter* 12 (19 Aug. 1982): 1256.

81. 47 *Fed. Reg.* 54,433 (1983).

82. Kim Masters, "Lead Exposure Limits to Be Retained," *Legal Times*, 30 May 1983, 1; *BNA Occupational Safety and Health Reporter* 13 (4 Aug. 1983): 211.

83. Leonard M. Apcar, "OSHA Signs Union-Backed ASARCO Plan to Control Steelworker Exposure to Lead," *Wall Street Journal*, 1 Feb. 1984, 10, col. 2.

84. *BNA Occupational Safety and Health Reporter* 13 (16 Feb. 1984): 990; ibid. (23 Feb. 1984): 1014.

85. Ibid. (12 Apr. 1984): 1196.

86. Ibid. (31 May 1984): 1357.

87. Ibid. 14 (12 July 1984): 155.

88. Ibid. 15 (13 Mar. 1986): 1028.

89. Staff of the Office of Management and Budget, *Summary of Reagan Administration's Regulatory Relief Action, a Report to the Presidential Task Force on Regulatory Relief* (Washington, D.C.: The Office, 1981), 50.

90. 46 *Fed. Reg.* 42,622 (1981).

91. Benjamin W. Mintz, "Occupational Safety and Health: The Regulatory Program—A History," in *Fundamentals of Industrial Hygiene*, 3d ed., ed. Barbara A. Plog (Washington, D.C.: National Safety Council, 1989), 718.

92. 48 *Fed. Reg.* 9738 (1983).

93. *BNA Daily Report for Executives* 43 (3 Mar. 1983): A6.

94. *BNA Occupational Safety and Health Reporter* 12 (17 Mar. 1983): 893.

95. *Forging Industry Ass'n.* v. *Secretary of Labor*, 748 F.2d 210 (4th Cir. 1984), *rev'd.*, 773 F.2d 1436 (4th Cir. 1985) (*en banc*).

96. *Forging Industry Ass'n.* v. *Secretary of Labor*, 773 F.2d 1435 (4th Cir. 1985) (*en banc*).

97. OSHA Instruction CPL 2–2.35A G (1983).

98. *Donovan* v. *Castle & Cooke Foods*, 692 F.2d 641 (9th Cir. 1982).

99. *Sun Ship Inc.*, 11 O.S.H. Cases (BNA) 1028 (Rev. Comm. 1982).

100. *BNA Occupational Safety and Health Reporter* 11 (11 June 1981): 41.

101. "A Shift Toward Protective Gear," *Business Week*, 13 Apr. 1981, 56.

102. *BNA Occupational Safety and Health Reporter* 10 (2 Apr. 1981): 1385.

103. "Memorandum for Policy Review Board from John A. Pendergrass, Addendum to the Options Memorandum Concerning Revision to the Methods of Compliance Requirements in Meeting OSHA's Permissible Exposure Limits" (n.d.), in U.S. Congress, Senate Committee on Labor and Human Resources, *Hearings on Oversight on the Administration of the Occupational Safety and Health Act*, 100th Cong., 2d sess., S.Hrg. 100–719, 1988, 260–61.

104. Peter Behr and Joanne Omang, "White House Targets 27 More Regulations for Review; More Regulations Target of Administration Review," *Washington Post*, 26 Mar. 1981, A1, col. 2.

105. "Protective Gear," *Business Week*, 56.

106. Ibid.

107. *BNA Occupational Safety and Health Reporter* 11 (11 June 1981): 41.

108. Ibid.

109. *Chemical Week*, 22 April 1981, 31.

110. Ibid.

111. *BNA Occupational Safety and Health Reporter* 11 (11 June 1981): 40.

112. Ibid.

113. "Protective Gear," *Business Week*, 56.

114. Sandra Teeley, "OSHA Under Siege," *Washington Post*, April 12, 1981, A1, col. 1 (emphasis added).

6

The Reagan Years: Inching Forward

OSHA's activity during the Carter administration left the agency with a full plate of regulatory initiatives for which the Reagan administration expressed little gratitude. The Chemical Manufacturer's Association put OSHA's carcinogen policy high on its proposed "hit list,"[1] and the new administration quietly withdrew the Bingham administration's proposed amendments to that policy in early 1981, thus ending a major four-year battle with a decisive victory for the chemical industry.[2] Other matters that had been pending for many years were put on the slow track while the agency attempted to rewrite rules that were already on the books.

Assistant Secretary Auchter did not eliminate his predecessor's "new directions" initiative for educating workers about health and safety and about their rights under the OSH Act, but he cut the program's funding so substantially and put such severe restrictions on outlays that it gradually faded away. The program's funding was reduced from $13.9 million in fiscal year 1981 to $6.9 million in fiscal year 1982 and $5.6 million by fiscal year 1985.[3] The agency in 1981 shifted the oversight of the program to OSHA's regional offices, and it terminated the peer review process for new directions grants, thereby introducing a greater political element into the process of selecting grant recipients.[4] OSHA changed the program even more drastically in 1983 by reducing the eligibility of educational and other nonprofit organizations. In particular, OSHA stopped funding activist groups that sought to educate workers about actions they could take in public forums to bring about safer workplaces.[5]

Early in his tenure Auchter initiated the Dormant Standards Project to prune the agency's existing rulemaking agenda. An agency task force recommended that OSHA delete more than 100 projects from the list of pending initiatives. Noting that publication of its recommendations would doubtless draw public attention to the fact that OSHA had not completed work on 116 hazardous substances, the task force warned that "[t]his cannot be good publicity for the agency."[6] When word of the task force's recommendations inevitably leaked to the press, a congressional subcommittee demanded that Auchter explain why the agency was abandoning the initiatives. Auchter explained that OSHA had not made a final decision, but he noted that most of the projects were pending when Eula Bingham took over the agency in 1976. Promising that OSHA and the National Institute of Occupational Safety and Health (NIOSH) would meet soon to discuss the list, Auchter testified that OSHA "never had any intention of allowing any part of the Dormant Standards Project to move forward if doing so would threaten the health of workers."[7] Although the project was soon abandoned, the incident left worker representatives and some congressmen wary of OSHA's intentions with respect to pending initiatives.

Despite OSHA's deregulatory bent, the agency did not stop work entirely on completing existing initiatives. Progress, however, was very slow. In fact, OSHA promulgated only two new safety standards (marine terminals and latch-open devices on gasoline pumps)[8] and two new health standards (hazard communication and ethylene oxide)[9] during Auchter's tenure. The two health standards resulted from irresistible outside pressure. The hazard communication standard was promulgated at the behest of employers who sought federal regulation as a way to avoid more stringent state regulation. The ethylene oxide standard was promulgated in response to a court order. Where OSHA was not under similar pressure, as in the cases of the formaldehyde and grain dust standards, Auchter or OMB successfully delayed final rules.

THE HAZARD COMMUNICATION STANDARD

One of the most significant rulemaking initiatives of the Bingham era ironically became the only real success story of the Auchter years. During the late 1970s, workers began to insist that they be apprised of workplace risks, so that they could make informed career choices and demand appropriate risk premiums for working under dangerous conditions.[10] Few employers, however, were willing to go to the trouble of informing workers when the predictable consequence was that employees would attempt to bid up wages. Many employers were also worried that telling employees about workplace hazards would require them to disclose the identities of workplace chemicals and thereby risk the loss of valuable trade secrets.

OSHA began actively considering options for a worker information standard not long after the agency was established. In 1974, NIOSH published a criteria document recommending a hazard communications standard,[11] and the agency established an advisory committee to develop guidelines for labeling requirements in standards for individual toxic substances. After that committee submitted its final report, Ralph Nader's Health Research Group petitioned the agency to issue a standard to require labeling of *all* workplace chemicals. In response, OSHA published an advanced notice of proposed rulemaking (ANPR) in January 1977.[12] After spending four years studying the comments on the ANPR, OSHA published a notice of proposed rulemaking for a generic hazard identification standard as one of the Carter administration's last-minute "midnight regulations."[13]

Soon after President Reagan "froze" the midnight regulations, OSHA withdrew the notice of proposed rulemaking and appointed an agency task force to develop alternatives to the proposal.[14] The unions predictably accused the administration of caving in to industry.[15] Not trusting the Reagan OSHA to promulgate an acceptable standard, they shifted their attention away from the federal arena and attempted to secure the enactment of state and local "worker-right-to-know" legislation. Although the chemical and manufacturing industries were initially happy to see the OSHA proposal withdrawn,[16] they soon realized that a uniform standard might be preferable to a potpourri of possibly inconsistent (and potentially more stringent) state and local standards.[17] OSHA soon initiated a new rulemaking effort to satisfy industry preemption demands.[18] The career staffers from the team that wrote the Carter administration proposal formed the nucleus of the new team that wrote the Reagan administration proposal. Perhaps because much of the work had already been done, the team proceeded expeditiously and a draft proposal was ready for Office of Management and Budget (OMB) review in early 1982.

Since this was the first major rule to come out of OSHA during the Reagan administration, OMB viewed it as an important test of its newly acquired regulatory review powers. The OMB staff drafted a 14-page "administratively confidential" memorandum to Vice President Bush's Task Force on Regulatory Relief, "in the spirit of lively internal debate,"[19] that offered three principal arguments against OSHA's proposal: (1) there was "no direct evidence of a need for universal labeling of chemicals" and "much indirect evidence that it is not needed"; (2) hazard identification was "not an appropriate area for federal preemption of state and local regulation"; and (3) "the potential costs of the proposal far exceed[ed] the benefits."[20] The economists in OMB acknowledged that there were some cases where better labeling would be worthwhile, but maintained that "neither OSHA nor anyone else knows even approximately the number of such cases or whether they justify a national policy of universal labeling."[21]

OSHA in turn accused OMB of relying upon "shaky arithmetic and faulty assumptions."[22] A point-by-point rebuttal of OMB's critique questioned the factual basis for its assumptions and the technical basis for its evaluation of the scientific evidence. The agency also stressed the not insignificant political point that both labor and industry were behind the standard.

After a meeting between top-level OMB and OSHA officials resulted in no movement on either side, the Bush task force met to discuss the standard. Unable to resolve the dispute, the task force asked both agencies to try one more time to reach an agreement.[23] OSHA then contracted with a prominent conservative academic economist, W. Kip Viscusi, to evaluate OMB's critique and to prepare his own estimate of the standard's benefits.[24] Viscusi took pains to find some merit in the position of both agencies, but his figures came closer to those of OSHA's economists.[25] Viscusi opined that it seemed "inappropriate [for OMB] to criticize a relatively new approach to job safety as being based on speculation since all new approaches of this kind could be subjected to similar criticism."[26] Viscusi was also perplexed by OMB's conclusion that "workers will not respond at all to hazard information."[27]

The materials from the interagency debate were leaked to Congress, and House Democrats were quick to seize on the issue.[28] An OSHA memorandum to the task force captured the essence of the political situation:

Labor and other groups have criticized the Administration for "gutting" environmental and safety and health laws. . . . Superimposing OMB over the regulatory process in a manner where they became the de facto regulator will lend credence to those criticism. This, in turn, portends significant political problems. . . . For 11 months organized labor has been saying that we are not coming out with a new proposal, and we have been saying that we are. . . . Labor has not yet been given a cudgel with which to beat this Administration. Failure to act on this matter will provide one. . . . Recent articles point to the Democratic party's efforts to rebuild its ties to the labor movement by painting this Administration as anti-worker. Let us not ignore political reality.[29]

Ultimately, the vice president sided with OSHA, and the proposal went out in March 1982 without significant change.[30] The new proposal accepted the fundamental tenet that workers should be informed about workplace hazards, but it limited its application to the manufacturing sector of the economy. Although the proposal addressed only "hazardous" chemicals, it did not follow the Carter administration approach of specifying the substances that it deemed hazardous. Instead, it gave employers discretion in the exercise of their "professional judgment" to determine if chemicals were hazardous by considering "scientifically well-established evidence,"[31] and it did not provide employees with a vehicle for challenging an employer's hazard determination.[32] The proposed warning requirements were also "performance-based" in that they defined the term "hazard warning" very broadly to include "any words, pictures, symbols, or combination thereof which convey the hazards of the chemical(s) in the container."[33] The Reagan proposal went beyond the Carter proposal, however, in requiring every manufacturer to obtain or develop a material safety data sheet (MSDS), based on the available literature, for each hazardous product that it produced or used, and it listed specific items that were to be included in every MSDS. In addition, employers were responsible for ensuring that any new and significant health hazard information that came to their attention was included in the appropriate MSDS within a reasonable period of time. The most drastic departure of the new proposal was its requirement that employers provide employee training in how to work with hazardous chemicals.[34] Finally, the 1982 proposal was much more protective of trade secrets than the 1981 proposal.

Reactions to the proposal were highly polarized, but the public comments did not persuade OSHA to vary its basic approach. The agency rejected union demands that the standard be extended beyond the manufacturing industry. But it did retreat somewhat from its performance-oriented approach to identifying hazardous chemicals in favor of an approach that specified some of the chemicals for which hazard assessments would have to be undertaken. For example, the agency decided to specify a chemical as a carcinogen when the National Toxicology Program, the International Agency for Research on Cancer, or OSHA published a finding that the substance was a carcinogen. Similarly, it required manufacturers and employers to consider as "hazardous" any chemicals for which OSHA promulgated standards or the American Council of Governmental Industrial Hygienists published threshold limit values. The final rule also reduced employer discretion by mandating that any substance that caused hazardous effects at a statistically significant level in a single species of laboratory animal in a study conducted in accordance with established scientific principles must be regarded as hazardous.[35] The agency, however, rejected union requests that it specify particularized hazard determination procedures.[36] One further change was the specification of an explicit mechanism for resolving trade secrecy disputes.

In the final analysis, Auchter's hazard identification standard was one of the most important rules ever promulgated by the agency. It addressed a significant health concern that had been high on OSHA's agenda from its inception. In some ways, it was an easier standard for a conservative Republican administration to write, because it emphasized the "free market" in workplace risks and recognized that the market could not function without adequate information. It was also significant that both labor and industry were urging the agency to write a hazard identification standard. Without strong industry support (albeit motivated by a desire to avoid even more stringent state and local standards), the hazard identification standard might well have languished with the other dying initiatives during Auchter's tenure.[37] OSHA's decision, however, to restrict the standard to workers in manufacturing industries significantly reduced the scope of protection the standard offered. As Chapter 8 discusses, OSHA did eventually expand the coverage of the standard to all industries, but only after a court ordered it to do so.

ETHYLENE OXIDE

The only other health standard promulgated during Auchter's tenure, the ethylene oxide (EtO) standard, was successfully opposed by Auchter and OMB until a court ordered OSHA to promulgate it. Even the court order, however, could not prevent OMB from substantially weakening the rule that OSHA ultimately issued.

One of the 25 most widely produced chemicals in the United States, EtO is used primarily as an intermediate in the production of other items such as antifreeze. EtO is also used as a sterilizing agent in hospitals for delicate instruments and heat-sensitive devices. Since it is a gas at room temperature, it is held in a sterilizing chamber with the equipment to be sterilized, usually under high pressure, long enough to penetrate thoroughly all articles in the chamber. After a sufficient exposure time, the gas is evacuated from the chamber, and the instruments are purged of EtO vapor through aeration. Since the sterilization process is usually undertaken only one to three times per day, employees are typically exposed to high doses of EtO over fairly infrequent periods of 15 minutes or less while the chambers are opened and while the instruments are being purged of excess gases.[38]

The 1971 "consensus" standard for EtO was 50 ppm over an eight-hour period, based on animal studies showing no adverse effects at that level. In 1977, however, NIOSH issued a "special occupational hazard review" that recommended the adoption of an additional 75 ppm ceiling over 15 minutes, based on studies indicating that EtO be mutagenic. In 1981 the American Council of Governmental Industrial Hygienists lowered its recommended threshold limit value to 10 ppm over eight hours in light of the mutagenicity studies and of the possibility that EtO was carcinogenic. In the same year NIOSH issued a "current intelligence bulletin" recommending that EtO be regarded as a carcinogen and that the existing OSHA standard be lowered. OSHA issued an ANPR requesting comments and information, but making no promises. In November 1982, a Finnish study of hospital workers exposed to EtO for short periods of time suggested that such exposure caused spontaneous abortions in pregnant women.[39] Since many of the nurses engaged in sterilization activities in hospitals were female, this was a matter of particular concern.

The Public Citizen Health Research Group (HRG), a Nader-affiliated organization, petitioned OSHA in August 1981 to issue an emergency temporary standard (ETS). After OSHA denied the petition a month later, HRG went to court and secured a court order requiring OSHA to issue the ETS by January 25, 1983.[40] The district court concluded that the scientific studies available to OSHA "presented a solid and certain foundation showing that workers are subjected to grave health dangers" and that OSHA's refusal to issue an ETS was an "abuse of discretion." In a one-sentence response to the January 5, 1983 decision, Auchter complained that "it appears the court is trying to set our regulatory agenda for us."[41] OSHA appealed, and the District of Columbia Circuit ruled that the district court had exceeded its authority in ordering that the ETS be issued. The appellate court, however, ruled that the 18-month interval between the ANPR and the district court's ruling was so lengthy, given the district court's findings, that OSHA had "unreasonably delayed" action on the standard. The court of appeals therefore ordered OSHA to issue a proposed rule for a permanent standard within 30 days.[42]

On April 21, 1983, OSHA published a proposed rule mandating a permissible exposure limit of 1 ppm over an eight-hour period.[43] The agency did not, however, propose a short-term exposure limit (STEL), even though the 1 ppm eight-hour average would allow an employee to be exposed to 480 ppm for one minute, as long as there was no exposure for the rest of the day.[44] The agency announced that more study was necessary before an STEL could be established.

Both affected interest groups were dissatisfied. OSHA received more than 158 written comments, and numerous employee and employer groups testified at OSHA's public hearings and at Congressional hearings on the standard. The American Federation of State, County and Municipal Employees noted that even the least conservative risk assessment predicted that hospital workers currently faced a 1 in 1,000 risk.[45] The union argued that an STEL was necessary and that the eight-hour level should be set at 0.1–0.5 ppm.[46] The Chemical Manufacturer's Association wanted a more flexible, performance-based proposal.[47] An organization of EtO users argued that because of "significant uncertainties" in extrapolating high-dose animal studies to humans, OSHA lacked sufficient evidence to justify the 1 ppm standard.

Although OSHA had cited the need for more study in justifying its refusal to set an STEL, Leonard Vance, the director of the Health Standards Directorate, blocked staff efforts to study an STEL for EtO in June 1983, immediately after meeting privately with a top official of the Union Carbide Corporation, a major manufacturer of the chemical. Dr. Robert Beliles, leader of the agency's EtO team, asked Dr. Peter Infante, the team's epidemiologist, to prepare a risk assessment based upon the Finnish spontaneous abortion study. Since Infante was leaving for a vacation, he asked a staff epidemiologist, Dr. Theodora Tsongas, to prepare the assessment. Before Infante returned, Vance ordered Tsongas not to prepare the risk assessment, explaining that the staff had more important things to do and that the risk assessment would cause too much controversy.[48] Beliles later testified to a congressional committee that Vance ordered him not to raise the issue of an STEL at the rulemaking hearings.[49]

When a congressional committee subsequently investigated Vance's role in the EtO standard-setting process, Vance promised to give the committee his office logs, which presumably would have documented Vance's meetings with companies affected by the proposed standard.[50] But he later reported that he had discarded some of them when his dog vomited on them during a hunting trip. Not everyone was convinced by this novel excuse, and Vance never explained what his office logs were doing in the back of his pickup truck in the middle of the woods.[51] Beliles later transferred to EPA to avoid friction with Vance.[52]

In accordance with a court-ordered deadline, OSHA sent the rule to OMB for review in late spring. OMB reacted strongly against the STEL requirement in the draft final rule. Its economists argued that OSHA had grossly overstated the health risks by relying on three allegedly flawed studies and by using erroneous assumptions in its risk assessment. OMB also argued that evidence of damage to chromosomes should not be used as the basis of regulation. Mimicking the hospital industry's contentions, OMB further maintained that there was no basis for establishing an STEL and that the standard was in any event too costly. As usual, OMB determined that the standard would be much cheaper if OSHA allowed greater use of respirators.[53]

Despite OMB's objections, OSHA prepared a final rule that contained an STEL, and the agency was prepared to publish it in the *Federal Register* on June 15. On June 14, however, OMB ordered OSHA to delete the STEL. OSHA, which was leaderless at the time (Auchter had resigned on March 6, 1984), caved in and excised the STEL and its lengthy justification from the final rule. OSHA's key conclusion that spontaneous abortions were linked to short-term exposures was unceremoniously glossed over.[54] NIOSH later concluded that "OMB's concerns regarding inclusion of a short term exposure limit in the ethylene oxide standard appears [*sic*] to conflict with the substantial scientific evidence collected by OSHA,"[55] and the National Institute of Environmental Health Sciences encouraged OSHA to establish the STEL in spite of OMB's objections.[56]

OMB denied having forced OSHA to delete the STEL. Christopher DeMuth, the head of OMB's Office of Information and Regulatory Affairs, said, "We raised the issue with policy level people, and they agreed with us. OMB did not make the final decision, the Secretary of Labor did." Beliles and Infante, however, had written a memorandum two days before the altered version was published, stating, "We are aware that [the deletion of the STEL] was dictated to the agency by OMB without input from Occupational Safety & Health Administration professionals. This raises concerns for us not only for the ethylene oxide standard but future standards."[57]

OSHA's final rule set a permissible exposure limit of 1 ppm averaged over an eight-hour period,[58] and the agency promised that it would consider whether to promulgate an STEL in a "mini-rulemaking" devoted exclusively to that question.[59] The rule was quickly appealed by the Association of Ethylene Oxide Users,[60] and HRG asked the district court to require OSHA to promulgate an STEL.[61] Calling OSHA's action "atrocious," the district judge ordered the agency to give the court a progress report on the "mini-rulemaking." The court warned OSHA that it would have to complete the proceeding by December 17, 1984.[62]

On January 2, 1985, OSHA issued its determination not to promulgate an STEL.[63] In reaching this decision, OSHA's management rejected the unanimous recommendation of the staff team that had performed the underlying analysis of the EtO standard.[64] HRG returned to court, alleging that OSHA's action was once again taken on orders from OMB.[65] The District of Columbia Circuit, on July 25, 1986, held that the record before the agency did not support its conclusion that an STEL was not necessary, but it declined to decide whether the OMB intervention was unlawful.[66] Almost a year after the judicial remand, OSHA still had not decided whether to publish an STEL, and HRG, in April 1987, asked the court to require OSHA to issue an STEL within two weeks.[67] In late July 1987, the District of Columbia Circuit ordered the agency to respond to its remand by March 1988 or be held in contempt of court. The court noted: "At some point, we must lean forward from the bench to let an agency know, in no uncertain terms, that enough is enough."[68]

Finally, on January 21, 1988, OSHA published a proposed rule establishing an STEL of 5 ppm averaged over a period of 15 minutes.[69] OMB predictably objected to the STEL, arguing that respirators would be more cost-effective.[70] After soliciting additional comments on the STEL, OSHA published a final rule identical to the proposed rule on April 6, 1988.[71] Once again, the Reagan administration was dragged, kicking and screaming, to a sensible accommodation of the contending interests that was both politically sound and scientifically supportable. Yet, in the final analysis, it took OSHA over six years to reach roughly the same result that HRG had originally requested.

FORMALDEHYDE

In contrast to the previous two initiatives, Auchter was able to prevent OSHA from promulgating a formaldehyde standard despite clear evidence that workers were at substantial risk. Formaldehyde has for decades been an inexpensive multipurpose solvent, preservative, and insecticide. Because it is widely used in many industries, the number of exposed workers is correspondingly high. In 1963, the American Council of Governmental Industrial Hygienists recommended a threshold limit value of 5 ppm for formaldehyde to protect against skin and nasal irritation, and OSHA promulgated a "consensus standard" of 3 ppm in 1971. Formaldehyde rose to the top of the regulatory agenda in the late 1970s when a test sponsored by the Formaldehyde Institute suggesting that formaldehyde caused nasal cancers in laboratory rats was confirmed by a second study conducted at New York University.[72] A special panel of government experts in November 1980 concluded that it was "prudent to regard formaldehyde as posing a carcinogenic risk to humans."[73]

In the midst of OSHA's preliminary investigation of formaldehyde, Dr. Peter Infante, a widely known cancer researcher who had recently joined OSHA's Health Standards Directorate, wrote a letter on OSHA letterhead to Dr. John Higginson, director of the International Agency for Research on Cancer (IARC), questioning IARC's February 1981 determination that the industry-sponsored study presented only "limited" and not "sufficient" evidence that formaldehyde was an animal carcinogen. At Auchter's insistence, Health Standards Director Bailus Walker, Jr., proposed to fire Dr. Infante for failing to make it clear that his letter did not represent the agency's official position.[74] When the affair attracted public and congressional attention, however, Auchter wrote to Infante, telling him the charges had been dropped.[75] Walker left the agency soon thereafter.

Although the formaldehyde issue subsequently dropped from the public spotlight, OSHA staffers continued to meet regularly with industry representatives as they attempted to formulate the agency's position. After a meeting with Formaldehyde Institute representatives at a Washington restaurant in early 1981, Deputy Assistant Secretary Mark Cowan recommended to Auchter that the agency should not release a "current intelligence bulletin" warning workers about formaldehyde cancer risks. He alluded to "significant evidence" that was presented to him at the breakfast meeting.[76]

In January 1982, OSHA denied an October 1981 petition from the United Auto Workers Union to establish an ETS for formaldehyde at the lowest feasible exposure level.[77] Later in 1982, NIOSH director J. Donald Millar wrote to OSHA to forward the final IARC monograph on formaldehyde. According to Millar, IARC had concluded that formaldehyde "must be regarded as if it were carcinogenic to man. . . . " Cowan dismissed Millar's letter, stating that OSHA had not yet determined that formaldehyde posed a "significant risk" to exposed workers.[78] Millar wondered publicly whether OSHA was now requiring evidence of carcinogenicity in humans before regulating a substance: "If so, it s bad news indeed for those who are interested in preventing work-related cancer and particularly for the estimated 1.6 million workers potentially at risk from exposure to formaldehyde." Cowan responded that his first letter was intended only "to indicate that OSHA cannot promulgate a regulation for a carcinogenic substance solely because a substance has been *identified* as a carcinogen. . . . "[79]

In fact, at the time Cowan wrote to NIOSH, OSHA possessed information suggesting that formaldehyde did indeed pose a significant risk to workers. A risk assessment performed by a respected consultant, Clement Associates, Inc., extrapolated from the recent animal data to conclude that workers faced a lifetime risk of 620 excess cancers per 100,000 workers at the current OSHA limit. Clement concluded that the risk could be reduced almost 27-fold by reducing the standard from 3 ppm to 1 ppm.[80] In addition, an OSHA scientist had recently determined that formaldehyde caused benign tumors in laboratory rats, and a well-known scientist from the National Cancer Institute found that "formaldehyde gas was carcinogenic by inhalation for rats at all three exposure levels used in his carcinogenicity tests."[81] One of the exposure levels tested was only one ppm above the current OSHA standard.

When this new information came to light several months later, the UAW renewed its demand for an ETS and accused OSHA of making "a deliberate policy decision to keep the information out of sight as long as possible."[82] After OSHA again denied the petition, the union sued.[83] OSHA replied that it could promulgate an ETS only upon finding that the risk to employees was "substantially greater than a 'significant risk.' "[84] A recent OSHA risk assessment had projected a 1.5 in 10,000 risk "for the great majority of workers" who were exposed to formaldehyde at levels lower than the 3 ppm standard. OSHA concluded that this risk did not approach the 1 in 1,000 risk that the Supreme Court in the *Benzene* case suggested might constitute a significant risk. Even the "minority" of workers exposed to levels near the existing 3 ppm exposure limit faced "only a four in 1,000 risk—a level not elevated dramatically above the Supreme Court's benchmark for permanent rulemaking."[85] Thus, the Supreme Court's embarrassingly inept hypothetical in the *Benzene* case provided OSHA with an excuse for failing to protect workers exposed to risks that were exceedingly high in comparison with risks that are routinely regulated in the environmental context.

Even when confronted with a chemical that posed very high risks to workers, Auchter's OSHA was unwilling to undertake a new rulemaking initiative. The formaldehyde question remained in limbo until a federal court ordered OSHA to take it up four months after Auchter left the agency. We will continue the formaldehyde saga in chapters 8 and 11.

GRAIN-HANDLING FACILITIES

Auchter did not seek to stymie every OSHA initiative. Even with his support, however, progress was slowed by OMB opposition. The grain-handling facilities rule was one of the more visible victims of White House oversight.

Grain dust is an amazing agglomeration of uninviting substances, including plant fragments, seeds, pollen, minerals, insects and insect parts, pesticides, molds, bacteria, and fungi. Although this stomach-turning mixture can pose health risks to workers, its primary hazard stems from the fact that, in the right sizes and concentrations, it can explode with extraordinary force when ignited by a spark.[86] Pound for pound, grain dust contains more explosive energy than TNT.[87]

OSHA's involvement with grain dust began in 1978, when a series of disastrous grain elevator explosions focused public attention on grain dust in elevators.[88] Although the agency published an ANPR in February 1980, the incoming Reagan administration put the grain elevator project on the back burner to make way for deregulatory initiatives. After several more highly publicized grain elevator explosions and the publication of a comprehensive report by the Academy of Sciences (NAS),[89] OSHA agreed in late 1982 to draft a proposed rule. Relying on the NAS panel recommendation,[90] the AFL-CIO argued that OSHA should require elevator operators to clean grain dust off surfaces before it accumulated to a depth of 1/64 inch. The grain-handling industry contended that a uniform standard was inappropriate, because the explosion hazard varied greatly with the composition of the dust.[91] On March 4, 1983, a proposed standard specifying a level of 1/8 inch was supposed to be sent to OMB. Noting that OMB had never held up a safety standard, the head of OSHA's Safety Standards Directorate predicted that the grain dust standard would sail through OMB review.[92] Unfortunately, the text of the proposed rule got lost on the way to the Department of Labor solicitor's office prior to being sent to OMB. Two months later, after some congressional prodding, the draft was located and sent to OMB,[93] where it was not well received. Promising that OMB's review of the standard "should be completed within the next several weeks," Budget Director David Stockman observed initially that OSHA had failed to provide an adequate justification for the 1/8-inch level, had relied on bad assumptions and poor data in predicting the benefits of the proposal, and had "not examined the cost-effectiveness of each provision on a uniform basis."[94]

OMB demanded from the outset that all communications between the agencies be kept entirely secret, and it insisted that no written document be exchanged and that no notes be kept of any meetings.[95] Indeed, at one point OMB insisted that a 27-page written response from OSHA be orally transmitted over the telephone by Department of Labor Deputy Solicitor Francis X. Lilly.[96] Yet at the same time, OMB staffers were meeting in private with representatives of the American Feed Manufacturers Association.[97] Like any good lobbying organization, the Millers' National Federation sent OMB a lengthy letter criticizing the OSHA proposal.[98] Debbie Berkowitz, a safety expert for the AFL-CIO, charged that OMB "bought lock, stock, and barrel the arguments by industry, which says, 'We are taking care of the problem; we don't need a standard.' "[99]

After a July 28, 1983, meeting between OSHA and OMB failed to iron out their differences, the AFL-CIO called on the Reagan administration to publish a proposed rule immediately.[100] AFL-CIO president Lane Kirkland also wrote to Vice President Bush, asking him to free up the grain elevator standard.[101] Robert Harbrant, president of the Food, Beverage and Trade Department of the union, charged that OMB was delaying the proposal for political purposes.[102]

An October 6, 1983 meeting between the two agencies resulted in another stalemate. OMB would still not agree to a ⅛-inch standard, and it insisted that the standard contain an exception for small grain elevators. Pointing out that the NAS panel had recommended a 1/64-inch level, OSHA indicated its willingness to change parts of the preamble to the standard, but it would not agree to change the standard itself.[103] Finally, on December 21, 1983, more than six months after receiving it, OMB cleared OSHA's proposed rule. In a significant concession to OMB and the grain industry, however, the agency proposed three options, including a ⅛-inch required level, a requirement that operators use pneumatic dust control systems, and a requirement that employers clean their facilities at least once a shift. Although the latter "housekeeping" option was added to satisfy OMB,[104] the proposal did not contain OMB's suggested exemption for small elevators.[105]

An outraged Berkowitz charged that, at OMB's insistence, OSHA had "gutted the standard to save a few dollars." She continued:

The whole point of the standard was to control the explosive dust. Now it says you can control the dust by keeping it below a certain level, or you can sweep once a day. You can sweep with a rake and sweep for five minutes and then leave, and in an hour there will be two inches of dust on the floor.[106]

She complained that the proposal was worse than no standard at all, because it would give rise to "a false sense of security."[107] An official OSHA spokesman denied that the proposal was watered down,[108] but another OSHA official said privately: "If we hadn't done it, OMB would never have let it out." Another

OSHA staffer noted that sweeping does not necessarily control the dust and that inches of dust can accumulate in a single shift.[109]

Despite intense criticism from labor groups and some members of Congress,[110] OMB was not done with the standard. In a letter of mid-May 1984, OMB told OSHA that the proposal "substantially overstated" the likelihood of explosions and the ability of the measures contained in the proposal to reduce the frequency of explosions.[111] The letter noted that the grain elevator handling system "already has strong natural incentives to reduce risks," pointing to property loss, workers' compensation, tort liability, and the possibility that workers would demand risk premiums. OMB thus remained committed to the market paradigm that Congress rejected when it enacted the OSH Act.

OSHA conducted informal hearings in the summer of 1984 on the proposal, allowed further comments during the fall of 1984, and closed the record on April 23, 1985.[112] The agency then spent two years assimilating the comments. By the summer of 1987, OSHA had completed its work on the final rule, and it was again bottled up in OMB. Although James Miller, the new head of OMB, promised Senator Tom Harkin on August 26, 1987, that OMB would "very shortly" complete its review, OMB economists would not budge from their insistence that OSHA had "grossly overstated" the risk of grain elevator explosions.[113] It took another grain elevator explosion in late October to pry the standard loose.

OSHA published the final rule on December 31, 1987, seven years after the agency's ANPR.[114] Notwithstanding OMB's heavy-handed review, the final standard retained the ⅛-inch dust level requirement of the original proposal, but it was limited to "priority areas" rather than being made applicable to all areas of the facility. In a concession to OMB and the industry, the standard allowed employers to come up with their own housekeeping programs for "reducing" dust levels (rather than "minimizing" them, as in the proposal), so long as they would provide "equivalent protection." OSHA continued to refuse to exempt small elevators, but it provided some flexibility in implementing the housekeeping program for some very small regulates. The rule also contained requirements for removing materials that might cause sparks or otherwise ignite accumulated grain dust.

Both the industry and the union appealed. Although the industry managed to locate the case in the usually friendly Fifth Circuit, the reviewing court held that OSHA did not have sufficient evidence to justify limiting the ⅛-inch action level to priority areas. It remanded the standard to OSHA either to adopt a facility-wide action level or explain adequately why it would be infeasible to do so.[115] The court, however, agreed with industry claims that OSHA may have underestimated the cost of compliance, and it remanded that issue back to the agency as well. After OSHA recalculated compliance costs, the court ordered elevators to comply with the ⅛-action level in priority areas while the possible extension of that rule was being decided.[116] In response to the court's remand, OSHA issued an ANPR in December 1990 requesting comments on the possibility of expanding the standard beyond priority areas.[117] As of the end of 1991, however, the agency had not issued a formal proposal.

The long-standing effort to write a rule to reduce the notorious risks of grain elevators was thus not quite completed more than a decade after the three explosions in 1978 that triggered OSHA's initiative. The extraordinarily time-consuming deliberations in OSHA and OMB in the end produced a standard that offered somewhat more protection than doing nothing, but a court that is generally sympathetic to industry found that OSHA lacked evidence to support the concessions that OMB forced upon it. The delay in promulgating the rule had its own tragic consequences. In the interim period between the publication of the ANPR in 1980 and the publication of the final rule on the last day of 1987, 124 grain elevators exploded, killing 39 workers and causing millions of dollars worth of property damage.[118]

CONCLUSIONS

On March 6, 1984, Auchter announced that he would resign to become president of the B. B. Anderson Construction Company. He believed that he had accomplished his mission to bring stability, balance, and a solid management system to the agency.[119] Although Auchter apparently took some pride in the rulemaking management system that he had imposed on the agency, it had, if anything, slowed down the agency's rulemaking pace. Four days after Auchter's resignation became effective, his deputy admitted in congressional testimony that no final standard had been issued during Auchter's tenure for any previously unregulated substance.[120] Auchter's promise in 1983 that the agency would issue more regulations under him than under any other assistant secretary was in the end an idle boast. To his credit, Auchter did go to bat for the OSHA position in battles with OMB. Once the institution decided to move forward with a rule, Auchter was not willing to allow White House economists to dictate OSHA policy.[121] Yet Auchter was not successful in prying rulemaking initiatives loose from OMB so that they could become law.

Auchter's effect on OSHA was not limited to the agency's lack of productivity. Auchter drove out of OSHA many of the agency's experienced scientists. Staff scientists were understandably frightened by Auchter's attempt to fire Dr. Peter Infante for writing to the IARC on agency letterhead about the risks of formaldehyde. Auchter's Director for Health Standards, Leonard Vance, stated that pressuring the staff to make scientific findings that conformed with the Reagan administration's political agenda was "just part of government."[122] By early 1982, four staff scientists had resigned. One doctor complained that since standard-setting decisions were no longer being made on the basis of health considerations, the "professional environment" at OSHA had become "unacceptable." Another doctor reported that health professionals were "no longer being sought out for advice," and they were "concerned about their reputations."[123] A 1984 General Accounting Office report found that between 1979 and 1983, OSHA suffered a net loss in its scientific work force of 14.9 percent, compared with a net loss of 2.3 percent in its nonscientific and engineering staff.[124]

Auchter had never been a favorite of labor and environmental groups. Not long after he was appointed, the AFL-CIO Executive Council accused the Reagan administration of engaging in a "broad attack" on OSHA regulations. They cited alleged attempts to "wipe-out" regulations concerning cotton dust, lead, hazard identification, walkaround compensation, hearing conservation, cancer policy, and access to medical records.[125] By late 1982, the American Public Health Association demanded that President Reagan fire Auchter.[126] An early 1983 report issued by several environmental groups claimed that OSHA under Auchter "ignored all evidence" in denying petitions to regulate formaldehyde, ethylene oxide, and ethylene dibromide, and in failing to impose stricter standards for asbestos and benzene.[127] They also criticized the reevaluations of the cotton dust and lead standards and the workplace cancer policy.[128] In late November 1983, Ralph Nader asked President Reagan to fire Auchter.[129] Even former Assistant Secretary Morton Corn criticized Auchter for "compromising the gains made at OSHA" from 1975 to 1980.[130]

Business groups were, on the other hand, quite satisfied with OSHA's performance under Auchter. Mark D. de Bernardo, a labor specialist for the U.S. Chamber of Commerce, said at the end of Auchter's term: "I don't think there's a regulatory agency in Washington that has delivered more on candidate Reagan's promises on regulatory reform—OSHA's way out in front in that respect. . . . The fact of the matter is OSHA, really for its first time, has widespread acceptance in the business community."[131] As the search for Auchter's successor began, Washington insiders speculated about whether President Reagan would be willing in an election year to appoint an OSHA head who was as committed to deregulation and industry cooperation as Auchter. To the great relief of Reagan's supporters in the business community, the answer was a resounding "Yes."

NOTES

1. *Pesticide and Toxic Chemical News* 9 (3 June 1981): 18.

2. 46 *Fed. Reg.* 19,000 (1981).

3. Benjamin W. Mintz, "Occupational Safety and Health: The Regulatory Program—A History," in *Fundamentals of Industrial Hygiene* 3d ed., ed. Barbara A. Plog (Washington, D.C.: National Safety Council, 1988), 716; BNA *Occupational Safety and Health Reporter* 13 (8 Sept. 1983): 348–49.

4. "OSHA Training Office Staff Members File Suit to Block Proposed Reassignment," BNA *Government Employee Relations Report* no. 969 (28 June 1982): 9.

5. Mintz, "A History," 716.

6. Cass Peterson, "OSHA May Drop Standard-Setting Efforts; Deletion of 116 Chemicals Urged," *Washington Post*, 21 Sept. 1983, A2, col. 1.

7. *Pesticide and Toxic Chemical News* 11 (5 Oct. 1983): 27.

8. 48 *Fed. Reg.* 30,886 (1983); 47 *Fed. Reg.* 39,161 (1982).

9. 49 *Fed. Reg.* 25,734 (1984); 46 *Fed. Reg.* 19,000 (1981).

10. See W. Kip Viscusi, *Employment Hazards: An Investigation of Market Performance* (Cambridge, Mass.: Harvard University Press, 1979); Susan Hadden, *Read the Label* (Boulder, Colo.: Westview Press, 1986); David Bollier and Joan Claybrook, *Freedom from Harm: The Civilizing Influence of Health, Safety, and Environmental Regulation* (Washington, D.C.: Public Citizen, 1986), 154–56.

11. 46 *Fed. Reg.* 4412 (1981).

12. 42 *Fed. Reg.* 5372 (1977).

13. 46 *Fed. Reg.* 4412 (1981).

14. 46 *Fed. Reg.* 12,214 (1981).

15. *BNA Occupational Safety and Health Reporter* 10 (9 April 1981): 1.

16. Ibid. (19 Feb. 1981): 1265–66.

17. *BNA Chemical Regulation Reporter* 4 (23 May 1980): 190; *BNA Occupational Safety and Health Reporter* 10 (19 Feb. 1981): 1274.

18. *BNA Occupational Safety and Health Reporter* 10 (28 May 1981): 1560.

19. Office of Management and Budget, *Executive Order 12,291 on Federal Regulation: Progress During 1981* (Washington, D.C.: the Office, 1982).

20. Christopher C. DeMuth, memorandum for members of the President's Task Force on Regulatory Relief on OSHA's hazardous communication proposal (Washington, D.C., n.d.).

21. Office of Management and Budget, *Executive Order 12,291 Progress*, 2.

22. Memorandum for the vice president and members of the President's Task Force on Regulatory Relief from Raymond J. Donovan on OSHA's proposed hazard communication standard (Washington, D.C., 1982), attachment 1, 2.

23. *BNA Occupational Safety and Health Reporter* 11 (25 March 1982): 844.

24. Ibid., 845; interview with Peggy Connerton, senior economist, Department of Labor, Washington, D.C., 17 May 1983.

25. W. Kip Viscusi, "Analysis of OMB and OSHA Evaluations of the Hazard Communication Proposal" (n.d.), 4. Mimeo.

26. Ibid.

27. Ibid., 8.

28. U.S. Congress, House Committee on Education and Labor, Subcommittee on Health and Safety, *OSHA Oversight Hearings on Proposed Rules on Hazards Identification*, 97th Cong., 1st sess., 1981, 1; House Committee on Government Operations, Subcommittee on Manpower and Housing, *Office of Management and Budget Control of OSHA Rulemaking: Hearings*, 96th Cong., 2d sess., 1982, 2; *BNA Occupational Safety and Health Reporter* 11 (18 Mar. 1982): 831.

29. *BNA Occupational Safety and Health Reporter* 11 (25 Mar. 1982): 844–45.

30. 47 *Fed. Reg.* 12,091 (1982).

31. 47 *Fed. Reg.* 12,123.

32. 47 *Fed. Reg.* 12,102.

33. 47 *Fed. Reg.* 12,121.

34. 47 *Fed. Reg.* 12,122.

35. 47 *Fed. Reg.* 53,342.

36. 47 *Fed. Reg.* 53,298–99.

37. "The Hazards of Hazard Labeling," *Regulation*, May/June 1982, 10.

38. U.S. Congress, House Committee on Education and Labor, Subcommittee on Labor Standards, *Hearings on Use and Control of Ethylene Oxide*, 98th Cong., 1st sess., 1983, 5 (hereafter cited as House, *Hearings on Ethylene Oxide*).

39. Kari Hemminski, P. Mutanen, I. Saloniemi, M.-L. Niemi, and H. Vainio, "Spontaneous Abortions in Hospital Staff Engaged in Sterlising Instruments with Chemical Agents," *British Medical Journal* 285 (20 Nov. 1982): 1461.

40. *Public Citizen Health Research Group* v. *Auchter*, 554 F. Supp. 242 (D.D.C. 1983), *rev'd in part*, 702 F.2d 1150 (D.C. Cir. 1983).

41. Felicity Barringer, "Judge Orders OSHA to Toughen Standard on Exposure to Gas," *Washington Post*, 7 Jan. 1983, A17, col. 3.

42. *Public Citizen Health Research Group* v. *Auchter*, 702 F.2d 1150 (D.C. Cir. 1983).

43. 48 *Fed. Reg.* 17, 284 (1983).

44. House, *Hearings on Ethylene Oxide*, 5.

45. *BNA Occupational Safety and Health Report* 13 (28 July 1983): 196.

46. Ibid. (4 Aug. 1983): 215.

47. House, *Hearings on Ethylene Oxide*, 138.

48. Ibid., 228–34.

49. Ibid., 257.

50. *BNA Occupational Safety and Health Reporter* 13 (3 Nov. 1983): 571.

51. Ibid. (29 Mar. 1984): 1167; Pete Earley, "Logbooks Dog-Gone, He Says," *Washington Post*, 27 Mar. 1984, A21, col. 1.

52. "OSHA Scientists Taken to Task," *Science* 225 (10 Aug. 1984): 603.

53. Marjorie Sun, "OSHA Rule Is Curbed by Budget Office," *Science* 225 (10 Aug. 1984): 603–04; *BNA Occupational Safety and Health Reporter* 14 (28 June 1984): 59.

54. *Public Citizen Health Research Group* v. *Rowland*, Civ. no. 84–1252 and no. 85–1014, Brief of Petitions for Review to the Occupational Safety and Health Administration, D.C. Cir., 4 Mar. 1985.

55. Ibid., 26; *BNA Occupational Safety and Health Reporter* 14 (20 Sept. 1984): 334.

56. *BNA Occupational Safety and Health Reporter* 14 (20 Sept. 1984): 334.

57. David Burnham, "Suit Challenges U.S. in Revision of a Safety Rule," *New York Times*, 10 Apr. 1985, A11, col. 1.

58. 49 *Fed. Reg.* 25,734 (1984).

59. Cathy Trost, "Average Exposure to Ethylene Oxide Reduced by OSHA," *Wall Street Journal*, 18 June 1984, 12, col. 1; Cass Peterson, "Tougher OSHA Rules on Exposure to Ethylene Oxide Still Criticized," *Washington Post*, 19 June 1984, A15, col. 2; *BNA Occupational Safety and Health Reporter* 14 (21 June 1984): 36.

60. *BNA Occupational Safety and Health Reporter* 14 (16 Aug. 1984): 244.

61. Ibid., 243.

62. Ibid. (30 Aug. 1984): 275–76.

63. 50 *Fed. Reg.* 64 (1985); Marjorie Sun, "Agency Scraps Plan to Limit Ethylene Oxide," *Science* 227 (25 Jan. 1985): 392.

64. Sun, "Agency Scraps Plan."

65. *BNA Occupational Safety and Health Reporter* 15 (8 Aug. 1985): 219.

66. *Public Citizen Health Research Group* v. *Tyson*, 796 F.2d 1479 (D.C. Cir. 1986).

67. *BNA Occupational Safety and Health Reporter* 16 (8 April 1987): 1180.

68. *Public Citizen Health Research Group* v. *Brock*, 827 F.2d 626 (D.C. Cir. 1987).

69. 53 *Fed. Reg.* 1724 (1988).

70. *BNA Occupational Safety and Health Reporter* 17 (16 March 1988): 1504.

71. 53 *Fed. Reg.* 11,414 (1988).

72. 52 *Fed. Reg.* 16,169–70 (1987).

73. 52 *Fed. Reg.* 46,170 (1987). Nicholas Ashford, William Ryan, and Charles Caldart, "Law and Science Policy in Federal Regulation of Formaldehyde," *Science* 222 (25 Nov. 1983): 894.

74. *BNA Occupational Safety and Health Reporter* 11 (9 July 1981): 108.

75. Ibid. (13 Aug. 1981): 205; ibid. (30 July 1981): 173.

76. Ibid. 12 (28 April 1983): 989.

77. Ashford et al., "Regulation of Formaldehyde," 898.

78. *BNA Chemical Regulation Reporter* 6 (4 June 1982): 335.

79. *BNA Occupational Safety and Health Reporter* 12 (15 July 1982): 148; *BNA Chemical Regulation Reporter* 6 (23 July 1982): 539.

80. *BNA Chemical Regulation Reporter* 6 (July 23, 1982): 539.

81. *BNA Occupational Safety and Health Reporter* 12 (12 Aug. 1982): 237.

82. Ibid.

83. *BNA Chemical Regulation Reporter* 6 (27 Aug. 1982): 664.

84. *BNA Occupational Safety and Health Reporter* 13 (17 Nov. 1983): 663.

85. Ibid.

86. 45 *Fed. Reg.* 10,732 (1980); U.S. Congress, House Committee on Education and Labor, Subcommittee on Health and Safety, *Staff Report on the Oversight of the Occupational Safety and Health Administration with Respect to Grain Elevator Fires and Explosions*, 96th Cong., 2d sess., 1980.

87. Eliot Marshall, "Deadlock over Explosive Dust," *Science* 222 (4 Nov. 1983): 485.

88. 45 *Fed. Reg.* 10,733 (1980).

89. National Academy of Sciences, National Research Council, *Prevention of Grain Elevator and Mill Explosions* (Washington, D.C.: National Academy of Science Press, 1982).

90. Marshall, "Deadlock."

91. Felicity Barringer, "OSHA; in Tug-of-War over Grain Safety Rules," *Washington Post*, 17 Dec. 1982, A19, col. 2.

92. *BNA Occupational Safety and Health Reporter* 12 (10 Mar. 1983): 828.

93. Felicity Barringer, "Mired Safety Standard Got Lost in the Shuffle," *Washington Post*, 12 May 1983, A21, col. 2.

94. *BNA Occupational Safety and Health Reporter* 13 (28 July 1983): 195.

95. Ibid.

96. Ibid. (17 Nov. 1983): 659.

97. Ibid. 13 (23 June 1983): 94.

98. Ibid.

99. Felicity Barringer, "OSHA's Grain Elevator Rule Delayed," *Washington Post*, 1 Aug. 1983, A13, col. 1.

100. *BNA Occupational Safety and Health Reporter* 13 (18 Aug. 1983): 293.

101. "Grain Safety Pressed," *Washington Post*, 26 Aug. 1983, A15, col. 1; *BNA Occupational Safety and Health Reporter* 13 (1 Sept. 1983): 324.

102. *BNA Occupational Safety and Health Reporter* 13 (29 Sept. 1983): 408; Marshall, "Deadlock."

103. Marshall, "Deadlock."

104. Felicity Barringer and Myron Struck, "AFL-CIO Blasts Grain Elevator," *Washington Post*, 9 Jan. 1984, A13, col. 1.

105. 49 *Fed. Reg.* 996 (1984).
106. *BNA Occupational Safety and Health Reporter* 13 (1 Jan. 1984): 812.
107. Barringer and Struck, "AFL-CIO Blasts."
108. Ibid., col. 4.
109. Eliot Marshall, "Regulators Agree on Grain Dust Standards," *Science* 223 (13 Jan. 1984): 151.
110. *BNA Occupational Safety and Health Reporter* 13 (19 Jan. 1984): 922.
111. Ibid. (17 May 1984): 1324.
112. 52 *Fed. Reg.* 49,592 (1987).
113. *BNA Occupational Safety and Health Reporter* 17 (2 Dec. 1987): 999.
114. 52 *Fed. Reg.* 49,592 (1987).
115. *National Grain and Feed Ass'n.* v. *OSHA*, 866 F.2d 717 (5th Cir. 1989).
116. *National Grain & Feed Assoc., Inc.* v. *OSHA*, 903 F.2d 308 (5th Cir. 1990).
117. *BNA Occupational Safety and Health Reporter* 20 (12 Dec. 1990): 1142.
118. Ibid. 17 (16 Dec. 1987): 1188.
119. Kathy Sawyer, "Leaving OSHA March 30; Job Safety Chief Says He Has Finished His Work," *Washington Post*, 7 Mar. 1984, A21, col. 3.
120. *BNA Occupational Safety and Health Reporter* 13 (19 Apr. 1984): 1251.
121. Michael Wines, "Auchter's Record at OSHA Leaves Labor Outraged, Business Satisfied," *National Journal* 15 (1 Oct. 1983): 2008.
122. Pete Earley, "OSHA Scientist See Standards from Other Side," *Washington Post*, 7 Dec. 1982, A21, col. 1.
123. *Washington Post*, 2 Apr. 1982, A27, col. 2.
124. *BNA Occupational Safety and Health Reporter* 14 (30 Aug. 1984): 281–82.
125. Ibid. 11 (13 Aug. 1981): 203.
126. Pete Earley, "Public Health Professionals' Group Urges President to Oust OSHA Chief," *Washington Post*, 24 Nov. 1982, A15, col. 1.
127. *BNA Occupational Safety and Health Reporter* 12 (31 Mar. 1983): 926–27.
128. Ibid.
129. Ibid. 13 (1 Dec. 1983): 697.
130. Ibid. 12 (26 May 1983): 1101.
131. Kenneth B. Noble, "OSHA; More Jeers by Critics and Cheers by Business," *New York Times*, 7 May 1985, 10, col. 5.

7

The Reagan Years: Killing Time

In July 1984, Robert Rowland was given a recess appointment as assistant secretary for OSHA. Rowland, an attorney from Austin, Texas, was vice chairman of Reagan's 1980 campaign in Texas, and he had been chairman of the OSHA Review Commission since 1981. Upon learning of the appointment, the AFL-CIO mused: "It is difficult to imagine leadership at OSHA . . . that could be more adulterated than that formerly provided by Thorne G. Auchter. . . . In Robert Rowland . . . the Reagan White House seems to have found precisely that person." Former Assistant Secretary Bingham characterized Rowland as "anti-worker and anti-people."[1]

The unions noted that Rowland had voted to uphold OSHA citations 16 percent of the time, compared with a 63 percent average for the commission's other members.[2] They also noted Rowland's disturbing tendency to attempt to rewrite OSHA standards at the enforcement stage. For example, in one enforcement action against an employer for violating the asbestos standard, Rowland took the position that the standard did not apply to workplaces where exposure to asbestos occurred only infrequently, even though the standard itself contained no such exemption.[3]

Rowland came to OSHA under a conflict-of-interest cloud because he owned sizable investments in several petroleum and chemical companies that could be affected by OSHA decisions. Although he placed the investments in a blind trust in late 1984, he later received a waiver from Labor Secretary Donovan granting him the right to set safety and health standards affecting companies in which he owned stock.[4] The comptroller general referred a complaint about Rowland's conflict of interest to President Reagan's counsel, Fred Fielding,[5] and in April 1985, the Office of Government Ethics said that it planned to investigate. To avoid giving the Democrats an election year issue, Senate Republicans delayed confirmation hearings on Rowland until after the 1984 elections. The confirmation hearings were never held because Rowland quickly became a political liability. He resigned in May 1985, shortly after he was exonerated on the conflict-of-interest charge.[6]

HEALTH AND SAFETY STANDARDS

During Rowland's ten-month tenure, the agency produced no new health or safety standards. Rowland denied a union petition for an emergency temporary standard for formaldehyde,[7] and he also sided with OMB against the OSHA staff in deciding not to propose a safety standard for the oil and gas well-drilling industry.[8] Rowland's greatest impact concerned the long-delayed standard for protecting field workers from unsanitary conditions. The history of the standard is a sad tale of an agency's abject failure to protect a powerless and poverty-ridden group of workers against well-established risks in the face of powerful political opposition. It is the story of OSHA at its very worst.

At the time Rowland took office, most outdoor workers were protected by sanitation standards,[9] but approximately 5 million farm workers (including 1.9 million migrant workers) lacked federal protection.[10] By 1984, farm workers had been pressing OSHA for nearly 15 years to give them the same type of protection available to other outdoor workers. They sought a standard that would provide such basic sanitary necessities as toilets and drinking water to reduce heat-induced injuries, infectious diseases, and pesticide poisoning.[11] Thousands of unprotected American farm workers at that time suffered parasitic infections rarely found in developed countries.[12] A worker who waits prolonged periods before urinating is at much higher risk of contracting a bacterial urinary tract infection.[13] Women are 30 times more likely to harbor such an infection, and they are vulnerable to pesticides and parasites that are introduced into their systems as a result of unwashed hands.[14]

The Department of Labor had recognized the deplorable working conditions of migrant workers in 1969, but no positive action was undertaken until several civil rights groups and farmworker organizations sued the department, seeking injunctive relief from alleged discriminatory action by state-operated labor services.[15] The lawsuit prompted OSHA to convene its Standards Advisory Committee on Agriculture. The committee solicited written and oral testimony from the agricultural and medical communities, and in December 1974 it recommended a standard to OSHA. After the agency still refused to take any positive action, the plaintiffs secured a court order requiring OSHA to promulgate a field sanitation standard.[16] Although it appealed this ruling, OSHA published a proposed standard in April 1976 that provided for potable drinking water and sanitary toilet facilities. The accompanying statement acknowledged that the standard was necessary to bring agricultural workers into the mainstream of the American labor force and to protect their health and safety.[17] This brief bit of progress came to an abrupt end, however, when the court of appeals reversed the district court, holding that the decision whether to complete the rulemaking was within the agency's discretion. On remand, the district court was directed to develop a timetable for completing the standard,[18] and OSHA reluctantly promised to write a final rule by December 28, 1979.[19] Once again OSHA appealed, and the appellate court held that OSHA must submit a timetable, but the district court should allow the agency to reconsider the previously submitted timetable.[20] It took two and a half more years for the parties to agree on a timetable. Under a settlement agreement, approved by the district court in July 1982, OSHA promised to make a "good faith" effort to complete the standard by February 1985.[21]

In March 1983, the secretary of labor announced that the proposed standard of 1976 was being revised, and in March 1984 a new standard was proposed. The new proposal looked very much like the old one, except that it applied only to farms employing 11 or more field laborers.[22] The proposal received extensive public comment from more than 200 witnesses.[23] In January 1985, OSHA submitted a final field sanitation standard to OMB, and simultaneously requested an extension of time from the court. Expressing some irritation over OSHA's failure to meet still another deadline, the court ordered the agency to submit a copy of its draft standard or face a contempt citation.[24] The district court then transferred the request for an extension to the District of Columbia Circuit Court, which granted the extension on March 29, 1985.[25]

On April 16, 1985, a decade after it was first proposed, Rowland determined that a field sanitation standard would not be adopted at all, because it "would not be appropriate to divert scarce agency resources from the enforcement of other OSHA standards protecting workers from more life-threatening toxic exposures."[26] Moreover, he believed that this area was more appropriate for individual state regulation.[27] According to an agency employee who attended the meeting in which Rowland made this decision, a primary motivating factor was Rowland's disinclination to face his Texas farmer friends after having been responsible for causing them so much inconvenience.[28] The agency's announcement that it was terminating the rulemaking effort precipitated a storm of protest.

The timing of the decision was especially bad for Rowland. Raymond Donovan had just resigned as secretary of labor to face a criminal trial on charges of grand larceny and falsifying business records, and Democrats in the Senate decided to use the confirmation hearings for incoming secretary William Brock as a platform for expressing their displeasure with Robert Rowland. They focused especially carefully on his field sanitation decision. Senator Howard Metzenbaum called Rowland's decision "one of the most shameful decisions ever made by the department [and] nothing more than a humiliating assault on the country's farmworkers."[29] Brock promised to review all recent OSHA decisions, including the field sanitation ruling.[30] Only eight days after Rowland's proposal, Brock agreed to reconsider the decision.[31]

Brock rescinded OSHA's decision on October 21, 1985, and reopened the record for public comment.[32] Instead of promulgating a standard, however, Brock set aside an 18-month period during which states could implement their own standards.[33] He committed the agency to promulgating a standard if, by April 1987, states representing a majority of unprotected field workers failed to enact sufficient regulations governing field sanitation.[34] To facilitate the implementation process, OSHA wrote guidelines for development of field sanitation standards requiring the states to promulgate standards that provided the same degree of protection as the 1984 proposed federal standard.[35]

Having addressed the field sanitation issue in a quasi-final way, OSHA requested the district court to dismiss the pending lawsuit. The court granted this motion and denied the farmworkers' motion to reinstate the original lawsuit.[36] Undaunted, several farm workers and farm labor groups petitioned the District of Columbia Circuit Court to instruct OSHA to issue a field sanitation standard, alleging that OSHA had acted in bad faith, thereby violating the good faith obligation of the 1982 settlement agreement. The petitioners asserted that Rowland acted in an "irrational, arbitrary and capricious" manner in rejecting the proposed standard.[37] The court agreed in February 1987, holding that the record "demonstrates beyond dispute that lack of drinking water and toilets" cause disease and heat-related illness among farm workers. The court ruled that Brock based his decision on factors he could not lawfully consider and that his reliance on his understanding of "federalism" violated the balance between state and federal governments that was established by Congress in the OSH Act. Emphasizing the compelling need to "end this chapter of legal neglect," the court ordered OSHA to promulgate a final standard within 30 days.[38]

Faced with a direct court order to promulgate the standard, OSHA still refused to obey. While seeking a rehearing, Labor Secretary Brock described the court's order as a "jackass decision" and suggested that the court should "reread the Constitution."[39] Finally, on March 11, 1987, the agency publis.ned a notice of the secretary's determination to issue a final federal field sanitation standard,[40] and the court vacated its February decision as moot.[41] With OSHA's concession, administrative law's "Bleak House" came to an end.

AGENCY MORALE

Because of cases like the field sanitation standard, staff morale fell to its lowest level ever under Assistant Secretary Rowland's brief tenure. Agency staffers complained that Rowland "was out of the office more than he was in."[42] The media also noted Rowland's reclusiveness, pointing out that he avoided public appearances and usually declined requests for interviews.[43] Agency staffers were disappointed that after several years of funding cutbacks under Auchter, Rowland presided over a further $7.7 million decrease in OSHA's $213 million budget.[44] Even employers, who generally supported Rowland's reluctance to regulate, were not sure "where he [was] coming from."[45]

In April 1985, the American Federation of Government Employees urged an investigation into remarks of Rowland's deputy, James R. Meadows, at a retreat for agency managers in which he allegedly "spent about ten minutes chastising

OSHA managers for not being aggressive enough in using [civil service] regulations to terminate problem employees." If the regulations got in the way, Meadows told the managers to "go ahead and terminate them and let them hire an attorney and spend the next three years trying to get their jobs back." Meadows demanded that senior managers "kick-ass and take names," and throughout the remainder of the motivational meeting the acronym KATN was frequently employed. Although the union argued that this conduct violated federal regulations and the Labor Department collective bargaining agreement, Rowland later testified that this "locker-room term" referred to a "widely used management technique."[46]

According to one inside source, Rowland himself told Labor Under Secretary Ford B. Ford and other Labor Department officials that "OSHA is full of communists, and I am going to root them out." In later House subcommittee hearings, Rowland admitted that there was an atmosphere of "fear" among some career employees in OSHA, but he attributed the morale problem to anonymous disgruntled employees who had distorted his record. Rowland acknowledged that he had heard the word "Commies" used around the agency and conceded that "I may have used the same phrase at one time or another."[47] Although teetering on the brink of disaster in the Soviet Union and eastern Europe, communism was apparently alive and well in the hallways of OSHA.

CONCLUSION

Robert Rowland's ill-fated resolution in the field sanitation proceeding was the beginning of the end of his very brief tenure as assistant secretary. He had an extremely negative impact on agency morale, and he had virtually no impact at all on the agency's growing backlog of rulemaking initiatives. Nevertheless, upon leaving the agency Rowland gamely announced that his "mission had been accomplished."[48] Whether one agreed with this assessment depended to some extent on one's view of the appropriate goals for the agency. Senator Edward Kennedy, for example, described OSHA's performance under assistant secretaries Auchter and Rowland as "a blueprint of how to effectively repeal a statute without changing the law."[49] Labor Secretary Brock, on the other hand, accepted the resignation "with regret."[50] The *New York Times* provided its own epitaph for Rowland's troubled tenure: "Perhaps the best that can be said of Robert Rowland's performance . . . is that he knew when to leave."[51]

NOTES

1. *BNA Occupational Safety and Health Reporter* 14 (20 Sept. 1984): 333.
2. Pete Early, "OSHA," *Washington Post*, 30 Aug. 1984, A25, col. 1.
3. *Duquesne Light Co.*, 11 O.S.H. Cases (BNA) 2033, 2039 (Rev. Comm'n 1984); *BNA Occupational Safety and Health Reporter* 14 (26 July 1984): 187.
4. Kathy Trost, "OSHA Chief's Stock Holdings in Blind Trust Prompt Conflict-of-Interest Criticism by Unions," *Wall Street Journal*, 10 Apr. 1985, 50, col. 1.

5. Kenneth B. Noble, "Inquiry Is Sought on a U.S. Official," *New York Times*, 13 Apr. 1985, sec. 1, 7, col. 1.

6. Kenneth B. Noble, "Head of Agency for Job Safety Resigns His Post," *New York Times*, 25 May 1985, 1, col. 5.

7. *BNA Daily Labor Report* (9 Jan. 1985): A–9.

8. "Safety Plan for Rig Workers May Be Abolished," Associated Press, 26 June 1983; "Oil Drilling Safety Rule Reported Delayed," Associated Press, 5 July 1985.

9. *BNA Occupational Safety and Health Reporter* 14 (31 Jan. 1985): 685; ibid. 15 (2 Feb. 1986): 849.

10. Ibid. 13 (16 Feb. 1984): 993.

11. *National Congress of Hispanic American Citizens (Hispanic I)* v. *Marshall*, 626 F.2d 882, 885 (D.C. Cir. 1979); *BNA Occupational Safety and Health Reporter* 13 (31 May 1984): 1361–62.

12. Kenneth R. Noble, "Labor Dept. Said to Kill Rule on Farm Sanitation," *New York Times*, 1 Apr. 1985, A20, col. 1.

13. *Occupational Safety and Health Reporter* 13 (31 May 1984): 1362; ibid. 15 (28 Nov. 1985): 535.

14. *Occupational Safety and Health Reporter* 13 (31 May 1984): 1362.

15. *NAACP, Western Region* v. *Brennan*, 360 F.Supp. 1006, 1007–09 (D.D.C. 1973).

16. *Hispanic I*, 626 F.2d at 885.

17. 41 *Fed. Reg.* 17,576 (1976).

18. *Hispanic I*, 626 F.2d at 1200.

19. *National Congress of Hispanic American Citizens (Hispanic II)* v. *Marshall*, 626 F.2d 882, 887 (D.C. Cir. 1979).

20. Ibid.

21. *Farmworker Justice Fund, Inc.* v. *Brock*, 811 F.2d 613, 617 (D.C. Cir. 1987) *vacated as moot*, 817 F.2d 890 (D.C. Cir. 1987).

22. Ibid.

23. 52 *Fed. Reg.* 16,050–51 (1987).

24. *Farmworker Justice Fund*, 811 F.2d at 617.

25. Ibid., at 617–18; 52 *Fed. Reg.* 16,051 (1987).

26. *Farmworkers Justice Fund*, 811 F.2d at 618; 52 *Fed. Reg.* 16,051 (1987).

27. *Farmworkers Justice Fund*, 811 F.2d at 618.

28. Arthur Gas, industrial hygienist, Health Standards Directorate, OSHA, telephone interview, 30 Oct. 1986.

29. Kenneth B. Noble, "Brock, at Confirmation Hearing, May Face Snag over Aide," *New York Times*, 21 Apr. 1985, 19, col. 1.

30. Kenneth B. Noble, "OSHA: More Jeers by Critics and Cheers by Business," *New York Times*, 7 May 1985, 10, col. 5.

31. *Farmworkers Justice Fund*, 811 F.2d at 618; 52 *Fed. Reg.* 16,051 (1987).

32. *Farmworkers Justice Fund*, 811 F.2d at 618; 50 *Fed. Reg.* 42,660 (1985).

33. Michael Wright and Caroline Rand Herron, "States to Police Field Sanitation," *New York Times*, 15 Sept. 1985, sec. 4, 4, col. 1.

34. *Farmworkers Justice Fund*, 811 F.2d at 618; 52 *Fed. Reg.* 16,051 (1981).

35. *BNA Occupational Safety and Health Reporter* 15 (24 Oct. 1985): 421.

36. 52 *Fed. Reg.* 16,052 (1987).

37. *BNA Occupational Safety and Health Reporter* 15 (20 June 1985): 35.

38. *Farmworkers Justice Fund*, 811 F.2d at 614; Kenneth B. Noble, "U.S. Told to Set Sanitation Rules for Field Hands," *New York Times*, 7 Feb. 1987, 1, col. 5.

39. *BNA Occupational Safety and Health Reporter* 16 (8 Apr. 1987): 1179.

40. 52 *Fed. Reg.* 7451 (1987).

41. *Farmworkers Justice Fund, Inc.* v. *Brock*, 817 F.2d 890 (D.C. Cir. 1987).

42. *Industry Week*, 22 July 1985, 42.

43. Cathy Trost, "Low-Key Style of Labor Agency's Chief Bolsters Complaints That Department Is Adrift," *Wall Street Journal*, 12 Feb. 1985, 54, col. 1; *Austin American Statesman*, 24 Mar. 1985, A11, col. 1.

44. *BNA Occupational Safety and Health Reporter* 14 (7 Feb. 1985): 699.

45. Trost, "Low-Key Style."

46. *BNA Occupational Safety and Health Reporter* 14 (16 May 1985): 987.

47. Ibid., 988.

48. *Facts on File*, 14 June 1985, 443, D3.

49. Peter Perl, "John A. Pendergrass: Hands-on Experience in Workplace Health," *Washington Post*, 25 Aug. 1986, A13, col. 1.

50. Noble, "Head of Agency."

51. "The OSHA Bone in Labor's Throat," *New York Times*, 30 May 1985, 22, col. 1.

8

The Reagan Years:
Tying Up Loose Ends

After Robert Rowland resigned in May 1985, Labor Secretary Bill Brock promised that the search for a successor would not take long. Finding a replacement
was not, however, as easy as Brock anticipated. Several potential candidates for
the OSHA assistant secretary position declined to be considered. Some of the
persons Brock sought were understandably concerned that the Office of Management and Budget (OMB) would continue to interfere with agency decisions.[1]
Brock did not name a proposed successor until September 1985, and the White
House did not make it official until February 28, 1986.[2] Some OSHA officials
suggested that the long delay indicated the low esteem in which the administration
held the agency.[3]

The eventual nominee was John A. Pendergrass, a 60-year-old industrial
hygienist who was the head of the 3M Corporation's hazard awareness unit.[4]
Although the unions "never viewed him as a major player in the health and
safety community,"[5] they did not actively oppose him in his confirmation
hearings. Without union opposition, Pendergrass received an easy Senate
confirmation.[6]

Under Pendergrass, OSHA awoke from its five-and-a-half year slumber and
began to clean up its backlog of pending standards. By the end of Pendergrass's
term, OSHA had completed 11 pending safety standards[7] and 4 pending health
standards.[8] Although Pendergrass did not have much to do with some of these
standards, he did not stand in the way of their promulgation. At the same time,
he began several important new initiatives. This chapter discusses OSHA's efforts
to tie up loose ends, and Chapter 9 describes the agency's fresh initiatives under
Pendergrass.

RESPONDING TO THE COURTS

One of Pendergrass's first jobs was to determine the agency's response to two lawsuits that sought to reverse two of Auchter's more controversial actions. The unions challenged OSHA's failure to extend the hazard communication rule to nonmanufacturing sectors, and they wanted to overturn Auchter's refusal to issue a formaldehyde standard. OSHA's responses in these court cases were tempered by OMB resistance and, in the case of the formaldehyde standard, by Pendergrass's own reluctance to issue the strongest regulation that the scientific evidence would support.

Hazard Communication

The hazard communication standard that was promulgated near the end of Auchter's tenure, over OMB's objections, was almost immediately challenged in court by both the unions and the manufacturing industries subject to it. The decision of the Third Circuit Court of Appeals came down on May 24, 1985, during Rowland's term. The court upheld much of the standard, but it remanded the trade secrets portion of the standard because the agency's definition of "trade secrets" was much too broad. More important, the court held that OSHA had been "arbitrary and capricious" in limiting the application of the standard to the manufacturing sector.[9]

OSHA had decided to limit coverage to the manufacturing sector because, according to OSHA's admittedly poor statistics, it included 30 percent of the total employment but accounted for more than 50 percent of the reported cases of chemically induced illness.[10] The court held that the agency did not adequately address the union's contention that the Department of Commerce's Standard Industrial Classification scheme, upon which it relied in distinguishing among industries, ignored the high levels of employee exposure occurring in specific jobs outside the manufacturing sector. The court held that the standard could remain in effect in the manufacturing sector, but it directed OSHA to reconsider the application of the standard to employees in other sectors "and to order its application to other sectors unless [the agency] can state reasons why such application would not be feasible."[11]

After OSHA failed to respond to the court's remand, the United Steelworkers Union petitioned the Third Circuit to require OSHA to promulgate a new rule by a date certain. On May 29, 1987, two years after the court's first ruling, it ordered OSHA to respond to its remand.[12] Not trusting the agency to adhere to another self-imposed schedule, the court directed it to publish a hazard communication standard applicable to all workers covered by the OSHA act or state within 60 days the reasons why, on the basis of the existing administrative record, the hazard communication standard would not be feasible in particular industrial categories. Having imposed this tight schedule upon the agency, the court denied the union's motion to hold Pendergrass, who had by now become the assistant secretary, in contempt of court.

With so little time to come up with reasons for excluding particular industries from the standard, the agency had little choice but to propose that the standard be extended to all industries.[13] Since the proposed standard covered 17.9 million exposed workers in 4.5 million workplaces,[14] labor representatives were very supportive. AFL-CIO representative Margaret Seminario said that the new regulation was "something we have been fighting for since 1973."[15] OMB officials, by comparison, were very critical of the standard and suggested many changes, including exempting the entire construction industry. Because OSHA was under pressure to meet its judicially imposed deadline, however, it issued a notice of proposed rulemaking without incorporating any significant OMB changes.[16]

OMB was not, however, done with the standard. For the first time in its history, it invoked its recently granted authority under the Paperwork Reduction Act to hold its own public hearing on an agency submission.[17] On September 30, 1987, OMB asked for public comment on the record-keeping, notification, and other "paperwork" requirements of the standard.[18] Not surprisingly, many employers complained about the paperwork burden that the standard would impose upon them. They were particularly concerned about the cost of updating the material safety data sheets.[19] The American Farm Bureau Federation complained that the paperwork requirements of the expanded standard would be very burdensome to small agricultural concerns, and representatives for the construction industry predicted that the standard was "unworkable in that industry."[20] On October 28, 1987, OMB conditionally approved OSHA's expanded hazard communication standard, but in a 14-page letter it ordered OSHA to delete three provisions and reconsider a key definition.[21] Interestingly, the lengthy letter did not attempt to estimate the amount of paperwork that would be saved by its deletions.

The labor unions condemned the Reagan administration for attempting to interfere with OSHA's promulgation of the expanded hazard communication standard. According to one labor leader, "It's incredible that a small group of administration economists think they can deny American workers the right to information about dangerous chemicals on the job."[22] Frank White, the deputy assistant secretary for OSHA, expressed disappointment with the OMB action, arguing that the agency's evaluation of the paperwork burden was "exceptionally well documented."[23] An options memorandum from the head of the Health Standards Directorate to Pendergrass complained: "The OMB letter ignores our record, distorts the issues, and contains a number of conclusions that are based on misstatement of fact."[24]

The Third Circuit eventually held that the communication requirements to which OMB had objected did not come within the Paperwork Reduction Act. The court stated flatly: "Nothing in the Paperwork Reduction Act suggests a congressional intention to allow OMB, in the guise of regulating collection of information, the authority to second guess other federal agencies with respect to the kind of disclosure needed to accomplish substantive policies entrusted to such agencies."[25] Displaying some frustration with the fact that the standard still had not been implemented in the nonmanufacturing sectors, the court ordered OSHA to "forthwith publish in the *Federal Register* a notice that those parts of the August 24th, 1987 hazard communication standard which were disapproved by OMB are now effective." Finally, on December 5, 1988, the Third Circuit unsurprisingly affirmed OSHA's extension of the standard to the nonmanufacturing sectors on the merits.[26]

On the advice of the solicitor of labor, Francis Lilly, OSHA decided not to appeal the court's ruling, and it published notice in the *Federal Register* making the standard applicable to all employers on February 15, 1989.[27] The Justice Department, however, decided to challenge the court's holding that OMB lacked authority under the Paperwork Reduction Act to order OSHA to amend its standard, and the Supreme Court agreed to hear the appeal. In February 1990, the Court affirmed the Third Circuit in all regards.[28] It was a stunning defeat for OMB and a great victory for OSHA and workers. After more than a decade of acrimonious debate and litigation, nearly all workers finally had a right to know the nature of the chemical risks that they faced on a day-to-day basis in their jobs.

Formaldehyde

OSHA's judicial troubles did not end with the hazard communication standard. Under pressure from the courts, OSHA reluctantly agreed to propose a formaldehyde standard. Although Pendergrass decided to propose an exposure limitation weaker than that requested by his scientific staff, OMB still strongly opposed the proposal. OMB opposition delayed the standard until OSHA was ordered by a court to promulgate it.

As Chapter 6 reported, Auchter did virtually everything within his power to forestall issuing a notice of proposed rulemaking for formaldehyde after receiving a petition from the United Auto Workers (UAW) in 1981. In July 1984, soon after Auchter left the agency, a federal district court ordered the agency to reconsider the need for an emergency temporary standard (ETS) for formaldehyde.[29] OSHA told the court that it could make the decision by December 15, 1984, and it promised to reach a decision whether to propose a permanent rule by April 15, 1985.[30] In mid-November, OSHA released a "preliminary assessment," based partially on the results of a "consensus workshop" attended by industry and union representatives, that estimated the risk associated with exposure to formaldehyde at 3 parts per million (ppm) to be 11,300 total tumors per 100,000 workers.[31] Commenting on the "startling clarity" of the numbers, a UAW spokesman ventured that "if one thousand foundry workers died in an explosion, that would be considered a national disaster." He could find "no reason why formaldehyde shouldn't be considered an emergency worthy of immediate attention."[32]

Still OSHA equivocated. It announced on January 7, 1985, that instead of promulgating an ETS, it would hold hearings on the risk assessment and decide whether it should propose a permanent standard by April 15, 1985.[33] Calling the OSHA response "a charade, a cynical tactic devised by OSHA perhaps in concert with the chemical industry,"[34] the union went back to court.[35] On April 15, 1985, OSHA equivocated once again, issuing an ANPR that merely solicited public comments "regarding OSHA's development of a new standard of formaldehyde and the appropriate scope of coverage."[36] Pointing out that the agency had neglected to specify a time frame within which it would decide whether to issue a proposed rule, the UAW asked the court to compel OSHA to issue a proposed rule within 30 days.[37]

The District Court for the District of Columbia granted the union's request during the interim between Rowland's resignation and Pendergrass's appointment. Noting that 43 months had passed since the union's original request for a formaldehyde standard, the court ordered OSHA to take "appropriate further action" toward the issuance of a permanent standard by October 1, 1985.[38] After OSHA promised to pursue an "intensive workplan" that included the assignment of three full-time staff members to the initiative,[39] the court ordered OSHA to promulgate a notice of proposed rulemaking by December 1.[40] The agency finally published a proposed rule on December 3, 1985.[41] Alluding to a "substantial controversy" over the carcinogenic effects of formaldehyde, the agency proposed to reduce airborne exposure to either 1.0 or 1.5 ppm.

While OSHA conducted hearings and evaluated the rulemaking record over the next 12 months, a debate broke out concerning two major epidemiological studies of workers and inhabitants of mobile homes. On March 3, 1986, the National Cancer Institute (NCI) announced the completion of a study of 26,561 industrial workers that, according to NCI, "provided little evidence" that exposure to formaldehyde in the workplace caused human cancer. A statistical reevaluation of the NCI study, however, found a "significantly elevated relative risk of death from all causes, all cancers, and lung cancer for hourly workers compared to salaried workers."[42] The second study, which was conducted by the Environmental Protection Agency (EPA), initially reported that "[n]o significant associations were found between occupational formaldehyde exposure and any of the cancer sites under study," but the study did detect a significant increase of cancer in people living in mobile homes containing formaldehyde-treated wood.[43] An NCI scientist, however, reinterpreted both studies to demonstrate a "striking trend" between formaldehyde exposure and cancer.[44] EPA finally concluded from all the available data that formaldehyde was a "probable human carcinogen."[45] Not surprisingly, the formaldehyde industry disagreed.[46]

In part on the basis of this new information, Dr. Imogene Rodgers, a health scientist in OSHA's Office of Risk Assessment, prepared a risk assessment for the final standard that concluded that the risks were higher than the agency had previously estimated. The cancer risk would still be significant even at the proposed exposure limit of 1 ppm. Dr. Peter Infante, of the Health Standards

Directorate and John Martonik, the deputy director of the Health Standards Directorate, agreed with this conclusion.[47] Dr. Michael Baroody, the head of the Department of Labor's policy office, however, was skeptical of the staff work, and he persuaded Pendergrass to avoid basing the agency's risk assessment on the new cancer data. Both Baroody and Pendergrass realized that the new risk assessment would make it much more difficult to justify the 1 ppm and 1.5 ppm options.[48] Over the vigorous objections of his scientific staff,[49] Pendergrass therefore decided not to use "best estimates," preferring instead to have the risk assessment present a range of possible risks at various exposure levels.[50]

Although it is easy to sympathize with the health scientists' view that the agency should use conservative point estimates of cancer risk, rather than broad ranges that allow considerable decision-making discretion, the science of risk assessment is not nearly so well developed that it can yield meaningful point estimates. Indeed, there are a host of competing risk assessment models that can yield dramatically different predictions, ranging over ten orders of magnitude. Given the huge uncertainties that plague the "art" of carcinogen risk assessment, it borders on deception to present a single point estimate of risk to the public, whether or not it is characterized as a "best estimate." Whether the agency chooses from the upper or the lower end of the risk range is a matter of policy, not science, and that policy should be drawn primarily from the agency's statute. Pendergrass was not making a scientific statement when he decided to use a range of risks and selected a standard from the upper range of the available options; he was making policy. The administration's policy was to be less protective of workers and more responsive to industry, and Pendergrass thought that he was dutifully implementing that policy. He had every right to tell the staff to characterize the risks as a range, rather than as a point estimate, and he deserved to be judged by the public according to the policy judgment that he thereby exercised.

Unfortunately for the workers, Dr. Pendergrass was not the only policymaker within the administration. As soon as it had completed a draft of the preamble for the final standard, OSHA sent it to OMB for review. OMB predictably objected to OSHA's risk assessment. Purporting to rely upon risk assessment techniques developed by the President's Office of Science and Technology Policy, OMB maintained that the most reliable estimate of carcinogenic risks of formaldehyde to workers was something less than one in a billion, which OMB characterized as "clearly *de minimis*." OMB did not explain the sharp variance between its estimates and those of virtually every other agency that had studied the matter. The variance can be explained at least partially by the inexperience of the three economists on OMB's staff who were assigned to review the rule.[51] Martonik later testified that he and Infante and Rodgers had to spend several hours giving OMB economists a lesson in elementary toxicology.[52]

OMB also proposed extensive changes in the substance of the final rule. OSHA accepted many of these changes, all of which had the effect of weakening the rule. Among the provisions that OSHA agreed to delete were requirements for exposure monitoring under particular predetermined conditions, a requirement that employees be evacuated in cases of formaldehyde spills until a cleanup could be accomplished, and a requirement that employers provide showers for employees who had to change from work clothing into protective clothing.[53] As usual, OMB criticized OSHA's preference for engineering controls over respirators.[54]

By the end of September 1987, OSHA still had not promulgated a final rule for formaldehyde, and the UAW set out on its well-worn trail to the courthouse. Pointing out that OSHA had promised that it would promulgate a standard in September, UAW concluded (probably accurately) that "OSHA is incapable of timely completing its regulatory obligations in the absence of a court order." OSHA responded that the regulation was undergoing final review within the agency and would soon be sent to OMB for review.[55] The court ordered the agency to issue a final rule by November 21, 1987.[56] On December 4, 1987, a full two years after the proposal had been published and more than six years after the UAW's original rulemaking petition, OSHA published the final rule for formaldehyde.[57] The standard required exposure to be reduced to 1 ppm, largely through the use of engineering controls. The rule also contained provisions for employee exposure monitoring, medical surveillance, record keeping, regulated areas, emergency procedures, maintenance and selection of personal protective equipment, and hazard communication.

Noting that it had hoped the agency would set a permissible exposure limit of 0.5 ppm, the UAW nevertheless viewed the regulation as a "partial victory." The Formaldehyde Institute was disappointed that the standard was not left at 3 ppm, but it found the new standard to be "reasonable."[58] The rule was nevertheless challenged by both the industry and the UAW.[59] In June 1989, the District of Columbia Circuit refused to accept Pendergrass's determination that a weaker formaldehyde standard was sufficient to protect workers. The court ruled that OSHA had not adequately justified its failure to promulgate a standard below 1 ppm, and it remanded the rule to the agency to promulgate a stricter standard or produce a better justification for refusing to do so.[60] As of the end of 1991, the agency had not responded to the remand.

ADDRESSING THE BACKLOG

Under Pendergrass, OSHA proposed two important safety standards without the spur of a judicial order. As in the case of the two previous standards, however, OSHA had to overcome substantial opposition from OMB. In addition, as in the case of the formaldehyde standard, Pendergrass proposed less stringent standards than the agency could have defended.

Lockout/Tagout

At least 144 workers die and 33,342 workdays are lost each year because the machines on which they are doing maintenance or other services unexpectedly

start running.[61] Craft workers, machine operators, and laborers, particularly in
the manufacturing sector, are especially at risk of being seriously injured when
equipment is accidentally switched on or replugged by an employee at controls
separate from the machinery.[62] They are also at risk from unexpected movements
of machinery parts that may contain residual energy from springs or hydraulic
pressure. In one typical case, an employee had crawled partway into an asphalt
mixing machine to change its paddles when another employee, while dusting in
the control room, accidentally hit a toggle switch that caused the mixer door to
close, striking the first employee on the head and killing him. Had the electrical
switches to activate the machine been locked out and air pressure to move the
doors shut off, the accident would not have happened.[63] In another, more severe
incident, a massive explosion at a Phillips Petroleum Company petrochemical
plant in which 23 workers were killed resulted from the failure of contractor
employees to close an air control valve prior to beginning maintenance work on
a polyethylene unit.[64] These accidents can be prevented either by disabling
machines while they are being serviced ("lockout") or by placing a warning
sign on the machines and relevant controls ("tagout").

OSHA promulgated national consensus standards for lockout/tagout in 1971,
but they were not uniform in their coverage and contained significant inconsistencies between industries and between different types of equipment in the
same industry.[65] In January 1977, OSHA published a notice in the *Federal
Register* asking whether it should promulgate a rule requiring a lockout or a
tagout whenever a machine was not in its normal operating mode.[66] After waiting
two years for OSHA to act, the United Automobile, Aerospace and Agricultural
Implement Workers of America (UAW) petitioned OSHA, in May 1979, to
establish an emergency temporary standard (ETS) requiring lockouts. In September 1979, OSHA declined to issue the ETS. It did publish an ANPR in June
1980,[67] but the issue assumed a low priority with upper-level decision makers
who were devoting their attention to health standards and the carcinogen policy.

The UAW again petitioned OSHA for an ETS in 1982, and OSHA again
denied the petition. When United Steelworkers Safety and Health Director
Adolph E. Schwartz warned of the "tragic consequences" that would attend
OSHA's failure to promulgate a lockout standard, the Safety Standards Directorate still balked, but James Scully, an OSHA occupational safety and health
specialist assigned to the project, put off his retirement for two years to enable
the agency to issue a lockout/tagout standard in a timely fashion.[68] Largely due
to Scully's efforts, the staff produced a draft standard by the end of 1984.

Although OSHA staffers favored a regulation that would be broadly applicable
to any industry where a lockout might prevent a serious accident, upper-level
decision makers ordered them to limit the standard to the few industries where
most lockout accidents occurred. As with all standards, OSHA sent the draft to
the solicitor of labor for review by the department's attorneys. The Solicitor's
Office was not satisfied with the agency's rationale for the regulation, and the
next two years were spent writing and reviewing four successive drafts of the

standard. During this process, Labor Department lawyers insisted that OSHA rewrite the standards to cover all of the industries where a lockout might arise, in effect countermanding the expressed preferences of OSHA's upper-level decision makers. This required the agency to amend its draft regulatory impact analysis at considerable additional time and expense.

When the UAW complained about the delays in a letter to Pendergrass in July 1986, he responded that a proposal would be published for public comment during the first part of 1987.[69] The Solicitor's Office finally approved the standard, but officials in the Labor Department's Policy Office objected to the standard's broad coverage. Although those officials finally agreed to keep the standard broad, it was delayed further because of the Departmental Policy Review Board's insistence that OSHA update the information upon which it had relied in its 1984 draft.[70]

In May 1987, OMB objected that OSHA did not have convincing evidence that any regulation at all was necessary, and OMB's economists opined that the analytical support for the standard was the weakest they had ever seen. OSHA met with OMB to discuss the lockout standard in August 1987 and February 1988, and they brought data compiled by the Bureau of Labor Statistics, work injury reports, and field studies to support them.[71] OMB finally approved a draft rule and preamble on April 14, 1988, on the eve of hearings conducted by Senator Kennedy in which the senator promised to look into delays in issuing the lockout/tagout standard.[72] OSHA published the proposed standard 15 days later.[73]

The proposed standard was immediately attacked by the unions and their political friends. The unions complained that the standard failed to incorporate the principle of "one person, one lock, one key," under which the worker servicing a machine must personally lock the machine's switch in the off position before beginning the maintenance work and must personally remove the lock on the way out.[74] In addition, the unions claimed that the scope of the rule was still too narrow, because OSHA exempted industries for which it was planning to develop separate lockout/tagout standards. Finally, the unions continued to push for employee participation in the formulation of lockout/tagout procedures and training programs.[75]

Senator Howard Metzenbaum criticized the agency for "eight years of unconscionable, and tragic, inactivity."[76] Using OSHA's own figures, he calculated that 1,200 workers—150 each year—had died in lockout accidents since OSHA first began considering the standard, and that thousands more had lost limbs and suffered other injuries. He pointed out that by "bickering over the standard's scope, [OSHA and OMB] delayed the rule by three years." Finally, Metzenbaum criticized the proposed rule as a "weak, exemption-riddled standard that leaves workers largely unprotected."

OSHA promulgated a final lockout/tagout standard on September 1, 1989.[77] Following its prior pattern, OSHA responded to some of the union concerns, but it was unwilling to issue as strong a rule as the unions sought. The standard required the use of lockouts and "the one person/one lock/one key" concept for most machines. OSHA, however, required only "tags" if installation of a lock would require an employer to dismantle, rebuild, or replace a machine. The standard rejected union demands to require employee participation in the development of lockout procedures and to extend the coverage of the standard to more industries.

If OSHA did not go far enough to please unions, it went too far for employers. Five industries or trade groups, including the National Association of Manufacturers, the American Petroleum Institute, and DuPont, immediately filed lawsuits challenging the standard.[78] They disputed OSHA's conclusion that locking equipment would better prevent accidents than tagging it. The UAW also filed a legal challenge to the rule.[79] The Court of Appeals for the District of Columbia remanded the standard to OSHA in September 1991, but it allowed it to remain in effect pending OSHA's response. The court's opinion is examined in detail in Chapter 17.

Confined Spaces

The second safety standard that OSHA considered addressed the hazards of confined spaces. A "confined space" is any space that can entrap workers and cause them to suffocate because of restricted air circulation.[80] OSHA estimates that about 224,000 establishments contain confined spaces and that about 2.1 million workers enter such spaces annually.[81] By some estimates, 300 workers per year die as a result of unprotected and unregulated entries into hazardous confined spaces.[82]

On July 24, 1975, OSHA published an ANPR seeking comments on 14 issues related to confined space regulation.[83] OSHA said that it intended to develop a proposed rule to amend the existing standards that addressed confined spaces.[84] The response from industry, union representatives, and other agencies was generally positive. Nevertheless, citing both "the complexity of the issues and the period of time since the previous Advance Notice," OSHA issued a second ANPR on October 19, 1979, containing similar but more detailed questions.[85] The confined spaces issue next surfaced on March 25, 1980, when OSHA issued an ANPR soliciting information on possible revisions to its existing standards on confined space activities in the construction industry.[86]

OSHA held public meetings in May 1980 in the confined spaces issue. By now many companies were afraid that OSHA would mandate a burdensome permitting process that would require advance scheduling for even minor maintenance jobs and cause costly labor delays.[87] The unions, on the other hand, strongly supported a tough confined spaces standard. Unlike the employers, the unions favored continuous monitoring of confined spaces rather than a single monitoring effort at the outset of the confined space activity, and they cited several fatalities that could have been prevented if continuous monitoring had been required.[88] After another two years passed without a confined spaces standard, the Allied Industrial Workers petitioned OSHA to issue an emergency temporary standard for confined spaces in late 1982. OSHA responded in 1985 by producing a 30-minute slide program to "aid employees in hazard recognition" and to provide instruction on the selection and proper use of protective clothing and equipment.[89]

OSHA's slides did not stem the tide of confined space fatalities. Prompted by the deaths of two of its members in a Pennsylvania zinc condenser in December 1985, the United Steelworkers petitioned OSHA to promulgate a comprehensive standard for confined spaces.[90] Since a draft standard was being circulated and was scheduled for general distribution in February 1986, the union requested immediate distribution of the draft to facilitate the standard-setting process. The agency responded that it would effectively grant the union's petition, but it would not publish a proposed rule until the spring.[91]

In early 1986, NIOSH published a hazard alert containing recommendations for employees entering confined spaces.[92] The alert was prompted by the "recurring occupational tragedy" of workers dying while OSHA debated whether standards should be applied to all industry sectors or just to the sectors where regulation was most needed.[93] Still in the final stages of drafting at this point, the proposed standard covered only a limited number of industrial sectors.[94] OSHA staffers spent the spring and summer debating about the scope of the proposal and attempting to come up with accurate numbers on fatalities related to confined spaces for its regulatory impact analysis.[95] Fearing that OSHA would never publish a proposed standard, NIOSH in 1987 distributed a new worker guide on safety in confined spaces highlighting the need for appropriate testing, sampling, and protective equipment and the necessity of attendant personnel.[96]

OSHA finally published a proposed rule nearly two years later, on June 5, 1989, that required fairly extensive permitting procedures for some work spaces, including signed entry and exit forms, and further required employers to establish and implement means, procedures, and practices for the control of hazards in such spaces.[97] The proposal exempted the agriculture, construction, and maritime industries upon OSHA's determination that they were adequately covered under existing industry-specific regulations.[98]

As of the end of 1991, OSHA had not issued a final rule for confined spaces. As with the lockout/tagout proposal, this deliberateness had its costs. By its own reckoning, 30–35 workers will die every year that OSHA delays the final implementation of the standard. At an OSHA hearing held in February 1990, the families of victims testified about the dimensions of this cost. The mother of Craig Fogle testified concerning how OSHA's failure to adopt a standard caused her son's death.

Five young men died as a result of the incident at Bastian. Four of them died trying to rescue Jeff Link, the first to be overcome by deadly hydrogen cyanide in the holding tank. One by one they died, almost instantly, as the gas locked their oxygen supply in their blood stream and it failed to reach their body tissues.[99]

Another mother summed up the experiences of all the families when she said of her son, Mark Dermoss, "There is not a day which goes by that we don't miss him. Not a day goes by that we don't feel anger and frustration that an accident like this could happen."[100]

Personal Protective Devices

The final pending initiative taken up by Assistant Secretary Pendergrass was one he would have preferred to ignore. We have observed on numerous occasions in this book that OMB economists have consistently expressed a strong preference for personal protective devices, such as respirators, over engineering controls for reducing employee exposure to airborne toxics. OSHA has traditionally been equally firmly wedded to engineering controls when such controls are feasible. Indeed, it is a rather well-established principle of industrial hygiene that engineering controls are to be preferred over personal protective devices. We saw in Chapter 5 that Vice President Bush's task force pressured OSHA into reexamining its policy on personal protective devices, but that initiative quickly died under strong employee resistance. Under renewed pressure from OMB, Pendergrass agreed to take up the topic again in 1986.

In late 1986, Pendergrass sent an options memorandum to the Departmental Policy Review Board on the question of engineering controls versus personal protective devices.[101] The memorandum restated OSHA's traditional policy favoring engineering controls, and it noted that "[p]rimary reliance on respirators is permitted where engineering controls are determined to be infeasible, where engineering controls do not achieve full compliance, and in other specific circumstances. . . ."[102] Pendergrass pointed out that "[t]his policy reflects a fundamental industrial hygiene principle that contaminants be controlled at their source, to the extent feasible."[103] The memorandum agreed that "there may be limited areas in which some modification to the policy would not compromise worker protection, but would permit more cost effective controls to be implemented."[104] In particular, OSHA identified five limited instances in which respirators might be the preferred means of compliance. Since these were the areas in which respirators would be allowed under OSHA's current policy, the agency saw no need to amend that policy.

The Department of Labor's Policy Review Board did not accept OSHA's recommendation that the standard remain unchanged. The head of the Department of Labor Policy Office, Michael Baroody, told OSHA that the department had reached an agreement with OMB under which OSHA would issue a proposed rule in September 1987 and a final rule in September 1988, and he demanded that OSHA fulfill the department's promise.[105]

Since OSHA was powerless to undo this agreement, it drafted a proposed rule that simply reaffirmed the traditional policy. When the Policy Review Board refused to accept the proposal, OSHA rewrote it to list the five specific situations where respirators would be permitted. A special assistant to the solicitor of labor,

Randall K. Johnson, then wrote to OSHA suggesting several more instances in which respirators would be appropriate.[106] Recognizing that he was arguably advocating the use of cost-benefit analysis in derogation of the Supreme Court's *Cotton Dust* opinion, the departmental attorney suggested that OSHA could disguise this lapse by "defining through compliance directives the term 'feasible' as used in the air contaminants method of control hierarchy with cost/benefit concepts."[107] At a subsequent Policy Review Board meeting, the Department of Labor economists pressured OSHA into accepting two of Johnson's proposals for inclusion in its notice of proposed rulemaking.[108]

This was not enough to satisfy OMB. At a meeting of the Bush task force on March 26, 1988, OMB singled out OSHA for strong criticism for its failure to act expeditiously on the methods of compliance rulemaking.[109] In response to OMB criticism, OSHA redrafted the proposal once again to request comments on the suggestion that employers should have the discretion to decide for themselves whether to use engineering controls or respirators.[110]

In June 1989, after Pendergrass had left the agency, OSHA issued a proposed respirator rule.[111] OSHA proposed to permit the use of respirators in lieu of engineering controls in five circumstances: (1) during installation of engineering controls; (2) where feasible engineering controls result in only a negligible reduction of exposure; (3) during emergencies; (4) where normal controls may fail; and (5) during entries into unknown atmospheres. As was to be expected, industry claimed the proposal "will enhance employee health and safety by clarifying circumstances where respirators have a history of effective use," while union representatives deplored it as "unnecessary, unjustified, and ill-advised."[112] OSHA also heard from health experts. Morton Corn, the former OSHA administrator, testified that there are "selected situations" in which respirators can be useful, but he warned OSHA against adopting broad exemptions.[113] An environmental health engineer from the Harvard School of Public Health told OSHA that, if anything, it should "insist on even greater reliance on engineering controls" rather than expand allowances for respirator use.[114]

The decade-long battle between OMB and Department of Labor economists and OSHA industrial hygienists clearly reflects a clash of professional perspectives, and it has thus far produced no tangible results. In a very real sense, personal protective devices have been an elusive "technological fix" for those who are concerned that protecting worker health is too expensive. In another rather disturbing sense the battle harks back to the nineteenth century common law in which workers themselves were viewed as the primary cause of industrial accidents. Yet absent dramatic new improvements in the technology of personal protective devices, it is unlikely that OSHA's policy can change very much without violating its statutory obligation to provide workers with a safe place of employment. In the end, Deputy Director of Health Standards John Martonik was probably correct in concluding in 1988 that the agency had "spent five needless years working on this project."[115]

CONCLUSIONS

John Pendergrass put OSHA back in business by allowing the agency to finish several pending health standards. In some cases, like formaldehyde and hazard communication, he had no choice because OSHA was under a court order to promulgate the standard. In other cases, such as lockout/tagout and confined spaces, OSHA issued the standards voluntarily. The last two standards are particularly noteworthy, because they had been stalled in the agency for years. OSHA, however, did not finish the confined spaces standard, despite its great potential for protecting workers.

Whether because of OMB pressure or as the result of his own conservatism, Pendergrass was generally unwilling to promulgate the most stringent regulation that OSHA could conceivably defend. He chose a less strict approach in the formaldehyde, lockout/tagout, and confined space rules. In the case of the formaldehyde standard, a court found that Pendergrass may not have had sufficient justification to refuse to issue a stricter standard. To his credit, Pendergrass did attempt to resist OMB pressure for a revised respirator rule, but a proposal issued soon after he left. Pendergrass was not content merely to finish what others had started. He was largely responsible for the first really new initiatives in the Reagan administration. Their fate is taken up next.

NOTES

1. Kenneth B. Noble, "U.S. Aides Report 3M Official Is Reagan Choice for OSHA," *New York Times*, 22 Oct. 1985, 9, col. 6.

2. Kenneth B. Noble, "OSHA; Agency Under a Cloud Awaits Its New Chief," *New York Times*, 6 Mar. 1986, 14, col. 4; *BNA Occupational Safety and Health Reporter* 15 (6 Mar. 1986): 1003.

3. Noble, "Agency Under a Cloud."

4. Cathy Trost, "Official at 3M to Be Nominated to Head OSHA," *Wall Street Journal*, 22 Oct. 1985, 12, col. 2; *BNA Occupational Safety and Health Reporter* 15 (6 Mar. 1986): 1003.

5. Noble, "3M Official."

6. *Engineering News-Record*, 29 May 1986, 100.

7. Electrical Standards for Construction, 51 *Fed. Reg.* 25,294 (1986); Accident Prevention Tags, 51 *Fed. Reg.* 33,251 (1986); Marine Terminal Servicing Single Piece Wire Rims, 52 *Fed. Reg.* 36,023 (1987); Grain Handling Facilities, 52 *Fed. Reg.* 49,592 (1987); Mechanical Power Presses, 53 *Fed. Reg.* 8322 (1988); Safety Testing Certification, 53 *Fed. Reg.* 12,102 (1988); Concrete and Masonry Construction, 52 *Fed. Reg.* 22,612 (1988); Shipyard Employment, 53 *Fed. Reg.* 12,102 (1988); Underground Construction, 54 *Fed. Reg.* 23,824 (1989); Excavations, 54 *Fed. Reg.* 45,894 (1989); Lockout/Tagout, 54 *Fed. Reg.* 36,644 (1989).

8. Asbestos, Tremolite, Anthophyllite, and Actinolite, 51 *Fed. Reg.* 22,612 (1986); Field Sanitation, 52 *Fed. Reg.* 16,095 (1987); Benzene II, 52 *Fed. Reg.* 34,460 (1987); Formaldehyde, 52 *Fed. Reg.* 46,168 (1987).

9. *United Steel Workers of America* v. *Auchter*, 763 F.2d 729 (3rd Cir. 1985).

10. Ibid., 736.
11. Ibid., 739.
12. *United Steelworkers of America* v. *Pendergrass*, 819 F.2d 1263 (3rd Cir. 1987).
13. 52 *Fed. Reg.* 3185 (1987).
14. *BNA Daily Report for Executives* (7 Apr. 1987): A1.
15. Henry Weinstein, "U.S. to Expand Right to Learn of Job Hazards," *Los Angeles Times*, 19 Aug. 1987, pt. 1, 1, col. 7.
16. U.S. Congress, Senate Committee on Labor and Human Resources, *Hearings on Oversight of the Occupational Safety and Health Administration*, 100th Cong., 2d sess., S. Hrg. 100–719, 1988, 403 (hereafter cited as Senate, *Oversight Hearings of 1988*).
17. Ibid.
18. 52 *Fed. Reg.* 36,652 (1987).
19. *BNA Occupational Safety and Health Reporter* 17 (3 June 1987): 700.
20. Ibid. (21 Oct. 1987): 846.
21. Senate, *Oversight Hearings of 1988*, 404, 975; *BNA Occupational Safety and Health Reporter* 17 (4 Nov. 1987): 907.
22. *BNA Occupational Safety and Health Reporter* 17 (4 Nov. 1987): 907.
23. Ibid.
24. Senate, *Oversight Hearings of 1988*, 977.
25. *United Steelworkers of America* v. *Pendergrass*, 855 F.2d 108, 113 (3rd Cir. 1987).
26. *Associated Builders and Contractors, Inc.* v. *Brock*, 862 Fed. 2d 63 (3rd Cir. 1988).
27. 54 *Fed. Reg.* 6,886 (1989).
28. *Dole* v. *United Steelworkers of America*, 110 S.Ct. 929 (1990).
29. *BNA Occupational Safety and Health Reporter* 14 (12 July 1984): 156.
30. Ibid. (13 Sept. 1984): 315.
31. Ibid. (22 Nov. 1984): 476.
32. Ibid.
33. 50 *Fed. Reg.* 1,547 (1985).
34. *BNA Chemical Regulation Reporter* 8 (22 Feb. 1985): 1389.
35. *BNA Occupational Safety and Health Reporter* 14 (31 Jan. 1985): 686.
36. 50 *Fed. Reg.* 15,179 (1985).
37. *BNA Occupational Safety and Health Reporter* 14 (9 May 1985): 971.
38. Ibid. 15 (13 June 1985): 19.
39. Ibid. (10 Oct. 1985): 387.
40. *BNA Chemical Regulation Reporter* 9 (15 Nov. 1985): 961.
41. 50 *Fed. Reg.* 50,412 (1985).
42. 51 *Fed. Reg.* 44,796 (1986).
43. Kenneth B. Noble, "Study Slights Risk of Formaldehyde," *New York Times*, 28 Sept. 1986, 17, col. 5.
44. *Inside EPA* 7 (12 Sept. 1986): 4.
45. *BNA Occupational Safety and Health Reporter* 16 (22 Apr. 1987): 1292; *Pesticide and Toxic Chemical News* 15 (15 Apr. 1987): 14.
46. *Pesticide and Toxic Chemical News* 15 (22 Apr. 1987): 6.
47. Senate, *Oversight Hearings of 1988*, 444–45.
48. Ibid., 445.

49. Memorandum to John Pendergrass from John Martonik and Imogene Rodgers on options for the assessment of risk from exposure to formaldehyde (n.d.), in ibid., 446–50; memorandum to John Pendergrass from Peter F. Infante through Charles E. Adkins, 6 Nov. 1987, ibid., 456–58.

50. Ibid., 452.

51. Judith Havemann, "Assessed Cancer Risk Is Inflated, OMB Says; Regulatory Agencies May Get Guidelines," *Washington Post*, 13 July 1986, A8.

52. Senate, *Oversight Hearings of 1988*, 513–14.

53. Ibid., 468.

54. *BNA Occupational Safety and Health Reporter* 15 (1 May 1986): 1203.

55. Ibid. 17 (7 Oct. 1987): 795.

56. Ibid. (21 Oct. 1987): 847.

57. 52 *Fed. Reg.* 46,168 (1987).

58. "U.S. Stiffens Rule on Formaldehyde Exposure," *New York Times*, 22 Nov. 1987, sec.1, 45, col. 1.

59. *BNA Occupational Safety and Health Reporter* 17 (12 Dec. 1987): 1043.

60. *United Automobile, Aerospace and Agricultural Implement Workers* v. *Pendergrass*, 878 F.2d 389 (D.C. Cir. 1989).

61. 54 *Fed. Reg.* 36,684 (1989).

62. 53 *Fed. Reg.* 15,499–502 (1988).

63. Ibid.

64. U.S. Congress, House Committee on Government Operations, Subcommittee on Employment and Housing, *Hearings on the Adequacy of OSHA Protections for Chemical Workers*, 101st Cong., 1st sess., 1989, 16–25 (testimony of Robert E. Wages, vice president, Oil, Chemical and Atomic Workers Union).

65. 53 *Fed. Reg.* 15,496 (1988): *BNA Occupational Health and Safety Reporter* 10 (2 Oct. 1980): 479.

66. 42 *Fed. Reg.* 1741 (1977).

67. 45 *Fed. Reg.* 41,012 (1980).

68. Senate, *Oversight Hearings of 1988*, 537.

69. Memorandum to Bernard Butsavage from John Pendergrass, dated 14 Oct. 1986, in ibid., 518.

70. Ibid., 519.

71. Ibid., 521 (statement of James Scully).

72. Ibid.

73. 53 *Fed. Reg.* 15,459 (1988).

74. *BNA Occupational Health and Safety Reporter* 17 (12 Apr. 1988): 1863; ibid. 18 (19 Oct. 1988): 1046.

75. Ibid. 18 (27 July 1988): 574.

76. Ibid. (5 Oct. 1988): 974.

77. 54 *Fed. Reg.* 36,644 (1989).

78. *BNA Occupational Safety and Health Reporter* 19 (8 Nov. 1989): 1063.

79. Ibid.

80. 54 *Fed. Reg.* 24,080–81 (1989).

81. 54 *Fed. Reg.* 24,097 (1989).

82. *BNA Occupational Safety and Health Reporter* 17 (12 Aug. 1987): 428.

83. 40 *Fed. Reg.* 30,980 (1975).

84. *BNA Occupational Safety and Health Reporter* 5 (31 July 1975): 286.

85. 44 *Fed. Reg.* 60,334 (1979).
86. 45 *Fed. Reg.* 19,266 (1980).
87. *BNA Occupational Safety and Health Reporter* 10 (5 June 1980): 8; ibid. (17 July 1980): 202.
88. Ibid. (5 June 1980): 8.
89. Ibid. 15 (22 Aug. 1985): 254.
90. Ibid. (19 Dec. 1985): 772.
91. Ibid. (9 Jan. 1986): 864.
92. Ibid. (13 Mar. 1986): 1033; 54 *Fed. Reg.* 24,081 (1989).
93. *BNA Occupational Safety and Health Reporter* 16 (1 Apr. 1987): 1131.
94. Ibid.
95. Ibid. 17 (12 Aug. 1987): 428.
96. NIOSH Publication no. 87–113; *BNA Occupational Safety and Health Reporter* 16 (16 Sept. 1987): 626.
97. 54 *Fed. Reg.* 24,080 (1989).
98. 54 *Fed. Reg.* 24,089 (1989).
99. National Safe Workplace Institute, *Confined Space Accidents: Frustration, Grief, Anger & Loss: Five Family Tragedies* (Chicago: The Institute, 1990), 13–14.
100. Ibid., 10.
101. Memorandum to Policy Review Board on options memorandum concerning revision to the methods of compliance requirements in meeting OSHA's permissible exposure limits, from John Pendergrass (n.d.) in Senate, *Oversight Hearings of 1988*, 247.
102. Ibid.
103. Ibid., 248.
104. Ibid., 247.
105. Ibid., 316.
106. Memorandum for Frank A. White and Roland Droitsch from Randel K. Johnson, special assistant to the solicitor, Department of Labor, dated 12 Jan. 1988, in ibid., 322.
107. Ibid., 325.
108. Ibid., 328.
109. Memorandum to John Pendergrass from Michael F. Baroody, on vice president's Task Force of Regulatory Relief (n.d.), in ibid., 331.
110. Ibid., 338.
111. 54 *Fed. Reg.* 23,991 (1989).
112. *BNA Occupational Safety and Health Reporter* 20 (6 June 1990): 6.
113. Ibid., 4.
114. Ibid.
115. Senate, *Oversight Hearings of 1988*, 339.

9

The Reagan Years: New Initiatives

OSHA mounted no new rulemaking initiatives during the first five years of the Reagan administration. For the most part, Auchter and Rowland were content to reexamine past OSHA standards and stall pending ones. Assistant Secretary Pendergrass, however, broke this pattern. He came to the job dedicated to updating the 1971 national consensus standards as rapidly as possible, and he quickly let the staff know that this project was his highest rulemaking priority. Pendergrass was also devoted to the idea of negotiated rulemaking, and he seized upon the nascent rulemaking on methylenedianiline to serve as a trial for that dispute resolution technique. Finally, events forced the agency, over some initial hesitancy on Pendegrass's part, to initiate a rulemaking to address bloodborne diseases, of which AIDS was the most notorious.

THE PEL UPDATE

Immediately upon assuming office, Pendergrass expressed his strong desire to have the agency update the permissible exposure limitations (PELs) (sometimes called the Table Z standards) that the agency had promulgated as "national consensus standards" for more than 400 substances in 1971. Although the PELs had their origin in the recommendations of private standard-setting organizations such as the American Council of Governmental Industrial Hygienists (ACGIH), they had not been updated to keep pace with changes that the various private standard-setting organizations had incorporated through the years. For some chemicals, an employee could legally be exposed to concentrations far in excess of the recommended threshold limit values. In addition, private standard-setting organizations and the National Institute of Occupational Safety and Health (NIOSH), had recommended exposure levels for a number of substances for which PELs had not been established in 1971. To Pendergrass, an industrial hygienist from a large company, this was an outrage. Although he believed that most companies that were aware of the ACGIH updates voluntarily complied with the new guidelines, he nevertheless decided that the primary goal for his tenure as assistant secretary would be to find a way to update the existing PELs in a legally binding way.[1] After exploring several options for accomplishing the PEL update, Pendergrass ultimately decided to initiate a generic rulemaking that would establish PELs for a large number of substances based primarily upon recommendations from NIOSH and ACGIH. He envisioned that later individual rulemakings would set complete, and presumably more stringent, standards for individual substances based on a more complete data base.

The staff quickly set to work on this high priority item. The scope of the project was expanded somewhat, however, when the Solicitor's Office advised OSHA that the *Benzene* decision required the agency to undertake at least a rudimentary hazard evaluation and risk assessment for each individual substance for which an update PEL would be promulgated. Despite the enormity of the project, OSHA moved with extraordinary speed, given its past experience with rulemaking on individual substances. A small team, lead by a scientist on loan from the Los Alamos National Laboratory, completed its job in just over a year. Although the Office of Management and Budget (OMB) expressed severe reservations about the legal validity of updating the PELs in a single generic proceeding and about the cost effectiveness of the project, it let the proposed rules out with less than usual resistance.[2] In a Notice of Proposed Rulemaking published on June 7, 1988, OSHA proposed to reduce the existing PELs for approximately 100 substances, raise the PEL for 1 substance, and set new PELs for approximately 205 substances not currently regulated by OSHA.[3]

Reaction to the proposal was mixed. Most companies and trade associations were mildly supportive of the generic approach and of the proposed PELs. Not surprisingly, a few companies objected to individual PELs for substances found in their workplaces, arguing either that the ACGIH or NIOSH recommendations were not supported by the scientific information or that the recommendations were not economically and technologically feasible.

Although the unions were not opposed to reducing the PELs in a single generic proceeding, they opposed the rulemaking on the ground that OSHA was obliged to promulgate more protective standards. Fearing that OSHA would breathe a heavy sigh of relief at the end of the generic proceeding and reduce efforts to promulgate more stringent standards for individual substances, the unions argued that the generic proceeding should include all relevant information on the regulated substances and that the agency should promulgate the most stringent standards feasible. Frank Mirer of the United Steelworkers Union complained that "an effort to adopt ACGIH limits would be a scatter-gun approach which will cover a great many chemicals of little interest without providing substantial or adequate protection against the highest priority chemicals."[4] The unions further argued that the agency should not rely at all on the ACGIH recommendations, because they believed that ACGIH was dominated by industry.[5] Indeed, the unions had traditionally refused to participate in the ACGIH recommendation process precisely for that reason, thus making their complaint a self-fulfilling prophecy. They were able to cite a published paper by an environmental safety and health consultant finding that the threshold limit values (TLVs) reflected undue industry influence.[6] Finally, the unions argued that OSHA's heavy reliance on private standard-setting organizations subverted NIOSH's role in the OSHA standard-setting process.[7] To bolster their case, the unions later pointed out that OSHA had overlooked or ignored evidence from other federal agencies indicating that at least 22 of the substances the PEL standards addressed were carcinogenic but were not treated as such by ACGIH. Karl Kronebush, of the Kennedy School of Government, and Silvia Tognetti, of the National Academy of Sciences/ National Research Council, found that OSHA had designated as carcinogenic fewer than half of the chemicals under consideration that were actually carcinogens.[8]

OSHA assimilated the thousands of pages of outside comments with extraordinary dispatch. Less than six months after the close of the hearing record, it published a final rule that reduced the existing PEL for 212 substances and set new PELs for 164 substances not currently regulated.[9] As in the proposed standard, the agency relied primarily upon the NIOSH and ACGIH recommendations in determining the levels for the PELs, but in response to the union comments it also made an independent "significant risk" determination based upon its limited literature survey and upon the information submitted during the comment period.

In setting PELs, the agency erred on the side of ensuring feasibility, apparently on the theory that if a PEL turned out to be insufficiently stringent, it could always adopt a more stringent PEL in an individual rulemaking proceeding. OSHA specifically acknowledged that it was not "attempting to force technology"[10] and that further regulation might be necessary to meet the agency's obligation to set limits at the lowest feasible level that eliminated significant risks in the workplace. Indeed, Robinson and Paxman noted that OSHA raised the final PEL from the proposed PEL for many substances solely because levels above the proposed PELs were detected in workplaces.[11] OSHA agreed to proceed with individual rulemaking initiatives for such substances (most of which were likely to be carcinogens) as its resources permitted. But it did not make any promises, and it did not set any deadlines for itself.

OSHA also softened the economic impact of the new PELs by giving companies four years to use respirators, rather than engineering controls, to meet the standards. For some substances in some workplaces, OSHA gave companies even longer than four years. Indeed, the agency did not provide any deadlines at all for industries for which compliance was currently infeasible. Thus, a company could theoretically maintain that compliance with engineering controls was always infeasible and thereby, as a practical matter, substitute respirators for engineering controls in perpetuity.

Twenty-seven separate judicial challenges to the PEL standard were filed in several courts of appeals.[12] After all of the appeals were consolidated in the Court of Appeals for the Eleventh Circuit,[13] OSHA began to negotiate with the challengers. Over the next year, OSHA reached settlements with most of the challengers, usually on terms favorable to the latter.[14] By the end of 1990, only 11 of the original 27 challenges remained,[15] but one of those was the AFL-CIO challenge alleging that the process was flawed by OSHA's reliance on private standard-setting agencies and by its failure to set more stringent PELs based on complete information.[16] Even though two prominent trade associations filed briefs in support of the OSHA generic standard, the Court of Appeals for the Eleventh Circuit vacated the entire standard in July 1992. The court held that OSHA had not supported with sufficiently detailed analysis its significant risk and feasibility determinations with respect to all of the permissible exposure limits set in the single generic proceeding. The court in no uncertain terms held that OSHA was obliged to make detailed individual findings for each of the chemicals in each of the affected industries. OSHA's generic findings of significant risk and feasibility were virtually ignored. In effect, the court held that OSHA could not use a generic approach to reduce its overall workload.[17]

OSHA's PEL project was a credible attempt to gain a handle on the problem of multiple chemicals in the workplace. The Eleventh Circuit's overly aggressive review of the standard will not only set the PEL update project back but may also spell doom for other innovative generic attempts to protect workers. The court's focus on the agency's failure to make individual significant risk and feasibility findings was misplaced. The rule's deficiencies did not lie in the agency's analytical inadequacies, but rather in its failure to provide more complete protections for workers. First, the PELs were based almost exclusively upon the TLVs generated by an industry-dominated group,[18] and they were not always based upon a consideration of chronic effects.[19] Second, as OSHA acknowledged, they did not press technology. One survey conducted just prior to the publication of the PEL update regulations concluded that out of 43,000 samples taken for 56 chemicals with established PELs, 92 percent complied with the PELs and 79 percent were less than half the PEL. The PEL update left the PELs for 70 percent of the 56 substances unaffected and reduced the PEL for 20 percent by less than half. The study supports the conclusion that the PEL update did not bring about many changes in the real world.[20] Third, the standard virtually ensured that laggard companies would not install engineering controls at a rapid pace by failing to provide a deadline after which respirators would no longer be appropriate. Fourth, the PELs did not include other important aspects of a full-fledged standard, such as monitoring and medical removal protection. Finally, as the court noted, the PELs did not represent a complete analysis by OSHA scientists and engineers. OSHA must now commit itself to promulgate as expeditiously as possible full-fledged standards that require the most stringent feasible installation of engineering controls. In the end, OSHA probably regrets spending more than $4 million on the effort.[21]

METHYLENEDIANILINE

When he assumed office, Assistant Secretary Pendergrass expressed a strong preference for negotiated rulemaking over the traditional adversarial process.[22] His first opportunity to experiment with negotiated rulemaking came during the agency's attempt to regulate worker exposure to 4,4' methylenedianiline (MDA), a large-volume industrial chemical used primarily as an intermediate in the production of polyurethane foams and similar products. Normally handled as a liquid or in the form of flakes, granules, or lumps, the greatest potential source of workplace exposure occurs as a result of spills during the handling of dry MDA rather than from the release of vapors of airborne dusts.[23] About 4,000 to 6,000 workers are exposed to MDA,[24] which, according to the National Toxicology Program (NTP), presents a significant risk of liver damage and cancer. OSHA's preliminary risk assessment, which was based on the NTP animal data, predicted that between 60 and 200 workers out of every 1,000 exposed to current levels would contract cancer.[25]

OSHA's rulemaking initiative began, interestingly enough, with the EPA's first ever determination, under section 4(f) of the Toxic Substances Control Act,[26] that MDA posed a "significant risk of serious or widespread harm to human beings from cancer."[27] Having made this finding, EPA had 180 days to decide whether to regulate MDA itself or refer the matter to another agency. Well within this time frame, EPA and OSHA published a joint ANPR in September 1983.[28] The matter then languished for nearly two years, until EPA, on July 5, 1985, published a *Federal Register* notice formally referring MDA to OSHA, based on its determination that MDA's risks were limited to the workplace.[29] Although OSHA did not respond affirmatively to EPA's referral until February 1986,[30] it published a notice in October 1985 of its intent to form a mediated rulemaking advisory committee to develop a proposed rule for MDA. The agency cautioned that the negotiated rulemaking process would supplement rather than replace traditional rulemaking procedures.[31]

The Public Citizen Health Research Group (HRG), a Nader-affiliated organization, strongly opposed OSHA's use of the mediated rulemaking procedure for developing occupational health standards.[32] HRG feared that the effort to induce the diametrically opposed parties to compromise implied a bargaining process that the OSH Act expressly prohibited. It was afraid that the agency might use negotiation "to circumvent customary rulemaking procedures."[33] Both HRG and the unions recalled OSHA's failed benzene mediation effort between August 1983 and May 1984.[34] In particular, the unions recalled the delay caused by the "improper interference" by the OMB in the benzene process, and made their participation in the MDA negotiated rulemaking procedures contingent on OMB's willingness to allow the rulemaking process to "progress as Congress intended."[35] Industry representatives had similar concerns. The Chemical Manufacturers Association (CMA) expressed doubts about the suitability of negotiated rulemaking procedures for MDA.[36] It sought specific assurances that OSHA would be taking an active role in the negotiating process rather than merely providing technical, legal, and administrative support.

Notwithstanding the benzene failure, OSHA was determined to demonstrate "that negotiated rulemaking can work if you're careful about choosing a chemical" to submit to the procedure.[37] MDA was selected for mediated rulemaking for several reasons: it was at the preproposal stage of development; affected interests were limited in number and readily identifiable; it was likely that the interested parties would negotiate in good faith; and sufficient information was available to address and resolve the key issues.[38]

OSHA appointed a 14-member committee composed of representatives of labor, industry, occupational health and safety professionals, federal agencies, and the public.[39] Representatives from three unions, three industry trade associations, three government agencies, two national laboratories, and one state agency agreed to participate.[40] HRG was not invited. Fortunately for the group, OSHA appointed an extremely dedicated staff member to provide support to the group. She spent much of the next year working late and on weekends to keep the group together and supplied with current information.[41] Unfortunately, OSHA provided her with virtually no clerical support, and she was reduced to hiring her children on weekends for 35 cents an hour to run the copying machine and collate documents.[42] A mediator from the Federal Mediation and Conciliation Service was appointed to chair the meetings, but he had no responsibilities for organizing the meetings or managing the schedules.[43]

Although it took an entire meeting and some extracurricular socializing for the members of the groups to get to know and trust each other, they soon began to negotiate in good faith with a minimum of posturing. The union representatives made it known early on that they were not prepared to compromise on the question of worker health. They came into the negotiations with a "bottom line" number for the MDA airborne exposure level that would be acceptable to them; when the industry representatives (to the surprise of the union representatives) relatively quickly accepted that number, the labor members were willing to negotiate about less important matters such as medical removal pay protection.[44] There were, of course, some difficulties with personality conflicts and the inability of representatives to make commitments until they had polled some of the people they represented. But for the most part the negotiations went smoothly.

At the first committee meeting, in July 1986, the group agreed that if it did not reach consensus within six months, OSHA would terminate the process and initiate the formal rulemaking process without delay.[45] The committee was able to speed things up by appointing subcommittees to meet on a more frequent basis to work on particular wording of agreed-upon concepts.[46] Yet although the committee worked diligently in a genuine attempt to adhere to the schedule, its progress was slowed by illness, scheduling problems, and poor weather. At the committee's request, the agency granted an additional six months to complete the negotiations.[47] The consensus recommendations were finally published on July 16, 1987.[48] Immediately thereafter, OSHA announced that it would publish a proposed standard based on the recommendations within 90 days, stating that it foresaw no complications that would delay publication.[49] As the deadline drew near, OSHA continued to hold to a November 1987 publication data, stressing the agency's "moral obligation" to promulgate the rule as quickly as possible and to continue with its "good faith" effort to bring the rulemaking to an expeditious conclusion.[50] The agency did, however, hold up the proposal in an ill-advised attempt to give its Advisory Committee on Construction Safety and Health a chance to review it. This new cast of characters quickly became confused about the implications of the proposed rule for the construction industry, and it successfully requested the agency to defer its review until February 1988, thus further delaying the publication of the proposal.[51]

The regulation was then submitted to OMB for review. Unfortunately, OSHA's priorities were not necessarily those of OMB, and the regulation was placed at the bottom of the "in" box of a busy junior official at OMB.[52] To the increasing disappointment of the committee members, the matter languished in OMB until the first anniversary of the mediation group's recommendations.[53] The CMA requested that the agency "convey to [OMB] the urgent need for prompt action" on the proposal,[54] and it began to put pressure on upper-level OMB officials to increase the rule's priority within that agency. Feeling betrayed, the United Steelworkers' representative reminded Pendergrass of his earlier prediction that the negotiated rulemaking process could speed the rulemaking process and possibly make public hearings and judicial review unnecessary. The union's health and safety specialist, Frank Grimes, concluded his letter to Pendergrass with a heartfelt "[t]hanks for nothing."[55] Perhaps the most bitter participant of all was the dedicated OSHA staffer who had sacrificed weekends and holidays to the process, only to see it held hostage to OMB's scheduling whims.[56] When OMB finally did get around to commenting on the regulation, its comments were substantive in nature and threatened to undo some of the delicate compromises underlying the proposal. For example, OMB wanted to provide that the standard's medical surveillance requirements would "sunset" after three years. Even the industry objected to this suggestion, observing that it would be pointless to begin a medical surveillance program if it would be terminated in three years.

In September 1988, Pendergrass reported that the proposal was in the "final stages of review," and he promised publication in a few weeks. The change of administrations in January delayed the initiative still further, because no upper-level decision maker within the agency wanted to take responsibility for issuing the proposal until the incoming assistant secretary had an opportunity to review it.[57] It was finally published in May 1989, almost three years after the initial committee meeting and well over four years after OSHA announced its intention of beginning a mediated rulemaking process.[58]

The proposal attracted only a few comments (significantly fewer than prior rulemakings), and they were generally supportive.[59] It seemed for a time that Pendergrass's prediction that the regulatory negotiation process would avoid lengthy hearings and judicial review would be borne out. Two companies, however, firmly opposed the proposed rule, and OSHA reopened the hearings in January 1990 for further comments on 17 specific issues.[60] As of the end of 1991, no further action had been taken on the standard.

While the MDA rulemaking, like the benzene effort that proceeded it, was intended to be a showcase for negotiated rulemaking, it likewise failed to produce a standard within a reasonable period of time. Part of the blame must fall on OSHA's doorstep. The agency did not give the effort the high priority that it promised; it mistakenly brought a second advisory committee into the process; and its refusal to provide even secretarial assistance to the one staff person it was willing to devote to the project was irresponsible from a managerial perspective. But the worst roadblock was the institution that the unions were dubious about from the outset. OMB was not at all attuned to the agency's priorities, and it burdened the process with substantive concerns that risked undoing the compromises that sustained the effort. The unions have now been burned twice; they will not lightly embark upon the regulatory negotiation road again. Unless significant improvements (of the sort suggested in Chapter 12) are made in the concept, so that beneficiary groups can be persuaded that negotiated rulemaking is not merely an excuse for inaction, it is doomed to failure in the highly contentious context of worker safety.

BLOODBORNE DISEASES

OSHA's other significant new initiative addressed bloodborne diseases. Although acquired immune deficiency syndrome (AIDS) is a widely recognized public health problem, few members of the general public realize that it is also an occupational health issue. At least 25 health care workers have reportedly become infected with the AIDS virus through occupational exposure to blood or other potentially infectious materials.[61] Other workers who are routinely exposed to the AIDS virus include postal workers (from the shipment of medical wastes), janitors and orderlies, policemen and fire fighters, and morticians. Yet AIDS is merely the most notorious of several bloodborne diseases that pose risks to workers, such as hospital orderlies and janitors, who must interact with persons carrying such diseases and with contaminated instruments and equipment. Hepatitis B, for example, is a serious disease of hospital workers, even though it lacks the notoriety of AIDS. Other less prevalent bloodborne diseases include syphilis and malaria. Over 5.5 million health care workers in the United States are at risk of becoming infected with bloodborne diseases.[62]

Good housekeeping procedures as well as disinfection and sterilization techniques are necessary to prevent the spread of a virus.[63] Wearing gloves is an obvious precaution, but like many other personal protective devices, this technique is hardly foolproof. Gloves may give workers a false sense of security. People who wear gloves often do not change them after each procedure or wash them as frequently as they would their hands. In any event, gloves do not effectively prevent needle-stick injuries.[64] By far the most effective technique for protecting workers from hepatitis B is a vaccine that was licensed in 1982. As of 1989, approximately 30 to 40 percent of high-risk health care workers had been vaccinated.[65] Unfortunately, there is no vaccine for AIDS.

OSHA attempts to protect workers from bloodborne diseases began in 1983, when it issued a set of voluntary guidelines designed to reduce the risk of occupational exposure to hepatitis B virus. These guidelines included a description of the disease, suggestions for work practices, and recommendations for use of the vaccine.[66] With the advent of the AIDS crisis in the mid-1980s, the Service Employee's International Union and the American Federation of State, County, and Municipal Employees (AFSCME) petitioned OSHA in September 1986 for an emergency temporary standard to protect workers from hepatitis B virus and the AIDS virus, but the unions received no response until OSHA rejected the petition in October 1987.[67]

Pressure for action began to mount when the Centers for Disease Control (CDC), on May 22, 1987, reported for the first time that health care employees became infected by the AIDS virus without sustaining needle-stick injuries.[68] AFSCME union president Gerald W. McEntee maintained that this new information "clearly shows that employers will not regulate themselves," and Bill Borwegen, safety and health director for the Service Employees International Union, warned that "[e]very day OSHA delays, more health care workers are at risk."[69] Police officers, who often participate in emergency medical care, began to pressure OSHA to put a regulatory regime in place.[70] In addition, the first case of AIDS infection of a research worker was reported on September 4, 1987.[71] Finally, Pendergrass, in testimony before a congressional subcommittee in July 1987, committed the agency to publishing an advance notice of proposed rulemaking (ANPR) for bloodborne diseases and to enforcing CDC's protective guidelines under the general duty clause in the interim.[72]

On October 30, 1987, OSHA and the CDC distributed a joint advisory notice to more than 600,000 employers, employee representatives, and trade and professional associations.[73] A month later, on November 17, 1987, OSHA published an ANPR asking for comments on whether it should propose an enforceable standard.[74] At OMB's insistence, the ANPR also asked whether the additional protection afforded by a permanent standard was warranted in light of the immediate ongoing activities of the departments of Labor and Health and Human Services.[75] The notice precipitated "an overwhelming response" of more than 350 comments.[76]

Additional impetus was provided by a June 1988 preliminary report of the President's Commission on the Human Immunodeficiency Virus Epidemic, a 13-member group established by President Reagan. Of the report's 579 recommendations, 20 related directly to protecting health care workers, and 12 recommended actions employers should take to educate and help employees deal with the epidemic. The report said that the current efforts to protect ambulance personnel, police, fire fighters, correctional officers, sanitation workers, and custodians were "less than adequate," and it urged OSHA to draft a final standard on AIDS in the workplace "expeditiously, within one year."[77]

At this point, OSHA had drafted a proposed rule, but it was undergoing OMB review.[78] Senator Edward M. Kennedy attempted to pry the rule out of OSHA with a letter urging the agency to commit publicly to a deadline for promulgating a rule.[79] On July 19, 1988, Pendergrass promised Senator Kennedy that the agency would soon issue a proposed standard for bloodborne diseases.[80]

Pendergrass could not, however, control the pace of OMB's review. OMB was quite critical of several aspects of the draft proposal. To OMB's concern that OSHA should not make the rule broadly applicable to all potentially exposed employees, such as laundry workers, OSHA responded that it did not want to have the regulation turn on its ability to identify and classify particular occupations. In addition, OSHA assured OMB that the standard was not intended to require emergency personnel to interrupt life-saving procedures to put on personal protective devices. To satisfy OMB's concerns, OSHA agreed not to require "universal precautions" (a term of art meaning that all human blood and certain human body fluids are treated as if known to be infectious) if they would "interfere with the proper delivery of health care or public safety services" in particular circumstances. At OMB's insistence, OSHA agreed to reduce the stringency of the rule's medical surveillance requirements so as not to require that it be undertaken by a physician in every instance.[81] By mid-March 1989, the unions were growing impatient, and they wrote to the secretary of labor to remind her that they had agreed not to sue OSHA on its promise that it would act expeditiously.[82]

On May 30, 1989, OSHA published its long-awaited proposed rule for bloodborne diseases.[83] It was OSHA's first attempt to regulate occupational exposure to biological hazards.[84] Rather than limit the standard to health care workers, who generally suffer the greatest exposures to bloodborne diseases, the agency proposed to make its provisions broadly applicable to all workers who have occupational exposures to blood or other infectious substances.[85] The proposal required covered employers to identify and document all tasks in which exposures could occur with or without personal protective devices, but it did not require that employers develop standard operating procedures for those tasks.[86] In addition, employers would be required to develop an infection control plan.

The proposal contained a general requirement that "universal precautions" be observed to prevent contact with blood and other infectious materials, but it also contained OMB's qualifier for cases in which such precautions would interfere with the proper delivery of health care or public safety services. The proposed rule set out broad requirements for engineering controls, work practice controls, and personal protective equipment. Engineering and work practice controls included hand washing, decontamination of personal protective equipment, and various prohibitions on use of needles and sharp objects and other potentially dangerous activities in areas where infections could occur. Personal protective equipment provisions included requirements for wearing gloves, masks, gowns, caps, and such but did not require the use of respirators. The proposal also included several broad housekeeping and waste disposal requirements. Superimposed on all of this was a general requirement that all employees occupationally exposed to hepatitis B virus be provided the opportunity to be vaccinated against hepatitis B at the employer's expense. Finally, the proposal included requirements for warnings and training programs.[87] OSHA predicted that the proposed rule would entail compliance costs of approximately $852 million per year,[88] making it by far the most expensive standard ever promulgated by OSHA (the hazard communication standard had an annual price tag of $500–600 million).[89]

Although the standard-setting process for bloodborne diseases did not break any speed records, it proceeded reasonably expeditiously. The issue was not near the top of OSHA's agenda when Pendergrass assumed office, but events outside the agency relentlessly prodded it toward writing regulations to protect health care workers. Interestingly, the agency proceeded at least to the proposal stage without the extra incentive of a court action. At the very least, the experience demonstrated that the threat of contempt of court is not an essential spur to agency action.

SMOKING IN THE WORKPLACE

At the same time that Pendergrass was undertaking the ambitious PEL update generic rulemaking, he declined to take up the exceedingly controversial topic of smoking in the workplace. On May 7, 1987, the American Public Health Association and the Public Citizen Health Research Group petitioned OSHA to promulgate an emergency temporary standard banning smoking in the workplace. They asserted that this would eliminate nearly 60 percent of the lung cancers that nonsmokers contract from inhaling tobacco smoke and would "protect at least 52 million nonsmoking Americans who work in over 4.8 million indoor workplaces regulated by OSHA and involuntarily breathe tobacco smoke." The petitioners pointed out that the General Services Administration had imposed new restrictions on 890,000 federal workers in 6,800 government buildings and that the Department of Health and Human Services banned all smoking in all of its buildings.[90]

Responding to a letter from Senator Jake Garn, Assistant Secretary Pendergrass in February 1989 said that smoking was not an OSHA priority, because "tobacco smoke is not generated by an industrial process, exposure to tobacco smoke also occurs during off duty hours over which OSHA has no control," and existing studies failed to distinguish workplace exposure from other exposures. Pendergrass suggested that the problem would be addressed more effectively "as a component of a larger public health effort dealing with smoking."[91] At the same time OSHA denied a citizen petition requesting it to issue an emergency temporary standard for smoking.[92] Thus, the workplace smoking initiative died aborning.

CONCLUSIONS

Soon after the election of George Bush, Pendergrass announced that he would resign to allow the new president to choose his own assistant secretary for OSHA. Pendergrass was satisfied with his accomplishments. He was especially proud of the successful completion of the PEL project prior to his departure, and he had reason to be proud of his efforts to reinvigorate the enforcement of existing OSHA standards, a topic that will be addressed in Chapter 10. In addition, by some counts OSHA issued more full-fledged standards during Pendergrass's tenure than under any other assistant secretary.[93] As we have seen, however, at least some of the credit for this last statistic goes to the courts of appeals that ordered OSHA to proceed expeditiously.

Although staff morale picked up somewhat during the Pendergrass years from the nadir of the Auchter and Rowland years, there was still considerable dissatisfaction and some outright rebellion among lower-level professionals. Pendergrass's first full budget, for fiscal year (FY) 1988, called for a 4.26 percent across-the-board decrease, and it required drastic reductions in staff travel.[94] When asked by Senator Lowell Weicker why he did not request more money, Pendergrass replied, "Senator, the resources of OSHA will always be finite." He added that OSHA must be responsive to American taxpayers, and "I feel compelled to do the most with what we have."[95] Pendergrass's FY 1989 budget request, however, asked for a 4.5 percent increase over the 1988 budget.[96]

When several long-time staff professionals testified at hearings held by Senator Edward Kennedy, they expressed years of pent-up frustrations. Dr. Imogene Rodgers, who was the project officer for the formaldehyde standard, testified:

Working for OSHA is almost professional suicide. When you cannot get anything out for so long, you have a bad reputation on the outside, like what's going on. And particularly in the proposal, where we had to put some very egregious things in that ignored cancer altogether, I had people call me from the outside and ask, "What has happened to your brain?" It is a very frustrating situation to have to take the fall for that.[97]

Dr. Peter Infante, who worked on formaldehyde and ethylene oxide, also found working for OSHA to be "extremely frustrating." He elaborated:

There are so many occupational health hazards that we have not dealt with yet today, that when we finally choose to deal with the hazard, there is tremendous information on that hazard. And then you go through and you do a lengthy evaluation, and at the end of gathering information, analysis, re-analysis and further re-analysis, if nothing comes from it, or if less than what you had hoped for comes from it, that is extremely frustrating, and you ask yourself the question why you are doing this.[98]

Jennifer Silk, who spent several years on the successful hazard communication standard and who was widely praised by both industry and labor for her diligence, reported:

I have always said you have to have strong masochistic tendencies to stay in health standards as long as most of us have, because it is very frustrating. You have to fight constantly just to get out the things that you are supposed to be doing.[99]

Dr. Susan Harwood, the project officer for the bloodborne disease initiative, was particularly critical of the role that OMB played in delaying OSHA standards:

I think the thing that keeps me awake at night is the idea of people dying unnecessarily because OSHA is delaying, or OMB has taken something out, or something like that. That is what I find most difficult to deal with.[100]

One of the employees who testified at the Kennedy hearings was allegedly denied a transfer request. OSHA referred the matter to the Department of Labor's inspector general, but nothing came of it.[101]

In defense of the agency and his management of it, Pendergrass testified:

I was not unaware that a number of staff members of the Standards Directorates were frustrated by the slow progress of the various standards on which they were working. I knew as well that some of them felt strongly that OMB review was an unwarranted intrusion into the rulemaking process. That is not to say that I agreed with them, though I understood how they felt. There is no mathematical or scientific formula that can be used to determine the contents of an OSHA standard. Judgments based on considerations of economic and technological feasibility are integral to our rulemaking process. As I stated, OMB has a legitimate role to play in that process. The statutory requirements that different interests be heard and that the public participate in rulemaking can certainly foster frustration. I recognize this, and so does [sic] the OSHA staff scientists who appeared before the committee, all of whom continue to produce excellent work for the agency.[102]

Although Pendergrass was correct to point out that OSHA decisions are complex and must reflect input from several interest groups, his response did not reach the heart of the professional staffers' complaints. OSHA staff professionals recognize that science cannot dictate most controversial OSHA decisions, but they are rightly concerned when they observe up close that politics (even starkly partisan politics) play a very large role in the decision-making process. Like any professional, an OSHA health scientist would like to believe that he or she is accomplishing something. But it is very hard to feel a sense of accomplishment when a regulation for which you are responsible sits on the desk of an upper-level manager or an OMB desk officer for two years.

While the assistant secretaries for OSHA cannot always play to the home crowd, they do have a responsibility to the institution itself to listen to the legitimate complaints of its career employees. Much more than his two predecessors, who often showed little more than contempt for OSHA professionals, Pendergrass tried to be sensitive to their concerns. He inherited an agency with very low self-esteem, and he tried to give it some confidence with an ambitious PEL update project and with significant new enforcement initiatives. To some extent he succeeded in reinvigorating the staff, but much more was required. Even a highly motivated staff could accomplish little without a substantial infusion of new resources and commitment to hire new professionals with a fresh commitment to OSHA's mission.

Pendergrass also had his critics outside of the agency. OMB excoriated OSHA in its annual regulatory program for failing to implement rulemaking designed to augment the "Reagan legacy."[103] At the same time, Senator Howard Metzenbaum harshly criticized Pendergrass for failing to proceed with individual rulemakings: "I can only say to you that when you say that you think you have been doing a good job, I say to you, Mr. Pendergrass, you have let down the workers of this country. You have not been doing a good job, by all of the objective evidence that is available."[104]

In his defense, Pendergrass invoked the dedication of OSHA's career staff:

I think we have accomplished a great deal. I think to characterize the agency as a failure is unfair; it is not accurate, and certainly does not in any way support the 2,000-plus people in the agency and their dedicated efforts to protect the health and safety of the workers in this country.[105]

It is hard to imagine Pendergrass's two predecessors invoking the dedication of the agency staff to its statutory mission as a measure of success. In a very real sense both criticisms were fair. OSHA under Pendergrass was not a dynamic agency striving to accomplish the job that Congress gave it. Yet because it was willing to move ahead cautiously on several fronts, it veered away from the course that the White House policymakers had set for it. OSHA did not steer a path down the middle of the road during Pendergrass's tenure, but it moved a considerable distance back toward the middle from the far right shoulder.

NOTES

1. *BNA Daily Report for Executives* (28 Aug. 1986): A2.
2. *Inside the Administration* 3 (21 Dec. 1984): 1.
3. 53 *Fed. Reg.* 20,960 (1988).
4. U.S. Congress, Senate Committee on Labor and Human Resources, *Hearings on Oversight on the Administration of the Occupational Safety and Health Act*, 100th Cong., 2d sess., S. Hrg. 100–719, 1988, 99 (hereafter cited as Senate, *Oversight Hearing of 1988*).
5. Ibid.
6. Barry I. Castleman and Grace E. Ziem, "Corporate Influence on Threshold Limit

Values," *American Journal of Industrial Medicine* 13 (1988): 531; see also *BNA Occupational Safety and Health Reporter* 17 (6 May 1988): 221

7. Senate, *Oversight Hearings* of 1988, 99. See also James C. Robinson, Dalton G. Paxman, and Stephen M. Rappaport, "Implications of OSHA's Reliance on TLVs in Developing the Air Contaminants Standard," *American Journal of Industrial Medicine* 19 (1991): 3 (arguing that NIOSH's recommended exposure limits were more appropriate than ACGIH TLVs for setting exposure limits).

8. *BNA Occupational Safety and Health Reporter* 18 (2 Dec. 1988): 1323. See also James C. Robinson, *Toil and Toxics: Workplace Struggles and Political Strategies for Occupational Health* (Berkeley: University of California Press, 1991), 160 (arguing that OSHA characterized as carcinogens only 11 of 78 actual carcinogens in the list of 326 substances).

9. 54 *Fed. Reg.* 2332 (1989).

10. Ibid., 2366.

11. James C. Robinson and Dalton G. Paxman, "Technological, Economic, and Political Feasibility in OSHA's Air Contaminants Standard," *Journal of Health Politics, Policy and Law* 16 (1991): 7.

12. *CCH Employment Safety and Health Guide*, 11 Apr. 1989, 1.

13. *BNA Occupational Safety and Health Reporter* 18 (24 Feb. 1989): 1701.

14. Charles Gordon, Office of the Solicitor, Department of Labor, telephone interview, 22 May 1990; *BNA Occupational Safety and Health Reporter* 19 (2 Aug. 1989): 454; ibid. (6 Sept. 1989): 623; ibid. (27 Sept. 1989): 756; ibid. (9 May 1990): 2155.

15. *BNA Occupational Safety and Health Reporter* 20 (13 June 1990): 36.

16. Ibid. (14 Nov. 1990): 1010–11.

17. *AFL-CIO v. OSHA*, 1992 WL 135775 (11th Cir. 1992).

18. John Mendeloff, *Regulating Safety: An Economic and Political Analysis of Occupational Safety and Health Policy* (Cambridge, Mass.: MIT Press, 1979), 45; Daniel M. Berman, *Death on the Job: Occupational Health and Safety Struggles in the United States* (New York: Monthly Review Press, 1978), 75–76; Joseph O. Page and Mary-Win O'Brien, *Bitter Wages: Ralph Nader's Study Group Report on Disease and Injury on the Job* (New York: Grossman, 1973), 159.

19. *BNA Occupational Safety and Health Reporter* 19 (23 May 1990): 2234 (reporting study conducted by Matthew Gillen).

20. Ibid. 20 (3 Oct. 1990): 797 (reporting a study by Eileen Senn Tarlav, an industrial hygienist for the New Jersey Department of Health).

21. Robinson and Paxman, "Technological, Economic, and Political Feasibility," 11.

22. *BNA Daily Report for Executives* (28 Aug. 1986): A2.

23. 52 *Fed. Reg.* 1021 (1986).

24. *BNA Occupational Safety and Health Reporter* 18 (17 May 1989): 2028; ibid. 17 (15 July 1987): 219.

25. Ibid. 15 (6 Mar. 1986): 1008.

26. 25 U.S.C. § 3608 (1988).

27. *BNA Occupational Safety and Health Reporter* 13 (28 Apr. 1983): 996.

28. 48 *Fed. Reg.* 42,836 (1983).

29. 50 *Fed. Reg.* 27,674 (1985).

30. 52 *Fed. Reg.* 6,748 (1987).

31. 50 *Fed. Reg.* 42,789 (1985).
32. *BNA Occupational Safety and Health Reporter* 15 (12 Dec. 1985): 594.
33. Ibid. (6 Feb. 1986): 942.
34. Philip J. Harter, "Dispute Resolution and Administrative Law: The History, Needs and Future of a Complex Relationship," *Villanova Law Review* 29 (1983–84): 1393: Mendeloff, *Regulating Safety*, 205; *BNA Occupational Safety and Health Reporter* 15 (12 Dec. 1985): 594.
35. *BNA Occupational Safety and Health Reporter* 15 (9 Jan. 1986): 870–71; ibid. (12 Dec. 1985): 594.
36. Ibid. (9 Jan. 1986): 870.
37. Ibid. (24 Apr. 1986): 1164.
38. Ibid. (24 Oct. 1985): 422.
39. Ibid. 16 (8 Apr. 1987): 1186.
40. 54 *Fed. Reg.* 20,672 (1989).
41. Roger Daniel, industrial hygiene consultant, Chemical Manufacturers Association, telephone interview, 3 Nov. 1986.
42. Daniel interview.
43. *BNA Occupational Safety and Health Reporter* 15 (24 Oct. 1985): 422.
44. Daniel interview.
45. Ibid.
46. Daniel interview.
47. *BNA Occupational Safety and Health Reporter* 16 (5 May 1987): 1437; Patti Waugh, senior industrial hygienist, OSHA, telephone interview, 30 Oct. 1936.
48. 52 *Fed. Reg.* 26,776 (1987).
49. *BNA Occupational and Safety Reporter* 17 (22 July 6 1987): 239.
50. Ibid. (30 Sept. 1987): 769.
51. Ibid. (11 Nov. 1987): 935.
52. Daniel interview.
53. *BNA Occupational Safety and Health Reporter* 181 (27 July 1988): 570.
54. Ibid., 571.
55. Ibid.
56. Waugh interview.
57. Ibid.
58. 54 *Fed. Reg.* 20,672 (1989).
59. *BNA Occupational Safety and Health Reporter* 19 (18 Aug. 1989): 665.
60. 55 *Fed. Reg.* 2101 (1990).
61. 54 *Fed. Reg.* 23, 051 (1989).
62. Senate, *Oversight Hearings of 1988*, 339.
63. 54 *Fed. Reg.* 23,050 (1989).
64. *BNA Occupational Safety and Health Reporter* 17 (13 Apr. 1988): 1668–69.
65. 54 *Fed. Reg.* 23,051 (1989).
66. Ibid., 23,047.
67. Ibid.; Senate, *Oversight Hearings of 1988*, 14, 339.
68. *BNA Occupational Safety and Health Reporter* 16 (27 May 1987): 1452.
69. Ibid., 1453.
70. Ibid. 17 (2 Aug. 1987): 437.
71. Ibid. (9 Sept. 1987): 565.
72. U.S. Congress, House Committee on Government Operations, *Hearings Before*

a Subcommittee on Need for Immediate OSHA Regulations to Protect Health Care Workers from AIDS, 100th Cong, 1st sess., 1987, 61.
73. 52 *Fed. Reg.* 41,818 (1987); 54 *Fed. Reg.* 23,047 (1989).
74. 52 *Fed. Reg.* 45,438 (1987); Senate, *Oversight Hearings of 1988*, 1027.
75. 54 *Fed. Reg.* 23,047 (1989); 52 *Fed. Reg.* 45,441 (1987).
76. 54 *Fed. Reg.* 23,047 (1989).
77. *BNA Occupational Safety and Health Reporter* 18 (8 June 1988): 22.
78. Ibid.
79. Ibid. (22 June 1988): 413.
80. Ibid. (27 July 1988): 572.
81. Ibid. (8 Feb. 1989): 1615.
82. Ibid. (22 Feb. 1989): 1657.
83. 54 *Fed. Reg.* 23,042 (1989).
84. Ibid.
85. 54 *Fed. Reg.* 23,111.
86. Ibid., 23,113.
87. Ibid., 23,135–39.
88. Ibid., 23,074.
89. *BNA Occupational Safety and Health Reporter* 18 (11 Jan. 1989): 1444.
90. "U.S. Is Urged to Ban Smoking in Workplace," *New York Times*, 7 May 1987, A29, col. 1.
91. *BNA Occupational Safety and Health Reporter* 16 (25 Feb. 1987): 1022.
92. Ibid.
93. Ibid. 18 (5 Apr. 1989): 1848.
94. Ibid. 17 (6 Jan. 1988): 1229.
95. Ibid. (27 Apr. 1988): 1723.
96. Ibid. (30 Mar. 1988): 1597.
97. Senate, *Oversight Hearings of 1988*, 513.
98. Ibid.
99. Ibid.
100. Ibid.
101. *BNA Daily Report for Executives*, 25 July 1988.
102. Senate, *Oversight Hearings of 1988*, 809–10.
103. *BNA Occupational Safety and Health Reporter* 17 (13 Apr. 1988): 1659–60.
104. Senate, *Oversight Hearings of 1988*, 921.
105. Ibid.

10

The Reagan Years: Weakening Enforcement

Many of OSHA's gains in the enforcement arena during the Bingham years quickly dissipated during Auchter's tenure and were only partially regained under Pendergrass. The net effect was that during the Reagan administration OSHA substantially weakened health and safety enforcement.

TARGETING INSPECTIONS

Early in its history, OSHA recognized that the key to effective enforcement was the ability to target inspections toward the most dangerous workplaces. By improving how OSHA targeted companies for inspection, the Bingham administration was able to increase significantly the number of serious violations that OSHA detected. One of Auchter's first actions was to modify these targeting criteria. Convinced that too many industries were covered by the Bingham approach, Auchter limited programmed inspections (inspections not based on employee complaints) to the manufacturing and construction sectors.[1] Auchter also believed that programmed inspections should be aimed only at the most dangerous individual firms in a given industry.[2] He therefore elected not to inspect any firm if its lost workday injury rate was below the national average of 4.9 days per 100 workers.[3]

OSHA's new programmed enforcement policy had at least six adverse impacts on worker safety. First, employers not in the manufacturing and construction sectors had very little reason to fear an OSHA inspection. The unions complained that "[m]any industries and job sites in these exempted nonmanufacturing industries, such as hospitals, hotels, and utilities had high injury rates and major hazards," and they stressed that more than half of all injuries occurred in those sectors.[4]

Second, the reduced threat of an OSHA inspection undercut safety incentives for better-than-average employers, thereby effectively freezing the level of safety for millions of workers. The AFL-CIO calculated that OSHA's new policy eliminated the threat of a random safety inspection for the employers of 86 percent of the workers in the manufacturing sector.[5] According to the union, the number of workers covered by actual inspections declined from 3.7 million in 1980 to 2.2 million in 1982, a drop of 40 percent. The unions further observed that OSHA's enforcement efforts were not noticeably more stringent in the targeted industries.[6]

Third, the policy required OSHA inspectors to spend an inordinate amount of their time in offices examining records rather than out in the workplaces searching for real hazards.[7] A Sierra Club report noted that the process of reviewing company records to determine if the employer's injury rate was greater than the national average consumed approximately eight hours of an inspector's time per employer.[8] The unions concluded that OSHA's enforcement targeting program was "nothing more than a public relations gimmick to increase inspection numbers through counting records review visits, while exempting most manufacturing employers from routine safety inspections."[9]

Fourth, the policy may have effectively shielded some of the most dangerous workplaces from inspections. Because OSHA took into account only a firm's lost workday rate, "an employer with a significant history of fatalities [stood] no greater chance of being inspected than other employers within the same industry with no history of fatalities."[10] For example, in 1983, OSHA inspectors conducted a "records only" inspection of a Chicago film recovery plant and decided on the basis of company records not to proceed with a full-fledged inspection. Not long thereafter, an immigrant worker, Stephan Golab, died of cyanide poisoning at the plant, and the firm was later convicted for the murder of Mr. Golab by an Illinois jury.[11] Had OSHA conducted a full inspection, it would undoubtedly have discovered the extremely unsafe conditions at the plant.

Fifth, companies that relied heavily upon outside contractors did not include deaths and injuries of outside employees in their statistics, even though the accidents occurred in their plants. The petrochemical industry, for example, relied very heavily upon the employees of outside contractors to provide a substantial proportion of construction and maintenance services. From the cold statistics, it appeared that the industry had an exemplary record, but the statistics did not account for all of the casualties of petrochemical plant explosions, because many of the dead and injured were employed by outside contractors.[12]

Sixth, especially dangerous firms could avoid inspections by the simple expedient of falsifying their accident logs.[13] For example, employees of Consolidation Coal Co. in Osage, West Virginia, agreed to help cover up their accidents by recording missed workdays as vacations or by recuperating at work. This allowed the company to report that employees had never actually missed work.[14]

The notorious Iowa Beef Packing (IBP) episode was a dramatic illustration of how good-looking records could mask devastatingly dangerous realities. In

1986, OSHA appeared at the IBP plant in Dakota City, Nebraska, but failed to conduct an inspection because the IBP records indicated that the company's lost workday rate was below the national average. In fact, the IBP plant was one of the most dangerous in the nation. IBP had 13,000 lost workdays in 1985, a rate twice as high as the average packing plant, and seven times as high as the average industry.[15] A congressman characterized testimony presented by current and former workers at the plant as " 'a story out of Charles Dickens': production-line employees working with knives at close quarters in cold, wet conditions; standing in a 'sea of blood' and slippery animal fat; and suffering crippling injuries because of unsafe working conditions and inadequate treatment by company medical personnel.''[16] The injuries were either never reported or grossly understated.[17] When workers complained about the conditions, the company threatened to fire them.[18] Indeed, the conditions at IBP were so abhorrent that the turnover rate was nearly 100 percent a year. OSHA discovered that IBP had falsified its safety records only after union representatives brought the matter to its attention. In July 1987, OSHA recommended a $2.6 million penalty for IBP, the largest fine at that time in OSHA history, for more than 1,000 alleged ''willful'' record-keeping violations.[19] The penalty did not, of course, heal any of the hundreds of worker injuries.

COMPLAINT INSPECTIONS

Auchter also moved to restrict the frequency and extent of inspections conducted in response to employee complaints. Much to the consternation of OSHA inspectors in the field, he eliminated the existing ''wall-to-wall'' policy under which an officer undertaking a complaint inspection was free to inspect any other area of the plant.[20] Except in especially dangerous industries, inspections were limited to the hazards specified in the complaint, unless the investigator discovered information ''indicating the likelihood of serious hazards in other portions of the plant.'' Not surprisingly, complaint inspections fell from 16,093 in 1980 to 5,728 in 1983, a decrease of 65 percent.[21] OSHA further decided to consider any complaint from a *former* employee as an ''informal'' complaint that yielded only a letter from OSHA to the employer repeating the worker's complaints as mere allegations, unless the former employee alleged that the workplace posed an imminent danger. Employers were free to respond in writing to such informal complaints, and only one in ten was ever inspected.[22]

INFORMAL SETTLEMENT CONFERENCES

Besides modifying its approach to choosing companies for inspection, OSHA increased its reliance on informal settlement conferences when violations were detected. Auchter's willingness to settle on terms favorable to employers further reduced the minimal impact of the small penalties actually assessed. Auchter enthusiastically instructed the troops, ''Whenever possible . . . arrive at a settlement agreement under which the employer agrees to obey OSHA's order and comply."[23] The percentage of contested cases correspondingly fell rapidly from 25 percent during the Bingham years to 2 percent.[24] Indeed, Auchter encouraged inspectors and area directors to enter into settlements before issuing citations, thereby allowing the agency and the employer to resolve the matter "quietly." One OSHA inspector complained that these informal approaches amounted to an open invitation to employers to "come and get your citation at bargain-basement discount prices."[25] Sensing this hostility, upper-level OSHA officials sometimes declined to invite the inspectors to the settlement conferences.[26] OSHA inspectors were not the only persons left at home. Union officials complained bitterly bout the agency's failure to allow employee representatives to participate in these behind-the-scenes negotiations, arguing that "[t]he issuance of the citation itself is fundamental to the process."[27]

Auchter believed that the policy of maximizing the number of settlements protected workers by bringing about earlier corrections of dangerous conditions.[28] He also felt that the policy created a climate in which employers, employees, and OSHA could work constructively to solve their mutual problems. A 1984 report of the General Accounting Office tended to bear Auchter out by concluding that the informal settlement policy had resulted in expedited correction of dangerous working conditions.[29] But worker representatives maintained that the informal settlements "failed to include adequate provisions to assure proper abatement."[30] In one case, an informal settlement with Scott Paper reduced penalties for record-keeping citations and eliminated penalties for hundreds of safety citations that had not yet been issued, but did not require the company to forgo contesting the safety citations or to abate the cited hazards. Several weeks after the settlement agreed was signed, Scott Paper contested all the safety violations.[31] In addition, the GAO report pointed out that OSHA conducted few follow-up inspections to determine whether employers actually corrected the violations as promised.[32]

FOLLOW-UP INSPECTIONS

When an OSHA inspection resulted in one or more significant citations, agency inspectors had traditionally conducted a follow-up inspection to determine whether the citation had produced any tangible results. Under Auchter, OSHA severely curtailed these follow-up inspections on the theory that they were usually a waste of the inspector's time.[33] As long as the employer sent a letter assuring OSHA that the violation had been remedied, it would not conduct a follow-up. The number of follow-up inspections predictably fell from 11,670 in 1980 to only 1,602 in 1983, a drop of 88 percent.[34] Auchter argued that the 18 percent overall decrease in the total number of inspections during his first year was mostly attributable to this decrease in follow-up inspections. He explained that more than 99 percent of firms that were visited in follow-up inspections were found to be in compliance with all OSHA standards.[35] He did not say what

OSHA inspectors found on the hundredth visit, nor did he speculate about whether the compliance rate would be as high once it became known to employers that OSHA would no longer be conducting follow-up inspections.

FROM TOUGH COP TO TRUSTED ADVISER

Auchter's primary motive for the aforementioned changes in OSHAs enforcement policies was to change fundamentally the role of the agency's inspectors. He firmly believed that OSHA inspectors could much more effectively reduce occupational accidents and diseases if they assumed the role of "consultant" rather than the adversarial "enforcer" role that, according to some employers, OSHA inspectors had assumed under Bingham.[36] In July 1983, Auchter announced to agency managers his desire "that OSHA field offices become community safety and health resource centers fully capable of assisting employers and employees and implementing effective health and safety programs in the workplace."[37] Each area director was obliged to develop an annual outreach program plan that included a list of OSHA experts, short courses addressing specific health and safety questions, and "handout" packages to be distributed to particular audiences. The programs were to stress voluntary compliance, labor-management cooperation, and employer abatement assistance. OSHA staffers were encouraged to join professional organizations and to attend meetings as a "vehicle for informing the public of OSHA's balanced program mix."[38] Regional managers were told that their performance would be judged in part by their ability to reduce the number of citations that were contested by employers.[39]

Under another enforcement policy initiative, inaugurated in late 1982, OSHA agreed to reduce or eliminate programmed inspections for companies with labor-management safety committees. Employers with safety committees could become part of STAR (Sharing the Accountability for Regulation) program. The PRIME (Positive Results through Intensive Management Efforts) program was available for nonunion employers who did not want to work with organized labor. The PRAISE (Positive Results Achieved in Safe Employment) program was created for smaller businesses and nonhazardous industries. Operation TRY, which OSHA created for companies with compliance problems, involved greater OSHA oversight.[40]

Unions opposed these attempts to achieve voluntary compliance through promises of reduced enforcement.[41] Workers preferred OSHA to be the "tough cop" rather than a "helpful consultant." According to one union official: "We don't want inspectors judged by how polite they are to the bosses. We want hazards uncovered."[42] Labor leaders were also very skeptical of programs in which employers were allowed to develop their own health protection programs in lieu of OSHA inspections. They suspected that such programs would rely heavily upon personal protective devices such as respirators. Surprisingly, employer interest in participating in these new programs was not especially high. One report speculated that employers had little reason to be interested; given OSHA's reduced enforcement resources, the likelihood of a citation was already so small that there was little incentive to join the programs.[43]

REDUCED CRIMINAL PROSECUTION

Consistent with the agency's new emphasis on cooperation, Auchter was reluctant to treat employers who violated OSHA standards as ordinary criminals. A Nader report, issued in September 1983, pointed out that the number of "willful" violations cited by OSHA dropped 90 percent, from 1,238 in 1980 to 112 in 1982.[44] Auchter called the report "a collection of lies, distortions and generalizations based on isolated and unrepresentative cases, wrapped in the philosophy that the free enterprise system is out to squeeze the profits from the very blood and bones of workers."[45] The fact remains, however, that OSHA did not refer a criminal case to the Justice Department until well over a year after Auchter assumed the helm.[46] In the first six years of the Reagan administration, the agency referred only ten cases to the Justice Department for possible criminal prosecution, compared with 24 during Bingham's last three years.[47] Chapter 14 describes how local district attorneys grew so impatient with OSHA's reluctance to file criminal charges against employers that they began to prosecute them under state homicide and manslaughter statutes.

REDUCED STATE ENFORCEMENT

Auchter's changes were not limited to OSHA's own enforcement efforts. He also reversed the prior administration's get-tough policy for approving state programs. In 1981, Auchter explained to a Senate committee that "local problems are best addressed by those closest to them," and he pledged to "resolve differences" that had previously existed between OSHA and the states in order to "develop a management and policy framework that will integrate the states into the overall OSHA program."[48] To implement this partnership, Auchter terminated proceedings initiated during the Bingham era to withdraw OSHA's prior approval of the Indiana plan and denied a petition to withdraw approval of the Virginia plan.[49] A labor official speculated that OSHA would certify any state plan "even if it was written on toilet paper."[50]

Auchter's second major achievement was to scrap a court-ordered program to require states to hire additional inspectors. Assistant Secretary Bingham's program would have required states with approved plans to hire 305 new safety inspectors and 1,351 new health inspectors.[51] These new hires would still leave substantial enforcement gaps: Firms in some of the most hazardous industries would likely be inspected only once every 4–5 years, and firms in the least hazardous industries would get inspected only once every 35–50 years.[52]

Auchter found these requirements to be demanding, and he promised that they would be recalculated "more closely [to] reflect current agency policies."[53] In 1982, OSHA successfully sought an appropriations rider prohibiting it from

spending any money to set staffing levels for states that were greater than "levels
. . . determined by the Secretary to be equivalent to federal staffing levels."[54] In
other words, the rider reestablished Assistant Secretary Stender's original policy
(discussed in Chapter 3) of requiring the states to provide the same staffing levels
as OSHA, even if OSHA's staff was too small for effective enforcement. Having
secured this legislation, Auchter issued an order requiring states with approved
plans to have a total of 463 safety inspectors and 289 health inspectors. Because
of OSHA budget cuts during the first two years of the Reagan administration, the
Auchter benchmarks were lower than before Bingham issued her order to increase
the numbers to 1,154 and 1,683 inspectors, respectively.[55] Auchter defended the
severely reduced goals on the ground that more ambitious requirements might
cause state legislatures to cede enforcement back to OSHA, thereby forcing the
federal government to bear an additional $100 million in funding for OSHA.[56]

AUCHTER'S IMPACT

The Auchter policies took their toll on OSHA's effectiveness. Under Auchter,
OSHA conducted about 10,000 more inspections in 1983 to 1984 (around 70,000)
than it did in Bingham's last year (around 60,000). In 1981 and 1982, it conducted
about the same number of inspections.[57] Yet, OSHA found far fewer violations
as compared to 1980. As Figure 10–1 documents, there was a decline of between
13 and 28 percent in the total number of citations from 1981 through 1984
compared with 1980, the last year of the Carter administration. More important,
as Figures 10–2 and 10–3 demonstrate, the number of citations for serious
violations and for willful and repeated violations declined even more drastically
in those years. Compared with 1981, the number of serious citations declined
between 31 and 47 percent and the number of willful and repeat citations declined
between 55 and 70 percent.

Auchter argued that much of the reduction was attributable to the fact that the
states were operating their own OSHA-approved job safety and health programs.[58] The state programs, however, were subject to less supervision under OS-
HA's new policy. Auchter also promised that the agency would "offset a slight
reduction in inspections with better management and a more effective mix of all
the means at the agency's disposal."[59] Another explanation for the combination
of increased numbers of inspections with decreased numbers of citations was the
enormous pressure on the shrinking OSHA inspectorate to engage in "bean counting." OSHA compliance officers testified that during the Auchter period they
were pressured to generate "numbers" of inspections, even though the inspections could not be done thoroughly and therefore did not result in citations.[60]

The lameness of Auchter's excuses for OSHA's poor performance is also
demonstrated by the record of John Pendergrass. Figure 10–1 reveals that OSHA
issued about the same total number of citations from 1986 through 1988 under
Pendergrass that it issued from 1978 through 1980 under Bingham. Figures 10–
2 and 10–3 reveal that in 1988, OSHA issued more serious citations and willful

Figure 10–1
Total Violations Cited (in thousands)

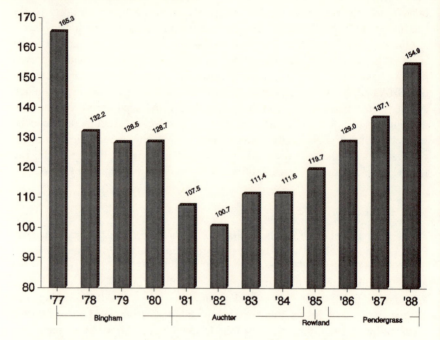

Source: The President's Report on Occupational Safety and Health, 1976–1988.

and repeat citations than in any year during the Carter administration. Unless one is prepared to believe that workplaces were temporarily safer when Auchter ran OSHA, the Pendergrass record strongly suggests that OSHA under Auchter simply failed to look hard enough to find violations.

The combined effect of Auchter's settlement policy and weak enforcement efforts was a dramatic reduction in the total amount of OSHA fines. Figure 10–4 indicates that total proposed penalties declined between 55 and 76 percent from 1981 through 1984 compared with 1980, the last year of the Carter administration. Once again, the abberational nature of Auchter's efforts is indicated by comparing OSHA under John Pendergrass. Figure 10–4 indicates that OSHA returned to the level of penalties assessed during the last year of the Carter administration in 1987 and that it almost doubled that amount by 1988.

As the total amount of the penalties assessed by OSHA during the Auchter administration dropped, OSHA lost its deterrent effect. OSHA inspectors were less likely to recommend stringent enforcement measures when they knew that a settlement reached by their superiors would probably undermine their effectiveness.[61] According to one OSHA expert, Auchter had "come very close to reducing OSHA to the level of irrelevance in the eyes of both business and labor."[62] An OSHA spokesman count-

Figure 10–2
Serious Violations Cited (in thousands)

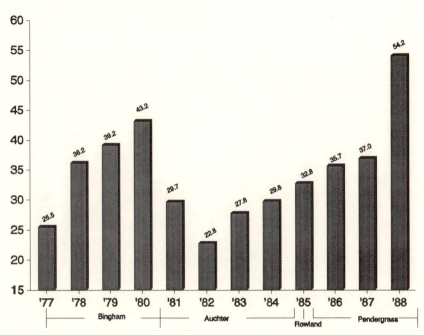

Source: President's Report on Occupational Safety and Health, 1976–1988.

ered that "OSHA's goal is neither to make money nor to punish employers but to abate a hazard as quickly as possible."[63] Auchter proudly announced: "Our philosophy is one of safety and health and not of crime and punishment."[64] Although the backlog of contested cases soon disappeared and the decibel level of employer complaints decreased dramatically, worker safety appeared to play second fiddle to OSHA's efforts to achieve industrial harmony.

For a time, it appeared that OSHA's more conciliatory policies were having a salutary effect. In May 1983, the National Safety Council reported that worker fatalities in 1982 were 35 percent fewer than in 1972. Auchter was quick to take credit for these results, noting that '[t]he idea that management, labor, and government are natural enemies in the workplace is outdated."[65] Auchter did not mention that the 1982 recession had increased unemployment to the highest level since the 1930s and that the decrease might well be attributable to the fact that many fewer workers were on the job in 1982. In any event, as Figure 1–2 in Chapter 1 indicates, workplace injury and fatality statistics were on their way back up by 1984. Former Assistant Secretary Bingham explained that workplace accidents tend to lag behind OSHA policy changes by about three to five years and suggested that the 1984 statistics were the leading ledge of the results of OSHA's enforcement policies under Auchter.[66] Bingham's prediction has proven

Figure 10–3
Willful and Repeat Violations Cited (in thousands)

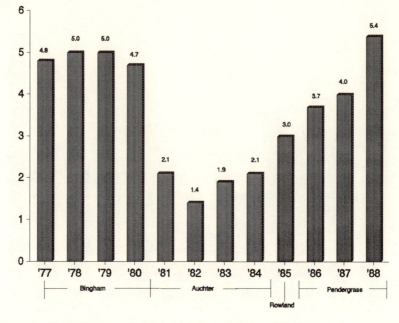

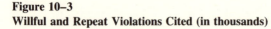

Source: President's Report on Occupational Safety and Health, 1976–1988.

to be accurate. As Chapter 1 discussed, workplace safety statistics remained at the same elevated levels in 1985 and 1986, before jumping again in 1987 and 1988. The number of workdays lost because of work-related injuries, a measure of the seriousness of injuries, was at an all-time high in 1988, four years after Auchter left the agency.

Employers were generally delighted with OSHA's new enforcement programs. An early 1983 survey found that 99 percent of the surveyed employers believed that OSHA inspectors treated them courteously, that inspections were conducted in an impartial manner, and that inspectors appeared knowledgeable about safety and health. The same high proportion of employers said that the inspections were accomplished with a minimal disruption of their work.[67] Employee representatives were less impressed. The vice president of the Oil, Chemical and Atomic Workers Union testified that the voluntary compliance program "has rendered itself impotent and taken away a large incentive for industry to maintain safe and healthful working conditions."[68] Auchter reacted defensively, and in a strongly worded letter to an AFL-CIO official, he announced that OSHA would no longer provide enforcement data to the union.[69]

In a lengthy and more objective report written at the end of Auchter's tenure, the Congressional Office of Technology Assessment reported that OSHA in-

Figure 10–4
Total Proposed Penalties (millions of dollars)

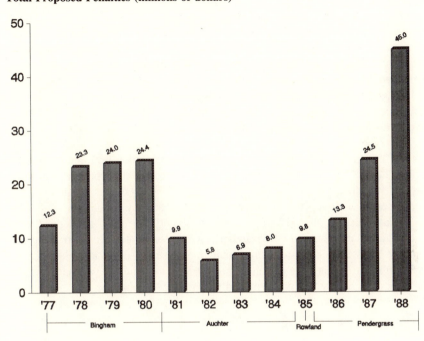

Source: *President's Report on Occupational Safety and Health*, 1976–1988.

spectors were able to visit only about 160,000 of the 4.6 million job sites every year and that the average penalty for a "serious violation" was about $172 in fiscal year 1983. The report concluded that OSHA's inspections were so infrequent and its penalties so low that companies had limited incentive to comply with its standards.[70]

POLITICS IN ENFORCEMENT

At the same time Auchter's deregulation of enforcement left most workers unprotected by OSHA, his obvious disdain for the opinions of the agency's compliance officers in informal settlement conferences had a predictable negative impact on the morale of career OSHA inspectors.[71] Morale was further diminished by Auchter's injection of politics into enforcement policy. He enraged many OSHA employees when he told the headquarters staff that he considered the agency's primary goal for 1984 to be the "campaign of President Reagan."[72] After his remark, reports circulated within the agency that Auchter had personally played a role in forcing the head of OSHA's Denver office, Curtis Foster, to resign because he had failed to halt a planned inspection of a facility run by

Joseph Coors, a prominent Republican and friend of President Reagan.[73] On the day of the attempted inspection, which was supposed to be low on OSHA's priority list, Joseph Coors told a group of his employees that Foster would have to be replaced. That same day, Auchter telephoned Foster and angrily complained that "we need this like we need a hole in the head."[74] Foster's attorney later produced several documents demonstrating that Auchter and his deputy, Mark D. Cowan, visited Coors officials privately before Foster was forced to resign.[75] Although both OSHA and Coors officials denied any favoritism or foul play,[76] the lesson that it was not wise to anger powerful friends of the administration was not lost on the remaining OSHA employees.

In another incident, OSHA inspectors presented a warrant at the B. B. Anderson Construction Company, a large Kansas construction firm, and demanded entry, despite an Auchter-inspired enforcement policy that forbade inspectors from demanding entry to any workplace until obtaining a contempt citation (and, incidentally, allowing the employer time to correct any problems). Auchter's aides later dismissed a $12,680, "extreme gravity" penalty and reprimanded the regional director who had authorized the search for "embarrassing the agency." After electing to retire rather than accept a demotion, the regional director reported that other regional administrators told him that they had "backed off" or "gone easy" on firms owned by wealthy Republicans.[77]

PENDERGRASS TAKES OVER

By the time John Pendergrass became assistant secretary in 1986, many of the deficiencies of Auchter's policies had become evident. One of the problems with OSHA's targeting policies—the exclusion of several dangerous industries—was brought to public attention in the wake of a tragedy at a fireworks plant in June 1985 near Hallett, Oklahoma, in which 21 persons were killed. Reporters discovered that OSHA had never inspected the plant, and it was not even on OSHA's inspection list. A deputy regional administrator in Dallas explained: "We only have so many resources and compliance officers to go around, so we try and focus our compliance and inspection activities on these industries where, as a whole, employees are at a great degree of risk." AFL-CIO Safety and Health Director Margaret Seminario, however, replied that "[t]he fact of the matter is that the agency has a small inspection staff—fewer than 1200 inspectors nationwide—and they've never really focused in a manner that insures adequate coverage."[78] In addition, Auchter's policy of basing inspections on employer safety records had predictable effects. Well-publicized congressional hearings revealed that employers kept fraudulent logs of employee injuries.[79]

Pendergrass acted to address both of these deficiencies. He expanded the basis for selecting employers beyond a "record review" comparison of the firm's lost workday rate against the average rate. Beginning in 1988, employers were also chosen for inspection based on their history of workplace fatalities.[80] In addition, every tenth programmed inspection in high-hazard industries was to be a comprehensive inspection, regardless of the firm's prior lost workday rate.[81] An inspector was also at liberty to inspect a firm with an above-average rate if he or she detected any discrepancies in its accident logs, if an imminent hazard was in open view, if the record review indicated an unusual number or type of injuries, or if an employee representative filed a safety complaint.[82] Record inspections were expanded to include a review not only of a firm's injury and health logs but also of its compliance with the hazard communication standard and of its safety and health management programs.[83] Finally, Pendergrass quickly reinstituted OSHA's "wall-to-wall" complaint inspection policy, which Auchter had repealed, so that inspections were not limited to the areas of the workplace identified by specific complaints.[84] These changes had a real impact. As noted earlier, Figures 10–1 to 10–3 reveal an increase in the total number of citations, serious citations, and willful and repeat citations. In 1988, Pendergrass's last year, the number of citations in the last two categories was the largest since 1977, and the number of total citations was the second largest.

Pendergrass also acted to stem the rash of false reporting of workplace injuries. OSHA sought to guarantee the accuracy of injury logs by levying large fines, often ranging from $100,000 to $1 million, against employers that deliberately failed to keep accurate records. For example, in September 1987, OSHA proposed a fine of $813,000 against Scott Paper Company because of willful underreporting of injuries at its Winslow, Maine, plant.[85] Although many union officials viewed the record-keeping crackdown as an image-building effort that diverted resources from actual health and safety problems,[86] others supported the effort as a necessary means of ensuring accurate occupational safety statistics.[87]

Pendergrass also acted against another type of cheating by modifying Auchter's follow-up policy to require that every tenth targeted safety inspection be a complete inspection, regardless of whether the injury rates were above the average, in order to "spot check" to ensure compliance.[88] Nevertheless, the agency continued to have problems securing abatement. A Department of Labor inspector general's report found that in the two regions it studied, there was insufficient or no evidence that abatement had occurred in 35 percent of the cases studied.[89] OSHA responded that it had already identified those two regions "as having severe problems," and it promised additional reforms.[90]

MEGA-FINES

Although the foregoing steps were essential for reestablishing a credible enforcement program, another Pendergrass initiative received more attention in the media. Early in his tenure, OSHA began the practice of proposing very large "mega-fines" in cases where employers had acted in a flagrant or egregious manner.[91] In such cases, OSHA did not "bundle" the violations but instead assessed a penalty for each violation of up to $10,000, the maximum amount for a willful violation.[92] The first evidence of the new policy came in April 1986, when OSHA assessed a $1.38 million fine against Union Carbide's Institute, West Virginia, plant.[93] By comparison, in the first six years of the Reagan administration, OSHA assessed no fine that exceeded $100,000. The fine was OSHA's first proposed penalty of more than $1 million, and it was quickly followed by additional "mega-fines." Between early 1986, when Pendergrass assumed office, and late 1988 the agency proposed penalties in excess of $500,000 12 times, and in 2 cases they ranged as high as $4 million and $5 million.[94] OSHA's largest proposed fine under Pendergrass was slightly more than $5 million against the contractors in the L'Ambience Plaza building collapse in Bridgeport, Connecticut, which took 28 lives.[95]

The mega-fine program dramatically increased the total amount of proposed penalties. Figure 10–4 indicates that OSHA proposed penalties totaling $45.0 million in 1988, almost double the $24.5 million dollars in proposed penalties that were assessed in 1987. While this dramatic increase earned OSHA headlines, it gradually became apparent that few companies actually paid those fines. Long before a company actually wrote a check to the United States Treasury, OSHA and company officials would meet to work out a mutually agreeable settlement of the dispute. From 1986 to 1988, OSHA settled 9 of 11 cases with proposed penalties that exceeded $100,000 for reductions ranging from a low of 31.8 percent to a high of 89.2 percent.[96] The L'Ambience Plaza enforcement action was settled for $437,000,[97] approximately $15,600 per lost life. OSHA's attitude toward settlement of the mega-fines was consistent with its general settlement policy during the Pendergrass years of reducing proposed penalties by as much as 50 percent[98] and providing that employers who settled did not have to admit any violations.[99]

PENDERGRASS'S IMPACT

Union representatives were generally supportive of Pendergrass's changes in OSHA's inspection practices.[100] Pendergrass not only surpassed the weak record of Thorne Auchter but he bettered OSHA's efforts during Eula Bingham's last year in all but one relevant statistical category. Yet, not all workers benefited from OSHA's renewed enforcement efforts. The United Steelworkers Union pointed out that "upon closer examination, it is clear that the majority of strong enforcement actions have come in response to a tragedy, a union complaint, a situation subject to media attention or where there is a particularly aggressive inspector or area director."[101] Enforcement activity in other areas continued to lag. The percentage of workplaces in compliance with the field sanitation standard declined from 60 percent to 45 percent from fiscal year 1987 to the middle of 1988.[102] Based on a survey of 21 farms in New York, the Farmworker Legal Services Corporation of New York found a "gross noncompliance" with the field sanitation regulations.[103] The agency admitted that compliance with the field sanitation standard was not high enough, and it attempted to put more resources into that effort.[104]

CONCLUSIONS

OSHA has stumbled through most of its history from program to inconsistent program in attempting to enforce its standards. During OSHA's early years, the agency's largely meaningless enforcement activities aroused the ire of the unions (because enforcement was weak) and of businesses (because they were constantly cited for minor violations). The substantial progress achieved under Eula Bingham quickly dissipated during Thorne Auchter's tenure. His changes in OSHA's programmed inspections, complaint-initiated inspections, and follow-up inspections all resulted in less effective enforcement. At the same time that he attempted to turn more enforcement authority over to the states, he reduced OSHA's oversight of state enforcement activities. Auchter virtually ignored OSHA's power to initiate criminal prosecutions. All of this made Auchter popular with business, but it did little or nothing to fulfill the agency's responsibility to protect workers. John Pendergrass quickly reversed the most egregious of Auchter's deregulatory initiatives. These changes and Pendergrass's mega-fine program projected a considerably tougher image than during the first five years of the Reagan administration, and they returned OSHA's enforcement activity to Carter administration levels. For workers, however, a return to the Carter era was not enough, because too many standards were poorly enforced even at that time. For all the good he accomplished, Pendergrass did not solve the fundamental dilemma of too few inspectors and too many employers to inspect.

NOTES

1. U.S. Congress, Senate Committee on Labor and Human Resources, *Hearings on Oversight on the Administration of the Occupational Safety and Health Act*, 100th Congress, 2d sess., S. Hrg. 100–719, 1988, 31 (hereafter Senate, *Oversight Hearings of 1988*).

2. National Safe Workplace Institute, *Safer Work: Job Safety and Health Challenges for the Next President and Congress* (Chicago: The Institute, 1988), 15.

3. *BNA Occupational Safety and Health Reporter* 11 (1 Oct. 1981): 339; Michael Wines, "Auchter's Record at OSHA Leaves Labor Outraged, Business Satisfied," *National Journal* 15 (1 Oct. 1983): 2008.

4. Senate, *Oversight Hearings of 1988*, 31.

5. U.S. Congress, Senate Committee on Labor and Human Resources, Subcommittee on Investigations and General Oversight and Subcommittee on Labor, *Administration of the Occupational Safety and Health Act*, 97th Cong., 1st sess., 1981, 171.

6. Wines, "Auchter's Record," 2008.

7. Senate, *Oversight Hearings of 1988*, 120–21.

8. Sierra Club, *Poisons on the Job: The Reagan Administration and American Workers* (San Francisco: Sierra Club Books, 1982), 19.

9. *BNA Occupational Safety and Health Reporter* 13 (17 Nov. 1983): 1660.

10. National Safe Workplace Institute, *Failed Opportunities: The Decline—U.S. Job Safety in the 1980's* (Chicago: The Institute, 1988), 10.

11. Senate, *Oversight Hearings of 1988*, 25.

12. U.S. Congress, House Committee on Government Operations, Subcommittee on Employment and Housing, *Hearings on the Adequacy of OSHA Protections for Chemical Workers*, pt. 2, 101st Cong., 2d sess., 1990, 72 (statement of Representative Tom Lantos).

13. Senate, *Oversight Hearings of 1988*, 540.

14. Bryan Burrough and Seth H. Lubove, "Credibility Gap: Some Concerns Fudge Their Safety Records to Cut Insurance Costs," *Wall Street Journal*, 2 Dec. 1986, 1, col. 6.

15. U.S. Congress, House Committee on Government Operations, *Hearings on Underreporting of Occupational Injuries and Its Impact on Workers' Safety*, pt. 1, 100th Cong., 1st sess., 1987, 10 (hereafter cited as House, *Underreporting*).

16. *BNA Occupational Safety and Health Reporter* 16 (25 Mar. 1987): 1107.

17. Ibid.

18. House, *Underreporting*, 44, 49–52.

19. *BNA Occupational Safety and Health Reporter* 17 (22 July 1987): 235.

20. Senate, *Oversight Hearings of 1988*, 125–26.

21. U.S. Congress, House Committee on Government Operations, *Hearings on OSHA Enforcement Policy*, 98th Cong., 1st sess., 1983, 105 (hereafter cited as House, *OSHA Enforcement*) (testimony of Margaret Seminario, associate director, Department of Occupational Safety, Health and Social Security, AFL-CIO)

22. Senate, *Oversight Hearings of 1988*, 126.

23. House, *OSHA Enforcement*, 22 (testimony of Thorne G. Auchter).

24. Ibid., 106 (testimony of Margaret Seminario); Benjamin W. Mintz, "Occupational Safety and Health: The Federal Regulatory Program—A History," in *Fundamentals of Industrial Hygiene*, 3d ed., ed. Barbara A. Plog (Washington, D.C.: National Safety Council, 1988), 715.

25. Felicity Barringer, " 'Bureaucratic Surrender'; OSHA Blasted by Nader Group," *Washington Post*, 5 Sept. 1983, A15, col. 3.

26. Senate, *Oversight Hearings of 1988*, 540.

27. Ibid., 65, 130; *BNA Occupational Safety and Health Reporter* 13 (17 Nov. 1983): 660.

28. Mark Rothstein, "OSHA After Ten Years: A Review and Some Proposed Reforms," *Vanderbilt Law Review* 34 (1981): 115–19.

29. General Accounting Office, *Informal Settlement of OSHA Citations: Comments on the Legal Basis and Other Selected Issues* (Washington, D.C.: United States Government Printing Office, 1984).

30. Senate, *Oversight Hearings of 1988*, 28–29.

31. Ibid.

32. General Accounting Office, *Informal Settlement*, 5.

33. Pete Early, "Glowing Reports," *Washington Post*, 14 July 1982, A19, col. 6.

34. House, *OSHA Enforcement*, 18 (testimony of Thorne G. Auchter).

35. Ibid.

36. Wines, "Auchter's Record," 2008.

37. *BNA Occupational Safety and Health Reporter* 13 (21 July 1983): 171.

38. Ibid.

39. Wines, "Auchter's Record," 2010.

40. Mintz, "A History," 716; Felicity Barringer, "Enforcers Proposed for OSHA: STAR, PRIME and PRAISE," *Washington Post*, 18 Jan. 1982, A9, col. 1.

41. Barringer, "Enforcers Proposed."

42. *BNA Occupational Safety and Health Reporter* 12 (21 Oct. 1982): 404–05.

43. Sierra Club, *Poisons on the Job*, 19–20.

44. Phillip Simon, *Reagan in the Workplace: Unraveling the Health and Safety Net*, Center for Study of Responsible Law, report no. 173, Sept. 1983, 1; Barringer, "Bureaucratic Surrender"; *BNA Occupational Safety and Health Reporter* 13 (8 Sept. 1983): 348.

45. Barringer, "Bureaucratic Surrender."

46. Philip J. Hilts, "Reagan's OSHA Files First Criminal Case," *Washington Post*, 30 Sept. 1982, A21, col. 5.

47. *BNA Occupational Safety and Health Reporter* 21 (21 Aug. 1991): 347.

48. U.S. Congress, Senate Committee on Government Affairs, Subcommittee on Intergovernmental Regulations, *Hearings on State Implementation of Federal Standards*, pt. 2, 97th Cong., 1st sess., 1981, 24–25 (hereafter cited as Senate, *State Implementation*).

49. *BNA Occupational Safety and Health Reporter* 11 (9 July 1981): 112.

50. Ibid. 14 (18 Apr. 1985): 896.

51. Mintz, "A History," 717; Benjamin W. Mintz, *OSHA: History, Law, and Policy* (Washington, D.C.: Bureau of National Affairs, 1984), 641, 644–45.

52. U.S. Congress, House Committee on Education and Labor, Subcommittee on Health and Safety, *Oversight Hearings on OSHA—Occupational Safety and Health Act for Federal Employees, Part 4, State Plans*, 96th Cong., 2d sess., 1980, 492–93.

53. Senate, *State Implementation*, 19.

54. Supplemental Appropriations Act of 1982, P.L. 97–257, tit. I, ch.IX, 96 Stat. 818, 844 (1982).

55. Mintz, *History, Law and Policy*, 644–45.

56. Ibid., 645.

57. Occupational Safety and Health Administration, *Report of the President to the Congress on Occupational Safety and Health for Calendar Year 1985* (Washington, D.C.: United States Government Printing Office, 42; Occupational Safety and Health Administration, *Report of the President to the Congress on Occupational Safety and Health for Calendar Year 1984* (Washington, D.C.: United States Government Printing Office, 1985), 53; Rothstein, "OSHA After Ten Years," 94.

58. Thorne Auchter, "OSHA Is Not Backsliding," *Washington Post*, 26 Dec. 1981, A19, col. 6.

59. Ibid.

60. Senate, *Oversight Hearings of 1988*, 572.

61. Ibid., 540–41.

62. Wines, "Auchter's Record," 2008.

63. Felicity Barringer, "Grain Elevator May Be Let Down Easy; $8,000 Would End Case," *Washington Post*, 31 Dec. 1981, A13.

64. Christine Russell, "Auchter Calls Report 'Hogwash'; Nader Group Study Calls OSHA Too Lax," *Washington Post*, 9 November 1982, A19.

65. *BNA Occupational Safety and Health Reporter* 12 (26 May 1983): 1105–06.

66. Robert L. Simison, "Safety Last: Job Deaths and Injuries Seem to Be Increasing After Years of Decline," *Wall Street Journal*, 18 Mar. 1986, 1, col. 6.

67. *BNA Occupational Safety and Health Reporter* 12 (21 Apr. 1983): 979.

68. Ibid. 14 (18 Apr. 1985): 896.

69. Ibid. 12 (10 June 1982): 27–28.

70. U.S. Congress, Office of Technology Assessment, *Preventing Illness and Injury*

in the Workplace (Washington, D.C.: The Office, 1985), 13–15; Kenneth B. Noble, "Study Faults U.S. on Safety Effort," *New York Times*, 18 Apr. 1985, 11, col. 1.

71. Senate, *Oversight Hearings of 1988*, 540.

72. *Pesticide and Toxic Chemical News* 11 (30 Nov. 1983): 6; *BNA Occupational Safety and Health Reporter* 13 (15 Dec. 1983): 781.

73. *BNA Occupational Safety and Health Reporter* 13 (19 Apr. 1984): 1254.

74. Ibid. (12 Apr. 1984): 1201.

75. Pete Earley, "The Skimmed-off Bureaucrat; Official Lays Plight to Brewery Magnate, Wants His Job Back," *Washington Post*, 21 Aug. 1984, A13, col. 4.

76., Ibid.; *BNA Occupational Safety and Health Reporter* 13 (19 Apr. 1984): 1251–52.

77. Pete Earley and Rick Atkinson, "'Auchter's Act Aided Company," *Washington Post*, 13 Mar. 1984, A2, col. 1; Leonard M. Apcar, "OSHA Chief Backed Killing Fine Against His New Employer," *Wall Street Journal*, 14 Mar. 1984, 13, col. 1; *BNA Occupational Safety and Health Reporter* 13 (31 May 1984): 1358–59.

78. Kenneth B. Noble, "Work Safety Agency Never Checked Fatal Factory," *New York Times*, 27 June 1985, 10, col. 1.

79. House, *Underreporting*.

80. *BNA Occupational Safety and Health Reporter* 17 (1 July 1987): 173.

81. Mintz, "A History," 715.

82. *OSHA Field Operations Manual*, Ch.III, General Inspection Policies, IID4b, in *BNA Occupational Safety and Health Reporter [Reference File]*, 77: 2516–17.

83. Ibid.; Senate, *Oversight Hearings of 1988*, 26.

84. "U.S. Safety Inspectors to Examine Factories, Not Just Injury Records," *New York Times*, 23 Mar. 1988, A.18, col. 1.

85. Albert R. Karr, "OSHA Proposes Fining Scott Paper Total of $813,000," *Wall Street Journal*, 28 Sept. 1987, 30, col. 5.

86. William Glaberson, "Is OSHA Falling Down on the Job?" *New York Times*. 2 Aug. 1987, sec. 3, 1, col. 2.

87. House, *Underreporting*, 163–64 (testimony of Mary-Win O'Brien, assistant General council, United Steelworkers of America).

88. Ibid., 118, 123 (testimony of John Pendergrass, assistant secretary for occupational safety and health).

89. National Safe Workplace Institute, *The Rising Wave: Death and Injury Among High Risk Workers in the 1980s* (Chicago: The Institute, 1987), 11; *BNA Occupational Safety and Health Reporter* 17 (1 July 1987): 171.

90. *BNA Occupational Safety and Health Reporter* 17 (23 Sept. 1987): 742.

91. Senate, *Oversight Hearings of 1988*, 746 (testimony of John Pendergrass).

92. *OSHA Field Operations Manual*, Ch. V, Citations, C, in *BNA Occupational Safety and Health Reporter [Reference File]*, 77:2910–11.

93. Kenneth B. Noble, "Union Carbide Faces Fine of $1.4 Million on Safety Violations," *New York Times*, 2 Apr. 1986, 1, col. 5; *BNA Occupational Safety and Health Reporter* 15 (10 Apr. 1986): 1115.

94. Senate, *Oversight Hearings of 1988*, 762 (testimony of John Pendergrass).

95. *BNA Occupational Safety and Health Reporter* 18 (23 Nov. 1988): 1171.

96. National Safe Workplace Institute, *Failed Opportunities*, 19.

97. *BNA Occupational Safety and Health Reporter* 18 (23 Nov. 1988): 1171.

98. Stephen Bokat and Horace Thompson III, eds., *Occupational Safety and Health Law* (Washington, D.C.: Bureau of National Affairs, 1988), 316.

99. *BNA Occupational Safety and Health Reporter* 16 (4 Feb. 1987): 963.

100. Senate, *Oversight Hearings of 1988*, 26.

101. Ibid.

102. Ibid., 843.

103. Ibid., 793–94.

104. Ibid., 843.

11

The Bush Years: An Identity Crisis

President Bush's record as head of the President's Task Force on Regulatory Relief did not inspire much optimism that he would make occupational safety and health a visible priority for his new administration. His appointment of Washington, D.C., veteran Elizabeth Dole as secretary of labor therefore came as a pleasant surprise to labor representatives. At her confirmation hearings, she promised to implement more effective OSHA rulemaking procedures, to enforce existing standards with greater vigor, and to attempt to clarify the Office of Management and Budget's role in standard-setting.[1] In a speech to labor unions, Dole lauded the extension of the hazard communication standard to the construction industry and the promulgation of the permissible exposure limit (PEL) update standard, and she promised even more intensive efforts to expedite the rulemaking process.[2] Secretary Dole, however, resigned after only 18 months to head the American Red Cross,[3] and her low-profile successor, Lynn Martin, made little of worker health and safety issues.

Notwithstanding her strong endorsement of OSHA, Secretary Dole was unable to find an immediate replacement for Assistant Secretary Pendergrass. By mid-April 1989, several important safety standards were awaiting the signature of the new assistant secretary, and the agency appeared rudderless.[4] Finally, in June 1989, President Bush nominated Gerard F. Scannell, the director of safety and environmental affairs for Johnson & Johnson Co., to be OSHA's head. He was very experienced in occupational safety and health issues, having served as director of the Office of Health and Safety Standards under Assistant Secretary Guenther. Scannell was not, however, confirmed by the Senate until October 10, 1989.[5]

Scannell continued OSHA's trend toward more vigorous enforcement, doling out mega-fines on a regular basis. Agency morale continued at a relatively high level, and Scannell's "open door" policy helped reduce criticisms from outsiders in business and labor.[6] Although Scannell mercifully declined to reorganize the agency, he did establish a Policy Review Board within OSHA to "centralize and formalize" agency decision making.[7] The agency's progress in the area of standard-setting was nevertheless quite disappointing. To some extent, OSHA's ponderous pace reflected the influence of a new oversight entity, created by President Bush in 1990, called the Council on Competitiveness. This institution, which was composed of several cabinet members (not including the secretary of labor) and chaired by Vice President Quayle, soon replaced OMB as the venue of choice for industries seeking to halt or overturn OSHA rules.[8] As we shall see in more detail in Chapter 15, the council relied heavily upon private meetings with the regulated industry to bring regulatory excesses to its attention.

TYING UP LOOSE ENDS

The agency had a full plate of pending actions when Scannell finally assumed the helm. Although OSHA made a good-faith effort to finish these projects in an expeditious fashion, OMB and the Competitiveness Council slowed things down considerably.

Formaldehyde

Despite strong evidence that formaldehyde posed a high cancer risk to thousands of workers, Thorne Auchter, and later OMB, successfully forestalled any action against this commercially valuable product until December 1987, when the agency promulgated a final rule. The rule was ultimately remanded by the District of Columbia Circuit Court of Appeals in June 1989. After Scannell inherited the remand of this controversial chemical, the agency continued to receive new evidence on formaldehyde's toxic effects. A NIOSH study of workers at a Kentucky garment manufacturing plant detected an elevated level of birth defects among female workers who were exposed to formaldehyde.[9]

During the summer of 1990, labor and industry representatives met on several occasions in an attempt to avoid further litigation, and they were able to hammer out an agreement under which OSHA would reduce the PEL for formaldehyde from 1 ppm to 0.75 ppm. OSHA drafted a proposed rule incorporating the substance of the agreed-upon changes and submitted it to OMB in August 1990. Unfortunately, OMB apparently was not interested in an amicable resolution of the controversy, and it returned the proposal to OSHA for reconsideration.

In addition to rejecting an agreed-upon resolution of a long-standing dispute, OMB's intervention into the formaldehyde rulemaking was extraordinary in two regards. First, it provided legal advice to OSHA about what the court of appeals had required of the agency when it remanded the standard. In a letter of November 28, 1990, to OSHA, OMB's economists interpreted the court's opinion merely to require OSHA to write an explanation for its 1987 rule, not to write a new standard. In particular, OMB criticized the agency for including provisions for hazard communication and worker training that were not part of the original rule.[10] OMB's letter did not explain how the decisions would be vulnerable if no one challenged them in court. Second, exchanging its attorney hat for its scientist cap, OMB opined that OSHA had not sufficiently demonstrated that formaldehyde posed a significant risk at the 1 ppm level. According to OMB, a recent EPA risk assessment had "proven" that OSHA's risk assessment was wrong. An internal EPA memorandum, however, called OMB's conclusions "rather severe misconceptions."[11] A representative for the United Auto Workers complained that OMB took a "narrow view of the remand issues," and noted that it was "typical of OMB's 'battle to the last man' approach to prevent improvement of OSHA standards."[12]

In April 1991, the union petitioned the court of appeals to order OSHA to respond to the court's two-year-old remand by a date certain. In OSHA's reply brief, the Justice Department argued that the union was "denigrat[ing] the importance of presidential oversight of executive branch agencies."[13] Secretary Dole's promise to "clarify" OMB's role in OSHA rulemaking had apparently succeeded—OMB was now clearly the boss. The court denied the union's petition on May 10, 1991 in a brief opinion that seemed to confirm OMB's authority to slow things down. The court found that OSHA had "adequately explained the delay complained of by setting forth the necessity of complying with Executive Order 12291, an assertion that has not been contested."[14]

It later became apparent that a new kid on the regulatory block stood behind OMB's reinvigorated authority. In the summer of 1990, President Bush replaced the defunct Task Force on Regulatory Relief, which he had headed, with the Council on Competitiveness, chaired by Vice President Quayle and staffed by an ardent deregulator and former businessman from Indiana, Allan Hubbard. Unlike the task force, the Competitiveness Council was not content to sit as an appellate body to resolve disputes between OMB and the other agencies. This new entity assumed a proactive role of seeking out offensive rules and destroying them. According to a highly critical report on the Competitiveness Council, the formaldehyde rule was the first OSHA rule to come before OMB after the council went into operation, and the council wanted to establish a strong deregulatory precedent, even though the regulated industry did not oppose the standard.[15]

The proposal was published on July 15, 1991.[16] Since the proposal was indistinguishable from the proposal that OSHA had sent to OMB almost a year earlier, Frank Mirer, director of occupational safety and health for the United Auto Workers, complained that "[t]he extra delay by OMB has needlessly prolonged the risk to workers," and that the process "proved to me how bankrupt an idea a negotiated standard is."[17] At the time that OSHA proposed the formaldehyde regulation, it had been under consideration for 11 years. The impact of the delay on workers was considerable. Although it is impossible to know how many cases of cancer could have been prevented if OSHA had acted more rapidly, one scientist has estimated that worker exposure to formaldehyde levels above 1 ppm during the delay produced nearly 6,000 cases of respiratory irritation and 11,000 cases of dermatitis.[18]

Bloodborne Diseases

OSHA under Scannell also completed a significant rulemaking concerning bloodborne diseases. The proposed bloodborne diseases standard attracted a great deal of public comment at hearings held at several locations during the fall of 1989 and winter of 1990. The unions were generally satisfied with the proposal, but they argued that the OMB-inspired exception from "universal precautions" when they would "interfere with the proper delivery of health care or public safety services" was "a loophole you could drive a truck through." They also objected to OSHA's deletion, at OMB insistence, of a general statement expressing a preference for engineering and work practice controls over personal protective devices,[19] and they suggested that OSHA's cost estimates were greatly inflated and its risk estimates were too low.[20] The health care industry was not as supportive. Many commentators objected to the requirement that employers provide free hepatitis B vaccinations and to the specificity of the protective clothing requirements.[21] One union spokesperson ridiculed the industry testimony, suggesting that it presented the absurd specter of "OSHA inspectors in dirty workboots breaking down the operating room door in the middle of brain surgery, passing out $10,000 citations like parking tickets, and then heading off to wreak similar havoc on the maternity ward."[22]

A study by the National Institutes of Health indicating that occupational groups in laboratory medicine experienced hepatitis B infections at a rate seven to ten times greater than the general public[23] gave renewed impetus to the rulemaking proceedings, as did reports of the death of the first health care worker accidentally infected with the HIV virus.[24] After the Senate passed an appropriations rider requiring OSHA to complete the proceeding by the end of 1991,[25] the agency promulgated the final rule on December 6, 1991, more than a year and a half after the close of the comment period.[26] The final rule closely resembled the proposal, except that it deleted the OMB-required proviso to the "universal precautions" section that had so angered the unions, and it specified somewhat more detailed provisions for personal protective devices.

Although it was a long time in coming, the bloodborne diseases rule must be regarded as another success for OSHA. The agency waded into the uncharted terrain of infectious diseases to address a pressing occupational health problem, and it came up with a mix of performance-oriented, engineering, and work practice controls that went considerably beyond a general injunction to employees to "be careful." At the same time OSHA successfully resisted OMB's attempts to weaken the rule with a large loophole and to use the initiative as an opportunity to signal a rejection of the agency's preference for engineering and work practice controls over personal protective devices. The nature of the hazard of bloodborne diseases demands that personal protective devices play a prominent role in ensuring employee safety, but OSHA identified many additional protections that could be engineered into the physical plant and into the standard operating procedures of workplaces in which employees could be exposed to infectious bloodborne diseases.

Smoking in the Workplace

We saw in Chapter 9 that Assistant Secretary Pendergrass was reluctant to take up the controversial issue of smoking in the workplace. In July 1989, an anti-smoking group, Action on Smoking and Health (ASH), filed a lawsuit challenging OSHA's failure to respond to its petition for an emergency temporary standard banning smoking in the workplace. On September 1, 1989, OSHA denied the petition, finding that the existing data did not establish that workplace smoking posed a "grave danger" to workers. Since the data did demonstrate a positive correlation between passive smoke and lung cancer in homes, however, OSHA agreed to study whether a full-fledged standard should be promulgated.[27] Recognizing that the smoking issue was "one which OSHA probably will have to face in the 1990s,"[28] Scannell announced almost a year later that OSHA was contemplating publishing an advance notice of proposed rulemaking (ANPR). Six months later, in October 1990, Scannell agreed that OSHA would have to address the smoking issue soon, but decided to wait until the completion of two studies that were undergoing review by EPA's Science Advisory Board (SAB).[29] In January 1991, the SAB approved the EPA reports, one of which estimated that 3,700 lung cancer deaths per year were attributable to environmental tobacco smoke.[30] Nevertheless, OSHA rejected ASH's renewed request that it issue an emergency temporary standard,[31] and the District of Columbia Circuit Court of Appeals upheld that refusal on May 10, 1991.[32]

Still, the issue refused to go away. A controversial study prepared by a University of California scientist concluding that passive smoking caused 53,000 deaths per year (including all kinds of cancer and heart disease)[33] and a National Institute of Occupational Safety and Health (NIOSH) recommendation that smoking should be eliminated from the workplace whenever possible[34] generated renewed calls for banning smoking in the workplace. Finally, on September 20, 1991, OSHA issued an ANPR inviting comments on whether it should promulgate a standard for workplace smoking.[35]

Although Scannell indicated at the outset of his term that OSHA would have to address workplace smoking sooner or later, the agency ultimately elected to do it later. One reason that OSHA has been very reluctant to regulate this well-recognized workplace hazard is that it has been opposed by employers and unions alike.[36] It is difficult enough for OSHA to promulgate an occupational health rule when the unions press ahead at full tilt. When the unions oppose a rulemaking initiative, a final rule may be impossible. In the case of smoking, the union representing tobacco workers came to the forefront of organized labor, and the scientists and health activists were pushed to the rear. Under such conditions, a comprehensive workplace smoking standard is highly unlikely.

Personal Protective Devices

The last issue that Scannell inherited from his predecessor was the always controversial question of personal protective devices. The initiative dated back to 1981, when the Task Force on Regulatory Relief demanded that OSHA reassess its traditional preference for engineering and work practice controls. As Chapter 8 discussed, OSHA quietly abandoned its reassessment effort in early 1983.

The issue was forcefully revived in the summer of 1989 when OSHA published a notice of proposed rulemaking that proposed several ways to "incorporate additional flexibility in its methods of compliance by more explicitly setting forth the circumstances under which respiratory protection may be used in lieu of engineering controls."[37] The proposal identified five generic situations in which the agency would allow employers to use respirators without demonstrating the infeasibility of engineering controls. In addition, OSHA floated as a tribal balloon the suggestion that each employer be allocated a "respirator budget" of man-years in which respirators could be substituted for engineering controls in situations in which exposure is normally brief and intermittent. Similarly, OSHA raised the possibility of using respirators as a substitute for engineering controls for meeting short-term exposure limits for especially dangerous chemicals.[38]

Although some of the generic situations that OSHA identified were relatively uncontroversial (e.g., emergency rescue situations), the unions opposed OSHA's other proposals. A spokesman for the Amalgamated Clothing and Textile Workers Union suggested: "Any effort on OSHA's part to carve out these exceptions to the primacy of engineering controls must be recognized for its true meaning: an attempt to whittle away at this otherwise well-established industrial hygiene principle in the hierarchy of methods to control exposure."[39] At hearings on the proposal, conducted in May 1990, NIOSH and outside experts, including former Assistant Secretary Morton Corn, spoke out against using respirators as a long-term substitute for engineering controls, arguing that it was impossible to identify generic situations in which engineering controls would not be preferable.[40] They also pointed out that respirator use requirements were much more difficult to enforce than engineering controls. Industry comments were generally favorable, but many companies argued that OSHA should go all the way and allow employers complete flexibility to substitute respirators for engineering controls in situations in which the employers determined that respirators afforded equivalent protection.[41]

After this brief flurry of activity, the proposal once again faded from public view. OSHA's ultimate disposition of this proposed rule will indicate whether OSHA will shed its longtime identity with a health and safety orientation, and substitute a more economic-oriented approach. The source of OSHA's opposition to personal protective devices is the professional judgment of the agency's industrial hygienists and other health professionals that such devices do not protect workers as well as engineering and work practice controls. Economists at OMB have continually taken potshots at this position, but OSHA has preferred to rely on the advice of its own scientists. Whether OMB will ultimately prevail remains to be seen.

NEW SAFETY INITIATIVES

Scannell was able to finish only one of the rulemaking initiatives that he inherited, and that regulation was the subject of a congressional deadline. He posted a similar record for new safety initiatives. The agency made some progress on a motor vehicle safety standard, made less progress on an ergonomics regulation, and completed a safety standard for the petrochemical industry—but only after Congress imposed a mandatory deadline.

Motor Vehicle Safety

Secretary Dole had been the secretary of transportation during the latter part of the Reagan administration, and she carried to her new job a commitment to seat belts for protecting the drivers and passengers of motor vehicles. She strongly believed that OSHA should also address the common hazard of motor vehicle accidents. Prior to his confirmation, Scannell promised that he would make motor vehicle safety a high OSHA priority.[42] A modest initiative was already under way at OSHA as a result of a 1988 petition from the National Safety Council.[43] With remarkable speed, OSHA published a notice of proposed rulemaking on July 12, 1990, about a year after Scannell's confirmation.[44] OSHA made a strong case for regulation. The preamble to the proposal estimated that approximately 2,100 fatalities and 91,000 lost workdays occurred annually as a result of motor vehicle accidents. In 1987 alone, motor vehicle crashes constituted around 36 percent of all occupational fatalities.[45]

The proposal required employers to adopt and enforce a vehicle occupant protection program that included requiring all employees to wear seat belts. The unions and safety organizations generally favored the proposal, while industry complained that it was "burdensome and unnecessary." The proposed regulation attracted surprisingly little resistance from OMB and the Competitiveness Council, perhaps because it focused primarily on employee conduct rather than requiring engineering solutions.[46] As a representative of the Insurance Institute for Highway Safety noted, "We're really not talking about brain surgery here; the U.S. has lagged behind industrial nations with mandatory belt use."[47] Nevertheless, the agency was unable to publish a final rule by its own deadline of January 1, 1992.

Ergonomics and Robotics

The science of ergonomics is the study of how workers relate physically and psychologically to their employment environment. Although engineers have been designing tools and work environments to fit the strengths and limitations of the human body for centuries, public attention has increasingly focused upon repetitive motion disorders and other cumulative trauma problems suffered by workers in the modern computerized workplace. Repetitive motion disorders, such as carpal tunnel syndrome, have been detected in a wide variety of workers, including poultry processors,[48] grocery checkers,[49] and users of video display terminals.[50] Indeed, Bureau of Labor Statistics data indicate that almost half of all occupational illnesses and injuries are cumulative trauma disorders.[51] Similarly, the new technology of robotics has focused attention on how best to design the workplace to avoid accidents caused by interactions between humans and robots.[52]

After several well-publicized incidents of cumulative trauma disorders in meat-packing plants, OSHA in 1990 issued voluntary guidelines for the meat-packing industry.[53] It had issued general informational guidelines on robotics in late 1987.[54] Although it circulated a draft ANPR on ergonomics in June 1991,[55] it accomplished little else during Scannell's term. The agency balked at the suggestion that it promulgate a legally binding ergonomics standard for all industries.

A congressional committee was not satisfied with the agency's slow pace in developing an enforceable ergonomics standard. Complaining of a "national epidemic" of cumulative trauma disorders, Representative Tom Lantos told Scannell that his promise to have a standard for the general industry by the end of 1991 was "not good enough." Lantos wondered aloud why it took OSHA much longer to promulgate a safety standard than it took the country to get half a million troops to Iraq.[56] When Scannell left the agency in early 1992, the agency had yet to issue even an ANPR on ergonomics or robotics.

Petrochemical Process Safety

On October 30, 1987, a crane at a Marathon Oil Company plant in Texas City, Texas, dropped a 30-ton heater onto a pipe, causing a release of more than 7,000 gallons of the highly toxic chemical hydrogen fluoride into the surrounding air. The leak forced the evacuation of hundreds of workers and thousands of Texas City residents. Ninety-seven persons were hospitalized.[57] Although no one was seriously poisoned, the accident evoked the stark image of the similar leak at a pesticide manufacturing plant in Bhopal, India, in which more than 2,000 workers and residents were killed and more than 200,000 were injured.[58] In the four years following the Marathon Oil accident, 14 separate releases and explosions in the petrochemical industry killed 79 workers, injured hundreds more, and caused billions of dollars in property damage.[59] The worst was an enormous explosion at a Phillips Petroleum plant in Pasadena, Texas, that killed

23 workers, injured 232 workers, and sent debris flying six miles from the plant. Some suggested that the extraordinary rash of catastrophic events in an industry that had previously boasted an exemplary safety record might have been attributable to aggressive cost-cutting by companies fearing hostile takeovers or struggling to make payments on loans used to finance leveraged buyouts,[60] Others suggested that it might have to do with the industry's increasing use of outside contractors to perform tasks that had been assigned to company employees.[61]

OSHA had begun the progress of drafting a chemical process safety standard not long after the Bhopal incident in 1984, but OMB put a stop to the initiative by refusing to add it to the administration's regulatory program. With the advent of the Bush administration, OSHA decided to have another go at writing a standard, but OMB still resisted. In September 1989, OSHA circulated a draft proposed rule that reflected many weakening changes required by OMB.[62] OMB continued to oppose the standard, but several external events forced OSHA's hand. The Phillips explosion triggered congressional hearings aimed at exploring the risks posed by catastrophic failures of process safety in the petrochemical industry.[63] Several more petrochemical explosions, including one on July 5, 1990, at an ARCO plant that killed 17 workers and injured many more, added more pressure for OSHA to act.[64] And an OSHA-commissioned study by the John Gray Institute at Lamar University found that the chemical industry was increasingly relying upon untrained workers of outside contractors, and recommended that OSHA adopt a chemical process safety standard.[65] Correctly anticipating another round of congressional hearings, OMB released OSHA's proposed chemical process safety rule the day after the ARCO explosion.[66]

A proposed rule was published in July 1991. It required each covered employer to develop a plan, called a process hazard analysis, that would identify, evaluate, and control potential hazards. The proposal was performance-oriented in the sense that it specified goals that an employer had to meet, but it left the design of a safety program to individual employers.[67] This pleased the regulated industry[68] but worried labor representatives, who felt that the proposal relied too heavily on vague performance-oriented criteria that would be difficult to enforce.[69] OMB, as might be expected, was critical. It objected that OSHA had failed to consider alternative and less costly regulatory options. It also urged OSHA to include a "sunset' provision under which the rules would expire if the number of accidents did not decrease.[70]

A final regulation was published in February 1991. OSHA was able to act with dispatch, despite OMB's opposition, because Congress, in the 1990 Clean Air Act Amendments, specified particular requirements that OSHA had to include in the rule and set a strict deadline for the rule's completion.[71] The final rule adopted the same basic approach as the proposed rule but added a congressionally mandated requirement that employers allow worker participation in the development of the process hazards analysis and the process safety management program.[72] The agency rejected OMB's suggested idea.

In the final analysis, the petrochemical process safety rule established a structure for employer-designed safety programs and, at Congress's behest, worker participation in the process. The performance-oriented nature of the most significant operative provisions, however, provides so much flexibility to employers that it is difficult to predict how effective the rule will be in reducing the incidence of catastrophic leaks and explosions. Although OMB was skeptical of the initiative, it was unable to derail it once it had attracted sustained congressional attention. Because Congress established a strict deadline for the final rule, the agency acted far more expeditiously than it usually does. The agency's faster-than-usual pace was of definite benefit to workers. OSHA estimated that the final standard would prevent 264 fatalities and 1,534 injuries each year.[73]

NEW HEALTH INITIATIVES

Lacking the spur of a congressional deadline, OSHA was unable to finish even one of its new health initiatives during Scannell's tenure. The agency's new proposed regulations for cadmium, methylene chloride, and butadiene all became bogged down in the seemingly interminable rulemaking process.

Cadmium

Cadmium and its associated compounds have a wide variety of industrial applications, including electroplating, pigment stabilizing, and use in battery electrodes and metal alloys.[74] NIOSH estimates that approximately 1.5 million workers are routinely exposed to cadmium while performing their jobs.[75] The scientific evidence strongly suggests that cadmium is an element that, when inhaled in large quantities over a long period of time, can cause serious health effects, including kidney disease and cancer.[76] Cadmium had been on OSHA's rulemaking agenda since the early 1970s, but it had never had a very high priority, and OSHA dropped the project altogether in February 1983.[77]

In June 1986, the Public Citizen Health Research Group (HRG) filed a petition with OSHA demanding an emergency temporary standard (ETS) for cadmium and a permanent standard lowering the permissible exposure limit (PEL) from its current 111 $\mu g/m^3$ for fumes and 200 $\mu g/m^3$ for dust to 1 $\mu g/m^3$ for fumes and dust. HRG prepared a risk assessment indicating that about 50 of every 1,000 workers exposed to cadmium over a working lifetime could be expected to contract cancer.[78]

After the agency failed for more than a year to respond to HRG's petition, it went to court. In its brief, HRG cited an internal OSHA memorandum concluding that for each six months of delay in lowering the PEL, approximately 250 cases of cancer and thousands of cases of kidney disease would result.[79] While the court petition was pending, OSHA denied the request for an ETS but agreed to issue a proposal for a permanent standard by December 1987 and a final rule within six months after that. Pointing out that, according to OSHA's own risk assessment, as many as 750 additional workers might contract cancer if the agency adhered to that timetable, HRG returned to court.[80] OSHA responded that cadmium exposure posed no "grave danger" because its risk assessment relied upon a questionable rat study and inaccurate exposure estimates.[81] In October 1987, the court declined to order OSHA to issue an ETS for cadmium, finding that the agency's determination that the exposure data were deficient was entitled to great deference.[82]

Although OSHA had promised to promulgate a permanent standard expeditiously, two years passed without any noticeable action. In June 1989, HRG returned to court to request that OSHA be ordered to promulgate a proposed standard within a month.[83] OSHA responded that it needed more time to evaluate new exposure studies indicating that employee exposure to cadmium was much lower than previous risk estimates had assumed.[84] OSHA also reminded the court that it was already busy responding to court remands for formaldehyde, asbestos, and grain-handling facilities. But when asked by the apparently frustrated judges at oral argument where cadmium ranked among OSHA's rulemaking priorities, OSHA's attorney could not respond.[85] OSHA further argued that it could not move the rule more quickly because OMB was reviewing a draft proposal that OSHA had just sent to it in July 1989.[86] Relying upon OSHA's promise that its dialogue with OMB would proceed on an expedited basis, the court in late October 1989 declined to set an absolute deadline for the issuance of a proposed rule, but it ordered the agency to file a progress report with the court in three months.[87]

Not surprisingly, OMB was not pleased with OSHA's draft proposal. Under a revised procedure that had been worked out to accommodate increasing congressional dissatisfaction with the intrusiveness of OMB review, OMB in October and November 1989 sent to OSHA formal comments on OSHA's draft notice of proposed rulemaking for inclusion in the public rulemaking docket. These documents expressed OMB's "concerns" about several substantive aspects of the standard and posed dozens of questions for OSHA to answer prior to publishing the proposal.[88] Permeating the OMB document were suggestions and demands that OSHA undertake further studies and analysis before publishing the notice.

At the same time that OMB was politely asking questions for the public record, it was privately drafting explicit changes in the language of the *Federal Register* notice that reflected OMB's views on all of the issues raised in the public documents.[89] Although OSHA accepted many of OMB's changes, its scientists drew the line at what they considered to be OMB's meddling in OSHA's interpretations of the scientific studies. In a privately communicated written response to OMB, OSHA stated that many of OMB's changes "misrepresent data in studies; show a lack of understanding of federal agency guidelines pertaining to evaluation of cancer data; request changes OSHA already made . . . ; conflict with the OSHA staff's scientific interpretation of studies; or conflict with current OSHA policy."[90]

The notice of proposed rulemaking that was published in February 1990 contained some, but not all, of the inserts that OMB had demanded.[91] The notice, however, failed to resolve a critical dispute between OMB and OSHA over the relative weight that OSHA should give to a laboratory rat study and an ongoing epidemiological study. In an extraordinary concession to OMB, OSHA proposed two PELs and invited comments on which it should adopt. One PEL reflected OSHA's understanding that the animal evidence indicated that a strict regulation was necessary, and the other reflected OMB's position that the epidemiological evidence justified a weaker regulation. HRG and the unions called OMB's position a "thinly veiled assault on the use of experimental animal data—an argument that was discredited long ago."[92] The Cadmium Council, by comparison, said it was "'shocked over the unreasonableness'" of OSHA's position.[93] NIOSH sided with OSHA on the rat versus epidemiology controversy.[94]

After conducting hearings during the summer of 1990, OSHA began to assimilate the comments and to resolve the outstanding issues. In a February 12, 1991, status report to the court of appeals, OSHA promised a final standard within a year.[95] But the agency agreed to reopen the record in April 1991, and again in September 1991, to consider additional evidence on cadmium in color pigments and to consider the Cadmium Council's arguments in favor of raising the PEL.[96] As of the end of 1991, OSHA had not promulgated a final rule for cadmium.

The cadmium rulemaking demonstrates very clearly that OMB's influence on OSHA's rulemaking did not diminish under President Bush. OMB's economists were just as eager as they had been during the Reagan administration to substitute their views of proper science and policy for those of the agency to which Congress had assigned those tasks. The result was predictable—the pace of rulemaking slowed to a crawl.

Methylene Chloride

Methylene chloride (MC) is a ubiquitous solvent that is used in everything from printer's ink to pesticides to nail polish remover. It is also used in pharmaceuticals and to clean printed circuit boards in high-tech electronics plants. MC is the primary blowing agent for making polyurethane foam. Approximately 500 million pounds of MC are produced annually.[97] Almost 100,000 workers are exposed to MC, nearly half of them in the metal cleaning industry.[98]

In 1971, OSHA promulgated a consensus standard for MC establishing a PEL of 500 ppm averaged over 8 hours, 1,000 ppm as a ceiling, and 2,000 ppm as a maximum 5-minute peak. These limits were based primarily upon the risks that MC posed of skin irritation and damage to the nervous system. Although NIOSH recommended an 8-hour average PEL of 75 ppm and a 500 ppm overall peak in March 1976, OSHA allowed the recommendation to languish for more than a decade. In February 1985, the National Toxicology Program reported the results of animal tests indicating that MC was carcinogenic in mice and rats. Based on these studies, EPA concluded in May 1985 that MC was a probable human carcinogen. The studies also prompted a July 19, 1985, petition from the unions demanding that OSHA establish an ETS for MC. T he unions claimed that MC exposure at existing allowable exposure levels would cause cancer in 1 out of every 100 hairdressers exposed to MC in hair sprays.[99] Nevertheless, OSHA denied the unions' petition on November 17, 1986, but the agency promised to consider whether to promulgate a permanent standard on an expedited basis, and it issued an ANPR on November 24, 1986. At that point the MC initiative disappeared from sight for five years, even though the Food and Drug Administration banned the use of MC in cosmetics in 1989.[100]

MC was a difficult subject for rulemaking because it was so heavily used in so many important industries. Before imposing stringent standards that might put United States companies at a competitive disadvantage, OSHA wanted to be especially confident that MC posed significant risks to workers. The solvents industry took this occasion to try out a new theory of animal carcinogenesis according to which MC posed much smaller risks to humans than to the laboratory animals in which it caused cancer. The new theory postulated that MC itself did not cause cancer in the laboratory animals. Instead, the cancer was caused by a metabolite of MC that was produced at high doses in the animals through a metabolic pathway that was more active in mice than in humans and that kicked in only after the primary metabolic pathway had been overloaded.[101] The industry relied on negative epidemiological studies to bolster its argument.

Using traditional risk assessment models, OSHA predicted that a standard of 25 ppm would reduce the number of expected cancers from a maximum of around 50 per 1,000 workers exposed to 1–2 cancers per 1,000. Even under the *Benzene* case's misconceived one-in-a-thousand suggestion for "significant risk," this would easily have passed muster. When discounted to reflect the industry's new theory, however, the carcinogenic risks posed by MC were 140–170 times lower than those predicted by OSHA's model.[102] Citing numerous criticisms of the industry model by EPA, the Consumer Product Safety Commission, and others, OSHA concluded that it might be premature to rely on that model in determining whether MC posed a significant risk to workers.[103]

OSHA sent a 700-page draft notice of proposed rulemaking to OMB on January 7, 1991.[104] Perhaps because this was the first assignment of a new analyst, OMB approved the draft with minimal suggestions on May 9, 1991. Publication of the proposed rule was delayed another six months, however, by OSHA's decision to refer the draft to its Advisory Committee on Construction Safety and Health.[105] The agency issued a notice of proposed rulemaking on November 7, 1991, proposing to lower the 8-hour average PEL to 25 ppm and to establish a short-term exposure limit (STEL) of 125 ppm for any 15-minute period.[106] OSHA predicted that this standard would save about ten lives per year at a cost of approximately $108 million annually.

Although it took far too long for OSHA to react to the National Toxicology Program (NTP) data and the NIOSH conclusions, the proposal that ultimately resulted was reasonably protective. For the moment the agency has successfully resisted industry efforts to challenge the general presumption that substances that cause cancer in laboratory animals at high doses pose carcinogenic risks to humans. It is entirely possible that the mechanism for MC's carcinogenic response is unique to rodents that are fed high doses of that material, but the industry-supplied studies did not establish that proposition with a sufficient degree of certainty to rebut the general presumption. OSHA rightly placed the burden of proof on the industry, and the industry's proof has so far come up lacking. Whether the agency will insist that the burden of proof remain on the industry as it considers the comments and scientific information prior to publishing the final rule remains to be seen.

Butadiene

The chemical 1,3-butadiene (BD) is a major commodity product of the petrochemical industry that is used primarily in the manufacture of synthetic rubber products and nylon resins. About 3 billion pounds of BD are produced and used each year in the United States.[107] In 1983, the NTP published the results of a mouse study indicating that BD caused cancer in laboratory mice. A later study conducted in England suggested that BD caused cancer in laboratory rats.[108] Both studies, however, were subject to criticism for unconventional protocols and testing procedures. In addition, several epidemiological studies of worker exposure to BD yielded equivocal results. Although industry and some academic scientists interpreted the studies to support no correlation between BD exposure and cancer, OSHA scientists and some academic scientists found that the studies supported the conclusion that BD exposure caused leukemia in humans.[109] BD exposure has also been linked to reproductive effects in animals, bone marrow toxicity in humans, and other systemic effects. Based on these studies, OSHA predicted that the risk of contracting cancer posed at the allowable exposure level of 1,000 ppm was between 1,300 and 1,900 deaths per 10,000 exposed workers. By any comparative estimation, this is an exceedingly high risk. Applying multiple risk assessment models to the data, OSHA determined that nearly all of the models predicted cancer risks of greater than 1 in 1,000 at an exposure level of 10 ppm, and most predicted risks that high at a 1 ppm exposure level.[110]

Soon after the NTP animal study was published in 1983, several unions petitioned OSHA to issue an ETS for BD. On March 4, 1984, the agency denied the petitions on the ground that it was still evaluating the health data.[111] EPA then seized the initiative by writing an ANPR requesting information on how it could best control the risks posed by BD under the Toxic Substances Control Act.[112] On October 10, 1985, EPA formally referred the matter to OSHA to determine whether the bulk of the risks posed by BD exposure could be addressed by an OSHA standard.[113] On April 11, 1986, OSHA responded that it could adequately address the risks, given that "the magnitude of the carcinogenicity evidence in the NTP animal studies [was] overwhelming,"[114] and it published an ANPR on October 1, 1986.[115] The agency did not get around to publishing a proposed rule for another four years, after Scannell had assumed the leadership of the agency.[116] One spur to more rapid action was the publication in 1989 of another mouse study showing that BD caused cancer in the laboratory animals at the very low exposure level of 6.25 ppm.[117] Since workers could lawfully be exposed to as much as 1,000 ppm, this study required no high dose-low dose extrapolation.

The proposed rule, which was published on August 10, 1990, proposed to lower the PEL for BD from 1,000 ppm to 2 ppm averaged over an 8-hour period and to establish a short term exposure limit of 10 ppm averaged over any 15-minute period. The proposal also established the usual monitoring and medical surveillance requirements and set out the conditions under which respirators could be substituted for engineering controls. Since only about 7,000 workers were routinely exposed to BD, OSHA predicted that the benefits of reduced exposure would be relatively small—approximately 25 cancer deaths prevented over a 45-year period. On the other hand, the costs of compliance were predicted to be fairly low. OSHA estimated that the 2 ppm proposal would cost only $3.2 million per year.

The BD story is still another study in bureaucratic neglect. OSHA had un-equivocal evidence in 1983 that BD caused cancer in laboratory animals. But the agency allowed the existence of equivocal epidemiological studies to persuade it to wait until more could be learned about the chemical. In other words, OSHA gave BD the benefit of the doubt. When the second set of studies confirmed the first set six years later, the agency still declined to act for another year. A year and a half after the publication of the proposed rule, OSHA had not published a final rule. Workers could still lawfully be exposed to BD at levels more than 150 times the levels that cause cancer in laboratory animals. Although compar-atively few workers were exposed to BD, those who were exposed faced very high risks indeed.

A GET-TOUGH ENFORCEMENT POLICY

When John Pendergrass took over OSHA, he rejected the "cooperative" enforcement approach of his predecessors Thorne Auchter and Robert Rowland. Under Scannell, OSHA continued the get-tough approach.[118] In 1990, the agency proposed a record $66.6 million in total fines, compared with $45 million in Pendergrass's final year.[119] In both administrations, the heart of the renewed emphasis on strong enforcement was the "egregious" case policy under which OSHA counted multiple violations of OSHA standards as separate violations when they were determined to be flagrant. From 1985 to 1990, OSHA issued about 100 egregious citations to some 90 employers with proposed penalties totaling more than $45 million.[120] Multimillion dollars fines in egregious cases included proposed fines of $7.3 million against USC Corporation for alleged safety violations at two Pennsylvania facilities, $5.6 million against Phillips Petroleum Company for its role in the October 1989 explosion that killed 23 workers, and $2.8 million against the Union Carbide Chemicals and Plastics Company following an explosion that killed 1 worker and injured 32.[121] OSHA also collected fines of $5.8 million from CITGO Petroleum Company after a fire and explosion that killed 6 workers, $3.48 million from the ARCO Chemical Company after an explosion that killed 17 workers, and a record 10 million dollar fine from IMC Fertilizer, Inc. after an explosion killed 8 workers and injured 42 employees and 70 residents.[122]

In many of these cases, Scannell publicly castigated employers for their behavior. For example, in conjunction with a proposed a $1.2 million penalty against a Birmingham company for failing to protect workers against overexposure to lead, Scannell said the company "showed a flagrant and intentional disregard for the health of [its] employees."[123] Similarly, in accusing the Samsonite Corporation of "willfully" and "knowingly" ignoring specific information that OSHA had brought to its attention concerning ergonomic injuries, Scannell emphasized that OSHA "cannot tolerate what appears to be blatant disregard by Samsonite for the health of its employees."[124]

OSHA developed the egregious case policy partly in response to the limited deterrent effect of the agency's maximum $10,000 fine. In 1990, Congress amended the OSH Act and increased the maximum fine to $70,000 for a willful or repeat violation and $7,000 for a serious violation.[125] OSHA quickly invoked this new authority to impose even larger fines, especially in egregious cases. In October 1991, for example, OSHA proposed a $2.78 million fine against the General Motors Corporation when a maintenance worker was killed in GM's Oklahoma City plant. The agency alleged that GM committed 57 willful violations, including 44 egregious violations, and it assessed the maximum $70,000 penalty per violation.[126]

OSHA's tough mega-fine policy, however, did not apply to the newly promulgated field sanitation standard. Throughout Scannell's tenure, worker groups complained of OSHA's failure to enforce this standard, which was designed to protect some of the least powerful workers in this society.[127] The Farmworker Justice Fund reported in a letter to OSHA that "[w]e routinely get reports from farmworkers, farmworker advocates, and even farmers around the country that many, many agricultural employers are not adequately addressing the problems that farmworkers face in the fields." The letter alluded to OSHA statistics showing that during the first 18 months of the field sanitation standard, OSHA inspectors had detected more than 1,800 nonserious violations, for which they had proposed fines of only $80. The Fund concluded: "It is no wonder that compliance continues to be a problem—at an average of 4.4 cents per violation, it is more cost effective to employers to ignore the standard."[128] In addition, a study conducted by Farmworker Legal Services of North Carolina on compliance with the field sanitation standard in North Carolina revealed that only about 4 percent of the farms complied with the requirements for toilets, potable drinking water, and hand-washing facilities.[129]

Although the press reports on OSHA's enforcement efforts emphasized the size of its proposed fines, Scannell often reduced the amount of the fine in return for immediate abatement of safety or health hazards. Scannell defended this practice, which often resulted in reductions of up to half, as being in the best interests of workers, pointing out that employers did not have to abate the hazards until after a full-fledged hearing before the Occupational Safety and Health Review Commission. He explained, "My goal is to protect the workers. I don't care about bringing the money into the federal coffers."[130] One innovation that Scannell did introduce was to link reduced penalties for violations at one plant to company-wide agreements to correct problems at all of the defendant's facilities.[131] Nevertheless, critics like Joseph Kinney of the National Safe Workplace Institute noted that these accommodations were conducted in secret, thereby precluding unbiased assessment of their effectiveness. Kinney complained that OSHA was "all too willing to cut deals with employers, particularly when there is no union involved, without any kind of external involvement to protect the public interest."[132]

Scannell also implemented his get-tough approach through criminal prosecutions. During the first six months of 1991, OSHA referred ten criminal cases to the Justice Department, more than in any other similar period in its history. The 24 cases referred by Scannell during his first 22 months constitute 30 percent of the total cases referred by OSHA in its history.[133]

A Tragic Loophole

Unfortunately, OSHA's get-tough policy had a significant loophole. Although OSHA adopted tough enforcement policies for employers under its jurisdiction, it did little or nothing to require states with their own plans to do the same for employers under state jurisdiction. The OSH Act permits states to undertake primary enforcement authority, but it also requires OSHA to ensure that state enforcement does not leave workers with less protection than federal enforcement would give. Throughout the history of this program, OSHA has failed to police state enforcement efforts.

The North Carolina program is a good example of OSHA's failure to get tough with the states. In July 1990, the agency concluded that, despite some deficiencies, the overall North Carolina program "continues to be effective."[134] The deficiencies, however, were scarcely minor ones. OSHA's evaluation found that North Carolina had only 35 health and safety inspectors; of these, only 22 were journeyman inspectors and the rest were trainees.[135] With so few inspectors, North Carolina was able to inspect only 100 manufacturing establishments in all of 1990. At that rate, the AFL-CIO calculated that the state's high-hazard employers would be inspected only once every 30 years. The state's record was even worse with respect to health inspections. The union charged that the state conducted only five general health inspections during all of 1990 and none of these were in the manufacturing sector, despite the existence of 1,854 high-hazard firms in the state.[136]

On September 13, 1991, the grossly inadequate North Carolina program bore bitter fruit in Hamlet, North Carolina, when a line at the Imperial Food Products Company ruptured, spraying gas into burners that heated vats of cooking oil in which chicken was being prepared. The fire that resulted killed 25 workers and injured 50 more. Most of the fire exists in the plant were locked or blocked, and workers charged that the plant had no sprinkler system, only a single fire extinguisher, and only one emergency light.[137] The Imperial Foods plant had never been inspected by the state of North Carolina in its 11 years of operation despite the fact that the poultry industry has a high-hazard classification because of high injury and illness rates.[138]

After visiting the burned-out plant, Scannell told a congressional committee, "The site reminded me of Dante's *Inferno*. I saw the footprints on the inside of the doors made by the people desperate for their lives."[139] Approximately one month later, OSHA changed its mind about the adequacy of the North Carolina program. It took the unprecedented step of unilaterally assuming partial control for enforcing North Carolina's workplace safety and health plan.[140] Since this was the first time in OSHA's history that it had taken such an action, labor union officials and experts familiar with the agency's procedures called it a clear rebuke of the state program.[141]

John C. Brooks, North Carolina's labor commissioner, the official responsible for running the state's occupational safety and health program, conceded that the state did not have enough inspectors, but he blamed OSHA for this deficiency. He asserted that OSHA's continued approval of his program despite its shortcomings relieved the North Carolina legislature of any pressure to increase funding for the program.[142] He also claimed that during a meeting with Scannell after the fire, Scannell told him, "I know you have one of the finest programs and always have had."[143] North Carolina's governor saw matters differently. He told a congressional committee that the state's enforcement program was "disgracefully deficient."[144]

OSHA's failure to get tough with the state-plan states dates back to Thorne Auchter. As Chapter 10 explained, he reversed policies put into place by Eula Bingham that would have required the states to increase staffing levels significantly. The General Accounting Office in April 1988 found several aspects of OSHA's state monitoring efforts to be deficient, and it recommended that OSHA improve its monitoring by setting performance levels, providing monetary incentives to the states to reach them, and assisting states to evaluate the adequacy of their programs.[145] A February 1989 audit by the inspector general of the Department of Labor found additional deficiencies in OSHA's oversight, including a failure by regional offices to perform timely annual evaluations, a failure by Washington to identify and correct those problems, and inadequacies in the statistical data that OSHA used to certify that the state programs were as effective as the federal program.[146]

Another Blind Spot

At the same time OSHA was proposing large fines and jail sentences, Scannell opposed amending the OSH Act to extend civil and criminal penalties. Congress's enactment of a sevenfold increase in the maximum penalties in 1990 came to pass over OSHA's objections.[147] Moreover, although OSHA supported longer jail sentences in cases of deaths caused by willful violations, it opposed legislation that would have extended criminal penalties to willful violations that caused serious bodily injury. Scannell testified that he was "still concerned that the expanded scope of criminal prosecution under the OSH Act would have the unacceptable side-effect of deterring our successful efforts at obtaining voluntary abatement of workplace hazards." The new criminal penalties could result in the prosecution of "many thousands of employers" each year and "[e]mployers who in the past were inclined to permit entry to an investigator, to cooperate with the investigation, would no longer do so." David Fortney, the deputy solicitor of labor, who also testified, acknowledged that OSHA could obtain a warrant if an inspector was denied entrance to a workplace, but he argued that the process was "extremely protracted and significantly hampers our efforts to go forward with enforcement."[148]

The inspector general of the Department of Labor, Julian De La Rosa, however, endorsed expanded criminal sanctions. So did E. Michael McCann, the Milwaukee County district attorney, who testified that expanded penalties would represent "an unequivocal statement of Congressional intent that the deaths and serious injuries sustained by working men and women from willful violations of the OSH Act are to be viewed with suitable gravity."[149] A majority of the Senate Committee on Labor and Human Resources accepted these views. In July 1991, the committee voted 11 to 5 to expand criminal penalties for workplace health and safety violations. Senator James Jeffords noted that the proposed legislation would "allow OSHA better ability to come in with criminal sanctions when appropriate, and at the same time wouldn't interfere with the relationship between business and OSHA to cooperate in reducing the amount of injuries." But Senator Orrin Hatch, who opposed the bill, claimed that it would "change the mission of OSHA from one of cooperation between employers and agency compliance officers to reduce workplace hazards to one of 'criminal deterrence.' "[150] The Senate did not vote on the bill in 1990 or 1991.

OSHA's adamant opposition to the proposed criminal penalties legislation was inconsistent with its own enforcement policies. Although Scannell sent more cases to the Department of Justice for criminal prosecution than any other administrator, he refused to support new laws that, as Chapter 14 will show, could have the effect of increasing OSHA's capacity to deter unlawful conduct. Scannell's opposition to additional civil and criminal penalties came at a time when the number of workdays lost because of injury and illness was steadily increasing. The lost workday rate is considered to be a crucial indicator of workplace health and safety, because the number of days a worker is off due to an injury or illness tends to correspond to the seriousness of the injury or illness. In 1989, the rate was at an all-time high. One inference that can be drawn from this statistic is that OSHA has failed to stem the tide of workplace accidents and illnesses despite its more aggressive enforcement policy. However, as suggested in Chapter 1, current accident and illness data may reflect OSHA's earlier enforcement policies. If so, the record number of lost workdays in 1989 may only be a vivid reminder of the abject failure of Thorne Auchter's cooperative approach, and a warning of things to come if OSHA continues to object to stiffer penalties.

CONCLUSIONS

The record of the Bush administration in occupational safety and health is quite mixed. Under Scannell, OSHA retained its emphasis on levying large penalties and seeking criminal convictions to send a strong message to employers that egregious violations of OSHA standards would not be tolerated. The Bush administration for the first time in many years attempted to steer significant additional resources in OSHA's direction. During its first two years, the Bush administration requested substantial increases in OSHA's budget.[151]

In the area of standard-setting, however, the kindest thing that can be said is that unlike its predecessor, the Bush administration did not attempt to slam the agency into reverse. Despite the strong urging of OMB and the Competitiveness Council, OSHA did not devote many of its limited resources to reevaluating standards that were already on the books. It resisted pressure from farmers to reduce the scope of the field sanitation standard[152] and from small businesses to modify the hazard communication standard[153] and to "restructure" the PEL update standard to reduce the burdens on small firms.[154]

After Secretary Dole resigned to head the American Red Cross, Scannell's activist enforcement posture did not play as well in the upper levels of the Department of Labor. The new secretary, Lynn Martin, quickly attempted to reign in Scannell by forcing him to accept Dorothy Strunk, a Republican political activist, as his deputy. Chafing under the watchful eyes of Martin and Strunk, Scannell resigned in January 1992 to rejoin his former employer, Johnson & Johnson. Martin immediately appointed Strunk as acting assistant secretary for OSHA. Scannell's departure was mourned more in labor circles than in industry trade associations. Despite Scannell's failure to increase the agency's standard-setting pace, Michael J. Wright, director of health, safety and environment for the United Steelworkers of America, concluded that "Scannell was one of the best administrators in the agency's history."[155] For labor representatives, Scannell's departure resurrected painful memories of the Auchter and Rowland years at OSHA.

NOTES

1. *BNA Occupational Safety and Health Reporter* 18 (25 Jan. 1989): 1516. See also Kirk Victor, "OSHA's Turnabout," *National Journal* 21 (25 Nov. 1989): 2889.

2. *BNA Occupational Safety and Health Reporter* 18 (19 Apr. 1989): 1883.

3. Ibid. 20 (31 Oct. 1990): 939.

4. Ibid. 18 (5 Apr. 1989): 1847.

5. Ibid. 19 (11 Oct. 1989): 811.
6. Victor, "OSHA's Turnabout," 2889.
7. *BNA Occupational Safety and Health Reporter* 19 (31 Jan. 1990): 1444.
8. See Christine Triano and Nancy Waltzman, *All the Vice President's Men: How the Quayle Council on Competitiveness Secretly Undermines Health, Safety, and Environmental Regulation* (Washington, D.C.: Public Citizen Congress Watch and OMB Watch, 1991).
9. *BNA Occupational Safety and Health Reporter* 19 (30 May 1990): 2271.
10. Ibid. 20 (5 Dec. 1990): 1115.
11. *Pesticide and Toxic Chemical News* 18 (2 Jan. 1990): 4.
12. *BNA Occupational Safety and Health Reporter* 20 (5 Dec. 1990): 1115.
13. Ibid. (24 Apr. 1991): 1616.
14. Ibid. (22 May 1991): 1711.
15. Triano and Watzman, *All the Vice President's Men*, 14–15.
16. 56 *Fed. Reg.* 32,301 (1991).
17. *BNA Occupational Safety and Health Reporter* 21 (19 June 1991): 52.
18. U.S. Congress, Senate Committee on Labor and Human Resources, *Hearings on Oversight on the Administration of the Occupational Safety and Health Act*, 100th Cong., 2d sess., S.Hrg. 100–719, 1988, 170.
19. *BNA Occupational Safety and Health Reporter* 18 (31 May 1989): 2147; ibid. 19 (23 Aug. 1989): 584.
20. Ibid. 19 (23 Aug. 1989): 584; ibid. (6 Sept. 1989): 626.
21. Ibid. (19 July 1989): 371; ibid. (16 Aug. 1989): 551.
22. Ibid. (8 Nov. 1989): 1071.
23. Ibid. 19 (4 Apr. 1990): 1920.
24. Ibid. 21 (12 June 1991): 37.
25. Ibid. (18 Sept. 1991): 437.
26. 56 *Fed. Reg.* 64,004 (1991).
27. *BNA Occupational Safety and Health Reporter* 19 (13 Sept. 1989): 694.
28. Ibid. (30 May 1990): 2260.
29. Ibid. 20 (17 Oct. 1990): 872; ibid. (12 Dec. 1990): 1140.
30. Ibid. (30 Jan. 1991): 1299; ibid. (24 Apr. 1991): 1620.
31. Ibid. (6 Mar. 1991): 1445.
32. Ibid. (15 May 1991): 1695.
33. Ibid. 21 (14 June 1991): 690.
34. Ibid. (24 July 1991): 232.
35. 56 *Fed. Reg.* 47,892 (1991).
36. *BNA Occupational Safety and Health Reporter* 19 (27 Sept. 1989): 771.
37. 54 *Fed. Reg.* 23,991 (1989).
38. Ibid. 23,995–96.
39. *BNA Occupational Safety and Health Reporter* 19 (13 Oct. 1989): 872.
40. Ibid. 20 (6 June 1990): 4–5.
41. Ibid. 19 (13 Oct. 1989): 871.
42. Ibid. (16 Aug. 1989): 603.
43. *BNA Daily Labor Report*, 28 July 1988, n.p.
44. 55 *Fed. Reg.* 28,728 (1990).
45. Ibid.
46. Ibid.

47. *BNA Occupational Safety and Health Reporter* 21 (16 Oct. 1991): 552.

48. Ibid. 19 (9 May 1990): 2162 (NIOSH study of cumulative trauma disorders at a poultry processing plant).

49. Ibid. 21 (7 Aug. 1991): 297.

50. Ibid. 17 (2 Sept. 1987): 550 (reporting that about 25 percent of the 500 workers at a Mountain Bell site in Denver were afflicted with carpal tunnel syndrome or precarpal tunnel syndrome symptoms).

51. Ibid. 20 (3 Oct. 1990): 796 (remarks of O. Bruce Dickerson).

52. Ibid. 17 (10 June 1987): 27 (reporting comments of Prof. Patrick D. Krolak of the University of Lowell's Center for Productivity Enhancement).

53. Ibid. 20 (5 Sept. 1990): 631.

54. Ibid. 17 (7 Oct. 1987): 798.

55. Ibid. 21 (23 Oct. 1991): 574.

56. Ibid. 20 (27 Mar. 1991): 1522.

57. George Stein, "Debate on Refinery Acid Report Delayed by AQMD Officials," *Los Angeles Times*, 28 Jan. 1990, B3, col. 5.

58. Robert Reinhold, "Disaster in Bhopal: Where Does Blame Lie?" *New York Times*, 31 Jan. 1985, A1, col. 4; Stuart Diamond, "The Bhopal Disaster: How It Happened," *New York Times*, 28 Jan. 1985, A1, col. 1; Stuart Taylor, Jr., "Bhopal Suits Combined in New York," *New York Times*, 7 Feb. 1985, D1, col. 3.

59. Keith Schneider, "Petrochemical Disasters Raise Alarm in Industry," *New York Times*, 19 June 1991, A22, col. 3.

60. Ibid.

61. U.S. Congress, House Committee on Government Operations, Subcommittee on Employment and Housing, *Hearings on Adequacy of OSHA Protections for Chemical Workers*, pt. 2, 101st Cong., 2d sess., 1990, 39 (testimony of Mr. Lynn Williams, president of United Steelworkers of America); ibid., 188 (testimony of Gerald V. Poje, National Wildlife Federation). (Hereafter cited as House, *Protections for Chemical Workers, Hearings of 1990*, pt. 2)

62. Ibid., 36 (testimony of Lynn Williams).

63. U.S. Congress, House Committee on Government Operations, Subcommittee on Employment and Housing, *Hearings on Adequacy of OSHA Protections for Chemical Workers*, 101st Cong., 1st sess., 1989.

64. House, *Protections for Chemical Workers, Hearings of 1990*, pt. 2, 57 (testimony of Gerard F. Scannell).

65. *BNA Occupational Safety and Health Reporter* 21 (7 Aug. 1991): 285; Keith Schneider, "Study Finds Links Between Chemical Plant Accidents and Contract Workers," *New York Times*, 30 July 1991, A10, col. 1. See also House, *Protections for Chemical Workers, Hearings of 1990*, pt. 2, 199 (testimony of Gerald V. Poje).

66. House, *Protections for Chemical Workers, Hearings of 1990*, pt. 2, 35–36 (testimony of Lynn Williams).

67. 55 *Fed. Reg.* 29,150 and 29,163–65 (1990).

68. *BNA Occupational Safety and Health Reporter* 21 (19 June 1991): 55.

69. Ibid. 20 (12 Dec. 1990): 1146–47.

70. Ibid. (24 Oct. 1990): 899.

71. P.L. no. 101–549, § 304, 104 Stat. 2576 (1990).

72. 57 *Fed. Reg.* 6356 (1992).

73. *BNA Occupational Safety and Health Reporter* 21 (26 Feb. 1992): 1267.

74. 55 *Fed. Reg.* 4052, 4058 (1990): *BNA Occupational Safety and Health Reporter* 16 (19 June 1986): 54.

75. *BNA Occupational Safety and Health Reporter* 16 (19 June 1986): 54.

76. 55 *Fed. Reg.* 4052, 4065–66 (1990).

77. *BNA Occupational Safety and Health Reporter* 13 (29 Sept. 1983): 405.

78. 55 *Fed. Reg.* 4052, 4056 (1990): *BNA Occupational Safety and Health Reporter* 16 (19 June 1986): 54.

79. *BNA Occupational Safety and Health Reporter* 17 (1 July 1987): 171.

80. Ibid. (8 July 1987): 197.

81. Ibid. (29 July 1987): 393.

82. Ibid. (14 Oct. 1987): 819.

83. Ibid. 19 (7 June 1989): 8.

84. Ibid. (21 June 1989): 120.

85. Ibid. (18 Oct. 1989): 853.

86. Ibid.

87. Ibid. (25 Oct. 1989): 917.

88. Office of Information and Regulatory Affairs, Office of Management and Budget, discussion paper for Department of Labor regarding DOL's Draft NPRM, "Occupational Exposure to Cadmium," memo dated 19 Oct. 1989; memorandum to Charles Adkins from Scott Jacobs re "Additional Questions Pertaining to OSHA's NPRM, 'Occupational Exposure to Cadmium," dated 20 Nov. 1989.

89. Occupational Safety and Health Administration, "Changes to the cadmium document that were given to Adkins at 9:30 A.M. on Dec. 8, 1989," undated memo; fax transmittal to Chuck Adkins from Scott Jacobs, dated 12 Dec. 1989; fax transmittal to Chuck Adkins from Scott Jacobs, dated 17 Jan. 1990; Occupational Safety and Health Administration, "Additions to the Cadmium NPRM Received from OMB," 18 Jan. 1990; fax transmittal to Alan McMillen from Scott Jacobs, dated 19 Jan. 1990.

90. Occupational Safety and Health Administration, "Response to OMB Submission of 12/12/89 Related to OSHA Cadmium Proposal," memo dated 18 Dec. 1989.

91. 55 *Fed. Reg.* 4052 (1990).

92. *BNA Occupational Safety and Health Reporter* 19 (30 May 1990): 2265.

93. Ibid. (7 Feb. 1990): 1494; ibid. 20 (13 June 1990): 41.

94. *BNA Chemical Regulation Reporter* 14 (3 Aug. 1990): 721–22.

95. *BNA Occupational Safety and Health Reporter* 20 (20 Feb. 1991): 1412.

96. 56 *Fed. Reg.* 47,348 (1991).

97. Ibid. 57,030 and 57,044–53.

98. Ibid. 57,104.

99. *BNA Occupational Safety and Health Reporter* 17 (17 June 1987): 87.

100. 56 *Fed. Reg.* 57,039 (1991); *BNA Occupational Safety and Health Reporter* 19 (5 July 1989): 182.

101. 56 *Fed. Reg.* 57,093–94 (1991).

102. Ibid. 57,094.

103. Ibid. 57,098.

104. *BNA Occupational Safety and Health Reporter* 20 (25 Jan. 1991): 1532.

105. Ibid. (15 May 1991): 1697.

106. 56 *Fed. Reg.* 57,117 (1991).

107. 55 *Fed. Reg.* 32,736 and 32,739–40 (1990).

108. Ibid. 32,740–45.

109. Ibid. 32,753.
110. Ibid. 32,771.
111. Ibid. 32,738.
112. 49 *Fed. Reg.* 20,524 (1984).
113. 50 *Fed. Reg.* 41,393 (1985).
114. 51 *Fed. Reg.* 12,526 (1986).
115. Ibid. 35,003.
116. 55 *Fed. Reg.* 32,739 (1990).
117. *BNA Occupational Safety and Health Reporter* 18 (24 Mar. 1989): 1872.
118. Gerard F. Scannell, "OSHA Pledges Tougher Enforcement," *Trial*, June 1991, 24.
119. Dena Bunis, "OSHA's Leader Walks Loudly, but Some Say He Needs a Bigger Stick," *Newsday*, 18 Aug. 1991, 86.
120. *BNA Occupational Safety and Health Reporter* 20 (10 Oct. 1990): 829.
121. Ibid. 21 (18 Sept. 1991): 427.
122. Ibid. 20 (9 Jan. 1991): 1203; *CCH Employment Safety and Health Guide*, 10 Sept. 1991, 1; *BNA Occupational Health and Safety Reporter* 21 (6 Nov. 1991): 635.
123. *BNA Occupational Safety and Health Reporter* 21 (11 Sept. 1991): 407.
124. Ibid., 403.
125. Omnibus Budget Reconciliation Act of 1990, P.L. no. 101–508, 104 Stat. 388–29 (1990).
126. *BNA Corporate Counsel Weekly* 6 (9 Oct. 1991): 7.
127. See Kenneth Noble, "Farm Workers Fault Lack of Enforcement of Sanitation Rules," *New York Times*, 4 Oct. 1988, A1, col. 1; *BNA Occupational Safety and Health Reporter* 18 (1 Feb. 1989): 1547.
128. *BNA Occupational Safety and Health Reporter* 19 (14 Feb. 1990): 1686.
129. Ibid. (9 May 1990): 2170.
130. Bunis, "OSHA's Leader," 86.
131. *BNA Occupational Health and Safety Reporter* 20 (10 Oct. 1990): 829.
132. Bunis, "OSHA's Leader," 86.
133. *BNA Occupational Health and Safety Reporter* 21 (21 Aug. 1991): 347.
134. Ibid. (18 Sept. 1991): 428.
135. Ibid.
136. Ibid.
137. Ibid. (23 Oct. 1991): 572.
138. Ibid. (18 Sept. 1991): 428.
139. Kirk Victor, "A Federal -State Standoff on Safety," *National Journal* 23 (28 Sept. 1991): 2381.
140. *BNA Occupational Health and Safety Reporter* 21 (23 Oct. 1991): 571.
141. Ronald Smothers, "U.S. to Assist Carolina Safety Inspectors," *New York Times*, 24 Oct. 1991, A14.
142. Ibid.
143. Victor, "Federal-State Standoff," 2381.
144. *CCH Employment Safety and Health Guide*, 17 Sept. 1991, 1.
145. *BNA Occupational Safety and Health Reporter* 17 (4 May 1988): 1771.
146. Ibid. 18 (8 Feb. 1989): 1619.
147. Ibid. 20 (7 Nov. 1990): 979.
148. Ibid. (6 Mar. 1991): 1439.

149. Ibid. 1440.

150. Ibid. (14 July 1990): 155–56.

151. Ibid. 19 (31 Jan. 1990): 1435 (requested increase of approximately 7 percent for fiscal year 1991); ibid. 20 (6 Mar. 1991): 1443 (requested increase of approximately 6 percent for fiscal year 1992).

152. Ibid. 19 (14 Feb. 1990): 1685.

153. Ibid. (28 June 1989): 139.

154. Ibid. 18 (5 Mar. 1989): 1752.

155. Kirk Victor, "Is the Honeymoon Over?" *National Journal* 24 (25 Jan. 1992): 214.

Part III

INTERNAL REFORMS: BETTER MANAGEMENT FOR OSHA

12

Making OSHA More Efficient: Setting Priorities and Eliminating Bottlenecks

If OSHA is to fulfill its statutory mandate to protect workers, a way must be found to increase its regulatory output. Although OSHA desperately needs additional resources, a significant budget increase is unlikely, given the fiscal constraints under which the federal government currently operates. Even during the Carter years, when OSHA was comparatively flush with resources, the agency lacked an adequate staff of qualified health professionals.[1] To avoid complete paralysis, OSHA must seek out ways to optimize its use of its admittedly meager resources. The decision-making process at OSHA might be viewed as a road that begins at the identification of a problem and ends with the promulgation of a standard. The speed at which OSHA traverses this road depends on the quality of gasoline it uses, but it also depends on the number and size of the roadblocks it must overcome. Some of the obstacles are internal impediments, such as OSHA's failure to set priorities and adopt an effective management process, and others are external impediments, placed there by Congress when it prescribed in the OSH Act how OSHA is to write health and safety standards. This chapter considers how to remove these hurdles or at least how to decrease their number and size.

OSSIFICATION OF RULEMAKING

OSHA takes a long time to promulgate most rules. Figure 12–1 shows that almost half of the 25 final health standards took 3 or more years to finish, 40 percent took 5 or more years, and 28 percent took 6 or more years. OSHA has been working on 60 percent of the 17 current pending health standards for 3 or more years, on 40 percent of them for 4 or more years, and on 30 percent of them for 5 or more years. The situation is almost as bad for safety standards.

Figure 12–1
Health Standards (elapsed time)

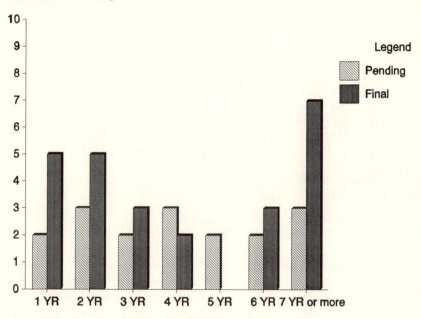

Source: *Federal Register*, Semiannual Regulatory Agenda.

Figure 12–2 shows that 37 percent of 37 final safety standards took 3 or more years, and OSHA has been working on 58 percent of the 19 pending safety standards for 4 or more years.

INADEQUATE BUDGETS

One reason for the ossification of OSHA's rulemaking process is not hard to find. Figure 12–3 indicates OSHA's actual budget authority and its budget adjusted for the effects of inflation. OSHA's actual budget has gradually increased each year, except for two years during the Reagan administration. But these increases have not been large enough to offset the effects of inflation. OSHA's budget adjusted for inflation has been around $200 million since 1982. The dramatic effects of this constant budget are revealed in Figure 12–4. Between 1981 and 1982, the number of permanent positions at OSHA declined from 3,000 to 2,350. By 1986, the number of permanent employees had dropped to 2,090. Although there has been an increase in the number of employees since 1986, OSHA still has more than 500 fewer employees than it had in 1981.

Although other governmental agencies have also suffered budget cuts, less of the federal budget goes to protecting workers than in the past. A study by the

Figure 12–2
Safety Standards (elapsed time)

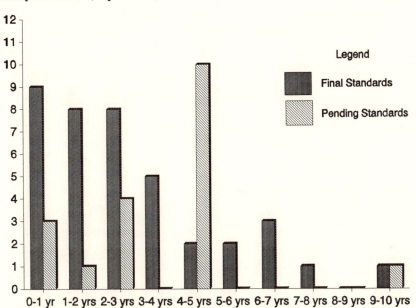

Source: *Federal Register*, Semiannual Regulatory Agenda

National Safe Workplace Institute (NSWI) compared the budgets of OSHA, the National Institute of Occupational Safety and Health (NIOSH), and the Mine Safety Health Administration (MSHA) with the total pattern of federal spending on health and safety agencies. It found that workplace-related spending grew only 21.2 percent between fiscal year (FY) 1981 and FY 1991, while federal spending overall increased by 92.4 percent. This means that while one out of $1,579 federal dollars went for workplace-related spending in FY 1981, only one out of $2,408 federal dollars went for this purpose in FY 1991. Moreover, work-related health and safety agencies have suffered deeper budget cuts than other health and safety agencies. In FY 1981, EPA's budget was 7.1 times larger than the combined budgets of OSHA, NIOSH, and MSHA. In FY 1991, it was 11.4 times larger. NSWI concludes, "It is obvious, based on almost any significant comparison, that workplace health spending has suffered during the 1980s."[2]

CHOOSING OSHA'S PRIORITIES

OSHA can and should seek additional resources, but it also must find ways to stretch its budget. The place to start is to establish a process for setting

Figure 12–3
OSHA's Budget Authority (in millions of dollars)

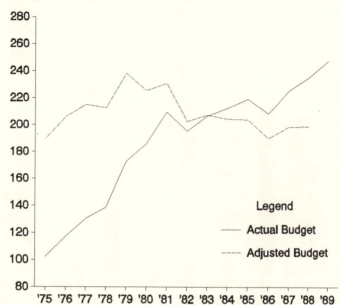

Source: Office of Management and Budget, *Budget of the United States*.

regulatory priorities. Since it can promulgate only a few regulations each year under existing resource constraints, it must develop a technique for focusing its attention on the most dangerous workplaces first. Currently, OSHA sets its regulatory agenda in reaction to interest group demands, congressional and White House pressure, and information from its employees and other regulatory agencies. OSHA presently has no way to choose among the many projects that are putatively on its agenda.

An appropriate metaphor for OSHA's relationship with the groups who contribute projects to its agenda is that of a business establishment with a front door, a side window, and a back door. Petitions, information from the field, and recommendations from private standard-setting groups all press at OSHA's front door, vying for the agency's attention. Meanwhile, the Office of Management and Budget (OMB) and the White House are constantly at the back door, demanding that OSHA reconsider some previously promulgated rules. At the same time, the courts are pushing some rulemaking petitions through the side window in response to lawsuits filed against OSHA because it has not acted on their request for a regulation.

In the last few years, the press of business from the back door and side window has been so great that OSHA has been able to accept very little business through

Figure 12–4
Number of Permanent OSHA Positions (in thousands)

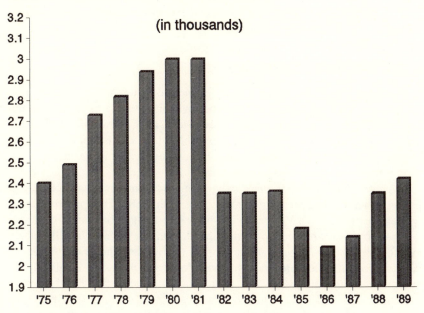

Source: Office of Management and Budget, *Budget of the United States*.

the front door. Instead of an orderly queue at the front door, there is now a great crowd of potential topics. The time is near when there will also be a disorderly crowd at the side window. Because it has no priority-setting process, OSHA long ago lost control of its front door agenda; it now risks total paralysis as its limited capacity to produce rules becomes overwhelmed by the press at the side window of applicants who have given up on the front door.

Despite its impending loss of control over its agenda, OSHA has vigorously resisted adopting a priority-setting process. One reason is that the agency wants to avoid destroying the carefully nurtured myth that everything that comes before it has a high priority. Agency managers are understandably reluctant to tell interest groups or politicians that their problem is less important than others on which the agency is working. At the same time, by avoiding a priority list or agenda, OSHA avoids resistance from those with an economic interest in the initiatives that would be on the list. OSHA's reluctance to engage in setting priorities is also attributable to conceptual difficulties inherent in the process. Although an ideal priority-setting scheme would emphasize risk to workers (including considerations of toxicity and extent of exposure) and would pay some attention to the practicality of controls, there is rarely enough high-quality information to make precise quantitative comparisons.

Despite these difficulties, OSHA has no alternative to priority setting if it hopes to regain control over its own agenda. Relying on the existing admittedly crude priority-setting techniques, it should attempt to rank-order its existing initiatives and adhere to that ranking.[3]

MORE EFFECTIVE MANAGEMENT

The second step in creating a more efficient decision-making process is to create a system for management and accountability capable of communicating upper-level management's priorities to lower-level staff, eliminating bottlenecks, and holding staffers accountable for inexcusable delays. Whether or not OSHA ever seizes control of its own agenda, it must invent an internal management system that makes the trains run on schedule.

At present, OSHA has in place only the most rudimentary system for establishing deadlines and measuring compliance with them. Time projections are typically arrived at on a "when-do-you-think-you-can-get-this-done" basis, and they are not always reduced to writing. In addition, they are continually subject to informal adjustment without explanation as priorities change due to outside pressures or other resource needs. These loose deadlines are communicated informally by the office directors to the staff members who are assigned to particular rules and who in turn communicate them to other staff members. OSHA also does not have any systematic approach tracking the progress of its rulemaking initiatives. As one official explained, "We keep it in our heads."[4]

OSHA's establishment of a management system capable of setting and enforcing deadlines can be contrasted with the Environmental Protection Agency's (EPA) "Action Tracking System" (ATS), which is a computerized accountability system that follows the progress of more than 200 items, approximately two-thirds of which are rulemaking actions. EPA has identified 13 "major milestones" that occur in most rulemaking initiatives, and unless the responsible staffers convincingly demonstrate why a particular rule is unique in its time requirements, agency managers assign standardize time intervals for each milestone. The computer on a biweekly basis pulls out all of the projects for which there are milestones within the next two weeks and all of the projects that are behind schedule. This "due or late" list is used by EPA's management to enforce compliance with the deadlines established for each rulemaking action.[5]

OSHA's managers have been reluctant for political reasons to adopt a tracking system like that used by EPA. The absence of closely monitored deadlines gives the false impression that OSHA is capable of doing more than it really can with its limited resources. Rather than disappoint a beneficiary group by declining to take on its preferred project, OSHA simply agrees to undertake it without saying when it will get done. In the long run, however, this tactic leads to the agency's disappointing many beneficiary groups when very little ultimately gets accomplished. And the focus at that point is inappropriately on the presumed lethargy of OSHA bureaucrats rather than on OSHA's lack of adequate resources.

OSHA administrators have also opposed an ATS out of fear that evidence of their inability to keep rules running on schedule will become public through Freedom of Information Act requests, congressional investigations, or the omnipresent "leak." Such revelations can be a serious tactical disadvantage to the agency when it is sued by a union or public interest group concerning its delay in promulgating a rule. Information about delays may also put the agency in an embarrassing position in its relationships with committees in Congress. It is always more comfortable for the agency to say "We are doing the best that we can," without having to worry about the possibility that its own ATS will undermine those assurances.

If OSHA is to be effectively managed, however, its administrators cannot ignore a tool as useful as the ATS, despite the political discomfort it may sometimes cause. An ATS would allow OSHA to uncover bottlenecks and determine causes of the delay, such as a particular unit's need for additional resources. Because the system would rely heavily upon computers, its personnel demands would be slight, and the simplicity of the program suggests that the computer resource needs would not be large. Revealing slippage to the world may be embarrassing, but it would also render the agency accountable to the public.

COORDINATION AMONG INSTITUTIONAL ACTORS

If OSHA is to do a better job of setting and enforcing deadlines, it must find better ways of coordinating the efforts of the various offices that have roles to play in the rulemaking process. Developing a rule requires the input of several institutional entities within OSHA and within the Department of Labor. The Health Directorate or Science Directorate gathers background information, administers contracts for technical information, assembles the record, drafts the proposed and final rules, and mines the outside comments for information and analysis. The Policy Office gathers information on the costs and economic and technological feasibility of complying with proposed rules. The Solicitors Office, which is a separate entity within the Department of Labor, reviews documents to be published in the *Federal Register*, drafts certain parts of those documents, and prepares expert witnesses for testimony at hearings. In the past, the functions of these various entities have been poorly coordinated.,

When OSHA initiates a rule, a project officer from the Health Directorate or Science Directorate is appointed to coordinate the input from the various parts of OSHA and the Department of Labor. Because this person has no authority to control the employees in the Policy Office and Solicitor's Office, however, there is very little he or she can do when workers in those offices fail to meet their deadlines. A project officer can bring the problem to the attention of the director of the Health Directorate or Safety Directorate, who may informally bring delays to the attention of the director of the Policy Directorate or the assistant solicitor for OSHA. This type of informal communication, however, has not prevented significant bottlenecks from arising. We saw an extreme example of this in Chapter 6 when the text of OSHA's draft rule for grain dust was lost in transmission between offices for several weeks before anyone realized that the document was missing.

An ATS could facilitate interoffice coordination and thereby reduce bottlenecks. The Health Directorate or Safety Directorate could enter a proposed schedule into the system at the time the project was approved by upper-level management, and any disputes over the proposed schedule could be resolved in one of the periodic meetings with the assistant secretary or deputy assistant secretary and midlevel managers. If a deadline was missed, the location of the bottleneck or delaying activity would become immediately apparent, and additional resource needs could be identified. Conflicts in priorities would also be revealed to upper-level managers, who would then be in a position to resolve such conflicts on the spot. Conflicts between the priorities of OSHA and of the Solicitor's Office would be less easily resolved, because of the location of the Solicitor's Office in the Department of Labor. But any conflicts would be apparent at a very high level within OSHA, and they could be resolved in meetings between the deputy assistant secretary for OSHA and the assistant solicitor for OSHA.

MORE EFFICIENT HEARING PROCEDURES

Although OSHA critics often point to its quasi-formal hearing procedures as a source of delay, the time actually consumed in formal hearings constitutes only a very small portion of the time required to promulgate a rule.[6] Still, a number of relatively easily implemented procedural reforms have a modest potential for speeding up OSHA rulemaking. The most promising reform would be to end the agency's overreliance on a procedure known as advance notice of proposed rulemaking (ANPR). Although OSHA seldom used an ANPR in its early history, its use has now become commonplace.

OSHA uses an ANPR to tell the public that it has recognized, and may in the future address, a certain problem area and to request interested persons to submit any information or ideas that they believe will help OSHA in deciding what type of action to take. Although the ANPR can be a useful source of information in some cases, there is a general feeling among agency staff and outside practitioners that this procedure has rarely resulted in the production of useful information for OSHA.[7] At the same time, the ANPR slows the progress of agency contractors, who are understandably reluctant to complete their reports until they have assimilated any information that the ANPR produces. Moreover, agency administrators can use the process, which can last from six months to a year, to avoid hard decisions. For these reasons, the ANPR should be used only when information that is not available through other vehicles is very likely to be forthcoming in response to the ANPR.

Many OSHA observers suggest that the agency could act faster if it stopped going to extreme lengths to perfect the record in rulemaking proceedings to avoid reversal on appeal. They point to 100-page preambles that discuss every nuance in the literature and every minor contention raised in the comments as evidence of "overpreparation" of the record. Most industry representatives forcefully dispute this notion and strongly maintain that OSHA must analyze the available information and comments exhaustively in order to establish a sound technical basis for its rules. OSHA's attorneys in the Solicitor's Office are also convinced that elaborate analysis and documentation are necessary to survive judicial review, and they explain that much of the delay caused by their office is prompted by concern for the quality of the agency's technical analysis.[8]

Although the Solicitor's Office should be free to determine the type of record that is necessary for the agency to prevail on judicial review, attorneys in that office should be subject to reasonable time constraints. Yet the Solicitor's Office cannot become more productive without additional resources. Given the current absence of any mechanism for holding the Solicitor's Office accountable for delays, it is impossible to say whether it has been underfunded inadvertently or as part of a deliberate attempt by budget managers in the Department of Labor or the Office of Management and Budget to slow down OSHA rulemaking. Whatever the reason, without additional resources, the Solicitor's Office will continue to be a bottleneck.

From a somewhat broader perspective, the source of the problem may be that the Supreme Court has encouraged "searching and careful" review on the part of the courts of appeals. Since the parties usually shop among all of the courts of appeals for the reviewing forum, OSHA attorneys must prepare the record under the assumption that it will be reviewed by the least sympathetic court. Although the advantages and disadvantages of strict judicial review will be examined in more detail in Chapter 17, it is worth noting at this point that the courts of appeals should not perform their essential institutional role in a vacuum, unaware of the consequences of intense judicial review.

CONGRESSIONALLY IMPOSED CONSTRAINTS

Not all of the delays at OSHA are the agency's fault. Congress has made OSHA's job more difficult by some of the choices it made when it passed the OSH Act. One of the most important of these decisions was to put the National Institute for Occupational Safety and Health (NIOSH) in a different executive department than OSHA. Congress also limited the usefulness to OSHA of technical advisory committees by placing severe restrictions on their membership.

NIOSH

Congress created NIOSH to give OSHA scientific advice, to generate new scientific data about health and safety problems, and to sponsor training and education programs.[9] Despite the fact that most, if not all, of NIOSH's functions require coordination with OSHA, Congress did not place it in the Department of Labor, where the secretary of labor could have ensured that the agencies worked closely together. Instead, NIOSH was located in the Department of Health, Education, and Welfare (HEW), which later became the Department of Health and Human Services (HHS).

The idea of establishing a separate research agency originated in the Senate after the House of Representatives had passed its version of the Act.[10] Although the legislative history does not indicate why the Senate put NIOSH in HEW, it may have been located there for one or more of four reasons. First, the Senate may have desired for convenience to create NIOSH to replace a bureau already located in HEW that conducted research concerning workplace health and safety. Second, the location may have been intended to coordinate with other agencies in the same department, such as the National Toxicology Program, the National Centers for Disease Control, and the National Institutes of Health.[11] Third, the Senate may have believed that locating NIOSH in HHS would assist in recruiting and retaining health scientists.[12] Finally, the Senate may have desired to protect NIOSH's "scientific integrity" by sheltering it from the day-to-day political and interest group pressures to which OSHA is constantly subjected, thereby allowing NIOSH to serve as a check on any propensity in OSHA to reach conclusions inconsistent with scientific knowledge.[13]

Although all of these reasons for locating NIOSH in a separate department were no doubt meritorious, NIOSH has as a result been of limited help to OSHA in accomplishing its goals. As related in Part II, OSHA and NIOSH have been unable to coordinate their efforts in a manner that permits NIOSH to serve as OSHA's scientific arm. As a result, OSHA has hired its own scientists, and it depends primarily on its own staff and outside consultants to generate the information necessary to promulgate its standards. This unsurprising development has resulted from the absence of any single administrator with the power to resolve disputes between the two organizations. Coordination therefore requires either agreement between the two agencies or the intervention of both secretaries. Since NIOSH and OSHA rarely elevate disputes to the secretarial level, the two agencies coexist in an uneasy, and often unproductive, relationship.

If NIOSH were transferred to the Department of Labor, the secretary of labor would be in a position to reconcile the goals and priorities of the two agencies, and NIOSH research efforts could be coordinated with OSHA's priority setting.[14] Moreover, OSHA employees could seek advice from NIOSH scientists when health and safety rules were being planned. Although such consultation can occur now, it is severely hampered by the fact that NIOSH is not located in Washington, D.C. Finally, a change could end duplicative activities.

If NIOSH were transferred to the Department of Labor, coordination with other health-related agencies in HHS might be more difficult. While such coordination is important, it is not as vital as the need for OSHA and NIOSH to coordinate their activities. Opponents of moving NIOSH justifiably worry that the agency would have more difficulty in maintaining its scientific integrity and

in hiring good scientists if it were located in the Department of Labor.[15] Ultimately, however, NIOSH's reputation, as well as its ability to hire good personnel, depends on the quality of its work. There is no inherent reason why
NIOSH could not maintain a reputation for independence and a high-quality
work product if it were located in the Department of Labor along with other
highly respected nonregulatory agencies like the Bureau of Labor Statistics.
When he left office in 1977, Assistant Secretary Morton Corn made a strong
case for folding NIOSH into the Department of Labor.[16] The case remains equally
strong in 1992.

Advisory Committees

Although other regulatory agencies routinely rely on advisory committees to
overcome resources limitations that prevent them from hiring and retaining outstanding scientists, Congress has placed restrictions on OSHA's use of advisory
committees that renders their use relatively impractical. Although OSHA may
form an advisory committee anytime it considers promulgating a health or safety
standard,[17] the agency has not appointed a committee since 1976. OSHA has
not explained its failure to use advisory committees, but others have reported
that advisory meetings "did little more than provide a forum for the contending
parties—labor and employers—to argue with each other,"[18] that the committees
became "tools for political manipulation,"[19] that committees were not "well
structured to resolve . . . differences [between labor and management],"[20] that
OSHA "depart[ed] greatly and with vigorous opposition" from committee recommendations,[21] and that, on balance, the agency found the use of such committees to be a burden.[22]

OSHA's disenchantment with advisory committees can be traced in part to
the unique structure that Congress established for OSHA's advisory committees.
In agencies that have had a more positive experience with advisory committees,
like the Food and Drug Administration, voting members are supposed to be
chosen on the basis of their expertise without regard to whether they represent
any particular constituency. At OSHA, however, advisory committees must
contain an equal number of representatives of management and labor, and the
agency is limited in the number of independent experts it can appoint.[23] Undoubtedly, this makeup has contributed to the politicized and adversarial nature
of OSHA committees, and it may have limited the range of expertise represented.
To remedy these problems, Congress should amend the OSH Act to eliminate
existing membership restrictions and to replace them with a simple requirement
that OSHA advisory committee membership be balanced.

Congress also set unrealistic deadlines for OSHA's use of advisory committees. An advisory committee must submit its recommendations within 90 days
of its appointment, although the secretary of labor can extend the deadline to
no more than 270 days.[24] In a study of deadlines for the Administrative Conference of the United States, Tomlinson found that because of logistical problems,

this deadline was difficult for OSHA to meet.[25] The Act also requires that OSHA
propose a standard within 60 days after receiving the recommendations of an
advisory committee.[26] OSHA has also had difficulty in complying with this
deadline because it is usually unable to write a proposed standard within the
time limits set for it.[27] As a remedy, Congress could eliminate the existing
deadlines.

If OSHA starts using advisory committees again, care must be taken to ensure
that it does not misuse the process. The primary disadvantage of advisory committees, beyond their not terribly burdensome expense to an agency, is their
potential for departing the confines of science, where technical expertise is
critical, and wandering into the realm of policy, where technical expertise has
no particular virtue. Most of the questions that come before a typical OSHA
scientific advisory committee are mixed questions of science and policy that
cannot easily be separated into their scientific and policy constituents.[28] A good
example is the level of certainty demanded before drawing a conclusion that a
possible cause is associated with a particular effect. Scientists are generally
unwilling to draw cause-effect conclusions from statistical data absent a high
degree of confidence that the observed association did not occur by chance. For
purposes of publishing scientific papers and establishing scientific reputations,
this degree of conservatism is entirely appropriate. But a policymaker may decide
not to demand such a high degree of confidence when the lives of hundreds of
workers are at stake. In other words, the policymaker may decide to err on the
side of safety. Another policymaker implementing a less protective policy might
require a greater degree of confidence. The important point is that the degree of
confidence required for drawing cause-effect relationships for regulatory purposes
is a question of policy, not of science.

Most agency policymakers understand the difficulty in separating questions
of pure science from their policy components and that scientific advisory committees are competent only to address purely scientific questions. Unfortunately,
scientific advisory committees can be useful to agency decisionmakers even when
operating beyond their competence. As long as the policy aspect of a science/
policy question is not immediately apparent to the public, the decision maker
can use scientific advisory committees as a shield from criticism for policy choices
by maintaining that the decision was made in accordance with the neutral advice
of an independent scientific advisory committee. For this strategy to work, the
decision maker must ensure that a majority of the committee will supply the
"proper" policy component to science/policy questions. This can be relatively
easily accomplished by "stacking" the committee with scientists whose past
actions indicate that they will generally resolve science/policy questions in accordance with the decision maker's policy preferences.[29]

The potential for misuse does not require that advisory committees never be
appointed, but only that appropriate precautions be taken to mitigate this danger.
One solution would be for Congress to require any advisory committee appointed
by OSHA to present a complete and full accounting of its deliberations, including

an explanation of each potential solution to an issue, which solution the committee recommended, and why that solution was preferable. The previously suggested requirement that advisory committees be balanced would also help ensure against programmed policy bias.

CONCLUSIONS

It may seem surprising that after two decades of existence, including one thoroughgoing management overhaul, OSHA still does not have in place an adequate management structure for establishing regulatory priorities and following through on them. Although OSHA has in recent years tried to put its house in order, the fact remains that its priorities are more often than not set by outside institutions like OMB and the courts. OSHA unquestionably needs greater resources, but it also needs to put into place a management system that is capable of saying "no" or at least "later" in a credible fashion. Other reforms suggested in this chapter, such as moving NIOSH into the Department of Labor and using advisory committees more effectively, should help improve the efficiency of the standard development process at OSHA. In the final analysis, however, these "patch and repair" changes will only marginally speed up the pace of OSHA rulemaking unless the agency adopts some of the more far-reaching changes suggested in Chapter 13.

NOTES

1. U.S. Congress, Senate Committee on Appropriations, *Hearings on Departments of Labor and Health Education and Welfare and Related Agencies Appropriations*, 95th Cong., 2d sess., pt. 1, p. 447 (1979); *BNA Occupational Safety and Health Reporter* 18 (5 Oct. 1978): 568.

2. National Safe Workplace Institute, *Beyond Neglect; The Problem of Occupational Disease in the U.S.—Labor Day '90 Report* (Chicago: The Institute, 1990), 40.

3. For a more detailed suggestion that OSHA establish a priority-setting process and a discussion of the available quantitative techniques for setting priorities, see Sidney A. Shapiro and Thomas O. McGarity, "Reorienting OSHA: Regulatory Alternatives and Legislative Reform," *Yale Journal on Regulation* 6 (Winter 1989): 1. Based on a report prepared by McGarity and Shapiro, the Administrative Conference of the United States has recommended that OSHA adopt a priority-setting process similar to the one described there. See ACUS, "Priority Setting and Management of Rulemaking by the Occupational Safety and Health Administration," Recommendation no. 87–1 (1987), 1 C.F.R. § 305.87–1 (1991).

4. Daniel Jacoby, Department of Labor, Office of the Solicitor, interview, Washington, D.C., 26 Sept. 1986; General Accounting Office, *Delays in Setting Workplace Standards for Cancer-Causing and Other Dangerous Substances* (Washington, D.C.: United States Government Printing Office, 1977), 23–24.

5. Memorandum from Alvin L. Alm to addresses on Action Tracking System, 20 Sept. 1983; Dan Fiorino, director, Regulations and Information Management Division, Office of Policy, Planning and Evaluation, EPA, telephone interview, 3 Nov. 1986;

Robert Curry, branch chief, Planning and Accountability Branch, Office of Standards and Regulations, EPA, telephone interview, 20 Nov. 1986.

6. Thomas O. McGarity, "OSHA's Generic Carcinogen Policy: Rulemaking Under Scientific and Legal Uncertainty," in *Law and Science in Collaboration: Resolving Regulatory Issues of Science and Technology*, ed. J. Daniel Nyhart and Milton M. Carrow (Lexington, Mass.: Lexington Books, 1983), 78, table 5–1; Elinor P. Schroeder and Sidney A. Shapiro, "Responses to Occupational Disease: The Role of Markets, Regulation, and Information," *Georgetown Law Journal* 72 (1984): 1305–09.

7. Susan Harwood, Office of Risk Assessment, OSHA, telephone interview, 21 Oct. 1986; Arthur Gas, industrial hygienist, Directorate of Health Studies Programs, OSHA, telephone interview, 30 Oct. 1986; George Cohen, telephone interview, 28 Oct. 1986; see ACUS, "Procedures in Addition to Notice and the Opportunity for Comment in Informal Rulemaking," Recommendation no. 76–3 (1976), 1 C.F.R. 305.76–3 (1991) (recommending that ANPRs are useful only in limited situations).

8. Harwood interview; Barry White, director, Directorate of Safety Standards Programs, OSHA, interview, Washington, D.C., 26 Sept. 1986; Daniel Jacoby, Department of Labor, Solicitors Office, interview, Washington, D.C., 26 Sept. 1986.

9. 29 U.S.C. §§ 669–71 (1988).

10. U.S. Congress, Senate, *Occupational Safety and Health Act of 1970: Senate Report no. 91–1282*, 91st Cong., 2d sess., 1970 (repr. in 1970 *U.S. Code Congressional and Administrative News*, 5196–97); U.S. Congress, *Occupational Safety and Health Act of 1970: Conference Report No. 91–1765*, 91st Cong., 2d sess., 1970 (repr. in 1970 *U.S. Code Congressional and Administrative News*, 5240).

11. U.S. Congress, House Committee on Education and Labor, Subcommittee on Manpower, Compensation, and Health and Safety, *Oversight Hearings on the Occupational Safety and Health Act*, pt. 2, 94th Cong., 2d sess., 267 (testimony of Dr. John Finklea, director, NIOSH).

12. Ted Greenwood, *Knowledge and Discretion in Government Regulation* (New York: Praeger, 1984), 116.

13. Ibid., 115; *BNA Occupational Safety and Health Reporter* 17 (14 Oct. 1987): 821.

14. Greenwood, *Knowledge and Discretion*, 123.

15. *BNA Occupational Safety and Health Reporter* 17 (14 Oct. 1987): 821.

16. Ibid. 6 (20 Jan. 1977): 1094.

17. 29 U.S.C. § 656(b) (1988).

18. Greenwood, *Knowledge and Discretion*, 125.

19. U.S. Congress, House Committee on Science and Technology, Subcommittee on Natural Resources, Agriculture Research and Environment, *Risk Assessment Research: Hearings on H.R. 4192*, 98th Cong., 2d sess., 145 (1985) (statement of Nicholas Ashford, MIT Center for Policy Alternatives).

20. Lawrence S. Bacow, *Bargaining for Job Safety and Health* (Cambridge, Mass.: MIT Press, 1980), 41–42.

21. Nicholas A. Ashford, "The Role of Advisory Committees in Resolving Regulatory Issues Involving Science and Technology: Experience from OSHA and EPA," in *Law and Science in Collaboration: Resolving Regulatory Issues of Science and Technology*, ed. J. Daniel Nyhart and Milton M. Carrow (Lexington, Mass.: Lexington Books, 1983), 165.

22. Mintz reports that no advisory committees were appointed in part because OSHA was bothered by the requirements for federal advisory committees established by OMB

during the Carter administration and by the requirements of the Federal Advisory Committee Act, 5 U.S.C. App. § 7 (1988). Benjamin W. Mintz, *OSHA: History, Law, and Policy* (Washington, D.C.: Bureau of National Affairs, 1984), 65.

23. 29 U.S.C. § 656(b) (1988).

24. 29 U.S.C. § 655(b)(1) (1988).

25. Edward Tomlinson, "Reporting on the Experience of Various Agencies with Statutory Time Limits Applicable to Licensing or Clearance Functions and to Rulemaking," in *Administrative Conference of the United States*, Recommendations and Reports (Washington, D.C.: United States Government Printing Office, 1978), 207.

26. 29 U.S.C. § (655(b)(2) (1988).

27. Tomlinson, "Experience of Various Agencies," 206.

28. Thomas O. McGarity, "Substantive and Procedural Discretion in Administrative Resolution of Science Policy Questions: Regulating Carcinogens in EPA and OSHA," *Georgetown Law Journal* 67 (1979): 729; Joel Yellin, "High Technology and the Courts: Nuclear Power and the Need for Institutional Reform," *Harvard Law Review* 94 (1981): 489.

29. See *Inside EPA Weekly Report* 7 (15 Aug. 1986): 1 (relating criticism of an EPA advisory committee for dioxin alleging a pro-industry bias).

13

More Bang for the Buck:
Alternative Methods of Regulation
and Implementation

Management reforms can carry OSHA only so far. Even a well-functioning priority-setting process will not substantially increase the number of regulations that OSHA issues. Assuming that OSHA will not receive a substantial infusion of new resources in the near future, any additional increases in regulatory protection will probably come from alternative methods of regulation and enforcement that are capable of yielding greater health and safety gains than OSHA's current approaches.

Like many health and environmental agencies, OSHA can choose from at least three sets of regulatory options in deciding how it will approach complex scientific rulemaking. First, it can choose a "case-by-case" approach that regulates only one hazard at a time or a "generic" approach that combines aspects of more than one hazard into a single proceeding. Second, it can adopt an adversarial orientation in which it chooses the "best" option indicated after a full public hearing or a consensus orientation in which its decision represents a compromise among the views of all the interested parties. Finally, it can select command solutions that protect workers by ordering employers to abate hazards or performance solutions that provide employers with incentives to pursue overall health and safety goals, but give them a certain degree of flexibility in determining exactly how to meet them.

In the past, OSHA had emphasized the case-by-case approach, an adversarial orientation, and command solutions. While these methods of regulation have their place in OSHA's quiver of regulatory arrows, the agency should look for opportunities to use generic regulations, a consensus orientation, and performance solutions. Although the alternative methods of regulation have problems of their own, OSHA can in many cases increase the number of regulations it promulgates by using a different mix of alternative approaches to regulation.

GENERIC REGULATIONS

As long as OSHA can adopt only a few regulations each year, it must maximize the extent to which each regulation protects workers. Generic regulations, which regulate more than one subject or problem in the same rulemaking proceeding, offer the greatest potential for maximizing worker protections for a given level of administrative resources. Generic rulemaking can sharply reduce administrative costs by allowing the agency to dispose of issues in a single hearing that would otherwise have to be decided repeatedly in individual proceedings. Similarly, it can reduce overall information costs, because the agency may not have to acquire detailed information about each regulatee. Finally, generic proceedings allow broader participation by small firms and public interest groups that might lack sufficient resources to participate on a case-by-case basis.

Generic regulations, however, also have some disadvantages. First, they can increase compliance costs, because they tend to gloss over differences between regulated firms. A variance procedure (providing exceptions to the generic rules for companies that can demonstrate unique compliance difficulties) can reduce the possibility of inefficient and inequitable generic regulations, but that procedure itself bears heavy administrative costs that might discourage small firms from taking advantage of it. Second, because the generic approach concentrates the agency's informational needs, the agency may find itself slighting its necessary day-to-day activities. Finally, since generic proceedings invariably involve high stakes, they are usually much more controversial. For the same reason, courts are probably inclined to review generic rulemakings more carefully.

Despite the disadvantages, most observers within and outside the agency agree that OSHA should make greater use of generic regulations.[1] A former OSHA acting administrator, Pat Tyson, observed, "[no] federal agency—be it OSHA, EPA, NIOSH, or any other—is going to be able to go through a regulatory process on a substance by substance approach and keep pace with the new data that is coming out."[2] An industry lawyer points out that "if OSHA's history indicates anything, it is that substance by substance regulation will not work."[3] A public interest lawyer agrees that "OSHA's only possibility of speeding decisionmaking is by use of generic rules."[4] And Frank Mirer, a union official, stresses:

There are several dozen widely used chemicals . . . for which there is overwhelming scientific data which shows that the current OSHA standard is inadequate. This is not an overwhelming number, and several groups of these chemicals could be regulated as classes (for example petroleum solvents, glycol ethers, isocyanates).[5]

OSHA has promulgated some generic regulations. By far its most ambitious generic undertaking was the effort, described in Chapter 9, to update the permissible exposure limits for approximately 400 airborne chemicals. The Eleventh

Circuit Court, however, cut short this commendable attempt to provide some additional protection to thousands of workers. In addition, OSHA has promulgated full-fledged standards regulating 14 carcinogens with similar properties. OSHA has also used the generic approach to address multiple problems in a single industry (such as telecommunications, commercial diving, and marine terminals) and common problems that occur in multiple industries (such as fire protection, noise exposure and hearing conservation, and employee access to medical and exposure records). Finally, OSHA used the generic approach quite successfully in the hazard communication standard (described in Chapter 6) to require employers to provide employees with information and training about exposure to hundreds of hazardous substances.

Despite some impressive generic initiatives, most of OSHA's efforts have been on a substance-by-substance basis. Only four of the agency's first 26 safety standards and only 5 of its first 18 health standards were generic.[6] In seeking out additional opportunities for using the generic approach to solve multiple problems, OSHA should recognize that three broad types of generic standards are available to address workplace risks: industrywide standards, multichemical standards, and work-practice standards.

Industrywide Standards

Industrywide standards, by which OSHA regulates the significant safety and health problems in an entire industry through a single standard, allow OSHA to focus its attention on the most dangerous industries and on the most significant risks in those industries. Industrywide standards can be especially useful where a limited number of risk reduction technologies are available and where industrial processes do not vary greatly among companies. This approach has the additional advantage of avoiding possible embarrassment if the most promising technology for reducing one kind of risk in the industry (e.g., inhalation of sulfur dioxide) increases another workplace hazard (e.g., electrocution hazards from scrubbers and vents).

Yet, industrywide standards have several disadvantages.[7] First, an industry-wide standard usually requires a great deal of information about the industry at issue. Second, if the agency must make a "significant risk" determination for each hazard that it addresses in the chosen industry, a generic standard may be impossible for some industries. Third, OSHA should expect significant and perhaps coordinated business resistance in the industries that it chooses to regulate generally. Fourth, OSHA may have difficulty defining what constitutes a discrete industry, a problem that frequently plagues the Environmental Protection Agency (EPA) in promulgating standards under the Clean Water Act.[8] Finally, the generic approach could create significant opposition from workers in other industries who were exposed to the same chemicals and claimed that the agency was discriminating against them by failing to reduce their exposures. To avoid judicial reversal, OSHA would have to provide a reasoned explanation for its distinctions.[9]

The industrywide approach will be cost-effective only when the foregoing disadvantages can be minimized. When the agency sets priorities, it should attempt to identify discrete industries in which the hazards to be regulated are unique (or where those hazards arise in other industries that can also be regulated), where such hazards are relatively stable over time, where industrywide regulation might save money for the industry, and where such regulation would be more effective for OSHA.

Multiple Chemical Standards

OSHA can also consider promulgating standards that regulate two or more chemicals at one time. The primary advantage of this approach is that OSHA may be able to prepare a generic risk assessment for all of the chemicals being regulated. For example, OSHA might be able to generate a single risk assessment for airborne exposure to all chemicals that may result in a particular disease end point such as chloracne or certain reproductive effects or nervous system disorders. Alternatively, OSHA could promulgate a single generic standard for a group of very similar chemicals, such as the glycol ethers.[10] The feasibility analysis might also be simplified if the same types of abatement techniques were available for all of the chemicals.

The Eleventh Circuit's opinion in the PEL rulemaking demonstrates, however, that there are limits on OSHA's ability to base a "significant risk" determination on a generic risk assessment for chemicals having dissimilar characteristics. Moreover, since there is no guarantee that chemicals with similar toxicological characteristics will be used to perform similar functions, separate feasibility analyses will also be necessary if the Eleventh Circuit opinion stands. Finally, since different chemicals may be used in many different industries, a multi-chemical standard might well attract a larger number of dissatisfied regulatees than either the traditional case-by-case chemical approach or industrywide generic standards. Despite these difficulties, OSHA should attempt to identify situations in which a multichemical approach would be cost-effective for the agency.

Work-Practice Standards

A final type of generic standard is a work-practice regulation, a standard that requires the use of some technology or work practice that protects workers. OSHA's hazard communication rule, its medical and exposure records access rule, and its proposed methods of compliance rule are good examples.[11] All of these rules apply to workers in many industries, and they apply regardless of the type of hazard to which the worker is exposed. Moreover, both seek to protect the worker by a method other than setting an exposure limitation.

OSHA can set work-practice standards in two ways. In many of its individual health standards, OSHA requires employers to provide general services such as exposure monitoring, employee training and education, record keeping, posting warning labels and signs, and the removal of susceptible workers to alternative work as a medical precaution. OSHA could require some of the same protections for any employer regulated by some or all of the recently updated Table Z "consensus" standards. In other cases, OSHA could specify what procedures constitute adequate protection of workers under certain general conditions. A good example is the personal protection device rule discussed in Chapter 11.[12]

Generic work-practice standards can protect a large number of workers in many industries, especially if they address activities that can reduce health and safety risks in numerous workplace contexts. They can also complement traditional chemical-by-chemical health standards by addressing work-practice requirements that are by and large independent of the toxicological effects of individual chemicals. Moreover, because the standards do not focus on a particular chemical or a particular industry, opposition to their implementation may be moderated. Work-practice standards, however, will probably not be successful in specifying practices that are foreign to particular industries or that are impossible to implement in some contexts. This suggests that OSHA should provide for variances in cases where the standards are clearly inappropriate. Finally, to the extent that work-practice standards tend to address relatively uncontroversial "boiler plate" aspects of individual standards, they are not likely to reduce OSHA's overall work load appreciably. Still, they can sometimes be quite useful in eliminating the need to address recurring issues in individual proceedings.

CONSENSUS APPROACHES TO REGULATION

In the past few years, several agencies have employed regulatory negotiation—a consensus approach to regulation—to speed up the rulemaking process. Negotiated rulemaking involves broad discussions among all interested parties with the goal of arriving at a consensus on a proposed rule. The agency's role can range from full participation as a negotiator to acting as an observer and commenting on possible agency reactions and concerns. The agency, however, must appoint an official to convene and organize the negotiations, and it can also appoint a mediator to facilitate agreements. Ground rules for the negotiations are established by the participants at the outset. The negotiators then meet until they have reached agreement, until they have agreed that they will not reach agreement, or until a previously imposed deadline has passed. Depending on how intensely the negotiators go about their work, the entire process can consume from six months to a year.

If the negotiations are successful, the agency should be able to promulgate the proposed rule with substantial cost and time savings. Other advantages include the avoidance of litigation, the possibility of more accurately identifying the real concerns of the parties (because they do not engage in the posturing that occurs in litigation), the opportunity to identify the intensity of the parties' concerns over various issues, and the legitimacy the promulgated rule will enjoy because it was a joint product of the agency and the parties.[13] Congress was sufficiently persuaded by the advantages of negotiated rulemaking that it enacted the Negotiated Rulemaking Act of 1990 to encourage agencies to try it in appropriate cases.[14]

OSHA has used some form of negotiations in rulemaking on four different occasions. In 1976, regulations controlling employee exposure to coke oven emissions were adopted in accordance with agreements reached among OSHA, industry, and organized labor. These efforts, however, did not forestall a legal challenge to the regulations.[15] In 1983, negotiations were used to a limited extent, without agency involvement, in resolving disagreements between industry and labor concerning the cotton dust standard. In the same year, OSHA sponsored more elaborate negotiations involving the steel, rubber, and petrochemical industries and labor to develop a revised standard for benzene. Although there were some significant agreements, the process ultimately failed. Finally, OSHA in 1986 completed a successful negotiated rulemaking proceeding for 4,4' methylenedianiline, a carcinogen, although those negotiations were nearly scuttled by OMB.[16]

Some observers believe that OSHA's mixed experience suggests that negotiated rulemaking will not work at OSHA, while others are more optimistic. The doubters argue that there is too much distrust between management and labor for this idea to function effectively, that its usefulness is limited because OSHA and labor have only a limited number of experts who can participate, and that OSHA and industry use regulatory negotiation for chemicals like benzene as an excuse to forestall difficult decisions. Skeptics fear that agency employees may attempt to torpedo the negotiations. Health professionals may object that the process compromises OSHA's statutory commitment to reducing risks, and agency lawyers may feel their role and influence are diminished.[17] Supporters counter that several conditions are required for a successful result and that many of those were missing in the benzene negotiations. They point out that labor and management reach agreements in collective bargaining, and they maintain that OSHA can achieve similar successes in appropriate cases, especially if it is a more active participant. They also observe that even if negotiations fail, OSHA can still gain a better understanding of the issues and a better feel for what the parties can accept.[18]

Negotiated rulemaking has great potential, but it will not work in all cases. In particular, negotiated rulemaking is not likely to be successful for large generic rulemaking efforts with precedent-setting potential. In addition, it is not likely to be useful in addressing issues, such as the use of respirators versus engineering controls, about which the positions of likely participants have already hardened. On the other hand, negotiated rulemaking might be entirely appropriate for new topics, such as regulating risks posed by genetically engineered microorganisms in the pharmaceutical industry, where positions have not been formed and where large investments have not yet been made. Negotiated rulemaking may also fail for topics in which a large number of parties have widely divergent interests. Finally, a precondition for a successful negotiated rulemaking may be a relative equivalence in the power of all participants to affect the outcome of the proceeding should the negotiations fail. A party that holds all the cards going into the negotiations is likely to have a disproportionate impact on the outcome. Knowing this, weaker parties may refrain from participating at the outset.

This suggests that OSHA should evaluate the possibility of using negotiated rulemaking on a case-by-case basis. In cases where the agency chooses to use the process, however, it must have some device for quickly jettisoning it when it appears to be failing. Otherwise, the already slow decision-making process at OSHA will become even slower. The best solution may be to set an irrevocable deadline for the completion of any regulatory negotiation. OSHA could also help to ensure a successful outcome if it held orientation for the negotiation committee to bring it up to speed concerning the industries involved, the scientific and technical issues to be covered, and the committee's latitude in writing a standard that is in compliance with the OSH Act.[19] OSHA should also ensure that the committee has adequate staffing.

The benefits to be gained from this consensus approach will evaporate if the Office of Management and Budget (OMB) insists on making changes in the negotiated rule. As Chapter 15 explains, OSHA must submit all proposed standards to OMB for review. OMB, as the president's agent, reviews the standards for compliance with the president's regulatory philosophy. In the MDA and formaldehyde rulemaking, however, OMB stuck to its ideological guns and insisted on changes in the rules, even though they were the products of delicate compromises. Chapter 15 discusses further the problem that OMB review presents for negotiated rulemaking.

PERFORMANCE STANDARDS

One traditional criticism of OSHA has been that it is too quick to order the use of a specific technique or technology (a design standard) to reduce workplace risks rather than allowing firms to meet mandatory safety goals by whatever design they choose (a performance standard). Although this criticism is not entirely accurate or fair, OSHA may benefit from the increased use of performance standards.

OSHA has not ignored performance standards. The permissible exposure limits (PELs) that are the core of OSHA's health regulations are performance-oriented, because employers are free to use any technology (other than respirators) that is capable of achieving the ambient concentration specified in the permissible exposure limit (PEL). Moreover, OSHA has attempted in recent years to expand its use of the performance-oriented approach beyond the use of PELs. The hazard communication standard (discussed in Chapters 6 and 8) permits firms to design their own labeling systems, and the grain-handling standard (discussed in Chapter 6) permits firms to use any one of several methods to decrease accumulations of grain dust.[20] Yet, almost all of OSHA's safety regulations are design standards. This choice is in part a legacy of the hundreds of consensus safety standards based on voluntary safety and health codes that Congress required OSHA to adopt in 1971. In doing so, OSHA converted discretionary guidelines into design standards, because the voluntary codes often contained specific design requirements.[21]

Since performance standards are usually less costly than design standards, greater reliance on them may reduce industry opposition to OSHA rules. A performance standard frees industry to choose the method of compliance with the lowest costs, to design methods of compliance that are easily understood, and to discover and adopt less expensive methods of compliance in the future.[22] Moreover, performance standards may be less resource-intensive for OSHA. OSHA must know a good deal about an industry when it promulgates a design standard, and this information usually comes from industry itself. These enormous information requirements virtually ensure that the pace of regulation will be slow. Performance standards require less information about risk-reduction technologies and therefore should require fewer agency resources. Yet, since OSHA ordinarily must examine the technological feasibility of complying with its standards in any case, these resource gains may be modest.

Performance standards, however, have significant disadvantages. Unless performance standards are as protective of workers as design standards, labor opposition could provoke considerable controversy. Design standards offer greater protection in some cases because they create precise expectations for employers, facilitate the ability of employees and OSHA inspectors to monitor compliance, and permit OSHA to require employers to implement new safety technologies. Performance standards are often unenforceable and therefore tend to shift the burden of risk avoidance from the employer to the worker. Finally, employers may lack the expertise and resources to translate performance criteria into suitable engineering designs, especially at small firms that cannot afford to hire outside expertise.[23]

OSHA should consider using performance standards, but only when they are appropriate in light of the problems identified above. A performance standard is appropriate only when it offers the same degree of protection as a design standard, it can be easily understood and monitored, and it is likely to lower industry compliance costs substantially.

INFORMATION STANDARDS

In the minds of some reformers, information-oriented standards provide a more flexible approach to regulation. Providing employees with greater information about health and safety hazards can assist private markets to promote health and safety more efficiently. In theory, workers will use this information to change their conduct in dangerous situations, bargain for wage premiums (extra pay) for dangerous work, and participate more effectively in relevant legislative and administrative proceedings. Proponents of information-oriented standards therefore applaud the hazard communication standard (discussed in Chapters 6 and 8) and urge OSHA to increase its efforts to make written materials and training programs available to workers.[24]

The discussion of wage premiums in Chapter 2 suggests that workers are rarely able to use information about safety and health hazards to bargain for significant wage premiums for job hazards. One reason for this is that workers lack bargaining power. Another is that they tend to discount workplace risks as a psychological reaction, and they therefore undervalue the danger they face. Finally, it is difficult to design effective programs to convey information to workers. For example, while communicating short-term safety risks to employees can be effective, long-term health risks are much more difficult to communicate. Moreover, OSHA cannot easily determine which industries should establish information programs addressing long-term risks because accurate information about those risks is so scarce.[25] In addition, complex problems of trade secrecy arise whenever information relevant to communicating workplace risks can be used by competitors to the employer's disadvantage.[26]

While increased reliance on information-oriented programs will no doubt aid workers, it is not enough, standing alone, to protect all workers adequately. Thus, while OSHA should continue to explore ways to increase the information available to workers, such solutions will never be a substitute for health and safety standards. Information-oriented approaches may prove more effective in the future when coupled with efforts (described in Chapters 22 and 23) aimed at empowering workers to make real choices about the acceptability of workplace risks.

RESOURCES

If OSHA is serious about increasing its ponderous standard-setting pace, it should rely more heavily upon generic approaches to standard-setting and use negotiated rulemaking and performance and information standards where appropriate. To maximize the risk-reduction potential of these reforms, OSHA badly needs additional resources and a regulatory plan.

The Reagan administration budget cuts left OSHA, and particularly the Health Standards Directorate, seriously understaffed, and the Bush administration has done little to remedy the problem. Individual health professionals in that directorate are responsible for multiple rulemaking projects and have numerous additional responsibilities. In addition, OSHA must have a significant infusion of new personnel. Many of OSHA's health scientists and industrial hygienists have been with the agency since the early 1970s, and a few are approaching retirement age. Although most are enthusiastic about their jobs, they have been around the block a few times and sometimes lack commitment to the agency's worker protection goals. The addition of fresh talent could have the synergistic effect of reinvigorating some of the long-term employees. It is, in the final analysis, hypocritical for Congress and OMB to criticize OSHA for poor work if they are unwilling to provide sufficient resources for the agency to do a good job.

NOTES

1. See, e.g., *BNA Occupational Safety and Health Reporter* 18 (11 Jan. 1989): 1445 (AFL-CIO recommends greater use of generic standards); ibid. 17 (29 Jan. 1988): 1750 (former Assistant Secretary Eula Bingham recommends generic standards); ibid. (23 Sept. 1987): 747 (industry health and safety director recommends generic standards).

2. U.S. Congress, House Committee on Science and Technology, *Neurotoxins at Home and the Workplace*, 99th Cong., 2d sess., 1986, H.R. Doc. 99–827, 33.

3. Scott Railton, interview, Washington, D.C., 30 Oct. 1986.

4. David Vladieck, interview, Washington, D.C., 26 Sept. 1986.

5. U.S. Congress, Senate Committee on Labor and Human Resources, *Hearings on Oversight on the Administration of the Occupational Safety and Health Act*, 100th Cong., 2d sess., S.Hrg. 100–719, 1988, 91–92 (testimony of Dr. Franklin E. Mirer, director, Health and Safety Department, International Union, UAW).

6. U.S. Congress, Office of Technology Assessment, *Preventing Illnesses and Injury in the Workplace* (Washington, D.C.: United States Government Printing Office, 1985), 363–64; Elinor Schroeder and Sidney Shapiro, "Responses to Occupational Disease: The Role of Markets, Regulation, and Information," *Georgetown Law Journal* 72 (1984): 1305–09.

7. Charles Gordon, Solicitors Office, Department of Labor, telephone conversation, 23 Oct. 1986; Margaret Seminario, Department of Occupational Safety, AFL-CIO, telephone conversation, 30 Oct. 1986; Imogene Sevin, Health Standards Directorate, OSHA, telephone conversations, 3 and 5 Nov. 1986; Frank Fordym, director, Directorate of Policy, interview, Washington, D.C., 26 Sept. 1986; Dan Jacoby, Solicitors Office, Department of Labor, interview, Washington, D.C., 26 Sept. 1986; Jack Sheehan, United Steelworkers of America, interview, Washington, D.C., 29 Oct. 1986.

8. Arthur Kneese and Charles Schultz, *Pollution, Prices and Society* (Washington, D.C.: Brookings Institution, 1975), 62, n.9.

9. In *United Steelworkers of Am.* v. *Auchter*, 763 F.2d (3rd Cir. 1985), OSHA had failed to explain adequately why it could not apply the coverage of the hazard communication rule to all employees instead of only those in certain industries.

10. 52 *Fed. Reg.* 10,586 (1987) (advance notice of proposed rulemaking for generic standard for glycol ethers).

11. 29 C.F.R. § 1910.1200, § 1910.120(f) (1991).

12. 56 *Fed. Reg.* 53,595 (1991).

13. Phillip Harter, "Dispute Resolution and Administrative Law: The History, Needs, and Future of a Complex Relationship," *Villanova Law Review* 29 (1984): 1393; Phillip Harter, "Negotiating Regulations: A Case of Malaise," *Georgetown Law Review* 71 (1982): 1.

14. 5 U.S.C. §§ 581–90 (West Supp. 1991).

15. *Iron & Steel Inst.* v. *OSHA*, 577 F.2d 825 (3rd Cir. 1978).

16. Hank Perritt, "Negotiated Rulemaking Before Federal Agencies: Evaluation of Recommendations by the Administrative Conference of the United States," *Georgetown*

Law Review 74 (1986): 1647–67, 1682–86; *BNA Occupational Safety and Health Reporter* 16 (26 May 1987): 1451.

17. Mark Rothstein, "Substantive and Procedural Obstacles to OSHA Rulemaking: Reproductive Hazards as an Example," *Boston College Environmental Affairs Law Review* 12 (1985): 663; Karl Kronebusch, Office of Technology Assessment, interview, Washington, D.C., 31 Oct. 1986; Benjamin Mintz, Catholic University, interview, Washington, D.C., 25 Sept. 1986.

18. Perritt, "Negotiated Rulemaking," 749; Rothstein, "Substantive and Procedural Obstacles," 663.

19. Roger Daniel, Chemical Manufacturers Association, telephone interview, 24 Oct. 1986.

20. 29 C.F.R. §§ 1910.272, 1910.1200 (1991).

21. W. Kip Viscusi, "Reforming OSHA Regulation of Workplace Risks," in *Regulatory Reform: What Actually Happened*, ed. Leonard Weiss and Michael Klass (Boston: Little, Brown, 1986), 248.

22. Albert Nichols and Richard Zeckhauser, "OSHA After a Decade: A Time for Reason," in *Case Studies in Regulation: Revolution and Reform*, ed. Leonard Weiss and Michael Klass (Boston: Little, Brown, 1981), 203; Paul MacAvoy, ed. *OSHA Safety Regulation: Report of the Presidential Taskforce* (Washington, D.C.: American Enterprise Institute, 1977), 14, 18; Robert Smith, *The Occupational Safety and Health Act: Its Goals and Achievements* (Washington, D.C.: American Enterprise Institute, 1976), 75–77.

23. MacAvoy, *OSHA Safety Regulation*, 18.

24. W. Kip Viscusi, *Risk by Choice: Regulating Health and Safety in the Workplace* (Cambridge, Mass.: Harvard University Press, 1983); Smith, *Goals and Achievements*, 27–28; Richard Zeckhauser and Albert Nichols, "The Occupational Safety and Health Administration—An Overview," in U.S. Congress, Senate Committee on Government Affairs, *Study on Federal Regulations*, 96th Cong., 1st sess., 1978, S. Doc. 96–14, 169, 172.

25. Susan Hadden, *Read the Label: Reducing Risk by Providing Information* (Boulder, Colo.: Westview Press, 1986), 101–13.

26. Thomas O. McGarity and Sidney Shapiro, "The Trade Secret Status of Health and Safety Testing Information: Reforming Agency Disclosure Policies," *Harvard Law Review* 93 (1980): 837.

14

Ensuring Compliance: The Puzzle of Enforcement

In November 1987, a jury in Brooklyn, New York, convicted the owners of the Pymm Thermometer Company, the nation's second largest manufacturer of mercury thermometers, of assault for exposing workers to high levels of mercury, an extremely toxic chemical that can cause permanent damage to the brain, lungs, liver, and kidneys. More than half of Pymm's approximately 100 employees, and several of their children, were victims of mercury poisoning. Pymm employees regularly suffered tremors, headaches, fatigue, and dizziness associated with their exposure to mercury.[1] One of the employees, Vidal Rodriguez, suffered permanent brain damage.[2] The workers had been removing the mercury from old thermometers in a windowless basement room filled with broken glass and noxious fumes from puddles of mercury on the floor. The room had almost no outside ventilation, and the workers did not wear respirators or protective clothing. Elizabeth Holtzman, the Brooklyn district attorney, told the jury, "If mercury can put holes in someone's brain, that's not much different from a gun putting a hole in someone's brain."[3]

OSHA had known about the conditions at the Pymm Company since January 1981, when Pymm was first cited for serious violations that resulted in overexposure to mercury.[4] The agency fined Pymm $1,400 and ordered it to abate the hazards within six months. Inexplicably, however, the agency granted four successive one-year compliance extensions, the last of which was allowed after the New York attorney general notified Rowland that the New York City Health Department had found elevated mercury levels in the bodies of employees. The fourth OSHA inspection, in October 1985, found mercury levels that ranged as high as ten times the permissible exposure limit of 0.1 milligram per cubic meter of air. Even after cleanup of the mercury, air samples showed levels greater than the permissible exposure limit. Fines of $30,100 were assessed.[5] In November and December 1986, after the company had been indicted by a state grand jury,[6] a fifth OSHA inspection again found violations, and this time assessed fines of $75,000.[7] OSHA officials conceded that federal inspectors failed to fine Pymm according to agency rules and overlooked the cellar because of irregular and insufficient inspections.[8]

Acting OSHA Director Patrick Tyson was flabbergasted: "How the hell could something like this happen? . . . It is clear to me that we made some mistakes."[9] Another OSHA official admitted that the agency's handling of the Pymm case was "not our finest hour."[10] This chapter examines what went wrong in the Pymm case and others like it. In brief, OSHA has failed to protect workers because it has too few inspectors, a faulty system for determining inspection priorities, and inadequate criminal penalties.

THE ENFORCEMENT PUZZLE

In attempting to devise an effective enforcement program, OSHA faces a crucial puzzle: How can it convince employers to achieve compliance despite the fact they are unlikely to be inspected? Although OSHA conducts about 60,000 inspections annually,[11] it has enforcement responsibility for more than five million employers. As a result, only one of every 25 job sites has ever been visited by an OSHA inspector.[12] An additional 100,000 inspections each year are conducted in states that run their own OSHA programs,[13] but the vast majority of employers remain uninspected in those jurisdictions as well.

Solving the puzzle requires an appraisal of the employers' incentive to comply with OSHA regulations. In deciding whether to comply, employers will compare the costs of compliance and noncompliance. Compliance costs include the expense of purchasing safety equipment or taking other preventive steps that OSHA requires. Noncompliance costs are related to the probability an employer will be inspected and the size of the penalties that will be assessed for any violations that are found.[14] For example, if an employer expects it will have 10 violations at $1,000 per violation, it is potentially liable for a total of $10,000. It will, however, take into account the likelihood it will be caught. If it has only a 1 in 1,000 chance of being inspected, it will calculate the cost of noncompliance as the probability of being inspected (1 in 1,000) times the amount of the fine ($10,000), or $10. Employers therefore often have an incentive not take safety precautions, because compliance costs often exceed such discounted noncompliance costs.

If OSHA is to have an effective enforcement program, it must increase the probability that dangerous workplaces will be inspected and, if violations are found, that stiff penalties will be assessed. OSHA's attitude concerning these critical elements of an effective enforcement policy has traditionally been one of complacency.

Size of the Inspectorate

If OSHA is to increase the number of dangerous workplaces that it inspects, it needs more inspectors. The number of compliance officers working for OSHA almost doubled from 1973 to 1980, from about 750 to nearly 1,400. By 1982, however, the number of inspectors had declined to 1,000, which is about the current number.[15] Arguably, these cutbacks brought about the Pymm Thermometer tragedy. The number of employees at OSHA's area offices in New York City declined from 63 to 42 during the first 5 years of the Reagan administration, largely a result of the closure of the Brooklyn area office that first cited Pymm for violations in 1981.[16] For the New York region as a whole—defined as New York, New Jersey, and Puerto Rico—the number of inspections generated by employee complaints dropped to 1,221 in 1985 from 2,692 in 1980.[17] Nevertheless, OSHA steadfastly refused during the Reagan administration to ask for more money to hire more compliance officers. John Pendergrass, OSHA's administrator from 1985 to 1988, defended this position by arguing that because OSHA must be responsive to the American taxpayers, ''I feel compelled to do the most with what we have.''[18] As the Pymm Thermometer case vividly demonstrates, however, what OSHA has is not nearly enough.

OSHA's reluctance to become an advocate for additional enforcement resources is unfortunate, because OSHA can make a good case for a substantial increase. For example, although the Mine Safety and Health Administration has far fewer employers to inspect, it has 1,290 inspectors (compared with OSHA's 1,000 inspectors).[19] Even fish and game animals are better protected than workers. The states and federal government employ over 7,000 fish and game wardens.[20]

Although OSHA should argue for more enforcement resources, any budget increases are likely to be modest in these days of stringency. OSHA must therefore take steps to use the resources available to it as effectively as possible. Even in the absence of severe budget constraints, OSHA will never have enough enforcement personnel to inspect more than a fraction of the country's employers in any one year.

Inspection Priorities

OSHA attempts to maximize its inspection resources through a two-pronged priority-setting system. It makes unprogrammed inspections in response to employee complaints or reports of accidents. Programmed inspections rely upon statistical data indicating which industries are the most dangerous.[21] Since OSHA cannot assume that it will always receive complaints about the most dangerous conditions, programmed inspections are essential to prevent accidents and illnesses. Unfortunately, the statistical data upon which the agency bases these program inspections are generally regarded as inaccurate and incomplete. Even if the data were accurate, OSHA would not have enough employees to inspect all of the truly dangerous workplaces. The General Accounting Office estimates that only 10 percent and 3 percent of the workplaces that OSHA identified as presenting high safety and health hazards, respectively, were actually inspected. And of those inspections, about half were conducted in response to specific evidence of hazardous conditions at a work site, such as complaints or referrals.[22]

Safety Inspections

OSHA prioritizes its safety programmed inspections on the basis of lost workdays as calculated by the Bureau of Labor Statistics (BLS), another agency in the Department of Labor. BLS relies upon an annual survey of employers to calculate the number of days employees in various industries missed work. As noted in Chapter 1, BLS concedes that its data understate lost workdays, because employers have an incentive to file inaccurate reports. If firms in an industry consistently underreport, OSHA is less likely to select that industry as a high-hazard industry subject to programmed inspections.

OSHA has attacked the problem of underreporting by levying significant fines against firms it catches with inaccurate records. Chapter 10 explained that under John Pendergrass, OSHA assessed millions of dollars in fines against major corporations for willfully failing to keep accurate injury logs. Although this effort should have resulted in better reporting, there is evidence that workplace fatality reporting is still inaccurate. An investigative reporter for the *Dayton Daily News*, who reviewed workers' compensation records in Arkansas and Oklahoma, easily discovered nearly three dozen workplace fatalities that were never reported to OSHA. The unreported fatalities constituted more than 25 percent of the total workplace fatalities in Arkansas, and 20 percent of fatalities in Oklahoma. When informed of the results of the newspaper's investigation, Assistant Secretary Gerard Scannell was not surprised and estimated that as many as "40 to 60 percent of all fatalities are underreported." When pressed to explain this extraordinary phenomenon, Scannell was stumped: "Why don't they report them? I wish I could give you an answer."[23] One somewhat less naive answer is that employers fail to report fatalities (and nonfatal accidents) to avoid programmed inspections.

A second problem with the data is that the number of "lost workdays" fails to indicate accurately the severity of the injuries that occur. A worker may recover quickly from a life-threatening accident in one case, while another person may lose months from a relatively minor injury that limits activity. For this reason, a National Academy of Sciences (NAS) report on occupational health and safety statistics recommended that the BLS require employers to report all injuries that result in death, hospitalization, or outpatient surgery. These data would indicate to OSHA which industries expose workers to the greatest number of life-threatening accidents.[24]

A third problem is that BLS statistics are available only for industries as a whole and not for individual firms. To obtain individual firm data, OSHA must inspect the records of each employer in an industry. If OSHA had a centralized data source that disaggregated industrywide data, it could eliminate this cumbersome procedure. BLS can produce data on individual firms, but it refuses to do so out of fear that disclosure to OSHA will reduce employer incentives to submit accurate information. The NAS report endorsed the BLS's position, although a minority of the report's authors disagreed. The majority of the authors recommended that OSHA develop its own system for generating data about individual firms.[25] OSHA has a computer system containing data obtained during OSHA inspections that it now uses to produce annual tabulations of its inspection activity. Although the agency hopes the system can also be used to target individual firms for safety and health inspections, OSHA employees have reported that the system is inaccessible or inoperable so much of the time that it usefulness is questionable.[26]

Health Inspections

OSHA does not use the BLS statistics on occupational illnesses for programming health inspections, because they are too unreliable. As with accidents, employers tend to underreport illnesses in order to avoid future inspections. In addition, it is very difficult to attribute occupational illnesses to workplace exposures to particular toxic chemicals. Furthermore, given the long latency period of many occupational illnesses and the mobility of the workforce, a system that relies upon individual employers to report illnesses caused by their workplaces is doomed to failure. The NAS report therefore recommended that the National Institute for Occupational Safety and Health (NIOSH) develop a surveillance system for illnesses that does not depend on employer reports.[27]

OSHA chooses industries for health inspections on the basis of the number of past violations of health-related regulations that OSHA has detected in those industries.[28] This approach has the capacity to weed out industries with good compliance records, but it does not ensure that especially unhealthy industries, like the thermometer manufacturing industry, get into the system in the first place. OSHA could enhance the effectiveness of its programmed inspection program if it also considered the identity and quantity of the chemicals used in an industry and how many workers are exposed to those chemicals. Although data concerning the location and quantity of chemicals have been difficult to obtain in the past, OSHA can now rely on the Emergency Planning and Community Right to Know Act, which requires companies to prepare forms listing the identity and quantity of the chemicals they use.[29]

Acquiring Better Safety and Health Data

The efficacy of OSHA's programmed inspection program depends upon the agency's ability to acquire better safety and health data for individual workplaces. Two easily implementable improvements would greatly enhance OSHA's programmed safety inspections. First, the secretary of labor should order BLS to implement the previously discussed NAS recommendations to improve accident data. This step would assist OSHA in identifying the most dangerous industries. Second, OSHA should consult workers' compensation payout data to choose individual employers for safety inspections. Firms with a poor safety record should have more successful workers' compensation claims filed against them. Most states maintain payout data in a form that could be used for targeting purposes, and some of them, like Washington, use the data to target their own inspections. Not all states, however, have readily available information, and the information from different states cannot be readily compared.[30] Nevertheless, OSHA has so little accurate information, it should not ignore this important source of data.

Programmed inspections for occupational disease would benefit if NIOSH adopted the NAS report's recommendation that it develop a comprehensive system of occupational disease data and if it carefully coordinated that function with OSHA. Congress could enhance NIOSH-OSHA coordination by moving NIOSH from the Department of Health and Human Services to the Department of Labor so that the secretary of labor can supervise both agencies and decrease coordination problems.

MONETARY PENALTIES

Better data will enable OSHA to find and inspect more dangerous workplaces. The willingness of employers to comply with OSHA regulations, however, is also a function of the size of the fines that violators pay. The increase in allowable fines that Congress enacted in 1990, discussed in Chapter 11, has the potential to increase significantly the deterrent effect of OSHA inspections, and OSHA has recently assessed several multimillion-dollar fines. But OSHA's record is spotty. While some violations receive severe treatment, others have been ignored. One reason for the apparent inconsistency is that OSHA's fines are by statute related to the number of violations instead of to their consequences. If a fatality results from a single violation of an OSHA regulation, the agency can fine the employer a maximum of $70,000, if the violation were willful or a repeat violation, and $7,000 if it were not.

In practice, OSHA has often failed to assess maximum penalties, even in cases involving fatalities. For example, OSHA inspected a chemical plant owned by the Phillips Petroleum Company in August 1989 after two workers were killed and two were hospitalized following a flash fire and explosion. Union investigators said undertrained contract workers triggered the explosion by mistakenly opening a valve. OSHA proposed penalties of $1,440 for the contractor and $720 for Phillips.[31] Two months later another explosion shook the same plant. This time 23 people died and 314 were injured. Again, union investigators attributed the explosion to undertrained contract workers who opened the wrong valve. OSHA proposed a $5.7 million fine for the second explosion. Noting that

OSHA investigators had uncovered internal documents showing that Phillips knew about and failed to correct the problem of undertrained contract workers, Secretary of Labor Dole complained: "This tragedy is magnified by the clear evidence that this explosion was avoidable had recognized safety procedures been followed."[32]

Unfortunately, OSHA is far more likely to impose a $720 fine than one of $5.7 million. The *Dayton Daily News* calculated that the median fine following a death or serious injury in 1990 was $890. Adjusted for inflation, that is less than half of the median fine in 1972.[33] In 1988, a workers' advocacy group calculated that the average fine assessed by OSHA in trenching accidents involving fatalities was $1,545.16 per fatality.[34]

Even in the more recent cases where OSHA has assessed significant penalties, it usually reduces their size in negotiations with employers after the press reports of the high fines are long forgotten. A good example is OSHA's mega-fine program. Started by John Pendergrass in 1985, the new policy authorized inspectors to assess a separate penalty for each instance an employer violated the same standard when engaging in "egregious conduct." As Chapter 10 explained, OSHA's prior policy had been to treat multiple violations of the same standard as a single violation. Critics of the mega-fine approach charged that OSHA lured the public into thinking it was taking a hard-line attitude, without actually doing so, by substantially reducing most of the mega-fines in subsequent settlement negotiations. OSHA reduced the fines in cases it closed in 1988 by 71 percent, from approximately $9.3 to $2.7 million. For cases closed in 1987, the reduction was 43 percent, from $2.7 to $1.6 million. OSHA's mega-fines apparently accounted for most of the reductions. OSHA reduced 9 of 11 mega-fines by amounts ranging from 25 to 89 percent in 1987 and 1988. The largest fine was reduced by 55 percent, from $2.8 million to $1.25 million. Another fine was reduced 72 percent, from $1.5 million to 0.4 million.[35]

The mega-fine reductions are part of a larger pattern. A computer analysis undertaken by the *Dayton Daily News* found that OSHA collects less than half of the fines it levies. The results of this study, reproduced in Figure 14–1, show that as OSHA has increased the size of its fines, it has collected a smaller percentage of the amounts originally assessed. Thus, while OSHA levied a record $66.5 million in fines in 1990, it actually collected only about 45 percent of that amount, or $30.479 million.[36]

OSHA defends these reductions on the ground that each settlement requires an employer to abate immediately the violations for which it was fined. When OSHA does not reach a settlement, abatement may not occur for several years because an employer has no legal obligation to abate a hazard until it has a hearing before the Occupational Safety and Health Review Commission. Thus, John Pendergrass defended OSHA's settlement policies because "[o]ur goal is abatement, and to achieve that, we enter into settlement agreements."[37] OSHA noted that although it has reduced most mega-fines, they are still larger than the largest fines assessed during the Bingham administration.[38]

Figure 14–1
OSHA Fines (millions of dollars)

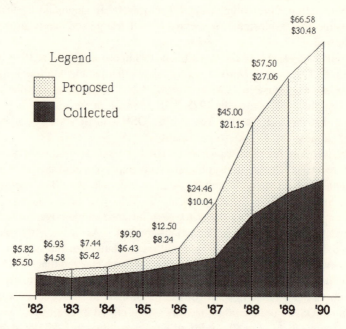

Source: Redrawn, with permission, from the *Dayton Daily News*.

It often makes sense for OSHA to trade fine reductions for immediate abatement of workplace hazards, given its inability otherwise to require immediate abatement. Not all of OSHA's reductions, however, are justifiable. For example, OSHA routinely reduces penalties for record-keeping violations, even though abatement is neither costly nor complex and the violations do not put workers in any immediate danger. OSHA can, in any event, maximize the deterrent effect of its fines by proposing the maximum fines for willful and egregious violations. Even if OSHA later reduced the fine to obtain immediate abatement of a hazard, the employer would still end up paying more than a token amount. Finally, OSHA needs to articulate a clear settlement policy to avoid reducing penalties in inappropriate cases. The Labor Department inspector general has concluded that the agency's failure to develop a settlement policy ''limit]s] the impact of OSHA's enforcement efforts by not sending the intended signal to all employers, both those already inspected and those not inspected.''[39]

Criminal Penalties

Besides increasing the size of the fines it assesses, OSHA can implement a ''get tough'' approach toward workplace fatalities through its power to seek criminal penalties. An employer can be sentenced to six months' imprisonment for the "willful" violation of a standard when the violation causes the death of an employee.[40] OSHA has, however, largely ignored the criminal prosecution enforcement option. In 20 years, only one employer has gone to jail. In that case, the owner of a construction company served 45 days after 2 workers died in Avon, South Dakota, when an unsupported trench collapsed in 1988.[41] By comparison, the Environmental Protection Agency has put 228 people in jail since 1987 for violating federal environmental laws.[42] OSHA's exceedingly weak criminal prosecution record lags far behind that of local prosecutors. In 1987, Ira Reiner, Los Angeles district attorney, told Congress that he filed more criminal cases in 2 years than the federal government had filed in 17 years.[43]

OSHA blames the Department of Justice (DOJ) for this lackadaisical record, and the DOJ blames OSHA. Both appear to be at fault. Although OSHA's field staff recommends approximately 100 cases for prosecution annually,[44] the agency's administrators referred a total of only 80 cases to the Justice Department from 1971 to 1991.[45] This record would have been much worse had not Gerald Scannell referred 24 cases (30 percent of the total) to DOJ during his first 22 months in office.[46] DOJ's record is equally meager. From 1980 to 1989, the department prosecuted only 4 of the 30 criminal cases that OSHA referred to it.[47]

These pitifully poor results have several explanations. A 1989 study concluded that whereas local prosecutors "routinely" bring charges within a few months of a complaint, poor coordination between OSHA and DOJ results in delays of as long as three years.[48] Because OSHA's enforcement resources are so strained (OSHA has no full-time criminal investigators on its staff),[49] two or more days often pass between a fatal accident and an OSHA investigation.[50] Stanley Twardy, Jr., a United States attorney, cited these reasons to explain his decision not to prosecute a building subcontractor for the 1987 collapse of a Bridgeport, Connecticut, building that killed 28 workers: "Simply put, the investigative process triggered by the collapse of L'Ambiance Plaza was not designed to gather the kind of evidence necessary for a criminal prosecution."[51] Finally, DOJ claims that it cannot justify spending resources on cases that involve such small penalties.[52] DOJ's attitude, however, underestimates the benefit of criminal prosecutions. Even a six-month jail sentence will likely have a substantial deterrent effect on employers. Nevertheless, the department has reduced the budget of its office that prosecutes workplace crimes by hundreds of thousands of dollars in order to increase the funding of the section responsible for the prosecution of child pornography.[53]

Congress should take three steps to expand OSHA's ability to rely upon criminal prosecutions. First, it should mandate longer sentences for employers in cases where willful violations cause employee deaths. Experience in other areas of white-collar crime, such as antitrust and environmental law, indicates that criminal penalties create a level of deterrence above and beyond that provided by civil penalties. Moreover, criminalizing a type of behavior sends a message to would-be lawbreakers that society finds such conduct intolerable. We should be no more willing to tolerate willful behavior by employers that results in the death of a worker than we are willing to tolerate violations of the Clean Water Act that endanger fish. Yet the former has a maximum penalty of only 6 months, while the later has a maximum penalty of 15 years.[54] An increase in authorized penalties should also undermine DOJ's reluctance to use its resources to pursue inconsequential penalties.

Second, Congress should extend criminal penalties to cases involving serious bodily injury. If a willful violation by an employer results in the death of a worker, OSHA can seek a criminal penalty. If the same behavior results in a serious bodily injury, the employer may not be punished criminally. Yet whether an employee is seriously injured or killed is often merely fortuitous. Since the employer's conduct is equally culpable in both cases, the available penalties should not vary.

In opposing the extension of criminal penalties to serious bodily injury cases, OSHA has argued that the change would hamper its enforcement efforts.[55] But the agency has not explained how adding an additional arrow to its quiver will reduce the number of available targets. The universal experience of other agencies and district attorneys is that increased penalties make it easier, not more difficult, to induce compliance with the law. Although OSHA has always had difficulty securing the cooperation of employers in abating safety hazards, the threat of criminal penalties for accidents involving serious bodily injury should inspire greater employer cooperation. As noted earlier, OSHA often agrees to cut penalties by more than half to achieve early abatement. A criminal penalty for bodily injury would give OSHA additional bargaining leverage to induce an early abatement of a dangerous hazard. The offer to drop a potential criminal charge should be even more persuasive to an employer than the offer to reduce civil penalties.

OSHA has argued that employers who may be subject to criminal prosecution will be less likely to agree to voluntary inspections of accident sites. OSHA can easily overcome this intransigence, however, by obtaining an administrative search warrant from a federal district court.[56] The courts have not been reluctant to grant OSHA warrants to investigate accidents involving death or serious bodily injury. If during the administrative inspection, OSHA finds probable cause that a criminal violation has occurred, it must obtain a special warrant applicable to criminal investigations.[57] But this is not a serious hurdle. Law enforcement officials routinely obtain search warrants from federal judges or magistrates in a matter of hours in similar circumstances.

Unless Congress is content to leave a significant loophole in the OSH Act, it should extend criminal penalties to violations of the General Duty Clause. Some of OSHA's most significant enforcement actions have been brought under that clause, and there is no reason to think this will change. One possible impediment to criminalizing General Duty Clause violations however, is the constitutional "void-for-vagueness" doctrine. The General Duty Clause has withstood such constitutional challenges when only civil penalties were at stake. In these cases, the constitutional requirement that fair warning be given of prohibited conduct was satisfied because the clause only obligates employers to address hazards that are "recognized."[58] The government can prove a hazard is "recognized" by showing that the employer had actual or constructive knowledge of it.[59] The employer has constructive knowledge whenever a danger is "common knowledge of safety experts who are familiar with the circumstances of the industry or the activity in question."[60] The government's burden of proof, however, is greater if an employer is charged with "willfully" violating the General Duty Clause, in which case the government must prove the employer's "intentional disregard of, or plain indifference to" the duty to furnish a place of employment free of recognized hazards.[61] The District of Columbia Circuit has held that this burden is met when an employer has actual and constructive knowledge of accepted industry standards and repeatedly ignores them.[62]

The Supreme Court would probably uphold criminal penalties for "willful" violations of the General Duty Clause. In *Boyce Motor Lines, Inc.* v. *United States*,[63] for example, the Supreme Court upheld the indictment of a motor carrier for driving through New York's Holland Tunnel in violation of a regulation that prohibited the transportation of explosive liquids through congested thoroughfares "so far as practicable" and "where feasible." The Court rejected the void-for-vagueness argument because the government was required to prove that the motor carrier "knew" there was a safer route and deliberately did not take it, or "willfully neglected to inquire into the availability of such an alternative route." This is almost the identical definition that the courts have applied in cases involving a charge that an employer has "willfully" violated the General Duty Clause.

State Prosecutions

OSHA's lax enforcement during the first five years of the Reagan administration created a large void that was filled in part by local prosecutors who began to use state laws to hold employers accountable for workplace fatalities and injuries. The Pymm Thermometer case described at the beginning of this chapter is a good example of this trend. By 1988, district attorneys from dozens of jurisdictions—including Austin, Chicago, Colorado Springs, Durham, and Milwaukee—had secured indictments against approximately 50 employers.[64] The charges included reckless endangerment, manslaughter, and even murder. The prosecutors saw their activity as a natural outgrowth of OSHA's weak regulation. One prosecutor explained it was "still cheaper to kill, maim, and injure, than to safeguard workers' lives," and until OSHA civil penalties are beefed up, state criminal prosecutions "are imperative."[65]

The future of state prosecutions depends on whether they have been preempted. Under the Supremacy Clause of the U.S. Constitution, Congress has the authority to establish federal law as the only legal regime that applies to a problem. Such a decision by Congress to prohibit state regulation is called preemption. Those who argue that the OSH Act preempts state criminal prosecutions focus on section 18(b), which provides that when a state wants to develop and enforce its own occupational safety and health standards relating to hazards for which OSHA has promulgated a standard, it must apply to OSHA for approval.[66] Although some courts have accepted this argument,[67] more recent decisions have gone the other way. The highest appellate courts in Illinois, New York, and Texas have ruled that state prosecution is not preempted, and the Supreme Court declined to review the New York and Illinois decisions.[68] Those courts concluded that there is nothing in OSHA's legislative history to indicate that Congress intended to preempt state criminal prosecutions. As one court explained, "To [find preemption] would in effect, convert the [OSH] statute, which was enacted to create a safe work environment for the nation's workers, into a grant of immunity for employers responsible for serious injuries or deaths of employees."[69]

The Supreme Court's refusal to hear the two cases does not necessarily indicate its approval of their reasoning. If the Court does not ultimately reject the preemption argument, Congress should amend the OSH Act to make it clear that it intended no preemption. State criminal enforcement has several advantages over federal enforcement. First, because there are hundreds of local prosecutors, the number of law enforcement personnel who can hold employers accountable for egregious behavior is increased significantly. Second, local prosecutors may have more incentive to bring criminal charges than OSHA officials, who are not as accountable to local citizens. Third, state prosecutions may be more effective because local prosecutors are closer to the scene of an accident, can conduct their own investigations, and can press charges quickly without the additional step of a referral to the Justice Department.[70] Fourth, the possibility of state prosecutions renders OSHA more accountable to the public. The Pymm Thermometer case shows how a local criminal prosecution can focus public attention on the inadequacy of OSHA's meager enforcement efforts. Finally, under current law, a state conviction for manslaughter or negligent homicide may be easier to obtain than a federal conviction for an OSHA violation. Under federal law, prosecutors must prove that a "willful" violation of the law directly caused a worker's death. A violation is "willful" when an employer knows the requirements of a standard and purposefully chooses not to comply with it.[71] Under many state laws, the prosecutors must prove only that the employer's actions contributed to the employee's death.[72] Moreover, state prosecutors can indict employers for lesser crimes in cases where workers are not killed.[73]

A Pluralistic Approach

An effective system of enforcement requires both that dangerous workplaces be inspected and that employers who commit violations be subjected to penalties that have a real deterrent effect. OSHA could do a better job of locating dangerous workplaces if it had better data, but its ability to obtain more information under its current resource constraints is problematic. This makes strict penalties even more important to OSHA's mission. The increase in penalties that Congress voted in 1990 will help, but only if OSHA uses this new authority to force violators to pay significant fines. In the past, it has seldom done so. Even if OSHA begins to assess larger fines, effective criminal penalties are still necessary, because they provide a level of deterrence that even very large fines cannot match. Congress should therefore increase the existing penalty for the death of a worker, extend the penalty to serious bodily injury, and create a penalty for violation of the General Duty Clause. Until Congress takes these steps, state prosecutions may be the best hope for achieving a viable system of criminal penalties, but more local prosecutors must join the battle.

NOTES

1. Kenneth B. Noble, "U.S. Cites Brooklyn Concern for Toxic Mercury Exposure," *New York Times*, 6 Feb. 1986, sec. B, 2, col. 5.

2. U.S. Congress, House Committee on Government Operations, Subcommittee on Employment and Housing, *Hearings on Criminal Penalties for OSHA Violations*, 100th Cong., 2d sess., 1988, 11–13 (hereafter House, *Criminal Penalties*).

3. Susan B. Garland, "This Safety Ruling Could Be Hazardous to Employer's Health," *Business Week*, 20 Feb. 1989, 34.

4. *BNA Daily Labor Report* (13 Feb. 1986): A–15.

5. *BNA Occupational Safety and Health Reporter* 15 (13 Feb. 1986): 955; Noble, "U.S. Cites Brooklyn Concern."

6. William G. Blair, "Brooklyn Company Named in Toxic Mercury Case," *New York Times*, 17 Oct. 1986, sec. B, 2.

7. *BNA Occupational Safety and Health Reporter* 16 (18 Mar. 1987): 1095.

8. "Criminal Statutes Weaved into Safety Violations Net," *Chicago Tribune*, 18 Jan. 1987, business sec., p. 4.

9. Peter Perl, "OSHA Probing Its New York Office; for 4 Years, No Action Taken on Health Problems at Factory," *Washington Post*, 6 Feb. 1986, A15, col. 1.

10. House, *Criminal Penalties*, 13.

11. Occupational Safety and Health Administration, *Report of the President to the Congress on Occupational Safety and Health for Calendar Year 1987* (Washington, D.C.: United States Government Printing Office, 1988), 44.

12. *BNA Occupational Safety and Health Reporter* 17 (25 Nov. 1987): 980.

13. Occupational Safety and Health Administration, *Report of the President*, 55.

14. W. Kip Viscusi, "The Structure and Enforcement of Job Safety Regulations," *Law and Contemporary Problems* 49 (1986): 127, 134.

15. Akio Konoshima, chief, Division of News Media Services, Occupational Safety and Health Administration, to Sidney A. Shapiro, 15 Sept. 1988.

16. Bill Sternberg, "Turmoil Ravages Local OSHA Office; Probes May Spark Tougher Inspections," *Crain's New York Business*, 24 Feb. 1986, 1.

17. Ibid.

18. *BNA Occupational Safety and Health Reporter* 17 (27 Apr. 1988): 1723.

19. Department of Labor, *Annual Report of the Secretary of Labor Under the Federal Mine Safety and Health Act of 1977* (Washington, D.C.: United States Government Printing Office, 1987), 98.

20. Mark Reef, resource specialist, International Association of Fish and Wildlife Agencies, telephone conversation, 5 Apr. 1989.

21. *OSHA Field Operations Manual*, ch. II, Compliance Programming, in *BNA Occupational Safety and Health Reporter Reference File* 77:2201–15; Benjamin Mintz, *OSHA: History, Law, and Policy* (Washington, D.C.: Bureau of National Affairs, 1984), 401.

22. General Accounting Office, *Occupational Safety and Health: Options for Improving Safety and Health in the Workplace* (Washington, D.C.: United States Government Printing Office, 1990), 28.

23. Russell Carollo, "OSHA Never Finds Out about Many Workplace Fatalities," in "Special Report: Dead Workers Do Not Matter," *Dayton Daily News*, 2–6 June 1991, 11.

24. National Academy of Sciences, National Research Council, *Counting Injuries and Illnesses in the Workplace: Proposals for a Better System* (Washington, D.C.: National Academy of Sciences Press, 1987), 103–07.

25. Ibid., 112–13.

26. National Safe Workplace Institute, *Failed Opportunities: The Decline—U.S. Job Safety in the 1980s* (Chicago: The Institute, 1988), 9.

27. National Academy of Sciences, *Counting Injuries*, 18.

28. *OSHA Field Operations Manual*, in *BNA Occupational Safety and Health Reporter Reference File* 77:2201–15.

29. 42 U.S.C. § 11022 (1988).

30. General Accounting Office, *Occupational Safety*, 20.

31. *BNA Occupational Safety and Health Reporter* 19 (8 Nov. 1989): 1061.

32. Ibid. 19 (25 Apr. 1990): 2083.

33. Mike Casey and Russell Carollo, "Workplace Safety: A Broken Promise," in "Special Report," 3.

34. National Safe Workplace Institute, *Failed Opportunities*, 20.

35. Ibid., 18–19.

36. Russell Carollo, "Workplace Inspections Few, Flawed," in "Special Report," 10.

37. *BNA Occupational Safety and Health Reporter* 18 (29 June 1988): 460–61.

38. Ronald E. Roel, "Are Cuts Crippling a Watchdog?" *Newsday*, 8 May 1988, 66.

39. National Safe Workplace Institute, *The Rising Wave: Death and Injury Among High Risk Workers in the 1980s* (Chicago: The Institute, 1987), 10.

40. 29 U.S.C. § 666(e) (1988).

41. Casey and Carollo, "Workplace Safety," 3.

42. Carollo, "Workplace Inspections," 10.

43. *BNA Occupational Safety and Health Reporter* 17 (25 Nov. 1987): 979.

44. National Safe Workplace Institute, *Ending Legalized Workplace Homicide: Barriers to Job Prosecution in the U.S.* (Chicago: 1988), 5.

45. *BNA Occupational Safety and Health Reporter* 21 (21 Aug. 1991): 347.

46. Ibid.

47. Ibid. 18 (3 May 1989): 1949.

48. Ibid.

49. National Safe Workplace Institute, *Legalized Workplace Homicide*, 8.

50. Ibid., 10.

51. *BNA Occupational Safety and Health Reporter* 18 (16 Nov. 1988): 1143.

52. National Safe Workplace Institute, *Legalized Workplace Homicide*, 8.

53. Carollo, "Workplace Inspections," 10.

54. 33 U.S.C. § 1319(c)(3)(A) (1988).

55. *BNA Occupational Safety and Health Reporter* 20 (6 Mar. 1991): 1439.

56. *Marshall* v. *Barlow's Inc.*, 436 U.S. 307 (1978).

57. *Michigan* v. *Tyler*, 436 U.S. 499, 511–12 (1978).

58. *Donovan* v. *Royal Logging Co.*, 645 F.2d 822 (9th Cir. 1981); *Bethlehem Steel Co.* v. *OSHRC*, 607 F.2d 871 (3rd Cir. 1979).

59. *Brennan* v. *OSHRC*, 494 F.2d 460 (8th Cir. 1974); *National Realty & Construction Co.* v. *OSHRC*, 489 F.2d 1257 (D.C. Cir. 1973).

60. 489 F.2d at 1265 n.32.

61. *St. Joe Minerals Corp.* v. *OSHRC*, 647 F.2d 840 (8th Cir. 1981).

62. *Ensign-Bickford Co.* v. *OSHRC*, 717 F.2d 1419 (D.C. Cir. 1983), *cert. denied* 466 U.S. 937 (1984).

63. 342 U.S. 337 (1952).

64. Ronald E. Roel, "OSHA Cases: Prosecution Turning into Frustration," *Newsday*, 29 July 1988, 47.

65. *BNA Occupational Safety and Health Reporter* 18 (24 May 1989): 2126 (statement of Kenneth Oden, county attorney, Travis County, Texas).

66. 29 U.S.C. § 667 (1988).

67. *People* v. *Hegedus*, 425 N.W.2d 729 (Mich. App. 1988); *Colorado* v. *Kelran Construction*, 13 O.S.H. Cases (BNA) 1898 (Colo. Dist. Ct. 1988).

68. *Sabine Consolidated, Inc.* v. *Texas*, 806 S.W.2d 553 (Tx. Ct. App. 1991): *Illinois* v. *Chicago Magnet Wire Corp.*, 534 N.E.2d 962 (Ill.1989), *cert. denied sub. nom. Astra* v. *Illinois*, 493 U.S. 809 (1989); *People* v. *Pymm*, 563 N.E.2d (N.Y.Ct. App. 1990) *cert. denied* 111 S.Ct. 3562 (1991).

69. 534 N.E.2d at 969.

70. *BNA Occupational Safety and Health Reporter* 18 (24 May 1989): 2123.

71. Stevan Bokat and Horace Thompson III, eds., *Occupational Safety and Health Law* (Washington D.C.: Bureau of National Affairs, 1988), 321.

72. Roel, "OSHA Cases," 51.

73. Ira Reiner and Han Chatten-Brown, "When It Is Not an Accident, but a Crime: Prosecutors Get Tough with OSHA Violations," *Northern Kentucky Law Review* 17 (1989): 83 (relating the experience of Los Angeles prosecutors under a California law that makes OSHA violations a crime).

Part IV

EXTERNAL REFORMS: WHO IS IN CHARGE?

15

The President's Role: OSHA and OMB

Although OSHA's assistant secretaries have come and gone, one notable constant since the beginning of the Reagan administration has been an almost constant opposition by White House underlings to the agency's attempts to write protective rules for workers. Time and again, regulations have run aground as officials from the Office of Management and Budget (OMB) and later the Competitiveness Council, chaired by Vice President Dan Quayle, demanded substantive changes. OMB's ambitious interventions into OSHA rulemaking are part of an extensive regulatory review process established by President Reagan and modified only slightly by President Bush, who himself played a role in the Reagan review process.[1] This chapter examines the acrimonious relationship that has developed between OMB and OSHA and draws some conclusions about the legitimacy of direct White House involvement in OSHA decision making.

OMB has consistently maintained a singularly one-sided approach to its oversight function. It has pressed OSHA hard to delay important new regulatory initiatives and to reduce the stringency of proposed regulations, at the same time urging OSHA to speed up its deregulatory efforts. Although convincing theoretical arguments can be made for some kind of centralized review of OSHA rulemaking by politically accountable officials, in practice OMB review has covertly deflected OSHA from its statutory mission. In more than a decade of painstaking review of OSHA regulations, OMB has not once urged the agency to change a standard in a way that would *increase* the protections afforded to workers.

OMB'S MANDATE

OMB's authority to review OSHA rulemaking stems from two primary sources. First, President Reagan promulgated several executive orders that lodged the centralized rulemaking review function in OMB and articulated the criteria that OMB was to use in reviewing rules. The most important of these was Executive Order 12291, which gave OMB authority to identify "duplicative, overlapping and conflicting rules" and rules that were "inconsistent with the policies underlying" the executive order.[2] OMB was empowered to require "appropriate interagency consultation to minimize or eliminate . . . duplication, overlap, or conflict." The primary vehicle for this review function was the regulatory impact analysis that the executive order required the agencies to prepare for major rules. Later in his administration, President Reagan issued another executive order that required executive agencies to place all of their rulemaking initiatives on a semiannual regulatory agenda for review and comment by OMB.[3] Absent exceptional circumstances, the agencies were not allowed to promulgate rules that OMB had not placed on the agenda. An OMB bulletin promulgated in early 1991 further required that all submissions of projects for inclusion on the regulatory agenda must be accompanied by a mini-analysis exploring the costs and benefits of several regulatory alternatives.[4] Second, OMB was given the responsibility for monitoring agency compliance with the Paperwork Reduction Act, a statute enacted near the end of the Carter administration that was intended to reduce the amount of paperwork that federal agencies required of regulated businesses.[5] Within OMB, the Office of Information and Regulatory Affairs (OIRA) has the general task of monitoring agency compliance with the executive orders and advising the president with respect to such compliance.[6] It is also responsible for monitoring agency compliance with the Paperwork Act.

During the Reagan administration, disputes between the agencies and OMB were resolved by an entity called the Presidential Task Force on Regulatory Relief, which was composed of high-ranking administration officials and chaired by Vice President Bush.[7] The task force was never very active (the only OSHA rule of any consequence in which it played a significant role was the first hazard identification standard promulgated near the beginning of the Reagan administration), and it gradually faded into oblivion. In 1991, President Bush revived the idea, and vested centralized review of interagency disputes in an entity called the Competitiveness Council, which was composed of the director of OMB, the secretary of commerce, the secretary of the treasury, the attorney general, the chairman of the Council of Economic Advisers, and the White House chief of staff, and chaired by Vice President Quayle. The Quayle council took a considerably more proactive role than the Bush task force, and it thereby engendered considerable controversy.

OMB REVIEW IN THEORY

Although the OSH Act makes no mention of any role for OMB in OSHA standard-setting, the head of OSHA does serve at the pleasure of the president, and the president has the authority as the chief executive to put in place mechanisms that ensure that the bureaucracy is implementing his policies. In theory, active presidential oversight has at least four attractive features. First, it can create much-needed coordination among federal agencies and thereby avoid the paralyzing inconsistency that can arise when one agency's unconstrained pursuit of its statutory goals clashes with another's similar pursuit of conflicting goals.[8] Second, presidential oversight can broaden agency perspectives and render them more accountable to the electorate. Advocates of presidential oversight maintain that the national policy perspective that the president brings to the decision-making process uniquely qualifies him to steer agencies in a direction that renders them accountable to the general electorate.[9] Third, presidential oversight can interject some flexibility into an agency regulatory culture that is often all too inclined to "go by the book."[10] Finally, presidential oversight can reduce the tendency of agencies to write arbitrary and unreasonable rules that are divorced from political reality.[11]

Although presidential oversight has some important theoretical benefits, they can be overstated, and the oversight process has some important disadvantages as well. Perhaps the most important disadvantage is the danger that it poses to the constitutional policy-making process. The policies that guide an agency in writing its regulations must emanate from a statute enacted by Congress and signed by the president or passed over his veto. When the president elevates one set of policies over another, he may be subverting congressional will as expressed in the statute. Since most regulatory statutes have multiple goals that are not crafted with crystal clarity, there may be considerable leeway within which the president or his subordinates can guide the agency's discretion. But the president may not require the agency to base its decision on factors that Congress deemed irrelevant or to ignore factors that Congress deemed relevant.

Although presidential oversight is touted as a roadway to greater account-ability, it will not achieve that goal if the president and his staff are able to intervene secretly into the regulatory process to demand that the agency reach a particular result. In such situations, the agency takes the political heat, and the president is able to avoid the criticism of disappointed regulatees or regulatory beneficiaries.[12] Moreover, the staff of OMB is not the president. OMB may have its own agenda that conflicts with that of the agency, and so long as it is able to impose its will, it is less accountable than the agency itself. Even assuming that OMB should have the power to identify inconsistencies in agency decision making, few would agree that it may legitimately advance its own extrastatutory policy preferences over another agency's statutory goals.[13]

Finally, ex parte, or secret, intervention into pending rulemaking initiatives by the president or his staff is inconsistent with broad public participation in the regulatory process. The procedural assumption underlying the Administrative Procedure Act's informal rulemaking model is that affected interests ought to have an effective opportunity to participate in governmental decisions in a direct way. Ex parte presidential influence over informal rulemaking is entirely contrary to the pluralistic values that underlie that procedure, and it therefore represents a step back toward autocracy.[14] Secret OMB intervention into the decision-making process robs the informal rulemaking model of its legitimacy.[15]

OMB REVIEW IN PRACTICE

Real-world experience with OMB oversight of OSHA rulemaking strongly bears out the skeptics' fears. Although OMB did bring a useful perspective to a few rules, it failed to achieve the potential advantages of presidential oversight because it engaged in micromanagement of OSHA's decision-making process. This micromanagement was especially inappropriate because OMB employees had little or no expertise to warrant substituting their judgment for that of OSHA officials. OMB's micromanagement had the further disadvantages of significantly delaying proposed rules and subverting the rulemaking process through secret communications.

Micromanagement

Because the White House is at the apex of the federal government, the president is the only government official in a position to ensure that agency policies are consistent with the overall policy perspectives of the national electorate. Few of OMB's attempts to influence OSHA, however, fit this image of broad presidential policy oversight. Instead, Frank White, who was deputy assistant secretary for occupational safety and health during the Reagan administration, reports that OMB's strategy was "one of reviewing in great detail each rule, reading line by line every provision, every preamble statement, and attempting to find vulnerabilities no matter how minor, in terms of the record support that the agency has generated for a particular provision in terms of internal consistency within the rule or in the nuances of preamble language."[16]

The history of OSHA rulemaking recounted in Part II supports White's description. We have seen that time and again OMB has extracted substantive concessions from OSHA and thereby determined the content of OSHA standards. OSHA relaxed the medical surveillance and exposure monitoring requirements of the cotton dust standard to meet OMB objections. For the same reason, OSHA watered down its grain dust standard, only to have its decision reversed on judicial appeal because it was not sufficiently protective of workers. When OMB objected to OSHA's formaldehyde standard, OSHA deleted requirements for exposure monitoring, employee evacuation, and showers for employees. And, in an especially notorious intervention, OSHA deleted the STEL for the ethylene oxide standard, literally at the last minute, in response to OMB pressure. Once again, OSHA's cave-in to OMB was reversed by a court that found OSHA could not defend the decision to delete the STEL.

In a more general way, OMB has insisted that OSHA use regulatory approaches that have the result of reducing both employer costs and employee protections. Before the Supreme Court held otherwise in the cotton dust case, OMB insisted that OSHA standards pass a stringent cost-benefit test, and OMB still requires that OSHA use cost-benefit analysis for safety standards. Despite the huge uncertainties inherent in that form of analysis, OMB has pressed OSHA to employ a very low value of $1 million for each human life saved by its safety standards.[17] OSHA professionals have consistently resisted such explicit thresholds for striking the unpleasant but inevitable balance between costs and mortality risks.

OMB has also consistently pressured OSHA to allow employers to require employees to use personal protective devices, rather than requiring employers to install feasible engineering controls. OMB's strong preference for performance-oriented standards is understandable, given the economics backgrounds of most of the OMB staff, and it is arguably desirable when the statute allows the agency the leeway to consider a performance-oriented approach. But OMB's single-minded devotion to respirators over engineering controls has probably exceeded statutory bounds, and it clearly has been counterproductive as a policy matter. We saw how OMB's insistence that OSHA allow employers to require respirators to meet the cotton dust standard precipitated a major confrontation that was not resolved until the White House science adviser concluded that a recent study on the effectiveness of respirator use did not support OMB's position. Moreover, OMB's strong advocacy of respirators to meet the lead standard almost undermined delicate negotiations between the agency enforcement staff and owners of lead facilities. According to OSHA's attorneys, the OSH Act expresses a definite preference for engineering controls and training over personal protective devices. And virtually all of the occupational health professional community is united behind the proposition that respirators are not as effective as engineering controls. Unless new breakthroughs in respirator technologies are achieved, it is inappropriate for OMB to continue to insist that OSHA devote substantial resources to studying that option.

Institutional Competence

The dispute over respirators reveals another endemic problem with OMB review of OSHA rulemaking—the tendency of OMB economists to range beyond their technical competence. For example, in the cotton dust proceeding, OMB was adamant in its insistence that OSHA allow employers to require employees to use respirators, until Dr. Imbus convinced the president's science adviser that his study could not be cited for the proposition that respirators were as effective as engineering controls and training. OMB likewise pressed OSHA to expand employer discretion to use respirators rather than engineering controls in the proceedings involving bloodborne diseases, ethylene oxide, formaldehyde, lead, and the generic rulemaking initiative on personal protective devices. OMB does not have any occupational hygienists in its employ, and its source of expertise on the effectiveness of respirators is not otherwise apparent.

OMB suffered a similar embarrassment when an outside economist with impeccable conservative credentials undermined OMB's critique of OSHA's original hazard communication standard. OMB later attempted to exempt entire industries from the expanded hazard communication standard, thus precipitating still another embarrassing defeat when the Supreme Court curtailed its attempt to expand its powers under the Paperwork Reduction Act.[18] OMB's economists even initiated a short-lived project to articulate uniform carcinogen assessment guidelines for OSHA and other executive agencies.[19] But after Congressman John Dingell announced that he would investigate OMB's role in developing EPA and OSHA cancer policy,[20] OMB quickly backed off.[21]

OMB has found the temptation to second-guess OSHA's science/policy determinations irresistible. In the formaldehyde proceeding OMB insisted that OSHA use the results of a risk assessment model selected by OMB's economists that predicted health effects orders of magnitude below those of models selected by EPA and OSHA. Although it purported to rely upon the expertise of the president's science adviser, the qualifications of OMB's staff economists to resolve modeling disputes were not apparent. Similarly, the credentials of the OMB staff to assess the risks posed by short-term exposures to ethylene oxide were not obvious, and OSHA's initial capitulation to OMB on the question of whether the standard should contain a short-term exposure limit had an immediate and lasting adverse impact on staff morale at OSHA. OMB used the cadmium proceeding as an opportunity to impose on OSHA its belief that laboratory animal studies were of little significance in light of negative epidemiological evidence. In the grain handling proceeding, OMB's economists became instant experts in the explosive properties of grain dust after meeting with industry representatives. Later, they became instant safety experts and confidently concluded that the technical support for OSHA's lockout/tagout regulation was inadequate. OMB economists even became instant attorneys when they objected to OSHA's proposed air contaminants update rule on the ground that OSHA did not have authority to address the hazards of multiple chemicals in a generic fashion and when they objected to OSHA's revisions to the remanded formaldehyde standard on the ground that the agency had misinterpreted the court's opinion.

OSHA's professional staff understandably resents OMB's tampering, and it distrusts OMB's motives. They have not devoted their lives to careers in occupational safety and health only to serve as cannon fodder for broadsides from OMB's economists. Like any professionals, OSHA health scientists would like to believe that they are making a positive contribution to society. But it is very hard to feel a sense of accomplishment when, after spending nights and weekends working on an important regulation, the OSHA staffer watches the result of her efforts languish on the desk of an OMB desk officer for two years, as happened during the MDA proceeding. More often than not, in the opinion of OSHA scientists, OMB's economists are much more concerned with reducing the costs of OSHA regulations than with improving the quality of the technical support for OSHA rulemaking initiatives.

Compared with OMB's unflagging attempts to weaken OSHA's rules, we found only one instance where the president's aides engaged in the type of macro-management for which presidential review is best suited. OMB's strong concern for federalism principles in the hazard communication proceeding represented an appropriate attempt to interject the policy preferences of the administration into the policy-making arena. Whether or not one agrees with OMB's position, which ultimately did not carry the day, it is hard to disagree with the proposition that some institutional actor with an interest in state autonomy should have played a role in the decision-making process. This was not a matter requiring any particular expertise, and the statute does not clearly dictate a policy on the question of preemption of state standards. The policy preferences of the president were thus entirely relevant to the decision.

Playing One Agency Against Another

Although policy coordination among the federal executive agencies is often cited as one of the virtues of OMB intervention, OMB can use its review powers to play one agency off against another to achieve particular substantive results. OMB's curious attempt to wrest the regulation of asbestos away from EPA and hand it to OSHA is a good example. In July 1984, OMB officials objected to EPA's preliminary decision to ban about half of all asbestos products.[22] Later congressional hearings revealed that the Canadian government had strongly encouraged OMB to take this position to protect the Canadian asbestos industry, and OMB regularly kept Canadian officials apprised of OMB's progress.[23] Under substantial OMB pressure, EPA announced in early 1985 that it would abandon its six-year-old attempt to ban most asbestos uses and refer the issue to OSHA and the Consumer Product Safety Commission.[24] After more than 100 outraged EPA employees wrote a letter to the EPA administrator criticizing the referral[25] and after receiving harsh criticism from several congressmen,[26] EPA reversed field and suspended its decision.[27] Having lost that battle, OMB began to pressure OSHA to reanalyze its risk assessment calculations and revise them downward. OMB officials hoped that OSHA's revised risk estimates would effectively preempt EPA's proposal to ban individual asbestos products, because EPA was required to take OSHA's estimates into account in issuing its own regulations under the Toxic Substances Control Act.[28] The Canadian embassy informed its home government via a telex that the deputy director of OIRA, Robert Bedell, had assured the Canadians that "OSHA regulation is a key element in OMB plan to avoid banning."[29] One OSHA staffer commented at the time that OSHA statisticians "will just have to swallow their professional judgments."[30]

Secrecy

The exact extent to which OMB has pressured OSHA to weaken proposed standards remains unknown because OMB's interactions with OSHA have for the most part remained hidden from public view. In virtually every instance, it took the forceful action of a congressional committee to expose the contents of

OSHA/OMB communications to public scrutiny. Indeed, OMB's obsession with secrecy so infuriated congressional committees that in late 1985 the Rulemaking Information Act of 1986 was introduced. This bill would have required agencies to maintain a file for every rule that would include drafts of regulations sent to OMB, any substantive changes in the proposals made in response to OMB, and a summary of all written or oral communications between EPA officials and OMB that resulted in recommendations for change to the rule.[31] The bill was, however, limited to EPA communications, and it stood virtually no chance of enactment over President Reagan's certain veto.

The chairmen of the House Appropriations and Energy and Commerce committees, however, accomplished roughly the same result as the bill proposed when they threatened to cut OMB's appropriation for regulatory review unless OMB exposed its interactions with EPA to greater public scrutiny. Under this substantial threat to the existence of the regulatory review program, OMB entered into a compromise agreement under which it agreed (1) to make draft notices sent to OMB available after publication in the *Federal Register*; (2) to make written communications between OMB and the agency available at the same time; and (3) to send EPA all materials that OMB received from outside parties and to invite EPA to all meetings with outside parties.[32] Like the proposed statute, however, this agreement did not apply to oral communications, and some aspects were limited to OMB communications with EPA.

In late 1986 the Department of Labor agreed to participate in the same "openness procedures" as EPA.[33] As we have seen, however, OMB in the past has gone to extremes to avoid this oversight by ensuring that its communications are oral and therefore not on the public record. In the grain handling proceeding, for example, OMB insisted that no notes be taken at OMB/OSHA meetings and that the contents of documents be read over the telephone, rather than transmitted in writing. More recently, the Competitiveness Council, which is not subject to the openness procedures, has assumed the primary role in communicating with the agencies behind closed doors.[34]

OMB as a Conduit

A problem related to the secrecy of presidential oversight is industry's use of that process as a private conduit for receiving the views of the regulated industry and conveying them to OSHA. When this happens, other participants in the rulemaking process are unaware of industry's real arguments and therefore do not have an opportunity to rebut them.

Although few instances of OMB's playing a conduit role have been documented, it has happened on occasion. We saw in Chapter 5 that the Bush task force staff, which included staffers from OMB, met privately with members of the commercial diving industry early in the Reagan administration to probe their interest in revising OSHA's commercial diving standard. OMB officials also met privately with representatives of the American Feed Manufacturers' Association during OSHA's consideration of the grain elevator standard. While OSHA's final lockout/tagout standard was pending before OMB, a copy was given to industry but not to labor representatives. As a result, two companies that had not participated in the rulemaking submitted highly critical data and analysis to OSHA and OMB, and OSHA changed the standard to meeting those objections.[35]

OIRA's leadership has recently taken the position that with the exception of the top two officials in OIRA, its staffers are prohibited from meeting with anyone outside of government concerning a regulation under review. Those officials have indicated that when they meet with any outside interest, they invite the agency involved to participate, make a summary of the meeting, and put that summary in the public record at the agency.[36] The Competitiveness Council, on the other hand, has made no promises not to serve as an industry conduit, and it has assumed the conduit role that OMB has apparently abandoned.[37]

Delay

OMB's constant interventions have made a slow OSHA decision-making process even slower.[38] We observed in Chapter 6 how OMB held up the proposed grain elevator standard for more than six months while it debated with OSHA about its merits and how it delayed the final standard for almost that long. In 1985, OMB indefinitely extended its review of OSHA's medical records access rule for the flavor and fragrance industry, thereby forcing OSHA to issue consecutive stays of the applicability of the regulation, which was already being enforced in other industries.[39] In Chapters 9 and 11 we saw how OMB may have dealt a death blow to future negotiated rulemaking efforts at OSHA by unnecessarily delaying the MDA and formaldehyde standards.

In addition to the direct delays caused by OMB's failure to review OSHA standards in a timely fashion, OMB review causes OSHA to spend thousands of hours preparing decision documents and analyses to meet predictable OMB objections. The added time that it takes OSHA to write rationales for rules capable of surviving OMB review must be counted as one of the costs of the review process.

By contrast, when OMB and the Bush task force ordered OSHA to reexamine existing rules, OMB was a forceful advocate of expedition. Early in the Reagan administration, for example, OMB and the task force urged OSHA quickly to amend the commercial diving standard, even though nobody was particularly dissatisfied with it. In 1982, the head of OIRA demanded that OSHA curtail its efforts to issue new regulations and devote greater attention to rewriting the old ones, including the cotton dust standard.[40] History repeated itself in 1992 when President Bush declared a three-month moratorium on new regulations and ordered the agencies to engage in a "top to bottom review of all regulations, old and new."[41]

Information Gathering Stumbling Block

OMB's control over OSHA does not end with its implementation of rulemaking review, because OIRA also oversees OSHA's compliance with the Paperwork Reduction Act. As mentioned earlier, OMB's efforts to control OSHA through this vehicle were dealt a setback by the Supreme Court in *Dole* v. *United Steelworkers of America*[42] when the Court held that OMB did not have authority to prohibit OSHA from ordering employers to keep records as part of their compliance with a health or safety standard.

Despite this limitation, OMB still retains the power to disapprove OSHA requests to obtain information from more than ten employers. It has frequently used this authority to limit the information that OSHA and NIOSH may request from industries concerning the risks posed by particular workplace hazards. We saw that in 1987 OMB disallowed an OSHA request to gather information on bloodborne diseases such as AIDS from health care facilities. In that same year, OMB also ordered OSHA to halt surveys of employee exposure to wood dust, arguing that the surveys constituted the unauthorized collection of information.[43] In 1990, OMB approved an OSHA survey probing the possible relationship between accident rates and the use of contractor employees, but OMB told the agency that the survey could not be used to draw cause-effect conclusions.[44] OMB has also tried to use the Paperwork Reduction Act to put OSHA on a short information-gathering leash by approving record-keeping requirements for very brief durations ranging from three to six months, so that the agency would constantly have to return to OMB for reapproval.[45] OMB has even attempted to use its Paperwork Reduction Act review powers to dictate the content of NIOSH workplace safety studies.[46]

Control over the Regulatory Agenda

OMB's ultimate tool for controlling OSHA is the regulatory agenda. After President Reagan's second election, he signed Executive Order 12,498, which established a regulatory agenda for all executive branch rulemaking initiatives. Each agency was obliged to submit to OMB for approval all regulatory initiatives that it planned to implement within the next year. Items that OMB did not include on the agenda could not be the subject of a notice of proposed rulemaking, absent unusual circumstances.

OMB has used its power to set the regulatory agenda to stifle OSHA initiatives at birth. For example, OSHA's very first regulatory agenda included a safety standard for the oil and gas industry. OMB tried to keep the standard off the agenda, arguing that a separate regulation for the oil and gas industry was not warranted.[47] Only after Labor Secretary William Brock's office intervened was OSHA allowed to retain the standard on its agenda.[48] OSHA did not fare as well when it announced that, in light of the Bhopal tragedy, it was adopting recommendations for management systems to ensure overall plant safety and that it was considering requiring mandatory self-audits of safety devices in chemical plants.[49] After OMB refused to place the initiative on the regulatory agenda, it was placed on the back burner[50] and it found its way onto the agenda only after a tragic explosion at a Phillips Petroleum Company plant in Pasadena, Texas, killed 23 workers and injured hundreds more.

CONCLUSION

Although there may be occasions on which OMB review of OSHA rulemaking has improved the agency's regulatory output, OMB intervention has on balance had a very negative impact. Throughout the lifetime of the OMB review process, that agency has invariably adopted the position of the employer and argued against protections for workers. A recommendation of John Morrall, a long-time OMB official charged with reviewing OSHA rules, in late 1981 gives a good indication of the deregulatory attitude that prevailed in OMB during the Reagan administration. Morrall suggested that Congress amend the OSH Act to require cost-benefit analysis for OSHA standard-setting and to relocate the agency in the Department of Health and Human Services, where it would play a largely informational role in protecting occupational health but not occupational safety.[51] Upon leaving his position as director of OMB in 1989, James C. Miller III opined that OSHA was the worst-performing regulatory agency in government.[52] That the head of OMB would thus cast stones at OSHA's meager attempts to fulfill its statutory mission at the same time that the Federal Home Loan Bank Board was overseeing a $500 billion savings and loan disaster speaks volumes about OMB's blinkered outlook during the Reagan years. It is therefore unsurprising that most OSHA staffers lack a warm spot in their hearts for OMB's economists.

Outside evaluations of OMB intervention in OSHA rulemaking initiatives are quite polar in nature. Business representatives are generally very supportive of OMB's role, finding it a necessary counterweight to an overly aggressive OSHA staff. They fear that, absent OMB review, even the most sympathetic assistant secretaries will become "captured" by the agency staff and begin to promulgate overly burdensome regulations. Employee representatives are unalterably opposed to OMB intervention, pointing out with considerable justification that OMB does not see OSHA's mission as that of protecting workers.[53] In their view, OMB review merely affords the regulated industry a second bite at the apple after OSHA has come a considerable distance in attempting to placate industry opposition.[54] Labor leaders have especially opposed OMB's aggressive use of the Paperwork Reduction Act to derail OSHA rulemaking initiatives.[55]

Former assistant secretaries have varying views of OMB's role. Former Assistant Secretary Eula Bingham testified that OMB review has sometimes made "a mockery of the rulemaking process." According to Bingham, OMB's oversight "tended to erode" the authority of the officials that Congress charged with implementing the act. She also complained that political considerations were being interjected into the standard-setting process "without the technical expertise necessary to evaluate scientific evidence and to make sound judgments when the scientific evidence is not conclusive."[56] Assistant Administrator Auchter disagreed with Bingham. While still in office, Auchter testified that OMB oversight was generally "helpful" and "meaningful," and he compared it to congressional oversight.[57] Former Assistant Secretary Pendergrass testified to a Senate subcommittee that OMB was not actively engaged in second-guessing OSHA:

OMB is not "substituting its judgment relevant to the content of health and safety standards over that of OSHA's health scientists" when it questions the methodology used in our regulatory impact analyses, or when it asks about scientific studies we have not referenced, or feasibility issues it believes we have not adequately considered. We are willing to listen and at times to ask for additional public comment at OMB's suggestion if that seems reasonable and does not reduce essential worker protection. When, however, we believe that OMB is in error and that a change it recommends would reduce essential worker protection, we insist on our position, and we prevail.[58]

The most recent assistant secretary, Gerard Scannell, was even rather complimentary of OMB: "I go over and meet with authorities over there who may have some questions . . . [but] they have never held anything up. The product that comes out of these [deliberations] is better than the product that went in."[59] Since executive agency congressional testimony must be approved by OMB, however, these latter endorsements must be taken with a grain of salt. Examples of OMB's substituting its judgment for that of the agency are simply too numerous to discount. Moreover, as discussed earlier, Frank White, who was Pendergrass's deputy, became highly critical of OMB review after he left OSHA.

The fact that White House input is often biased and uninformed does not inspire confidence in the review process. The fact that it is nearly always clandestine ensures that labor representatives will distrust it. Critics have charged, though often with little documentation, that OMB's instant expertise is more often than not gleaned from the regulated industry. Although OMB has implemented procedures to reduce ex parte contacts with industry, the Competitiveness Council and its staff apparently do not feel similarly constrained. In any event, it is clear that the White House, with only very rare exceptions like the preemption issue in the hazard identification proceeding, has consistently adopted the policy preferences of the regulatees. At the very least, the White House review process should be opened up to public scrutiny. All White House written communications should be placed in the rulemaking record so that affected parties may comment on it. All oral communications should be reduced to writing and likewise placed in the record.

OMB-inspired delays could be eliminated by placing deadlines on the time that OMB may take to review a rule. Indeed, if OSHA itself faced real deadlines, time constraints on OMB would probably be more realistic. For example, OMB's ability to delay the EPA's rulemaking efforts under the Resource Conservation and Recovery Act are severely hampered by the fact that EPA itself faces statutory deadlines. At least one court has held that OMB is powerless to delay rulemaking initiatives that are subject to such statutory deadlines.[60] In Chapter 12, we recommended that Congress put OSHA under similar deadlines. Implementation of that recommendation could have the added value of speeding up presidential review.

Finally, while the White House should continue to offer input on important questions of national policy, the micro-management that has characterized its relationship with OSHA in the past should cease. Congress did not delegate rulemaking power to the OMB, the Competitiveness Council, or even the president; it delegated it to the secretary of labor. Although OSHA should consult with the White House on important policy questions, presidential advisers should not be allowed to tell OSHA whether or not a short-term exposure limit is warranted for a carcinogenic chemical or whether or not the chemical is in fact carcinogenic. If legislation is required to keep OMB from imposing its will on OSHA decision makers, then it should be enacted.

NOTES

1. This experience is not at all unique to OSHA. See Thomas O. McGarity, *Reinventing Rationality: The Role of Regulatory Analysis in the Federal Bureaucracy* (Cambridge: Cambridge University Press, 1991), ch. 18; Jeffrey H. Howard and Linda E. Benfield, "Rulemaking in the Shadows: The Rise of OMB and Cost-Benefit Analysis in Environmental Decisionmaking," *Columbia Journal of Environmental Law* 16 (1991): 143; Oliver Houck, "President X and the New (Approved) Decisionmaking," *American University Law Review* 36 (1987): 535; Eric D. Olson "The Quiet Shift of Power: Office of Management and Budget Supervision of Environmental Protection Agency Rulemaking Under Executive Order 12291," *Virginia Journal of Natural Resource Law* 4 (1984): 1; Robert V. Percival, "Checks Without Balance: Executive Oversight of the Environmental Protection Agency," *Law and Contemporary Problems* 54 (Autumn 1991): 127.

2. Executive Order, 12,291 3 C.F.R. 127 (1982), repr. 5 U.S.C. § 601 (1988).

3. Executive Order 12,498, 13 C.F.R. 323 (1986), repr. 5 U.S.C. § 601 (1988).

4. *BNA Chemical Regulation Reporter* 14 (4 Jan. 1991): 1399.

5. Executive Order 12,291, 3 C.F.R. 127, § 6(b) (1982); Paperwork Reduction Act of 1980, 44 U.S.C. § 3501–20 (1988).

6. Executive Order 12,291, 3 C.F.R. 127 § 6(a)(8) (1982).

7. Executive Order 12,291, 3 C.F.R. 127 § 3(e)(1) (1982).

8. Lloyd N. Cutler and David R. Johnson, "Regulation and the Political Process," *Yale Law Journal* 84 (1975): 1395. See also Boyden Gray, "Presidential Involvement in Informal Rulemaking," *Tulane Law Review* 56 (1982): 863; Peter Shane, "Presidential Regulatory Oversight and the Separation of Powers: The Constitutionality of Executive Order 12291," *Arizona Law Review* 23 (1981) 1235.

9. Harold Bruff, "Presidential Power and Administrative Rulemaking," *Yale Law Review* 88 (1979): 451, 462–64; Richard Pierce, "The Role of Constitutional and Political Theory in Administrative Law," *Texas Law Review* 64 (1985): 520–21; Peter Strauss

and Cass Sunstein, "The Role of the President and OMB in Informal Rulemaking," *Administrative Law Review* 38 (1986): 190.

10. Eugene Bardach and Robert Kagan, *Going by the Book: The Problem of Regulatory Unreasonableness* (Philadelphia: Temple University Press, 1981), 58–92.

11. Bruff, "Presidential Power," 455; Cutler and Johnson, "Regulation," 1405–06; Christopher DeMuth and Douglas Ginsberg, "White House Review of Agency Rulemaking," *Harvard Law Review* 99 (1986): 1079–80.

12. Olson, "Quiet Shift," 14; Houck, "President X," 552–53.

13. Jonathan Lash, Katherine Gillman, and David Sheridan, *A Season of Spoils: The Reagan Administration's Attack on the Environment* (New York: Pantheon, 1984), 72; Alan Morrison, "OMB Interference with Agency Rulemaking: The Wrong Way to Write a Regulation," *Harvard Law Review* 99 (1986): 1067.

14. Bruff, "Presidential Power," 469; Olsen, "Quiet Shift," 31.

15. Kenneth Culp Davis, *Administrative Law Treatise*, 2d ed., vol. 1 (San Diego: University of San Diego, 1978) § 6:24; Morton Rosenberg, "Presidential Control of Agency Rulemaking: An Analysis of Constitutional Issues That May Be Raised by Executive Order 12,291," *Arizona Law Review* 23 (1981): 1200.

16. "Colloquium: Comments of Frank White," *Administrative Law Journal* 4 (Spring 1990): 25.

17. Pete Earley, "OMB Accused of Impeding Safety Rules," *Washington Post*, 24 Oct. 1984, A15, col. 1; "White House Duels with Labor Agency over Value of Life," *Wall Street Journal*, 24 Oct. 1984, 14, col. 2.

18. *Dole* v. *United Steelworkers of America*, 110 S. Ct. 929 (1990).

19. Judith Havemann, "Assessed Cancer Risk Is Inflated, OMB Says; Regulatory Agencies May Get Guidelines," *Washington Post*, 13 July 1986, A8.

20. *Inside EPA* 7 (25 July 1986): 1.

21. *BNA Chemical Regulation Reporter* 10 (25 July 1986): 516.

22. *Inside EPA* 5 (27 July 1984): 1.

23. *Inside the Administration* 5 (15 May 1986): 6–7.

24. *BNA Product Safety and Liability Reporter* 13 (1 Feb. 1985): 73.

25. *Pesticide and Toxic Chemical News* 13 (20 Feb. 1985): 39; *BNA Chemical Regulation Reporter* 8 (22 Feb. 1985): 1380.

26. "Florio Asserts E.P.A. Gave In on School Asbestos Removal," *New York Times*, 16 Apr. 1985, 9, col. 1; Phillip Shabecoff, "E.P.A. Pulls Back on Asbestos Rules," *New York Times*, 9 Mar. 1985, 7, col. 5; Robert S. Taylor, "EPA's Plan to Drop Asbestos Restriction Is Reconsidered in Response to Criticism," *Wall Street Journal*, 11 Mar. 1985, 8, col. 3.

27. *Inside EPA* 6 (19 Apr. 1985): 3.

28. Ibid. 7 (23 May 1986): 1.

29. *Inside the Administration* 5 (15 May 1986): 7.

30. *Inside EPA* 7 (23 May 1986): 9.

31. Ibid. (31 Jan. 1986): 5; *BNA Environment Reporter* 16 (31 Jan. 1986): 1807.

32. Wendy Gramm, memorandum for the heads of departments and agencies subject to executive orders 12,291 and 12,498 on additional procedures concerning OIRA review under executive orders nos. 12,291 and 12,498, 13 June 1986.

33. *BNA Occupational Safety and Health Reporter* 16 (5 Nov. 1986): 601.

34. See Christine Triano and Nancy Watzman, *All the Vice President's Men: How the Quayle Council on Competitiveness Secretly Undermines Health, Safety, and Environ-*

mental Programs (Washington, D.C.: Public Citizen Congress Watch and OMB Watch, 1991), 2–3.

35. U.S. Congress, Senate Committee on Governmental Affairs, *Hearings on the Role of the Council on Competitiveness on Regulatory Review*, 102d Cong., 1st sess., 1991, 102 (testimony of Frank Mirer, director of health and safety, United Auto Workers).

36. "Colloquium, Comments of the Honorable S. Jay Plager," *Administrative Law Journal* 4 (Spring 1990): 16.

37. Triano and Watzman, *All the Vice President's Men*, 6–7; Kirk Victor, "Quayle's Quiet Coup," *National Journal* 23 (6 July 1991): 1676; Michael Duffy, "Need Friends in High Places?" *Time*, 4 Nov. 1991, 25.

38. Olsen, "Quiet Shift," 6; Houck, "President X," 542–43; Percival, "Checks Without Balance," 157–61; *BNA Occupational Safety and Health Reporter* 13 (16 Feb. 1984): 993; Ibid. 12 (4 Nov. 1982): 438.

39. *BNA Occupational Safety and Health Reporter* 15 (15 May 1986): 1243.

40. Ibid. 12 (16 Sept. 1982): 323.

41. "State of the Union Address by the President of the United States," *Congressional Record*, 102d Cong., 2d sess., 1992, 138: H109.

42. 110 S. Ct. 929 (1990).

43. *BNA Occupational Safety and Health Reporter* 16 (28 Jan. 1987): 939.

44. Ibid. 19 (4 Apr. 1990): 1915.

45. Ibid. 15 (10 Apr. 1986): 1117.

46. Barry Meier, "Companies Wrestle with Threats to Workers' Reproductive Health," *Wall Street Journal*, 5 Feb. 1987, 21, col. 4.

47. "Budget Office Moves to Kill Draft of Oil Well Safety Rule," *New York Times*, 26 June 1985, 18, col. 5.

48. *BNA Occupational Health and Safety Reporter* 15 (11 July 1985): 91.

49. *Chemical Engineering* 94 (13 Apr. 1987): 12.

50. U.S. Congress, Senate Committee on Labor and Human Resources, *Hearings on Oversight of the Administration of the Occupational Safety and Health Act*, 100th Cong., 2d sess., S.Hrg. 100–719, 1988, 19 (hereafter cited as Senate, *Oversight Hearings of 1988*.)

51. *BNA Occupational Safety and Health Reporter* 11 (3 Dec. 1981): 510.

52. Carole Shifrin, "Weidenbaum Lists Traits Regulators Should Have," *Washington Post*, 10 Dec. 1980, B1, col. 2.

53. *BNA Occupational Safety and Health Reporter* 18 (1 Mar. 1989): 1677; Ibid. (19 Oct. 1988): 1042.

54. Senate, *Oversight Hearings of 1988*, 19 (Testimony of Lynn Williams, United Steelworkers).

55. Ibid.

56. *BNA Occupational Safety and Health Reporter* 13 (23 June 1983): 91.

57. Ibid., 92.

58. Senate, *Oversight Hearings of 1988*, 808–09.

59. Kirk Victor, "Is the Honeymoon Over?" *National Journal* 24 (25 Jan. 1992): 214.

60. *Environmental Defense Fund* v. *Thomas*, 627 F. Supp. 566, 571 (D.D.C. 1986).

16

OSHRC's Role: The Failure of the Split-Enforcement Arrangement

OSHA's efforts to establish a credible enforcement policy have been hindered by the structure that Congress established for adjudicating OSHA citations. Congress assigned OSHA, which is in the Department of Labor (DOL), the responsibility for promulgating health and safety standards and enforcing those standards by inspecting facilities and filing complaints against employers, but it gave the Occupational Safety and Health Review Commission (OSHRC), an independent commission, the responsibility for adjudicating such complaints. This split enforcement arrangement has created numerous conflicts between OSHA and OSHRC that have severely impeded OSHA's attempts to implement its statutory mission.

A UNIQUE ARRANGEMENT

Under the OSH Act, an employer has the right to appeal a citation to OSHRC for an adjudication of its validity. The commission is composed of three members who are appointed by the president, with the advice and consent of the Senate, and who serve six-year staggered terms. Any proceeding before the commission is initially heard by an administrative law judge (ALJ), who conducts a hearing at which the employer, OSHA, and, in many cases, a union introduce documents, present testimony, and cross-examine each other's witnesses. At the hearing, OSHA has the burden of proving by a preponderance of the evidence that a violation has occurred. The ALJ's decision is final unless one of the commissioners directs that the decision be reviewed by the full commission. If the commission hears a case, the parties have an opportunity to present briefs and make an oral argument before that body. The parties on the losing side can appeal a final order to a United States Court of Appeals.[1]

The unique split-enforcement arrangement is used at only one other federal administrative agency, the Mine Safety and Health Administration (MSHA). More typically, the same agency is responsible for both prosecuting violators and adjudicating the validity of those claims. Not surprisingly, the subjects of government regulation have long complained of the potential tyranny of administrators who are at the same time prosecutor, judge, and jury. Dean James Landis, one of the architects of the New Deal, responded that the idea of separation of functions was anachronistic in a modern industrial society, because without the combination of functions, government regulation could not be efficient. He explained, "If in private life we were to organize a firm for the operation of an industry, it would scarcely follow Montesquieu's lines. . . . Yet, the problems of operating a private industry resemble to a great degree those entailed by its regulation."[2] For this reason, the Supreme Court permits the combination of the adjudicatory and prosecutorial function as long as regulatees can seek judicial review to ensure that the agency used fair procedures and that its decision was consistent with its statutory mandate.[3] Additional protections are afforded the Administrative Procedure Act (APA), enacted at the end of the New Deal, which prohibits agency employees who are engaged in the prosecution of a case from discussing the matter with other agency employees who are involved in its adjudication. The APA also prohibits the ALJ and the commissioners from discussing a case with any of the parties involved in it outside of a hearing at which all parties are present.[4]

Despite these protections, Congress adopted the split-enforcement arrangement for OSHA as a political compromise. Business groups favored placing the rulemaking, prosecutorial, and adjudicatory functions of the OSH Act into three different agencies, while labor favored placing all of the functions in OSHA. Congressional debate concerning these choices centered on the trade-off between "fairness" and "efficiency." Business groups and their congressional supporters complained that combining functions in the DOL would be unfair because DOL would tend to favor organized labor in disputes between employees and employers.[5] Unions and their congressional supporters argued along with Landis that agency government is most efficient when an agency is in charge of all phases of enforcement. The creation of OSHRC was a compromise because it removed the adjudicatory function from DOL, which protected employers, but it retained the rulemaking and prosecution functions in DOL, which made the department more efficient.

LIMITS ON OSHA'S AUTHORITY

Congress's decision to adopt a split-enforcement model has not worked out well in practice. A primary reason for this failure is OSHRC's inability to confine its role to the narrow task of adjudicating disputes over alleged violations of existing OSHA standards. From the outset, OSHRC has attempted to narrow the range of OSHA's regulatory authority, a function that is beyond OSHRC's statutory authority and institutional competence. For example, OSHRC in 1976 sided with the employer's view that OSHA was required to use a cost-benefit test in promulgating health standards,[6] and did not abandon that position until after the Supreme Court held otherwise in 1981.[7] In addition, OSHRC for a time hamstrung OSHA's attempts to ensure the veracity of employer injury and illness reporting by holding that the Fourth Amendment required OSHA to obtain a warrant before undertaking inspections of employer records.[8] In addition, OSHRC and OSHA disagreed from the beginning on interpreting OSHA's safety standards. OSHRC often refused to accede to OSHA's interpretation of what its standards meant, even in cases where OSHA's interpretation was sensible and served to protect workers.

In 1991, the Supreme Court clarified which agency—OSHA or OSHRC— was to receive deference concerning the interpretation of OSHA's standards.[9] Writing for a unanimous court, Justice Marshall explained that an agency's interpretation of its own regulation traditionally is entitled to substantial deference, and there was no indication that Congress intended a different result when it enacted the OSH Act. He noted that because OSHA promulgates these standards, it is in a better position than OSHRC to develop the expertise relevant to assessing the effectiveness of a particular regulatory interpretation. Justice Marshall concluded, "Because historical familiarity and policymaking expertise account in the first instance for the presumption that Congress delegates interpretative lawmaking power to the agency rather than to the reviewing court . . . we presume here that Congress intended to invest interpretive power in the administrative actor in the best position to develop these attributes."

The Supreme Court's decision should assist OSHA in protecting workers by protecting it from hostile OSHRC interpretations. Unfortunately, it took the Court 20 years to settle the dispute whether OSHA or OSHRC should get deference, during which time OSHA's efforts to protect workers were disrupted by the commission's narrow interpretation of OSHA's authority. Nevertheless, as the remainder of the chapter indicates, the split-enforcement model still poses significant impediments to OSHA's enforcement efforts.

OSHRC INEFFICIENCY

The commission's performance during the Carter administration revealed that it was unable to keep up with the hundreds of appeals presented to it. This backlog endangered workers because an employer is not required to take corrective actions until OSHRC decides its case. From fiscal year (FY) 1973 through FY 1981, OSHRC had a substantial backlog of cases. The number grew from near zero in 1973 to over 750 in FY 1977. The backlog remained at between 300 and 400 cases through FY 1981. During the same period, the number of cases pending before the ALJ's grew from 500 in 1973 to nearly 2,500 in 1980.[10] OSHRC's failure to eliminate its backlog during this period had two related causes. First, the number of cases appealed to the commission doubled in the

Carter administration. Between 1977 and 1979, the percentage of contested citations rose from 12 percent to 21 percent of all citations.[11] In some industries, such as the oil and chemical industry, the contest rate rose as much as 90 percent.[12] One reason for this increase was that OSHA increased the frequency of citations for health hazards, which are more costly to abate than safety hazards.[13] OSHA also increased the number of citations for serious, willful, and repeated violations,[14] which correspondingly increased the size of the fines it imposed. A second reason for the backlog was the length of time that it took OSHRC to decide a case. In 1978, the General Accounting Office found that the ALJs at the commission took an average of 437 days. This compared with 281 days at the Department of Labor and 386 days at the Interstate Commerce Commission.[15]

OSHRC's slow pace at this time can be attributed to several factors. Because the filing of a notice of contest stays an employer's abatement duty,[16] employers have little incentive to have their cases decided promptly, and they may try to delay a decision as long as possible.[17] In addition, one of the commissioners charged that "understaffing and perhaps incompetence in the Department of Labor" caused delays because DOL lawyers almost always sought continuances in the cases they were prosecuting. Some of the delay was also attributable to the fact that more of the citations involved complex matters, such as the time-consuming evaluation of health hazards. Finally, disagreements among the commissioners slowed the decision-making process. Over 90 percent of the commission's decisions contained a concurrence, a dissent, or both.[18]

The commission was able to eliminate most of its backlog after FY 1981. The number of cases pending fell from about 250 in FY 1982 to a low of 39 in FY 1988. Likewise, the number of cases pending before the ALJs declined remarkably from over 2,000 in FY 1981 to 500 in FY 1983. The number remained between approximately 500 and 750 from FY 1982 to FY 1988. Both of these trends reflect the substantial reduction in OSHA's enforcement activity during the first five years of the Reagan administration (as Chapter 10 detailed). The backlog, however, started to increase with OSHA's renewed emphasis on enforcement in 1986 under John Pendergrass. In FY 1989, the commission's backlog increased from 39 to 77, and the ALJ's backlog increased from less than 750 to over 1,000 cases.[19]

The recent upturn in the commission's backlog is cause for concern, because the commission's efficiency is a crucial element in the protection of workers. Chapter 14 pointed out that vigorous enforcement is a key to increasing the deterrent effect of OSHA's health and safety standards. But increased enforcement also increases the number of cases that employers will appeal. OSHRC's efficiency is therefore critical to OSHA's effectiveness. A large backlog at OSHRC will not only place workers in danger, it will also delay the impact of OSHA's fines and thereby decrease their deterrent effect.

IDEOLOGICAL OPPOSITION

The commissioners appointed by President Reagan were so ideologically opposed to OSHA's mission that OSHRC became the center of a prolonged battle between the White House and organized labor and its allies in the Senate. The battle became so fierce that the Senate Committee on Labor and Human Resources refused to vote on many of President Reagan's nominations to the commission. As a result, the commission was unable to function the last year and a half of President Reagan's term because it lacked a quorum.

The Reagan administration's first appointment to the commission was Robert Rowland, who replaced Frank Barnako in 1981. Rowland had been active in President Reagan's primary election campaign in 1980 and was on the Reagan-Bush steering committee for Texas in the general election. Despite his lack of experience in health and safety law, Rowland faced no difficulty in clearing the Senate because the Republicans were the majority party. His lack of experience and his job performance became a political issue, however, in June 1983, when the president nominated E. Ross Buckley to fill the vacancy created when Bertram Cottine left the commission. The nomination was opposed by the AFL-CIO, which took the position that Buckley did not have qualifications "by way of experience and training" to be a commissioner. At the time of his nomination, Buckley had been OSHRC's general counsel, but the AFL-CIO argued that his responsibilities were only administrative in nature. None of Buckley's prior jobs were related to occupational safety and health law. The AFL-CIO feared that Buckley might simply mimic Rowland, who, according to the union, had demonstrated "a total lack of understanding" of the "serious nature of health and safety hazards in the workplace."[20] The AFL-CIO's criticisms of Rowland were echoed by a Carter appointee, Bertram Cottine, who described Rowland as a "political zealot" who would take "irresponsible" positions in order to exonerate employers. Cottine noted that President Reagan could have reappointed Frank Barnako, a conservative Republican with more than 40 years' experience in job safety and health, instead of appointing Rowland, who had no experience in health and safety law.[21]

After the AFL-CIO announced its opposition, the White House and the Senate engaged in a tug-of-war over the nomination. The Labor and Human Resources Committee took no action on the nomination for the remaining eight months of the congressional session. After the Senate adjourned in November 1983 without a vote, the president gave Buckley a recess appointment.[22] The Constitution authorizes the president to make "recess appointments" when Congress is not in session, but the appointment ends when the next session of the Senate adjourns at the end of the following year. In March 1984, the Labor and Human Resources Committee approved Buckley's nomination and the Senate concurred without debate.[23]

In July 1984, Rowland's term on the commission was cut short when President Reagan gave him a recess appointment as OSHA administrator. The appointment was hailed by the U.S. Chamber of Commerce, which called Rowland an "outstanding choice" to head OSHA.[24] Organized labor, however, was furious over the president's choice and his use of a recess appointment to bypass Senate confirmation. The AFL-CIO produced a statistical analysis of Rowland's voting record indicating that he voted to uphold OSHA, in full or in part, in only 23 of 179 cases, 12.8 percent of the time. During the same period, the commission as a whole affirmed OSHA in 111 cases, 72 percent of the time. The AFL-CIO also claimed that the data confirmed its fears about Buckley and Rowland forming an anti-OSHA coalition. They pointed out that OSHA was upheld in only 4 of the 20 cases decided after Buckley joined the commission, and Rowland voted for OSHA in only 1 of these cases.[25]

The administration took no action to fill the vacancy created by Rowland's departure until July 1985, when it nominated John R. Wall to serve the remainder of Rowland's term. Wall was employed by the Republic Steel Corporation, where he had served as assistant general traffic manager, director of personnel for labor relations, and vice president for labor relations.[26] A short time earlier, in April 1985, Timothy Cleary's term had expired, and the administration nominated Robert E. Rader, Jr., as his replacement. Rader was a partner in an Ennis, Texas, law firm that had represented numerous employers before the commission and the federal courts.[27] In August 1985, the administration made recess appointments to the commission for Wall and Rader after the Labor and Human Resources Committee had delayed its consideration of the nominees for several months.[28]

Although the administration argued that the recess appointments were necessary to create a quorum, they infuriated Senate Minority Leader Robert Byrd, who protested by holding up votes on nominations for 17 judgeships, approximately 5,600 military positions, and over 100 executive branch positions. The White House characterized Byrd's tactic as "the largest backlog of presidential nominations in modern history." Byrd responded that the White House was misusing recess appointments, because they had "all too often been made in situations which were not of an emergency nature or of a nature that such recess appointments could be justified."[29]

In March 1986, the Senate Committee on Labor and Human Resources approved by a voice vote the nomination of Wall to the commission, because he was regarded as a noncontroversial nominee.[30] The treatment of Rader, however, was an entirely different matter. Opponents claimed that Rader's voting record at OSHRC during his recess appointment indicated an anti-OSHA bias. According to Senator Paul Simon, Rader upheld OSHA's position in only 1 of 11 cases in which he participated, and in that case he upheld only 1 count of the citation. Rader claimed that he had voted for OSHA approximately 40 percent of the time. Senator Howard Metzenbaum argued that Rader's past performance in private practice demonstrated that he could not be "fairminded and unbiased" as a commissioner, because when he was a private lawyer, Rader had advised two of his clients to deny entrance to their workplaces to OSHA inspectors, even though they had a warrant. Rader replied that he was concerned about the constitutional rights of his clients. When it came time to vote on Rader, the committee defeated his nomination on an eight-to-eight vote. Rader described the vote as "politicized" and based on "differences in philosophy."[31]

Rader's accusation was probably accurate, but it did not respond to the senators' complaints that he and his fellow commissioners were biased in favor of employers. A 1985 case, *Schwarz-Jordan, Inc.*, is a good example. An OSHA compliance officer cited a drywall contractor for using a manually propelled scaffolding with no guard rails. The scaffold platform was only five feet, eight inches above its base, which rested on the floor, but the scaffold was positioned on the second floor of a building and placed next to an open four-foot-high window. A worker falling from the side of the platform that was next to the window would travel more than 16 feet before hitting the ground outside. OSHA alleged that the scaffold platform violated a standard that required guard rails for scaffolding "more than ten feet above the ground or floor because the platform was 16 feet above the ground." The ALJ affirmed the citation on that ground "because the fall distance was greater than ten feet." The Commission, in a two-to-one vote, reversed, deciding that "[a] manually propelled mobile scaffold has its base on the ground or floor, so the natural interpretation of 'above the ground or floor' would be the distance between the scaffold platform and the base of the scaffold."[32] On appeal, OSHA argued that the ALJ's interpretation was the "most likely to effectuate the purpose of the regulation to protect employees exposed to the hazard of falling more than ten feet from a scaffold platform." The Fifth Circuit reversed the commission's decision and affirmed the citation.[33]

Decisions like this caused organized labor and its political supporters to conclude that workers were better off without a commission, a result they accomplished when the administration made two additional appointments to OSHRC. In February 1987, Douglas Ehlke was nominated to replace Rader, who had resigned from his recess appointment. Ehlke had been in private practice in the state of Washington, representing employers in health and safety matters.[34] While Ehlke's nomination was pending, John Wall's term on the commission (in reality, Rowland's unexpired term) had expired, and in April 1987 he was renominated.[35] The Labor and Human Resources Committee refused to vote on the Ehlke and Wall nominations. In April 1988, one year after he was nominated, Wall asked that his name be withdrawn because of the delay.[36] Similarly discouraged with the prospect of confirmation by a hostile Senate during an election year, Ehlke withdrew his name in the summer of 1988.[37]

The committee's failure to vote on the nominations put the commission out of business for the last year and a half of the Reagan administration. From April 1987 until November 1988, it lacked the necessary two-person quorum, and it was therefore unable to conduct any business.[38] During this period, all of the cases that were pending before the commission remained undecided and Commissioner Buckley refused to order any new cases for review.[39] The Senate committee's failure to act was both criticized and praised. Critics claimed that

Senator Edward Kennedy, chair of the committee, put workers in danger by failing to hold a vote. A prominent labor lawyer, Scott Railton, claimed that "Kennedy is playing hardball. He is saying, 'If you don't give me what I want, you won't have a commission.' But what he forgets is that to the extent a case pends, employers have no obligation to abate the [safety or health] violation affecting employees. He is playing politics and the public be damned."[40] Supporters countered that Kennedy and the committee had a responsibility to ensure that nominees were "impartial and qualified." David McAteer, the head of the Occupational Safety and Health Law Center, a worker advocacy group, argued, "When [the Reagan administration] appoints people who vote against [OSHA] law, and they vote so consistently to make it a travesty, it is an injustice [to the public]."[41] Railton also objected that "the function of the commission is abdicated to the ALJs, which means employers and employees have their judicial rights determined by government officials not responsible to the public—that is a said commentary."[42] David Vladick, an attorney for Ralph Nader's Public Citizen responded, "It's not like the Review Commission has done a lot of people any good." He believed that in the absence of a quorum, "[t]he world is a better place."[43]

On October 21, 1988, President Reagan nominated Linda Arey to replace John Wall.[44] Arey was sworn in on November 22, 1988, under a recess appointment by President Reagan.[45] She had previously served in public affairs positions in the White House, Department of Transportation, and the Justice Department. The AFL-CIO opposed the nomination because she had no experience in occupational safety and health. Margaret Seminario, speaking for the AFL-CIO noted, "We've been through this before with a political appointee. The one thing that the [OSH Act] does specify [for appointment as a commissioner] is safety and health experience."[46] President Bush allowed the nomination to languish.

The commission remained without a quorum during the Bush administration until May 17, 1990, when the Senate confirmed Donald Wideman to fill the position last held by Linda Arey and Velma Montoya to fill the position last held by Robert Rader.[47] At the time of his appointment, Wideman was an administrator for safety and training for ElectriCities of North Carolina, Inc.[48] At the time of her appointment, Montoya was an associate professor of finance at the School of Business Administration at California State Polytechnic University in Pomona, California. She had also served as an economist in OMB.[49] The Senate had previously approved Edwin Foulke, Jr., who had been an attorney in Columbia, South Carolina, to serve as chairman of the commission.[50] The appointments of Wiseman and Montoya meant the commission had a full complement of members for the first time since September 1986.

THE FUTURE OF OSHRC

The fate of OSHRC is important to American workers. As Chapter 11 discussed, the Bush administration has adopted aggressive enforcement policies that can be expected to increase significantly the number of cases appealed to the commission. The commission can blunt the deterrent effect of these efforts if it is hostile to OSHA's interpretation of its regulations, falls behind in the adjudication of citations, or follows rigid ideological preconceptions concerning the role of OSHA. The commission has committed all of these sins in the past, and it has thereby rendered OSHA less effective.

Congress should reconsider the split-enforcement model. Whatever slight degree of additional fairness the model provides to employers is more than offset by its lack of efficiency. Furthermore, fairness can be adequately preserved if Congress abolishes OSHRC and transfers the adjudicatory function to OSHA. Congress could specifically require OSHA to separate its functions to guarantee fairness and to create internal barriers to insulate employees who work on the adjudication of citations from those who investigate and prosecute those citations. In addition, Congress could extend the prohibitions on ex parte contacts now present in the APA to include the assistant secretary for OSHA.[51] This would guarantee that ALJ decisions would be made independent of the assistant secretary's supervision or control.

If Congress elects not to abolish OSHRC, it could at least limit the incentive to delay by giving OSHA the power to mandate compliance during the pendency of OSHRC proceedings or allowing fines to accumulate during losing appeals. The best remedy, however, is to discard the split-enforcement model as an experiment that was tried and found wanting.

NOTES

1. Steven Bokat and Horace Thompson III, eds., *Occupational Safety and Health Law* (Washington, D.C.: Bureau of National Affairs, 1988), 442–85.
2. James Landis, *The Administrative Process* (New Haven: Yale University Press, 1938), 10.
3. *Crowell* v. *Benson*, 285 U.S. 22 (1932).
4. 5 U.S.C. §§ 554(d), 557(d)(1) (1988).
5. Bokat and Thompson, *Occupational Safety*, 442–47.
6. *Continental Can Co.*, 4 O.S.H. Cases (BNA) 1541 (Rev. Comm'n. 1976).
7. *American Textile Mfrs. Inc. v. Donovan*, 452 U.S. 490 (1981).
8. Compare *Secretary of Labor v. A. B. Chance Co.*, 842 F.2d 724 (4th Cir. 1988) (reversing the commission) with *Secretary of Labor v. Emerson Electric Co.*, 834 F.2d)94, 13 O.S.H. Cases (BNA) 1521 (11th Cir. 1987) (upholding the commission).
9. *Martin v. OSHRC*, 111 S.Ct. 1171 (1991).
10. *BNA Occupational Safety and Health Reporter* 18 (10 May 1989): 1997.
11. U.S. Congress, Senate Committee on Labor and Human Resources, Hearings on Oversight on the Administration of the Occupational Safety and Health Act, pt. 1, 96th Cong., 2d sess., 1980, 297 (hereafter Senate, *Oversight Hearings of 1980*) (statement of Basil Whiting, assistant secretary of labor for occupational safety and health).
12. Ibid., 879 (statement of Nolan W. Hancock, citizenship-legislative director, Oil, Chemical and Atomic Workers International Union).
13. Senate, *Oversight Hearings of 1980*, 297.

14. Ibid., 298.

15. General Accounting Office, *Administrative Law Process: Better Management Is Needed* (Washington, D.C.: United States Government Printing Office, 1978), 11.

16. 29 U.S.C. § 659(b) (1988).

17. Senate, *Oversight Hearings of 1980*, 878.

18. Mark Rothstein, "OSHA After Ten Years: A Review and Some Proposed Reforms," *Vanderbilt Law Review* 34 (1981): 117.

19. *BNA Occupational Safety and Health Reporter* 18 (10 May 1989): 1997.

20. Ibid., 13 (17 Nov. 1983): 665; *BNA Labor Relations Reporter* (9 Nov. 1983): A14; ibid. (1 Dec. 1984): A8.

21. *BNA Occupational Safety and Health Reporter* 13 (8 Sept. 1983): 353–54.

22. Ibid. (29 Mar. 1984): 1164.

23. Ibid. (5 Apr. 1984): 1180.

24. Ibid. 14 (26 July 1984): 187.

25. Ibid. *BNA Labor Reporter* (14 Sept. 1984): A6; ibid. (3 Aug. 1984): A2.

26. *BNA Occupational Safety and Health Reporter* 15 (15 Aug. 1985): 239.

27. Ibid.

28. Ibid. (24 Oct. 1985): 428.

29. Ibid. 427–28.

30. Ibid. (30 March 1986): 1045.

31. Ibid. 16 (26 June 1986): 75–76; ibid. 15 (30 March 1986): 1045.

32. *Schwarz-Jordan, Inc.*, 1984–85 O.S.H. Dec. (CCH) ¶26,989 (Rev. Comm'n. 1984).

33. *Brock v. Schwarz-Jordan, Inc.*, 777 F.2d 195, 198 (5th Cir. 1985).

34. *BNA Occupational Safety and Health Reporter* 16 (2 Feb. 1987): 1019–20.

35. Ibid. (29 Apr. 1987): 1319.

36. Ibid. 17 (4 May 1988): 1765.

37. Ibid. 18 (29 June 1988): 463.

38. Ibid. (30 Nov. 1988): 95. Linda A. Arey was sworn in 22 Nov. as a recess appointee by President Reagan.

39. Ibid. 17 (11 May 1988): 1835.

40. Ibid.

41. Ibid.

42. Ibid., 1839.

43. Ibid.

44. Ibid. 18 (26 Oct. 1988): 1059.

45. Ibid. (30 Nov. 1988): 1195.

46. Ibid. (26 Oct. 1988): 1059.

47. Ibid. 19 (23 May 1990): 2227.

48. Ibid.

49. Ibid. (20 Sept. 1989): 721.

50. Ibid. (27 Sept. 1989): 760.

51. Richard J. Pierce, Jr., Sidney A. Shapiro, and Paul R. Verkuil, *Administrative Law and Process* (Mineola, N.Y.: Foundation Press, 1985), § 9.3.6.

17

The Courts' Role: Judicial Review and OSHA

OSHA has been working for years on a lockout/tagout standard to protect workers from easily avoidable accidents. Although it started working on the standard in 1977, we learned in Chapter 8 that it did not promulgate a final standard until 1989. Sadly, that greatly delayed action did not end the matter. In July 1991, a three-judge panel of the District of Columbia Court of Appeals decided *International Union, UAW* v. *OSHA*, which remanded the standard to OSHA with instructions to supply evidence to support the rule.[1]

OSHA standards must pass judicial muster before they become effective if an affected party mounts a legal challenge, which almost always happens for health standards and often happens for safety standards like the lockout/tagout rule. Although OSHA has won most of these cases, the manner in which the courts review OSHA decisions is a primary factor in explaining why it takes the agency so long to promulgate standards. This chapter argues that unless Congress and the judiciary rethink how courts review the decisions of administrative agencies like OSHA, there may be little hope of speeding up the rulemaking process, no matter how committed the agencies are to expeditious action.

THE LOCKOUT/TAGOUT CASE

The lockout/tagout standard, as explained in Chapter 8, addressed the problem that at least 144 workers die and some 33,342 workdays are lost each year because machines under repair are accidentally started by an employee.[2] OSHA's standard requires employers to lock machines that are under repair and to provide the only key to the employee repairing or servicing the machine. When the installation of a lock would require an employer to dismantle, rebuild, or replace a machine, however, OSHA only requires a tagout, the posting of a sign warning employees that a machine is under repair and that it should not be turned on.

Judge Stephen Williams, writing for a three-judge panel in *International Union*, reached two important conclusions about OSHA's long awaited lockout/tagout standard. First, he found that because the lockout/tagout standard was not a health standard, OSHA's authority to promulgate the rule was Section 3(8) of the OSH Act, and not Section 6(b)(5). This distinction is important because of two Supreme Court decisions discussed in Chapters 4 and 5. The *Benzene* case held that once OSHA proves a toxic substance poses a significant risk, Section 6(b)(5) requires it to reduce workers' exposure to the risk to the extent that is feasible,[3] while the *Cotton Dust* case held that OSHA was not limited in the reduction of *health* hazards by a cost-benefit standard.[4] In the latter case, however, the Court expressly left open the issue of whether Section 3(8) established a cost-benefit test for *safety* standards. Judge Williams agreed with three prior circuit court findings that Congress did impose such a requirement,[5] but the District of Columbia Circuit nevertheless remanded the standard to OSHA to permit it to argue that it was not bound by a cost-benefit test. In so ruling, however, the court made it clear that it would not accept OSHA's argument that a feasibility-based standard applied to safety standards as well as to health standards.[6]

Second, because Judge Williams anticipated that OSHA would have to defend the standard under a cost-benefit test, he warned the agency that the existing record could not support the rule on that basis. OSHA had estimated that the final rule would cost industry $214.3 million during the first year of operation and $135 million in each subsequent year. The agency also found that the rule would likely save 122 lives, which meant that the standard would cost $1.2 million per fatality avoided. When OSHA included the economic benefits to employers of a reduction in fatalities and injuries, such as fewer lost production days, the cost of each fatality avoided fell to $0.19 million. Finally, when the agency included the benefits to workers from injuries that would be avoided, it found that the cost per injury was "extremely low." Based on this data, the agency had no trouble concluding that the rule was highly cost-effective.[7]

Judge Williams objected, however, that OSHA had not presented industry-by-industry comparisons of costs and benefits and that OSHA "nowhere explain[ed] its logic" for failing to do so. He considered this to be a significant failing, because he thought there might be some industries where the costs of compliance were relatively high and the benefits relatively low. Without such "disaggregated" data, Judge Williams believed that the court had no way of knowing whether the standard was justified.[8]

Judge Williams was applying a judicial approach to reviewing administrative decisions called the "hard look" doctrine. This doctrine requires an agency to explain adequately all of the important aspects of its justification for a rule and to provide data and analysis to back up that explanation. An inadequate explanation indicates that the agency has not taken a "hard look" at whether the proposed standard is necessary and appropriate, and a court will remand the standard to an agency to reevaluate the standard in such cases. In addition, the reviewing court will take its own "hard look" at the information and analysis in the record, and it will remand the standard if it is not convinced that the record supports the agency's conclusions. The agency is free to promulgate the same standard again, but if it is to survive judicial review the second time, it must offer an adequate explanation, provide better factual support, or both.

The "hard look" doctrine is the principal vehicle through which the courts review agency decision making. While the doctrine has the potential to ensure that agencies act in a rational and nonarbitrary manner, it also has the potential to subvert agency policy decisions. As will be explained below, this is exactly what the District of Columbia Circuit did in the lockout/tagout case. This subversion has two aspects. First, it delays useful and appropriate rules in cases where a standard is remanded to an agency. Second, it forces agencies to spend enormous amounts of time and resources assembling the factual and analytical support for a standard before it is issued, in an attempt to avoid a judicial remand. The doctrine thus slows down the rulemaking process even in those cases where the agency successfully defends its standard in court. To understand these impacts, it is necessary to review the relationship that Congress has created between the courts and administrative agencies.

THE DEFERENCE PRINCIPLE

In the Administrative Procedure Act (APA), which specifies the procedures that agencies use to develop and promulgate rules, Congress also established the relationship between the courts and agencies. Congress instructed the courts to "hold unlawful and set aside agency action, findings, and conclusions found to be . . . arbitrary [or] capricious. . . ."[9] For some kinds of more formal agency actions, Congress told the courts to set aside the actions if they were not supported by "substantial evidence." In a historical curiosity, the OSH Act requires the reviewing court to use the "substantial evidence" test for OSHA rules,[10] and the courts are divided as to whether this means that the courts should show less deference to such rules.[11] An action is "arbitrary" when it is the product of willful and unreasoning conduct, without regard to or consideration of the facts and circumstances of a case. In short, an action is arbitrary and capricious if it is not based on a consideration of the "relevant factors as it manifests a 'clear error of judgement.' "[12] The "substantial evidence" test requires the reviewing court to be sure that credible evidence in the record supports the agency's decision. The court must consider both the evidence that supports the agency's decision and the evidence that fairly detracts from it.[13]

Under either test, this division of authority between courts and agencies gives the primary responsibility to agencies to choose among competing policies and to resolve interpretational disputes about the data underlying agency rules. Congress thought this arrangement advisable for two primary reasons. First, agency officials and employees generally have greater expertise than federal judges to address regulatory subjects. Agency scientists, engineers, and economists are far better qualified to resolve complex science/policy disputes than are the lawyers assigned to the federal bench. Second, agency officials are subject to supervision by the political branches of government—the White House and Congress—while federal judges, who have lifetime appointments, are not. Assigning agencies the primary responsibility to make policy decisions therefore gives voters the power to influence those decisions through their elected officials.

Under the scope of review established by Congress, a court can set aside agency action if the agency has failed to justify its decision adequately. According to the Supreme Court, a decision is not the "product of reasoned decisionmaking" if it relies on factors that Congress has not intended it to consider, has entirely failed to consider an important aspect of the problem, has offered an explanation that runs counter to the evidence before the agency, or has offered an explanation that "is so implausible that it could not be ascribed to a difference in view or the product of its expertise."[14] The courts always couch their review function in deferential terms, sometimes invoking a partnership metaphor under which the courts and agencies are partners in the pursuit of sound administrative policy-making. It is, however, usually pretty clear who the senior partner is.

Presumably Judge Williams's objections to OSHA's failure to disaggregate its data was that the agency failed to consider an important aspect of the problem—the possibility that costs might outweigh benefits in some individual industries. The court's remand on this point, however, is wholly unwarranted under the deferential standard of review prescribed by the APA. OSHA's calculations indicated that the standard was highly cost-effective. The cost per fatality avoided was $190,000, and this calculation did not take into account the benefits to be gained from the elimination of over 37,000 lost workdays. The fact that the standard was so highly cost-effective strongly suggests that its benefits would exceed its costs in any industry. Judge Williams thought that a remand was necessary because injury rates varied widely among industries, but this ignores OSHA's finding that compliance costs were directly related to the injury rate. An industry will have a low injury rate only if it has few machines that present a lockout/tagout problem. This means the costs of meeting OSHA's standard will likewise be low. Indeed, OSHA found that the average cost of compliance in industries with low injury rates was approximately $169 per firm.[15]

THE EFFECT OF OVERZEALOUS REVIEW

Although OSHA is undoubtedly capable of assembling a record that supports a conclusion that the benefits of the lockout/tagout standard exceed its costs on an industry-by-industry basis, the court's insistence that OSHA prove the obvious will divert precious time and resources from rulemaking initiatives. This particular type of remand, however, has an even more pernicious effect. Remanding a case to respond to a flaw that a judge perceives in the agency's explanation for a rule is an easy way for a court to dispose of a rulemaking challenge without appearing to extend itself beyond the range of its institutional competence. In demanding additional explanation, the court is not technically ruling that the agency is wrong or irrational; it is merely holding that the agency's analysis is incomplete. Yet the message that the agencies hear is that their written rationales must be exceedingly thoroughgoing in every regard, or activist courts may send rulemaking initiatives back to the drawing board. Savvy program managers know that in the complex and constantly shifting institutional environment of modern rulemaking, a trip back to the drawing board can send the project spinning off in odd directions or, worse, consign the standard to oblivion as the agency commits limited staff resources to other projects, institutional memory fades, and more immediate priorities press rulemaking initiatives to the bottom of the agenda. As we saw in Chapter 11, a remand can also invite OMB to use its interpretation of the court's opinion as an excuse to deflect or derail the initiative. The key to successful rulemaking is therefore to make every effort to render the rule capable of withstanding the most strenuous possible judicial scrutiny the first time around. As a result, the process of assimilating the record and drafting the preambles to proposed and final rules has become the most time-consuming aspect of informal rulemaking.

The impact of having to dot every i and cross every t for fear of a judicial remand has had a dramatic effect on OSHA. Chapter 12 documented how long it takes OSHA to promulgate a rule. Sixty percent of the agency's health standards have taken three years or longer; 48 percent have taken four years or longer; and 40 percent have taken five years or longer. OSHA has been working three or more years on 70 percent of its pending health standards and five years or more on 40 percent of its pending health standards. It has acted somewhat more quickly on its safety standards—only 30 percent have taken three or more years— but it has been working four or more years on 57 percent of its pending safety standards. Of course, there have been other causes of delay, including a chronic lack of resources and a lackadaisical attitude during the early years of the Reagan administration. Nevertheless, the effect of judicial review undoubtedly is a primary cause of this delay.

A DELICATE BALANCE

Before OSHA can seriously aspire to fulfill its rulemaking mandate, the problem of overzealous review must be seriously addressed. The problem, however, is not an easy one. The requirement that agencies justify their actions with data, analysis, and adequate reasons serves a useful purpose. Agency decision makers are less likely to act irrationally when they know that a body composed of intelligent, neutral laypersons must feel comfortable in concluding that the agency applied its expertise to technical problems in a bona fide way and responded to significant objections from affected persons. Indeed, the mere possibility of substantive judicial review alone can be a great hedge against arbitrariness, even if it does not occur in every case. In sum, judicial review can perform a necessary "quality control" function.[16]

Moreover, the requirement that an agency give adequate reasons for its decisions is related to the constitutional legitimacy of the agency's actions.[17] An agency has constitutional authority to regulate private conduct only if its actions serve the statutory purposes for which it was created. The requirement that an agency adequately explain the connection between its rule and those purposes legitimizes its actions. Eliminating the adequate explanations requirement would make it more difficult for the courts to ensure that the agency's decision was true to its statutory mandate.

Reducing the intensity of rulemaking would in time speed up agency decision making, but it would also open the door to administrative arbitrariness. The courts must therefore strike a delicate balance between engaging in judicial review that is too intrusive on the one hand, and judicial review that is too deferential on the other.

AN APPROPRIATE BALANCE

Congress could assist the judiciary in striking an appropriate balance between guarding against arbitrary agency action and subverting an agency's mission by amending the APA to establish a new scope of review. The Administrative Law Section of the American Bar Association has adopted a "Restatement of the Scope of Review Doctrine" that contains some suggestions for congressional action.[18] The Restatement lists the type of legal, policy, and factual conclusions that agencies typically reach in rulemaking and indicates what scope of review is to be applied to each. Agency "policy judgments" are subjected to a standard of "arbitrariness"; the factual premises upon which policy judgments are based are subject to a standard of "substantial support in the administrative record viewed as a whole." Congress could amend the OSH Act to reflect this dichotomy between policy and facts.

This change would constantly remind courts of their institutional roles in reviewing agency standards. First, it indicates that an agency's policy decisions are to receive substantial deference since they are to be overruled only in cases where they are arbitrary. Second, it tells courts that agency fact-finding need not be perfect, and should be affirmed as long as the agency's conclusions have "substantial support." This is what the District of Columbia Circuit opinion in the lockout/tagout case did not do. Although OSHA's conclusions that its standard was highly cost-effective had substantial support, Judge Williams insisted that OSHA produce additional evidence anyway.

Whether such legislation would produce a more appropriate balance depends on how the courts would implement the new scope of review. Unless the Supreme Court insists that the lower federal courts give agencies appropriate deference, tinkering with the wording of the statute's scope of review requirement will not be effective. Moreover, even if Congress does not amend the OSH Act, the

Supreme Court could still signal the lower federal courts that they are not striking an appropriate balance. With or without congressional action, the Supreme Court could take two useful actions.

First, the Court should replace the "hard look" metaphor for describing the agency's obligation to provide adequate data, analysis, and reasons to justify a standard. Judge Patricia Wald, one of the most thoughtful students of administrative law on the District of Columbia Circuit, has suggested that a more appropriate metaphor might assign the courts the role of "nursemaid" for regulatory programs.[19] This metaphor suggests that the courts should assist an agency in providing reasons that would justify its actions. But this metaphor fails to suggest to the courts how much "nursing" they should provide and how thorough an explanation they should require the agency to assemble.

A better metaphor might be a "pass-fail" test for adequacy. According to this metaphor, the judge is like the professor who is vaguely familiar with the subject matter of a paper and must determine whether the paper meets minimum standards for passable work. The professor's disagreement with the paper's conclusions is not a reason for the student to flunk. Moreover, a check of the citations may reveal that the student could have found more sources or that the student may have mischaracterized one of the cited sources, and still the paper may pass. Only where there is an inexcusable gap in the analysis, an obvious misquote, or evidence of intellectual dishonesty will the professor put an "F" on the paper and send it back to the student. When courts engage in substantive judicial review of OSHA rulemaking, they should, like the professor, see their role as screening out bad decisions rather than ensuring that agencies reach the "best" decisions.

Second, the Supreme Court could explain the requirement of adequate reasons in a way that would strike a more appropriate balance between overly intrusive and too deferential judicial review. As noted earlier, two reasons are commonly given for deference. Agency employees have greater expertise than judges, and agency officials are more accountable than judges to elected officials. A third reason for deference is the unavoidable fact that agencies operate under a set of constraints that make it difficult, if not impossible, to meet high judicial expectations for the administrative "reasoning process." Because unrealistic judicial demands for agency data, explanations, and analysis slow the rulemaking process to a crawl, the congressional desire to ameliorate the adverse social impacts of an unconstrained labor market is defeated. Congress intended that health and safety agencies like OSHA act with dispatch to protect the beneficiaries of the agency's mandate. When courts fail to give agencies sufficient deference, because they do not recognize the difficult conditions under which agencies operate, they are, perhaps unintentionally, undermining the progressive policies of the OSH Act.

OSHA's rulemaking experience provides ample evidence of the difficulties that health and safety agencies face in attempting to promulgate rules. First, OSHA must continually make complex scientific, engineering, and policy judgments under conditions of insufficient data and lack of scientific consensus about the essential technical questions that underlie agency rulemaking efforts. Second, since OSHA has a limited number of scientists, engineers, and economists to undertake rigorous scientific and policy analysis, only a few chemicals or products can be considered for regulation at any one time. As Chapter 12 discussed, OSHA's budget has been increasing slowly in recent years, but the agency still has fewer constant dollar resources than it had during the last year of the Carter administration. Third, OSHA must contend with a difficult political environment. Regulatory decisions are normally controversial because they both affect Congress, the White House, and various interest groups, and involve difficult moral and philosophical choices. OSHA is guaranteed an unusual amount of political controversy because its decision-making process is like a zero-sum game: any decision that significantly affects worker interests will just as significantly affect employer interests in the opposite direction. As one study of the politics at OSHA has explained. "[T]he whole bitter nature of U.S. labor history—the mutual distrust, management's desire to run its business with minimal interference, labor's belief that employers cannot be trusted to do 'right things' without a gun at their heads—has been loaded onto OSHA."[20] These constraints have had a significant impact on OSHA's output. Indeed, given these restraints, it is surprising that OSHA has been able to regulate at all.

Recently appointed activist federal judges fail to take account of these factors when they order agencies to do a better job of explaining themselves. This failure, however, is not surprising because the conception of the purposes of judicial review, as currently understood by many judges, does not include assisting the agency to carry out its mission. Instead, more and more judges are convinced that the purpose of judicial review is to protect the property rights and managerial prerogatives of the companies that are adversely affected by such review. This is a seriously mistaken view of the proper role for the courts in reviewing administrative action. The courts should instead attempt to strike an appropriate balance between the protection of property rights from arbitrary government action and the protection of statutory beneficiaries in the manner Congress intended.

Professor Cass Sunstein, who has studied the tendency of judges to equate the purposes of judicial review with protection of private property rights, suggests that this approach reflects the failure of judges to take account of the changes in government brought about by the New Deal.[21] Sunstein explains that in the early twentieth century, nineteenth-century principles of private markets and private rights provided the baseline against which regulatory measures were assessed and interpreted. Starting with principles of laissez-faire, courts understood their role as that of "damage control" or limiting the reach of government regulation. Sunstein argues that since the New Deal the public has accepted the legitimacy of government regulation such as that provided by OSHA: "The national regulatory state, which originated in the New Deal and culminated in the rights revolution of the 1960s and 1970s, has renovated the American constitutional structure."[22] He therefore calls on the courts to develop a "sympathetic understanding of the functions of social and economic regulation'' that reflects the voters' acceptance of the goals and purposes of such regulation. In particular, the task is to develop a "set of background understandings" that are "sensitive" to the country's constitutional structure, the institutional design of agency government, and the role of government after the New Deal.[23]

As noted, one way to strike an appropriate balance between protecting private rights and ensuring that agencies can carry out their statutory mission is to view the aim of judicial review as administering a "pass/fail" test. When a reviewing court spots a potential gap in an agency's analysis or an oversight in an agency's justification for a regulation, it should ask whether the oversight is so fundamental that the agency could not have seriously addressed the problem it is regulating *in light of the resource and other constraints under which the agency is operating.* If the agency's failure to dot an i or cross a t stems from demonstrably sloppy thinking or obvious bureaucratic laziness, the rule should be remanded. But if the failure of explanation or analysis is plausibly related to a lack of resources, limitations in the available data, or similar constraints, the court should allow the agency to follow its congressional mandate. If the Supreme Court adopted their approach, the delay that overly intrusive judicial review causes should decrease and agencies should be less hesitant to promulgate protective rules as Congress intended.

BIFURCATED REVIEW

The three principles—agency expertise, political accountability, and Congress's desire to solve regulatory problems—that require deferential judicial review of agency rules also justify more stringent judicial review of agency failures to initiate rulemaking. When an agency refuses to regulate despite the obvious existence of a regulatory problem, courts ought to be dubious about the agency's failure to act. Unfortunately, as Chapter 21 will demonstrate, the courts all too often adopt the opposite approach, showing a high degree of deference to OSHA's failure to set protective standards.

The Supreme Court's opinion in *Motor Vehicle Manufacturers Association* v. *State Farm Mutual Insurance Company* suggests why the courts give more deference to the failure to act.[24] *State Farm* reviewed a decision by the National Highway Traffic Safety Administration (NHTSA) soon after President Reagan took office to rescind a regulation promulgated by the agency during the Carter administration. The regulation required the installation of automatic seatbelts or airbags in all new cars. The automobile makers had argued that NHTSA's decision to rescind the rule should be judged by the same highly deferential standard that a court uses to judge an agency's refusal to promulgate a rule. The Court rejected this argument on the grounds that a revocation of an extant regulation is substantially different from a failure to act, because revocation "constitutes a reversal of the agency's former views as to the proper course." In other words, having once decided that a regulation is desirable, the agency is in a different position than in cases where it has never acted. Accordingly, the court decided that "an agency changing its course by rescinding a rule is obligated to supply a reasonable analysis for the change beyond that which may be required when an agency does not act in the first instance." The Court was highly skeptical of NHTSA's reasons for recission, looked carefully at the evidence it cited in support of its position, and remanded the decision to the agency because it failed to give "adequate reasons" for its action.

The Court's explanation for treating recission and failure to act differently misperceives congressional intent. When Congress adopts a regulatory statute, it intends that an agency act to solve regulatory problems. Whether an agency rescinds an existing regulation or fails to address an obvious regulatory problem, the beneficiaries of a statutory scheme remain unprotected. Either result frustrates the intent of Congress. We therefore propose in Chapter 21 that the courts review more carefully those cases where OSHA refuses to act.

CONCLUSIONS

The challenge of devising an appropriate theory of judicial review is as old as administrative law itself. It is especially difficult to achieve a level of judicial review that is neither too deferential nor too intrusive. In reviewing OSHA rules, the courts have failed to strike the proper balance. While the requirement that agencies give adequate reasons for their actions is a desirable one, some judges have employed an unduly strict concept of adequacy, showing too little tolerance for unimportant errors. This hypercritical posture may reflect a failure to make proper allowances for the substantial constraints under which agencies work. Agencies that face significant resource constraints, limitations in their data, and constant political fights, either will be unable to perfect their justifications for an action, or will take so long to do so that other work is precluded.

Both Congress and the Supreme Court can act to establish an appropriate balance between guarding against arbitrary action and preventing agencies from regulating. Congress should clarify the scope of review in the APA. And the Court, for its part, should explicitly adopt as a reason for deference the difficult circumstances under which agencies must write rules. Both these actions would telegraph to federal judges that they are to balance effective implementation of congressional will against the danger of arbitrary action.

The steps suggested here may not end overly intrusive judicial review. The refusal of some judges to accept agency explanations is rooted in an ideological opposition to an expanded role of regulation in American society. These judges can easily mask this ideology in "hard look" jargon and thereby avoid public scrutiny of de facto judicial policy-making. The recommendations set out in this chapter and Chapter 21 would provide some benefit nevertheless. When judges fail to approve agency decisions that meet a "pass/fail" test, their ideological motives should be more apparent, and they can be criticized for inappropriately interjecting their political views into the review process. While such criticism may not change judicial behavior in every case, it should help persuade activist judges to apply the proper scope of review.

NOTES

1. 938 F.2d 1310 (D.C. Cir. 1991).
2. 54 *Fed. Reg.* 36,684 (1989).
3. *Industrial Union Dep't. AFL-CIO* v. *American Petroleum Institute*, 448 U.S. 607 (1980).
4. *Textile Mfrs. Inst.* v. *Donovan*, 452 U.S. 490 (1981).
5. *Donovan* v. *Castle & Cooke Foods*, 692 F.2d 641 (9th Cir. 1982); *International Harvester* v. *OSHRC*, 628 F.2d 982 (7th Cir. 1980); *RMI* v. *Secretary of Labor*, 594 F.2d 566 (6th Cir. 1979).
6. 938 F.2d at 1318.
7. 54 *Fed. Reg.* 36,684–85 (1989).
8. 938 F.2d at 1322–24.
9. 5 U.S.C. § 706(2)(A) (1988).
10. 29 U.S.C. § 660(a) (1988).
11. Compare *Associated Industries of New York, Inc.* v. *Department of Labor*, 487 F.2d 342, 347–50 (2nd Cir. 1973) (substantial evidence test in OSH Act is roughly equivalent to arbitrary and capricious review in other contexts) with *Corrosion Proof Fittings* v. *EPA*, 947 F.2d 1201, 1213–14 (5th Cir. 1991) (substantial evidence review is more stringent than arbitrary and capricious review).
12. *Citizens to Preserve Overton Park* v. *Volpe*, 401 U.S. 402 (1971).
13. Richard J. Pierce Jr., Sidney A. Shapiro, and Paul R. Verkuil, *Administrative Law and Process* (Mineola, N.Y.: Foundation Press, 1985), 357–60.
14. *Motor Vehicle Manufacturers Ass'n.* v. *State Farm Mutual Automobile Insurance Co.*, 463 U.S. 29 (1983).
15. 54 *Fed. Reg.* 36,684 (1989).
16. Stephen Breyer and Richard Stewart, *Administrative Law and Regulatory Policy* (Boston: Little, Brown, 1979), 307.
17. Sidney Shapiro and Richard Levy, "Heightened Scrutiny of the Fourth Branch: Separation of Powers and the Requirement of Adequate Reasons for Agency Decisions," *Duke Law Review*, 1987, 387.
18. American Bar Association, "Restatement of the Scope of the Review Doctrine," *Administrative Law Review* 38 (Summer 1986): 235–37; Ronald M. Levin, "Scope-of-Review Doctrine Restated: An Administrative Law Section Report," ibid., 239.
19. Patricia M. Wald, "Making 'Informed Decisions' on the District of Columbia Circuit," *George Washington Law Review* 50 (January 1982): 138.
20. Michael Levin, "Politics and Polarity: The Limits of OSHA Reform," *Regulation*, 3 (Nov./Dec. 1979): 34.
21. Cass Sunstein, *After the Rights Revolution: Reconceiving the Regulatory State* (Cambridge, Mass.: Harvard Univ. Press, 1990), 5–8.
22. Ibid., 227.
23. Ibid., 231.
24. 463 U.S. 29 (1983).

Part V

EXTERNAL REFORMS: CHANGING OSHA'S MANDATE

18

OSHA and Overregulation: Should Cost-Benefit Analysis Apply?

No occupational safety and health issue divides employers and the unions more dramatically than whether OSHA health standards should be subjected to a cost-benefit test. Employers can point to economic studies that purport to show that the costs of OSHA's health standards exceed the benefits by hundreds of millions of dollars. They attribute this discrepancy in part to the agency's insistence that employers use expensive engineering controls instead of less expensive respirators. Employers contend that OSHA "overregulates" when it mandates employee protections that cannot pass a cost-benefit test. Acknowledging that OSHA's current mandate requires it to protect workers beyond the point at which marginal costs equal marginal benefits, businesses and their allies in academe and the think tanks have lobbied Congress to amend the OSH Act to require OSHA to apply cost-benefit analysis to its health standards.

Expressing substantial doubts about the capacity of cost-benefit analysis to yield objective insights into the sufficiency of OSHA proposals, the unions tenaciously defend the current "feasibility-based" approach to health regulation. An AFL-CIO spokesman explained, "Cost-benefit studies are basically political documents and always have been."[1] To the unions, demanding cost-benefit analysis is merely a subtle way of advocating a return to less civilized days at the turn of the century, when businesses had the power to replace injured and diseased workers instead of protecting them.

This chapter considers the cost-benefit analysis debate. A close look at cost-benefit methodology reveals that beneath the precise-looking calculations lies a mine field of speculation, untested assumptions, and hidden value judgments. This chapter will also suggest that even if cost-benefit analysis is an appropriate test for "overregulation" in society, a highly debatable proposition, OSHA's critics fail in the final analysis to demonstrate that OSHA has in fact overregulated.

COST-BENEFIT ANALYSIS AS THE TEST FOR OVERREGULATION

Cost-benefit analysis attempts to achieve through regulation the result that would obtain in a hypothetical "efficient" labor market in which bargaining about workplace risks is not impeded by employers' market power, employees' lack of information, and the other problems identified in Chapter 2. In an efficient market, an employer would compensate workers for the consequences of exposure to toxic substances in the form of wage premiums (ex ante compensation) or workers' compensation payments (ex post compensation). To maximize its profits, the employer would protect workers from health risks up to the point at which the cost of preventive measures exceeded the wage premiums and workers' compensation thereby avoided. Phrased somewhat differently, the rational employer would install the prevention technology that minimized the sum of prevention costs and compensation costs.[2] In actual practice, however, employers underinvest in prevention because, as Chapter 2 demonstrated, workers rarely obtain full compensation for work-related diseases and seldom negotiate significant risk premiums.

Economists generally support occupational health regulation because of this underinvestment in prevention, but only insofar as it passes a cost-benefit test. One of the more forceful and articulate of OSHA's recent critics, John Mendeloff, has reiterated the conventional economic wisdom that OSHA "overregulates" when it forces employers to spend more on occupational safety and health than is warranted by the reduction in the probability of worker deaths multiplied by the value of their lives to society. Claiming that all but one of OSHA's health standards have failed the cost-benefit test, Mendeloff concludes that OSHA has an irresistible tendency to "overregulate." Yet, although Mendeloff's analysis has a surface plausibility, it glosses over a number of devastating analytical difficulties. In brief, attempts to calculate a regulation's costs are bedeviled by the unavailability of accurate cost information, while benefits estimates fall prey to insurmountable empirical and analytical obstacles in predicting the number of lives saved, determining the value of workers' lives, and discounting future benefits to present value.

COST CALCULATIONS

When economists analyze how much OSHA's previous health standards have cost, they usually rely on before-the-fact predictions that are notoriously inaccurate.[3] Since both OSHA and industry preimplementation cost projections rely heavily upon industry input, they are nearly always much higher than actual implementation costs. For example, a former Department of Labor economist determined that the actual cost of complying with OSHA's vinyl chloride standard was only about 7 percent of the predicted cost.[4] Since few postimplementation cost studies have been undertaken, economists have little choice but to rely on preimplementation cost projections. Retrospective cost studies are very difficult to undertake because companies do not always keep their books in a manner that facilitates cost comparisons and because some health-related capital expenditures would have been taken even in the absence of the OSHA standards.[5] For example, much of the money spent on complying with OSHA's cotton dust standard would have been spent in any event to retool the textile industry to meet foreign competition.[6]

Mendeloff acknowledges that the available retrospective studies show that the initial cost estimates were usually overestimates (usually by at least a factor of two), and he uses existing retrospective studies for about half of the standards that he analyzes, but his cost estimates remain on the high side.[7] To some extent, this is attributable to Mendeloff's heavy reliance upon cost calculations published in papers by John Morrall, the OMB economist who made a career of criticizing OSHA standards.[8]

BENEFITS CALCULATIONS

The difficulties in determining the costs of complying with OSHA standards pale by comparison with the uncertainties encountered in calculating the number of lives that OSHA standards save.[9] Current risk assessment techniques simply do not have the power to permit even marginally precise calculations of the number of lives a standard might save. And the analytical difficulties and moral dilemmas posed by attempts to place a value on credible risks to life ensure that the ultimate result is ideologically, not scientifically, determined.

Estimating the Number of Lives Saved

Scientists understand the complex cause-effect relationships between exposure to chemicals and adverse health effects in only the most rudimentary ways.[10] Ethical considerations preclude the human experimentation that could definitively establish whether a chemical causes particular diseases.[11] As Chapter 1 explained, the available epidemiological and animal evidence does not fill this void. Epidemiological studies of groups of humans who have historically received greater than normal exposures to chemicals (often the workers themselves) can provide some direct evidence of risk, but these studies are notoriously inconclusive.[12] Moreover, it is sometimes difficult to extrapolate the results of an epidemiological study conducted under one set of conditions to human exposures in different circumstances. Animal testing can help fill the gaps in knowledge, but such tests are expensive and often inconclusive. An agency proposing to rely upon animal studies must be prepared to answer difficult questions concerning the appropriateness of particular species, the validity of test designs, the applicability of exposure routes, and a host of other technical considerations.[13] The validity of virtually any animal study can easily be challenged in one or more significant ways, and the agency must always be prepared to defend the propriety of extrapolating from high-dose animal exposures to low-dose human exposures. Information on worker exposure is also expensive to obtain, and the agency must rely heavily upon employers for this critical piece of the puzzle.[14]

Risk assessment is the art of applying quantitative techniques to all of this unruly data in an attempt to arrive at a quantitative prediction of the magnitude of the risk that exposure to a chemical substance poses to workers. After the Supreme Court's *Benzene* decision, OSHA feels obliged to use risk assessment techniques to determine whether workers are exposed to a "significant" risk. Yet the predictive power of the available mathematical models is quite poor. For example, the predictions of cancer risk assessment models can vary over ten orders of magnitude.[15] If the magnitude of these variations could be translated into economic terms, the difference between the low and high estimates of cancer risk would be the equivalent of the difference between the price of a cup of coffee and the burden of the national debt.

Even attempts to determine retrospectively the improvement in worker health attributable to OSHA standards are fraught with uncertainty. Thus, the application of such quantitative techniques to past or future employee exposures should always be taken with a large grain of salt. One should be particularly suspicious of tables that use point estimates or ranges of less than an order of magnitude to depict the number of lives saved (or to be saved) by reduced exposures to workplace chemicals.

Valuing Lives

As mentioned earlier, calculations of the benefits of a health standard are based on estimates of the number of lives saved multiplied by the value of each of those lives. Economists employ a variety of techniques for specifying the value of a human life, the two most prominent of which are the "human capital" method and the "willingness to pay" approach. Both methods tread on treacherous moral and empirical terrain.

Human life is least valuable under the "human capital" approach, under which the economist simply estimates the total future earnings of the person whose life is being valued and discounts that number to present value.[16] Some even deduct "maintenance costs" such as food and living expenses.[17] This approach yields values ranging from $100,000 to $500,000 for the life of a worker. Most modern students of this morbid art agree, however, that the human capital approach severely undervalues human life.[18] A person's value to society is clearly greater than his or her salary.

Most economists believe that the most accurate approach to valuing life is the "willingness-to-pay" test that attempts to ascertain what the person at risk would be willing to pay for reduced mortality risks. One measure of willingness to pay is the wage premiums that workers receive for working in dangerous conditions. Since any worker would have to sacrifice that premium to work in safer conditions, workers who leave the job are willing to pay (in terms of forgone compensation) no more than the premium to work in safer conditions. Relying his own and other economists' studies of wage premiums, Mendeloff calculates the value of a human life at $2.5 million.[19] This estimate is somewhat higher than OMB's rule of thumb that a human life is worth about $1 million.[20] Both estimates are considerably lower than Moore and Viscusi's more recent estimate, based on more accurate National Institute of Occupational Safety and Health data, of somewhere between $5.4 million and $6.8 million.[21]

VALUATION DIFFICULTIES

Using the willingness to pay measure, the economist can calculate the dollar value of a risk-reduction technology and compare it against the cost of installing the technology to determine whether the cost outweighs the benefit. Using wage premiums to value the benefit of OSHA standards, however, presents two problems. First, the estimates are based on flawed wage premium studies. Second, the results of those studies are so heavily discounted that they erroneously suggest that little or no regulation is necessary.

Problems with Wage Premium Studies

Existing wage premium studies present at least three serious analytical difficulties. First, they are based upon safety hazards, not health risks. Mendeloff hypothesizes workers would pay less for reductions in health risks than in safety risks (because illnesses, compared with accidents, occur later in life), but he concedes that workers might pay more to reduce health risks because cancer is a painful and dreaded disease.[22] Second, using wage premium studies assumes that in the past workers were fully informed of all of the risks they encountered in the workplace and fully appreciated the magnitude of those risks. Yet even after OSHA's implementation of the hazard communication standard, which occurred long after most of the wage premium studies were completed, workers are not fully apprised of most of the risks to which they are exposed. Even if full information were available, most workers would not be able to wade through the extraordinarily complex data and form rational conclusions about the extent of the risks. Workers generally undervalue low-probability/high-consequence risks on the "it can't happen to me" theory, in which case "risk premium" measures of the value of small risks to life are generally too low.[23]

Finally, wage premium studies assume that workers are making free and unconstrained risk decisions when in fact low-paid workers in hazardous industries may be acting more out of desperation than of choice.[24] In an era of chronically high unemployment, walking away from a job is not an easy choice, because it usually entails the loss of the worker's income stream, personal and family pension benefits, and health insurance. The worker may also have to undergo retraining costs, relocating costs, and other inconveniences associated with finding a new job. In those sectors of the economy where collective bargaining plays little or no role in adjusting power relationships, individual workers are in no position to demand higher wages for hazardous work. Moreover, as James Robinson perceptively observes, employers have adopted strategies to ensure that the most hazardous jobs go to the least skilled and least organized workers:

[M]anagement has sought to organize the process of production in many hazardous industries so as to reduce the need for highly skilled workers. To the extent possible management replaces these workers with a combination of less skilled employees and increased supervision and control. Over time, managerial responses produce a pattern in which hazardous jobs require less education achievement, provide less on-the-job training, and offer fewer opportunities for worker autonomy, responsibility and creativity in the work process. These unskilled hazardous jobs pay lower wages than skilled safe jobs.[25]

As one union leader has explained (perhaps hyperbolically), relying upon wage premiums as a measure of workers' willingness to accept risks in the context of a "society that historically prides itself on a less than full employment economy" is "the conventional expression of cannibalism in America."[26] Guido Calabrese makes the same point somewhat less colorfully: "The willingness of a poor man, confronting a tragic situation, to choose money rather than the tragically scarce resources [his health or safety] always represents an unquiet indictment of society's distribution of wealth."[27]

Discounting Lives

After deriving a valuation from life wage studies, the economist makes another adjustment in calculating the benefits of health standards. Most economists believe that benefits that arise in the future must be discounted to present value by the application of some discount rate to the predicted benefits. At the 10 percent discount rate that OMB insists on, for example, a worker's life would be worth only $142,500 today if the person's whole life were valued at $2.5 million at the end of 30 years.[28] It would be worth $57,000 today if it were valued at $1.0 million at the end of 30 years. Since the latency period between employee exposure and the onset of disease can be as long as 30 years or more, discounting means that the present value of most health standards will be quite small compared with the current cost of reducing exposure. In other words, discounting effectively means ignoring the risk altogether.[29] Yet economists are untroubled by the practice, arguing without empirical evidence that people probably place a lower value on reducing risks that materialize in the future.[30]

POLITICAL VALUE JUDGMENTS

After examining some of the foregoing deficiencies, a skeptical journalist concluded that cost-benefit analysis is "Ouija-board science" with "roots deeply embedded in politics."[31] This cynical view of cost-benefit analysis reflects a conclusion, shared by other observers of its real-world applications, that it contains two hidden value judgments of highly questionable validity. First, practitioners of cost-benefit analysis invariably adopt a "willingness to pay" measure of the value of things not typically traded in markets, rather than a "willingness to sell" approach. Second, they usually derive the value of things by reference to the choices that consumers make in economic markets, rather than by examining the (usually more aspirational) behavior of citizens in political contexts where society determines and applies important collective values.

Willingness to Pay Versus Willingness to Sell

Economists justify their use of a "willingness to pay" measure on the ground that since workers are the primary beneficiaries of safety and health regulation, their assessment of the value of a regulatory requirement should correspond well to its social value.[32] A more appropriate measurement, however, would be a "willingness to sell" criterion that would determine how much workers would accept to sell the right to be free from occupational illnesses. The general tendency of individuals to buy and sell goods for roughly the same price (the market price) does not hold when the items being traded are credible risks to health and safety. Individuals are usually willing to sell the right to be free from increased mortality risks for considerably more money than they are willing to pay for reduced mortality risks. This is true for the simple reason that most of us can demand much more in a bargain in which we are asked to sacrifice something of great value to which we have a "right" than we can afford to pay for that same thing if someone else has the right to take it from us.

The "willingness to pay" and "willingness to sell" measurements are thus based on opposite a priori assumptions about legal rights or entitlements.[33] Using a "willingness to pay" measurement is the equivalent of a rule of law that an employer has the "right" to expose its workers to toxic substances, and the workers must pay the employer to reduce their exposure. By comparison, the "willingness to sell" measurement assumes a rule of law that an employer cannot expose its workers to toxic substances unless the workers agree to be exposed. Under the "willingness to sell" approach, the employer must justify exposing its workers to a toxic substance by showing that its employees would be willing freely to accept the risk in return for a payment equivalent to the amount of money the employer saves by not having to control the exposure.

The "willingness to sell" criterion is a more appropriate measurement of the value of human life, because under that test the wealth of workers will not affect the type of bargain they will make with employers. There is little reason to believe that a poor person will sell the right to be safe for any less than a rich person would. There is every reason to believe that a person's wealth will affect how much he or she can pay to purchase the right to be safe. Indeed, one of the studies that Mendeloff cites in support of his conclusion that OSHA is guilty of overregulation bears out this observation. Marin and Psacharopoulos found that the best estimate of the value of life using a "willingness to pay" criterion was $2.5 million for manual workers and $9.0 million for nonmanual workers.[34] Presumably the estimate for company presidents and board chairman would be even higher.

Despite the bias introduced by using a "willingness to pay" criterion, most economists show no hesitation making policy recommendations based on that measure of human life. Mendeloff acknowledges the problem but ignores its consequences when he adopts the $2.5 million estimate to support his conclusion that the costs of OSHA's standards are larger than the benefits. Far from being an objective assessment of the facts, this dogmatic adherence to the "willingness to pay" measure is in reality a subjective commentary on how power should be distributed in society. Since manual workers cannot purchase as much safety as nonmanual workers or board chairmen, their lives are not worth as much.

Other economists hark back to Knights' extraordinary conclusion that such disparities are easily explained by the fact that workers desire to risk their health while the chairman of the board prefers to risk his capital. Marin and Psacharopoulos, for example, surmise, without the benefit of empirical evidence, that "those prepared to work in . . . exceptionally risky jobs may well have a lower dislike of danger."[35] W. Kip Viscusi, a professor of business at Northwestern University, is even less hesitant to conclude that discrepancies in wage premiums are attributable to attitudes toward risk rather than disparities in wealth and opportunities. In a book with the revealing title of *Risk by Choice*, Viscusi explains:

Those individuals who are least averse to [safety] risks are willing to accept a lower compensation per unit of risk than the rest of the working population. As a result, they are inclined to accept larger risks with lower wage premiums per unit of risk. . . . Those who price their life the cheapest are drawn into the market first; higher wages must be paid to lure additional workers into risky jobs.[36]

If economists cannot see the connection between wealth and the amount of safety that a person can purchase, workers can. When Dorothy Nelkin and Michael Brown interviewed 75 workers about the experience of being exposed to toxic chemicals, Arnie, a chemical operator in a food processing plant, replied:

You never balance the wage against the risk; you balance the wage against the alternative. And the alternative is starving when you are put in this situation. That's what's so phony about this cost/benefit analysis. A worker in a plant doesn't say, "Well, I'm getting $6.50 an hour so I'm gonna take this risk." The worker in the plant says, "I'm getting $6.50 an hour. If I open my mouth I might get nothing an hour, or I might get the minimum wage. In that case, I can't afford to live."

For example, at the job I had before the food processing plant, there was a guy who had a perforated septum. He showed it to me and says, "Look, it's the fuckin' fumes." I asked, "Why don't you quit?" He says, "Well, I'm 46 years old and you're 18. I've got a third grade education, three kids . . . where the hell am I gonna go?"[37]

Sandy, a rigger in a chemical plant, also had something to say about "risk by choice":

Every worker has a choice. Any worker can quit his job. I mean, when you come down to brass tacks, anyone can quit. But the realities of life—the family, the children, mortgage payment—impose certain limitations on a worker's right to just quit. I don't feel personally that people should have to quit to protect their health. I feel the employer by obligation, by law, must provide a safe and healthful workplace. And if the employers live up to their obligations, then there would be no reason for a worker to make the choice.[38]

In a country that holds equality of opportunity as a primary value, perhaps the better measure for the value of a worker's life is how much it would take to induce the chairman of the board to leave his current job and undertake hazardous employment for a year.

Private Versus Public Decisions

Relying on "willingness to pay" to measure the value of OSHA's health benefits is objectionable from still another perspective. Those who use figures obtained from *private* transactions to provide guidance for *public* decisions assume there is no different between the price people pay for things in private markets and the value they wish those same things to be assigned in collective public decisions. Equating the two constitutes a hidden value judgment that there should be no difference between private behavior and the behavior we display in social life. Yet, as Steven Kelman argues, in many contexts, the public probably believes that "social decisions provide an opportunity to give things a higher valuation than we choose, for one reason or another, to give them in our private activities."[39]

Mendeloff and other economists generally concede Kelman's point that markets do not reflect "altruistic preferences" and acknowledge that "[s]ome situations do call for restricting the sway of the market." Mendeloff sees the need for such restrictions, however, only in a very limited set of circumstances, such as buying and selling votes and human beings, where markets would "undermine the legitimacy of democratic institutions" or where there is a consensus that particular transactions are immoral.[40] Significantly, these exceptional circumstances do not include risk markets. Even assuming that Mendeloff's reading of public attitudes is correct, the restrictions that he places on the occasions in which public values ought to outweigh private preferences are so strict as to render his concession virtually meaningless. Only regulators with a political death wish would look to a market for guidance when there is a concensus that transactions in that market ought to be banned. In any case, Kelman and others are not arguing that private markets for risk ought to be banned. They are maintaining that when public officials make decisions about risk, those decisions should be based on values other than those dictated by private risk markets. In Chapter 20, we suggest a new mandate for OSHA that is based on nonmarket values and explain why those values are appropriate.

DOES OSHA OVERREGULATE?

Relying on the "willingness to pay" measure of benefits, OSHA critics assert that the costs of most of OSHA's health standards substantially exceed their benefits. Using a $2.5 million value for a worker's life, Mendeloff suggests that seven of eight OSHA health standards fail the test.[41] Only OSHA's asbestos standard, in Mendeloff's judgment, was warranted. It may be only coincidental that this standard addresses a substance with undeniable health risks for which tort liability costs alone have bankrupted an entire industry.

Mendeloff's conclusions with respect to the rest of OSHA's standards are highly debatable for many of the reasons discussed earlier. First, although he acknowledges the huge uncertainties inherent in risk assessment, he chooses extraordinarily narrow ranges of predictions for the annual number of cancer deaths prevented by OSHA standards. For example, to support his conclusion that only one death per year was prevented by OSHA's standards for vinyl chloride, Mendeloff cites a study based on the astounding assumption that the 21 angiosarcoma deaths that had been definitively attributed to vinyl chloride exposure through 1976 constituted all of the deaths caused by vinyl chloride during the preceding 40 years. Mendeloff also reads an EPA risk assessment (based upon animal bioassays) to conclude that only two cancers per year would have been prevented. But to reach this result, he reduced EPA's predictions by a factor of 8 to take into account the fact that workers are exposed for 8 hours per day for 45 years.[42] Yet given that the EPA risk assessment could very easily be off by a factor of 10, that estimate might just as easily be 20 or even 40 cancers per year.

Such relatively minor adjustments in highly uncertain risk assessments can easily spell the difference between a standard that passes Mendeloff's cost-benefit test and one that fails it. The vinyl chloride standard, which Mendeloff estimates costs industry $40 million per year per life saved, badly flunked his test. Yet adjusting the risk estimate by a minor factor of 10 reduces the cost per life saved to $4 million, which might flunk Mendeloff's $2.5 million test but would not flunk everyone's test. It certainly does not exceed the $9 million value that the richer nonmanual workers assigned to their lives.

The point here is that, given the vast uncertainties involved in cancer risk assessment, it is foolhardy to hinge a cost-benefit test on whether a standard costs more or less than $2.5 million per predicted life saved. Since even the most accurate risk estimates may range over one or two orders of magnitude, one need not conclude with Mendeloff that "[s]pending 10 million or probably even 5 million dollars to prevent an occupational disease death is excessive."[43] A $10 million death under one risk estimate may be a $500,000 death under another, equally plausible estimate. Encountering a world characterized by such a higher degree of uncertainty is no doubt frustrating to economists searching for a finely tuned cost-benefit calculus for evaluating governmental interventions into the private marketplace, but it is an unavoidable fact of life (and death).

Mendeloff also inexplicably fails to take into account many of the lesser benefits of OSHA's health standards. He does not attempt to measure the value of a reduction in the number of nonfatal illnesses, a reduction in lost productivity attributable to occupational disease, or a reduction in welfare and Social Security payments to workers who become ill. Savings associated with the last benefit may be considerable. In fiscal year 1989, Social Security payments to disabled workers (for injuries and illnesses) totaled $7.65 billion.[44] Mendeloff also fails adequately to consider other "soft variables," such as the loss to people other than the workers themselves. For example, family members obviously suffer emotional harm when a worker is killed or injured. Mendeloff, like most economists, argues that the worker factors this into his or her "willingness to pay" measure.[45] There is no empirical basis for this claim, and the suggestion that people take into account the loss of grieving relatives when they engage in risky conduct seems highly implausible on its face. Rather than attempt to measure and place a dollar value upon the pain of a wife who must care for and ultimately grieve over a cancer-stricken husband, the economists simply ignore this factor.

This blinkered view is typical of the economists' tendency to "dwarf soft variables" that do not lend themselves to precise quantitative analysis.[46] Like most economists, Mendeloff acknowledges the existence of soft variables, then strains to find some rationale for ignoring them. The reader may be forgiven if he or she concludes that the economists' bottom line is likewise to be ignored.

CONCLUSIONS

When pressed hard to respond to the innumerable analytical difficulties and political biases in cost-benefit analysis, economists eventually resort to their goal-line defense that it is better than doing nothing. They observe that absolute safety is beyond the financial capability of any society, that trade-offs are therefore inevitable, and that it borders on dishonesty to suggest otherwise.[47] They also argue that regulations that cost too much deprive society of resources with which to support different safety or health improvements or other desirable activities. As Peter Asch puts it: "Those who are 'done dirty' by the system are not likely to be helped by rendering the system more wasteful."[48] One can, however, acknowledge that trade-offs must inevitably take place without accepting the economists' narrow cost-benefit approach to that trade-off. In Chapter 20, we suggest an alternative way of managing such trade-offs. Before we reach our proposal, however, Chapter 19 considers Mendeloff's innovative new argument in favor of less stringent OSHA standards.

NOTES

1. Pete Early, "What's a Life Worth?" *Washington Post Magazine*, 9 June 1985, 11.

2. John Mendeloff, *The Dilemma of Toxic Substance Regulation: How Overregulation Causes Underregulation at OSHA* (Cambridge, Mass.: MIT Press, 1988), 223.

3. Thomas O. McGarity, "Regulatory Analysis and Regulatory Reform," *Texas Law Review* 65 (1987): 1243.

4. Marguerite Connerton and Mark MacCarthy, *Cost-Benefit Analysis & Regulation: Expressway to Reform or Blind Alley?* (Washington D.C.: Center for National Policy, 1982), 21.

5. McGarity, "Regulatory Analysis," 1278–79.

6. David Bollier and Joan Claybrook, *Freedom from Harm: The Civilizing Influence of Health, Safety, and Environmental Regulation* (Washington D.C.: Public Citizen and Democracy Project, 1986), 148; Anne Smith-MacKay, "Cotton-Dust Ruling Is Expected to Spur Industry Trend Toward Modernization", *Wall Street Journal*, 18 June 1981, 21, col. 1.

7. Mendeloff, Dilemma, 58.

8. Ibid., 22, Table 2.1, note a.

9. See Sanford E. Gaines, "Science, Politics, and the Management of Toxic Risks Through Law," *Jurimetrics Journal* 30 (1990): 276–91 (elaborating on the synergy of scientific, legal, and political uncertainties).

10. Thomas O. McGarity, "Media Quality, Technology and Cost-Benefit Balancing Strategies for Health and Environmental Regulation," *Law and Contemporary Problems* 46 (Summer 1983): 159; Alvin M. Weinberg, "Science and Trans-Science," *Minerva* 10 (1972): 209; Armory B. Lovins, "Cost-Risk Benefit Assessments in Energy Policy," *George Washington Law Review* 45 (1977): 911; Richard Merrill, "Report on Federal Regulation of Cancer-Causing Chemicals," Administrative Conference of the United States, *Recommendations and Reports*, report 82–5 (Washington, D.C.: ACUS, 1982); U.S. Congress, Office of Technology Assessment, *Assessment of Technologies for Determining Cancer Risks from the Environment*, OTA-H138 (Washington, D.C.: United States Government Printing Office, 1981).

11. Department of Health and Human Services, "Protection of Human Subjects," 45 C.F.R. 46 (1991).

12. Carl F. Cranor, "Epidemiology and Procedural Protections for Workplace Health in the Aftermath of the Benzene Case," *Industrial Relations Law Journal* 5 (1983): 372; Howard A. Latin, "The 'Significance' of Toxic Health Risks: An Essay on Legal Decisionmaking Under Uncertainty," *Ecology Law Quarterly* 10 (1982): 339; Thomas O. McGarity, "Substantive and Procedural Discretion in Administrative Resolution of Science Policy Questions: Regulating Carcinogens in EPA and OSHA," *Georgetown Law Journal* 67 (1979): 729.

13. Merrill, "Federal Regulation," 58–71; Office of Science and Technology Policy, "Chemical Carcinogens: A Review of the Science and Its Associated Principles," 50 Fed. Reg. 10,372 (1985).

14. McGarity, "Media Quality," 138; Merrill, "Federal Regulation," 74–82; Office of Science and Technology Policy, "Chemical Carcinogens," 10,424.

15. Comment, "The Significant Risk Requirement in OSHA Regulation of Carcinogens," Stanford Law Review 33 (1981): 551; Latin, "Toxic Health Risks," 370–71; Cranor, "Epidemiology," 381.

16. Mark Sagoff, "The Principles of Federal Pollution Control Law," Minnesota Law Review 71 (1986): 19; Connerton and MacCarthy, Cost-Benefit Analysis; James W. Vaupel, "On the Benefits of Health and Safety Regulation," in The Benefits of Health and Safety Regulation, ed. Allen R. Ferguson and E. Phillip LeVeen (Cambridge, Mass: Ballinger, 1981).

17. Joanne Linnerooth, "The Evaluation of Life-Saving: A Survey" (No city: International Institute for Applied Systems Analysis, 1975) (Mimeo).

18. Ibid., 12–14; John D. Graham and James W. Vaupel, "The Value of a Life: What Difference Does It Make?" in What Role for Government? Lessons from Policy Research, ed. Richard J. Zeckhauser and Derek Leebart (Durham, N.C.: Duke University Press 1983), 176.

19. Mendeloff, Dilemma, 51.

20. Early, "Life Worth," 11.

21. Michael J. Moore and W. Kip Viscusi, Compensation Mechanisms for Job Risks: Wages, Worker's Compensation, and Product Liability (Princeton: Princeton University Press, 1990): 80.

22. Mendeloff, Dilemma, 48–49.

23. Russell F. Settle and Burton A. Weisbrod, Governmentally-Imposed Standards: Some Normative Aspects, Institute for Research on Poverty Discussion Paper no. 439–77 (Madison: University of Wisconsin, 1977), 31.

24. Sagoff, "Principles," 72; Arthur M. Okun, Equality and Efficiency: The Big Tradeoff (Washington, D.C.: The Brookings Institution, 1975), 21; Steven Kelman, "Cost Benefit Analysis and Environmental, Safety, and Health Regulation: Ethical and Philosophical Considerations," in Cost-Benefit Analysis and Environmental Regulations: Politics, Ethics, and Methods, ed. Daniel Swartzmann, Richard A. Liroff, and Kevin G. Crooke (Washington, D.C.: Conservation Foundation, 1982).

25. James C. Robinson, Toil and Toxics: Workplace Struggles and Political Strategies for Occupational Health (Berkeley: University of California Press, 1991), 75–76.

26. Sheldon Samuels, "The Role of Scientific Data in Health Decisions," Environmental Health Perspectives 32 (1979): 305.

27. U.S. Congress, House Committee on Interstate and Foreign Commerce, Subcommittee on Oversight and Investigations and Subcommittee on Consumer Protection and Finance, Joint Hearings on the Use of Cost-Benefit Analysis by Regulatory Agencies, 96th Cong., 1st sess., no. 96–157, 1979, 27.

28. At a 10 percent discount rate, a dollar's worth of benefits 50 years from now is worth slightly less than a penny today. Milton Russell, " 'Discounting Human Life' (Or, The Anatomy of a Moral-Economic Issue)," Resources 82 (1986): 8.

29. Ibid.

30. Mendeloff, Dilemma, 49.

31. Early, "Life Worth," 11.

32. Mendeloff, *Dilemma*, 44.

33. McGarity, "Media Quality," 171.

34. Mendeloff, *Dilemma*, 28.

35. Alan Marin and George Psacharopoulos, "The Reward for Risk in the Labor Market: Evidence from the United Kingdom and a Reconciliation with Other Studies," *Journal of Political Economy* 90 (1982): 841.

36. W. Kip Viscusi, *Risk by Choice: Regulating Health and Safety in the Workplace* (Cambridge, Mass.: Harvard Press, 1983), 103.

37. Dorothy Nelkin and Michael Brown, *Workers at Risk: Voices from the Workplace* (Chicago: University of Chicago Press, 1984), 91.

38. Ibid., 92.

39. Steven Kelman, "Cost-Benefit Analysis—An Ethical Critique," *Regulation*, 5 (Jan./Feb. 1981): 38.

40. Mendeloff, *Dilemma*, 42–43.

41. Ibid.

42. Ibid., 288, no. 21.

43. Ibid., 51.

44. National Safe Workplace Institute, *Safer Work: Job Safety and Health Challenges for the Next President and Congress* (Chicago: The Institute, 1988), 7.

45. Mendeloff, *Dilemma*, 34.

46. Laurence H. Tribe, "Ways Not to Think About Plastic Trees: New Foundations for Environmental Law," *Yale Law Journal* 83 (1974): 1318–19.

47. Mendeloff, *Dilemma*, 31.

48. Peter Asch, *Consumer Safety Regulation: Putting a Price on Life and Limb* (New York: Oxford University Press, 1988), 59.

19

Economics and OSHA: Cost-Benefit Analysis and Underregulation

Professor John Mendeloff contends that OSHA could more effectively protect workers from toxic substances if it promulgated a greater number of less stringent standards capable of passing a cost-benefit test.[1] Thus, in addition to the arguments for cost-benefit analysis considered in the last chapter, Mendeloff claims that OSHA's greater reliance on cost-benefit analysis will ultimately benefit *workers*, as well as business. Employee resistance to cost-benefit analysis is therefore misguided and should be reconsidered. This counterinuitive proposition, which has been uncritically accepted in the legal and public policy literature, is worthy of careful attention.

Mendeloff summarizes his argument with the catchy observation that "overregulation" causes "underregulation." As Chapter 18 indicated, a substance is overregulated when the costs of a regulation exceed its benefits. Mendeloff adds that it is underregulated to the extent that the costs of additional regulation are less than the benefits.[2] From this starting point, Mendeloff argues that many health hazards in the workplace are underregulated because OSHA insists on promulgating standards that are not justified under his cost-benefit test. If OSHA would only promulgate standards for which costs more nearly approximated benefits, it could promulgate many more standards, each of which would protect individual workers less than a stringent standard. OSHA could promulgate more standards, if they were less stringent, because industry would be less likely to challenge them in court and, if they were challenged, the courts would be more likely to approve them. Thus, although each standard promulgated by OSHA might be less protective of workers, the sum total of protection for workers would be greater because there would be many more standards overall.

Mendeloff reasons that since OSHA must assume that all of its standards will be appealed by well-financed regulatees and since the agency must bear the burden of justifying each standard to a skeptical court, it will spend inordinate amounts of time and resources studying the problem and preparing ornate documents explaining its standards. The more stringent the standard, the harder the industry will resist by refusing to provide important data, taking its case to the Office of Management and Budget (OMB) and Congress, and ultimately hiring expensive lawyers to challenge the standards in court. Because OSHA has only very limited resources (due to industry resistance to OSHA during the appropriations process), it is able to promulgate only a very few stringent standards per year under these adversarial conditions.[3]

As we observed in Part II, this analysis of OSHA's rulemaking dilemma is by and large accurate. Mendeloff's surprising solution, however, is for OSHA to accept the power of a determined industry to hamstring its standard-setting process, assume that less stringent standards will produce happier regulatees who will resist the process less doggedly, and end two decades of industry extortion by promulgating standards that the regulated inndustries can "live with." Yet it is extremely naive to expect that promulgating a greater number of less stringent standards will provide a greater degree of overall protection. Even assuming that such a strategy would work, a better solution would be to change the system (e.g., by shifting the burden of justification) so that OSHA need not allow industry resistance to impede its progress.

THE BENEFITS OF MILD STANDARDS

Mendeloff's argument rests on the debatable proposition that "mild" standards that meet his cost-benefit test will actually produce significant health benefits. He attempts to prove this point by comparing the permissible exposure limits (PELs) of the national consensus standards that were promulgated in 1971 with the current recommendations of the American Conference of Governmental Industrial Hygienists (ACGIH), which (by hypothesis) meet his cost-benefit test. Mendeloff argues that if OSHA merely turned the ACGIH recommendations into enforceable OSHA standards, thousands more workers would receive slightly more protection. Although a few workers would receive a great deal less protection than provided by feasibility-based standards, there would be a net gain in overall public health. Mendeloff attempts to prove this by showing that adopting the ACGIH standards would reduce the levels of employee exposure to a large number of chemicals from current allowed levels and that this "will often prevent deaths at a cost that seems reasonable, no more than $1 million or $2 million each."[4] This low cost would be ensured by Mendeloff's related recommendation that for the first five to ten years, employers would be allowed to meet the new standards through the use of respirators rather than engineering controls.[5] He does not suggest how the agency would muster the political will to require engineering controls after the regulatees had become comfortable with the respirator alternative.

Relying upon relatively old data from 1979–81, Mendeloff attempts to prove that a large number of workplaces existed during those years in which employees were exposed to toxic chemicals at levels above the ACGIH recommendations.[6] Yet when he looks at OSHA inspection data, he finds that industry was in compliance with the ACGIH standards two-thirds of the time. He is therefore forced to admit that "for many of the hazards adoption of the ACGIH limits would make little difference."[7]

Mendeloff contends, however, that for the other one-third of the chemicals for which there is some evidence of exposure above the ACGIH levels, a million workers would be protected by adoption and enforcement of the ACGIH limits.[8] To reach this conclusion, Mendeloff looks at the 15 chemicals that OSHA inspectors found most often were above the ACGIH limits but below the OSHA PELs. Although these data indicate the number of times an inspector found exposures above the ACGIH levels, they do not indicate how many workers were exposed in each case. Relying on other data for only 3 of the 15 chemicals, Mendeloff concludes that an average of 1,000 workers were exposed each time an OSHA inspector identified an exposure level above the ACGIH limits. Mendeloff estimates that 500,000 workers would be protected if OSHA adopted the ACGIH limits for the 15 chemicals. Since this estimate only involves 15 chemicals, Mendeloff "feel[s] that an estimate of a million workers would be conservative."[9]

Once the underlying basis for his calculations is revealed, it becomes apparent that Mendeloff's claim of 1 million exposed workers is highly speculative. More important, the data on which he relies indicate that only 4 of the 15 chemicals involve a high degree of worker exposure, and 3 of them are already on OSHA's current rulemaking agenda. Even if his estimate is reasonable, however, it is still not clear that compliance with the ACGIH levels would produce significant health benefits. Mendeloff acknowledges that the ACGIH standard-setting criteria do not stress the carcinogenicity of a substance nearly as heavily as OSHA's criteria.[10] Indeed, he observes that ACGIH is unlikely to characterize a substance as a carcinogen unless there is epidemiological data indicating that it has caused cancer in human beings, a position that all of the health-oriented federal agencies abandoned decades ago as the "body counting" approach to standard-setting. Mendeloff also concedes that the ACGIH recommendations rely much more heavily upon industry-supplied data than do OSHA standards.[11] Thus, he greatly understates the matter when he concludes that the ACGIH criteria are "somewhat more tolerant of illness than section 6(b)(5) of the OSH Act."[12]

Moreover, if Mendeloff's plan were followed, and the ACGIH standards became the basis of OSHA regulation, ACGIH would no doubt come under increasing pressure in the future to recommend threshold limit values (TLVs) that could easily be met by the vast majority of employers. Since labor does not actively participate in the ACGIH process and since all of the pressures will be coming from employers, this should ensure that the ACGIH TLVs would rarely be stringent enough to provide significant additional protection.

Our objections to the ACGIH standards do not mean that OSHA should not have attempted to amend the 1971 consensus permissible exposure limits (PELs) to meet the revised ACGIH TLVs as described in Chapter 19. That rulemaking attempted to provide some significant benefits to some employees of the comparatively few employers who were not already voluntarily complying with the TLVs. This does not mean, however, that the ACGIH standards should become the permanent basis for OSHA's health regulations. Although requiring companies as a legal matter to meet the ACGIH levels may be sufficiently cost-free to reduce some industry resistance, the operation is apparently benefit-free as well. To the extent that OSHA trades the undeniable benefits of more stringent feasibility-based standards for the chimeral benefits of weaker standards that most companies already achieve, employee health will suffer overall.

REDUCING INDUSTRY RESISTANCE

To a very large extent, Mendeloff's conclusion that promulgating less stringent standards will accomplish greater worker protection depends upon his views about the nature of admnistrative rulemaking in the context of scientific uncertainty. Accepting the current legal regime as a given, Mendeloff concludes that industry resistance will inevitably doom to failure OSHA's efforts to write stringent standards. For example, Mendeloff concludes that OSHA's attempt during the Bingham years to write a generic carcinogen policy was misguided:

OSHA's regulation of carcinogens has drawn fire because it is viewed by powerful and articulate sectors of the population as costly and inefficient. Given that perception, it was naive to believe that an effort to speed up the pace of *that manner* of regulation would not generate opposition in the White House, Congress, and the courts. Under those conditions, speedy rulemaking—always at risk of becoming an oxymoron—is not possible.[13]

So long as "powerful and articulate sectors of the population" have the resources available to make life extremely difficult for the agency, OSHA should make life less difficult for its regulatees. In other words, OSHA must "go along to get along."

Mendeloff is confident that "[p]recautionary measures should be accepted [by industry and other "powerful and articulate" interests] with relatively little evidence so long as the stringency of the measures seems reasonable."[14] Yet this idea contains an inherent contradiction. The cost-benefit analysis through which OSHA would demonstrate to industry that its proposed standard is "reasonable" itself requires a large amount of information and analysis, all of which is inevitably subject to legitimate debate. In other words, it will take a lot of evidence to convince industry, OMB, and other powerful interests that a proposed standard is reasonable if that standard is likely to require significant implementation costs. Mendeloff may instead be using a political test of "reasonableness"—a measure is "reasonable" so long as the industry does not object. But regulations that pass that test will not protect workers to any significant degree.

If a mild standard does produce significant protection for workers, some companies will be required to spend additional money on worker protection. Yet Mendeloff's solution depends upon the wishful assumption that a regulated company will gracefully accept the corresponding shift in wealth from its treasury to its workers. Rather than fighting expensive standards tooth and nail, the companies will be so convinced that greater worker protections are for the overall good of society that they will take out their checkbooks and start making arrangements to meet the standards. Mendeloff's limited evidence for this unlikely proposition is unpersuasive, and there is considerable evidence to the contrary.

By way of offering indirect evidence that industry will not appeal "reasonable" standards, Mendeloff points out that all but two of OSHA's health standards (acrylonitrile and dibromachloropropene [DBCP]) have been appealed, and those two were not especially burdensome to the industry.[15] The DBCP regulation, however, *was* burdensome to the small companies subject to it, although its total cost was only $3.65 million a year. The companies probably decided not to appeal the standard because there was very strong human evidence of its adverse reproductive effects and because EPA was in the process of banning the pesticide in any event. Mendeloff surprisingly neglects to mention that the most "reasonable" of all of OSHA's early standards—the asbestos standards—was fiercely challenged by the industry, even though the adverse effects of asbestos on workers were incontrovertible. By Mendeloff's own calculations, a substantial reduction in exposure was warranted under his cost-benefit test. The industry reduced its opposition to an OSHA asbestos standard only when EPA decided to go to the heart of the problem by banning the substance altogether under the Toxic Substances Control Act. At that point, industry pressured OMB to force EPA to refer the standard to OSHA, but even then, the industry did not stop resisting a stringent standard. The amended standard that OSHA finally promulgated was remanded by the District of Columbia Circuit because OSHA had not adequately addressed *union* objections.[16]

Perhaps the clearest contradiction of Mendeloff's postulate is the fate of OSHA's attempt to implement his recommendation that it update the standards for air contaminants to require industry to meet the ACGIH TLVs.[17] That standard, which by Mendeloff's own criteria is not unduly stringent, was challenged by 27 different companies and trade associations.[18] OSHA then attempted to settle the cases by reaching accommodations with the challengers, most of which involved concessions by OSHA or reductions in the stringency of the PELs. Despite OSHA's willingness to make significant concessions to avoid a court challenge to the validity of its use of generic procedures, 11 challengers insisted on going to court.

The fact that so many companies seem willing to go the substantial expense of a judicial challenge is understandable, given the economics of the situation. For example, in the PEL proceedings, OSHA estimated that the average annual cost of complying with each of the 376 PELs in the standard was about $2 million.[19] Since judicial review delays the average OSHA standard by two years,[20] a trade association would save its industry $320,000 by filing an appeal (assuming an interest rate of 8 percent). If the trade association limited the costs of appealing to $70,000, which finances 1,000 hours of attorney time,[21] an appeal nets $250,000, which represents about a 300 percent return on the cost of the appeal. The financial return to an industry would be even greater if the cost of the standard were more than $2 million, if industry reduced the amount it spent on the appeal, if it had higher-yield investments, and if it won the lawsuit.

Mendeloff argues that industry's financial incentives to fight a proposed regulation may be reduced to the extent that some members of a trade association are unwilling to fund an appeal for a standard that does not affect them or gives them a competitive advantage.[22] Moreover, he argues, some industries may decide not to appeal because "[a] reputation for unreasonableness is likely to play poorly not only with regulators, who may mistrust the industry and harass it, but also with political leaders and media who have helped to create a pervasive system of chemical regulation."[23] On the other hand, some companies and trade associations may perceive that fighting OSHA will discourage it from regulating in the future or at least slow the agency's efforts, and many companies object to OSHA regulation as a matter of principle. These latter factors no doubt explain some of the appeals of the mild standards in the generic PEL proceedings. It is therefore safer to predict that industry will generally resist *any* OSHA regulation, and to the extent that companies find it beneficial to invest resources in litigation as opposed to safety, they will do so, however cost-beneficial OSHA's standards appear to disinterested economists.

UNION RESISTANCE

If Mendeloff overestimates the degree to which mild standards will reduce industry resistance, he probably underestimates the significance of union and public interest group resistance to standards that do not meet the statutory "feasibility" criterion. Mendeloff argues that proponents of stringent regulation do not have as many resources available as industry to challenge OSHA standards. In addition, unions have less incentive to sue, because the implementation delays that inevitably accompany judicial challenges would be counterproductive from their point of view.[24] Mendeloff also notes that the unions have been growing weaker in recent years, and this should further reduce their power to make life difficult for OSHA when it promulgates less stringent standards.[25] Finally, Mendeloff believes that the position of organized labor may not be the most beneficial from the workers' perspective because "nonunionized workers have suffered disproportionately from underregulation."[26]

While it is unquestionably true that the delay inherent in court challenges can discourage union appeals, the fact that unions and/or public interest groups have challenged nearly every existing OSHA standard suggests that worker representatives often conclude that the increased protection resulting from a stringent permanent standard is worth the delay. Similarly, the fact that unions and public interest groups lack industry's substantial litigative resources does not mean that workers are utterly powerless to make life difficult for the agency. Worker representatives have proven remarkably successful in persuading courts to overturn OSHA standards that were not sufficiently stringent and to force the agency to regulate where it had arbitrarily declined to do so.

In any event, the fact that workers can or will litigate OSHA standards less frequently does not necessarily compel the conclusion that OSHA should promulgate mild standards to avoid litigation. When it passed the OSH Act, Congress was well aware of the fact that workers are not as economically powerful as employers, and it consequently charged OSHA with the duty to ensure that employers provided feasibly safe workplaces even if their employees lacked the economic power to achieve that result through private bargaining. For OSHA to agree with Mendeloff that it should sacrifice worker protection out of deference to the economic power of employers would be to shirk that statutory responsibility.

THE REAGAN EXPERIENCE

The fact that OSHA did not promulgate many regulations during the Reagan years may not be fairly cited as evidence that stringent regulation is doomed to failure, for the simple reason that OSHA did not try very hard during the Reagan administration. Mendeloff agrees that OSHA's slow pace during those years reflected "a strongly held view of many of its leaders that most rules were, on net, undesirable."[27] Thus, Mendeloff's complaint that OSHA usually fails to regulate carcinogens until it has evidence of carcinogenicity in human beings is easily explained by the Reagan administration's general reluctance to regulate *any* chemical substances absent almost certain proof of harm.[28] This was clearly not the case in the administrations prior to Reagan. The 14 carcinogens rulemaking during the Nixon administration was based on OSHA's conclusion, supported by an ad hoc committee of government scientists, that substances causing cancer in laboratory animals pose a carcinogenic risk to humans, and the Third Circuit Court of Appeals even elevated that principle to a rule of law.[29] OSHA's generic carcinogen policy during the Carter administration built strongly upon this same presumption. Indeed, during the latter part of the Reagan administration, when it was no longer politically feasible to be adamantly opposed to regulation, OSHA began to regulate substances, such as ethylene oxide, solely on the basis of laboratory animal studies.

There is very little evidence that OSHA's career employees have been especially reluctant to regulate in light of industry opposition. In Part II of this book, we repeatedly observed the inability of an increasingly frustrated staff to push rulemaking efforts through upper-level OSHA management and OMB. At the very same time that lower-level OSHA employees were trying to speed up the agency's efforts to regulate carcinogens like ethylene oxide, MDA, and formaldehyde, upper-level political appointees were "kicking ass and taking names" and rejecting technical documents because they "looked like they were drafted in Moscow." At the very same time that the courts were ordering OSHA's reluctant leaders to initiate rulemaking initiatives, OMB officials were drafting a new carcinogen policy for OSHA that would discourage the agency from regulating on the basis of animal studies alone, and one OMB economist was attempting to publish an article arguing that there was no scientific support for using animal studies to regulate chemicals.[30] If Mendeloff is suggesting that there is something inherent in the present statutory scheme that makes OSHA reluctant to regulate chemicals, he is mistaken. The reluctance is of relatively recent vintage, and its exists only at very high levels in OSHA and in OMB. If OSHA has for the last few years insisted upon waiting "for the toxicological equivalent of the smoking gun," it is because that was the policy of OMB and high-level political appointees in OSHA. Before giving up on stringent regulation, the agency might first make a good-faith attempt to try it.

STRICT JUDICIAL REVIEW

Mendeloff argues that the adoption of standards that can survive a cost-benefit test not only will reduce business opposition but also will reduce the likelihood that the courts will reject OSHA's health standards. His assessment of judicial review is not unlike that of the radical practitioners of the "critical legal studies" approach to legal interpretation.[31] Like many critical legal studies scholars, Mendeloff apparently believes that the best barometer of judicial conduct is the political predispositions of the individual judges on the panel deciding the case. In the special case of judicial review of agency rulemaking, this view holds that the judge's personal views about the political foundation of the statute at issue may be more important than the technical support for the regulation. Therefore, the prospect for judicial reversal of rules that do not meet the cost-benefit test is higher than for those that do.[32]

Although there is some evidence to support Mendeloff's view that the judges do at times allow their judgment to be affected by their political predilections, such conduct is radically contrary to articulated judicial norms. As we observed in Chapter 17, according to "black letter" administrative law, a court's review of the legal, factual, and policy basis for a rule is to be "searching and careful," but the court is forbidden to substitute its judgment for that of the agency. Under the "substantial evidence" test that is applicable to OSHA rules, the agency must be able to point to facts, analyses, and arguments that support its resolution of difficult technical questions, but the agency, not the court, is the primary determinant of technical controversies.[33] It is especially inappropriate for judges to substitute their ideas about the appropriate degree of "balance" required by an agency's statute for that of Congress or to allow their concerns about "over-regulation" to affect their judicial function.

It is entirely possible, as many critical legal studies scholars maintain, that the courts say one thing and do another. But in OSHA's case the record is mixed.

With a few notable exceptions, the courts have either affirmed OSHA's health standards, affirmed them in most important respects, or remanded the standards to the agency to be made stricter. Five standards (asbestos, vinyl chloride, arsenic, cotton dust, and noise) were entirely affirmed. Three additional standards (14 carcinogens, coke ovens, and lead) were substantially affirmed. Four standards were affirmed and remanded (grain dust, hazard communications, EtO, formaldehyde), but in each case the remand required OSHA to justify why it weakened some aspect of the rule. Another standard (field sanitation) was issued only after it was forced out by a court. OSHA did, however, lose appeals involving stringent standards in the benzene and lockout/tagout proceedings, and it has suffered partial remands at the industries' behest in a few others.

As Mendeloff observes, the Fifth Circuit, which is based in New Orleans and covers Texas, Louisiana, and Mississippi, has been especially skeptical of governmental regulation in general, and its past conduct offers some support for Mendeloff's view of judicial review.[34] That court has never allowed an OSHA emergency temporary standard (ETS) to go into effect. In several instances, the court, without even hearing OSHA's arguments for promulgating the ETS, has stayed the ETS until the court could schedule a full hearing and then simply declined to hold that hearing until the ETS automatically expired. Mendeloff suggests that OSHA's failure rate is attributable to judicial skepticism about the actual need for the standards, but in fact the judges never even considered the agency's reasons. The ETSs died from judicial neglect. This grossly inappropriate use of the judicial stay should be condemned, not accepted as an inevitable constraint that can be overcome only by declining to issue ETSs until the evidence that workers are dying is overwhelming.

If the lower courts adhere to the extremely deferential approach that the Supreme Court took toward the record support for OSHA's cotton dust standard, OSHA should not expect too many future judicial remands of standards that do not pass Mendeloff's cost-benefit test. The Court in the *Cotton Dust* case rejected industry contentions that OSHA had not adequately supported its cost projections and its determination that the standard would not threaten the economic viability of the textile industry. In doing so, the Court held that the agency could reject the conclusions of one of its contractors' studies because they rested upon erroneous assumptions and relied upon outdated industry-supplied data. At the same time, the Court held that OSHA could properly rely upon the results of an industry-sponsored study that estimated the costs of a less stringent standard than the one the agency ultimately promulgated. The agency believed that several erroneous assumptions in the latter study offset any underestimates resulting from its assumption that the standard would be less stringent. In effect, the Court allowed OSHA to reject its own study because of erroneous assumptions at the same time that it relied upon similar erroneous assumptions to justify its reliance on an industry-sponsored study of the costs of meeting a different standard. The Court adopted a similarly deferential view of the agency's feasibility determination. This aspect of the *Cotton Dust* case, which completely eludes Mendeloff, is important for the message that it sends to the lower courts that OSHA may "err on the side of safety" in interpreting data and drawing inferences from existing studies.

Mendeloff is critical of the Supreme Court's approach to reviewing agency rulemaking. He is especially critical of its review of the National Highway Traffic Safety Administration's recission of a standard that would have required airbags in automobiles. Applying the "arbitrary and capricious" test, the Court held that it should review rule recissions with the same degree of stringency as original rule promulgations.[35] Mendeloff argues that it was inappropriate for the court to place the burden on the agency to justify its recission of the rule.[36] He is similarly critical of the lower court cases that have forced OSHA to respond within a reasonable time to union petitions for emergency temporary standards.[37]

Mendeloff is undoubtedly correct to point the finger at the reviewing courts in explaining the ponderous pace of OSHA regulations. There can be little doubt that OSHA could write many more regulations in much less time if it did not have to prepare technical supporting documents capable of surviving judicial review under the stringent "hard look" test that evolved during the late 1970s. OSHA's problems are compounded by the fact that its statute prescribes a "substantial evidence" standard of review, as opposed to the "arbitrary and capricious" standard that ordinarily applies to review of informal rulemaking.

But Mendeloff seems rather clearly to *approve* of the stringent judicial scrutiny to which OSHA has been subjected, and he is generally critical of the court opinions that are either inclined to allow OSHA to regulate stringently or that push OSHA to regulate where it has failed to regulate. This is critical, because it reveals precisely where Mendeloff's sentiments really lie. In his heart of hearts, Mendeloff is not nearly as concerned about underregulation as he is about what he views as overregulation. He does not want so much to empower OSHA to protect more workers as he wants to take from the agency the power to protect any worker with standards that do not meet his narrow cost-benefit litmus test. He makes this very clear when he urges Congress to overturn the *Cotton Dust* case to require that OSHA engage in cost-benefit balancing in writing occupational health standards,[38] rather than urging Congress to reduce the stringency of judicial review for all OSHA standards.

Those genuinely concerned about the plight of workers need not accept stringent judicial review of OSHA standards as a given. If the courts are preventing OSHA from protecting workers, Congress can reduce the strictness with which the courts view OSHA standards. Yet, as we have seen, the problem is only to a limited extent one of insufficient deference to OSHA. Most courts have been deferential to agency technical and policy judgments, but the detail in which they probe the agency's technical rationale for aggressive regulation sends the wrong signal to OSHA. The agency is told that unless it spends millions of dollars and countless hours preparing its analysis of the record and its response to the public comments, there is a realistic possibility that a reviewing court will send it back to the drawing board. This inevitably increases agency caution and decreases the pace of rulemaking.

Mendeloff's answer to this problem—that OSHA should promulgate weaker standards—is not responsive to the real problem. OSHA would have to prepare the same elaborate record to defend a weaker standard as it does to support a stronger one. For that reason, we suggest in Chapter 20 that if Congress adjusted OSHA's burden of proof, it could free the agency from some of its current time-consuming obligations.

CONCLUSIONS

Mendeloff correctly concludes that the fundamental cause of delay in OSHA standard-setting is the fact that OSHA bears the burden of demonstrating the necessity of any additional changes to the status quo.[39] This strongly suggests that the solution to the problem lies in finding ways to relieve OSHA of its burden. But Mendeloff is unwilling to reduce OSHA's burden unless the standards that it promulgates can pass the cost-benefit test that he advocates.[40] His real target is not underregulation; it is "overregulation" as measured by a cost-benefit yardstick. Reducing OSHA's burden can help cure underregulation without necessarily reducing the stringency of OSHA standards. But Mendeloff maintains that it would be a mistake to tackle underregulation unless one accepts his argument that the current feasibility-based approach "overregulates." Those more committed to worker protection, however, need not agree that attacking underregulation alone would be a mistake. In Chapter 20, we will examine some vehicles for reducing underregulation that are more in line with OSHA's overall goal of protecting workers.

NOTES

1. John Mendeloff, *The Dilemma of Toxic Substances Regulation: How Overregulation Causes Underregulation at OSHA* (Cambridge, Mass.: MIT Press, 1988).
2. Ibid., 24–26.
3. Ibid., 9–10.
4. Ibid., 101–02.
5. Ibid., 240.
6. Ibid., 91, Table 4.6
7. Ibid., 90.
8. Ibid., 92.
9. Ibid.
10. Ibid., 85.
11. Ibid., 89.
12. Ibid., 83.
13. Ibid., 133.
14. Ibid., 13.

15. Ibid., 109.

16. *Building and Construction Trades Dept.* v. *Brock*, 838 F.2d 1258 (D.C. Cir. 1988).

17. Final Rule, 54 *Fed Reg.* 2332 (1989).

18. Charles Gordon, Office of the Solicitor, Department of Labor, telephone interview, 22 May 1990; 54 *Fed. Reg.* 36,766 (1989).

19. 54 *Fed. Reg.* at 2851–53.

20. Elinor Schroeder and Sidney Shapiro, "Responses to Occupational Disease: The Role of Markets, Regulation, and Information," *Georgetown Law Review* 72 (1984): 1258.

21. The cost of the appeal is a function of the number of hours it takes and legal costs per hour. The calculation in the text is based on 1,000 hours at an average of $70 per hour. Cases involving court-ordered legal fees in environmental cases indicate that even complicated appeals involve no more than 900 hours. See, e.g., *Sierra Club* v. *Gorsuch*, 684 F.2d 972, 973, 974, 976 (D.C. Cir. 1982). Sierra Club spent 442 hours and the Environmental Defense Fund spent 398 hours litigating "important, complex, and novel issues" in a controversial environment case. Although law firms may charge an average of $150 per hour or more, some (or even all) of the legal work for an appeal can be done by corporate legal departments of the members of a trade association or of the association itself. Attorneys in these departments typically earn less than an average of $150 per hour. If the industry pays an average of $100 per hour, it can deduct 38 percent of its legal costs from its taxes. The deduction makes the actual cost of appealing the standard approximately $70 per hour.

22. Mendeloff, *Dilemma*, 264.

23. Ibid.

24. Ibid., 10–11.

25. Ibid., 163.

26. Ibid., 244.

27. Ibid., 5.

28. Ibid., 101–02.

29. *Dry Color Manufacturers' Association* v. *Dept. of Labor*, 486 F.2d 98 (3rd Cir. 1973).

30. *BNA Chemical Regulation Reporter* 13 (23 Feb. 1990): 1507 (reporting on a draft paper submitted for publication by Richard Belzer, OMB economist).

31. Duncan Kennedy and Karl E. Klare, "A Bibliography of Critical Legal Studies," *Yale Law Journal* 94 (1984): 461; Duncan Kennedy, "Distributive and Paternalist Motives in Contract and Tort Law, with Special Reference to Comulsory Terms and Unequal Bargaining Power," *Maryland Law Review* 41 (Fall 1982): 563.

32. Mendeloff, *Dilemma*, 115–16.

33. Richard J. Pierce, Jr., Sidney A. Shapiro, and Paul R. Verkuil, *Administrative Law and Process* (Mineola, N.Y.: Foundation Press, 1985), 357–58; *Universal Camera Corp.* v. *NLRB*, 340 U.S. 454, 488 (1951).

34. Mendeloff, *Dilemma*, 110–11.

35. *Motor Vehicle Mfrs. Assn.* v. *State Farm Mutual Automobile Insurance Co.*, 463 U.S. 29 (1983).

36. Mendeloff, *Dilemma*, 171.

37. Ibid., 150.

38. Ibid., 172.

39. Ibid., 137–38.

40. Ibid., 240.

20

Modeling EPA: A New Mandate for OSHA

Among the several health and safety agencies that Congress created in the 1960s and early 1970s, the Environmental Protection Agency (EPA) has been one of the most successful. While many factors account for EPA's record, including broad public support for environmental protection, one aspect of EPA's history is particularly relevant to OSHA's experience. When EPA began to flounder in its early years, Congress adjusted its mandate under both the Clean Air Act and the Clean Water Act to make it easier for the agency to regulate. Congress gave EPA a more flexible regulatory scheme that permitted it to some extent to adjust the stringency of regulation to the level of danger posed by a hazard. Congress also lowered EPA's burden of proof by permitting it to supplement "health-based" standards with "technology-based" requirements. Notably, when Congress adopted these changes, it did not require EPA to adopt a cost-benefit approach.

The time has come for Congress to model OSHA, which has a similar mission, after EPA. Like EPA in its early years, OSHA's standard-setting is greatly hampered by its difficult "health-based" burden of proof, and a "technology-based" mandate should speed up regulation. OSHA would also benefit from a regulatory system that permits it to match the level of regulation to the level of danger posed by a substance. At present, OSHA is between a rock and a hard place—it must regulate health hazards that pose significant risks down to the lowest feasible level, or it may not regulate at all. The agency either struggles for years to produce sufficient proof that a substance poses a significant risk and that the controls it mandates will not bankrupt much of the industry, during which time workers are unprotected, or it decides not to regulate, which still leaves workers unprotected.

This chapter makes a case for a new standard for OSHA. OSHA should have the authority and the duty to mandate both strict regulations and mild regulations.

OSHA should have the authority to regulate strictly, because when there is sufficient evidence that a substance is hazardous, preventive regulation is ethically preferable to compensating workers and their families. OSHA should also be obligated to mandate less stringent health and safety technologies across the board even in the absence of clear proof of danger. A combined regime of health and technology-based requirements would speed the promulgation of standards and permit a more rational matching of the level of regulation to the degree of the risk presented without engaging in the meaningless and time-consuming charade of calculating cost and benefits.

JUSTIFICATION FOR STRINGENT STANDARDS

There are good reasons why OSHA should not be restricted by a cost-benefit test, the most important of which may be that cost-benefit analysis ignores the distributional consequences of regulatory policy. The economists' defense of cost-benefit-based standards is that it is less expensive for employers to pay compensation for some illnesses and injuries than it is to prevent them. This response, however, ignores the ethical distinction between preventing a death and compensating the victim's family after it occurs. Congress apparently had this in mind when it rejected the cost-benefit-based approach in the OSH Act. The Supreme Court's reading of the legislative history of the OSH Act in the *Cotton Dust* case, discussed in Chapter 18, indicates a congressional determination that even if the costs of a health standard exceed its benefits, it is preferable to engage in preventive action than to allow illnesses to occur.[1]

Many economists have trouble believing that Congress could have really meant what it said—that workers were to be protected beyond the point indicated by a cost-benefit test—because they subscribe to the notion that absolute safety is beyond the financial means of any society and therefore trade-offs between cost and safety are inevitable.[2] Since these trade-offs are inevitable, many economists believe it only makes sense to set standards at the level at which their costs just equal their benefits. While trade-offs are indeed inevitable, what escapes these critics is that there are other equally rational ways to write standards.

Acknowledging that society cannot vest workers with an unqualified right to an absolutely safe workplace, one may rationally take the position that workers do have a right to insist that employers do the best they can to protect human health. Employers can be required to install available risk reduction technologies, even though the cost of such technologies might exceed the benefits as calculated under the ''willingness to pay'' approach to valuing lives discussed in Chapter 19. This ''technology-based'' approach to regulation has a long history in the area of environmental protection, and it is reflected in the ''feasibility'' requirement of section 6(b)(5) of the OSH Act.

Partial Versus Complete Compensation

Besides the ethical superiority of preventing illnesses and accidents over compensating for them, it is inequitable to place upon workers the entire burden of less stringent cost-benefit-based standards. Economists generally maintain, however, that the distributional consequences of their prescriptions are beyond their bailiwick. Professor Mendeloff, for example, recognizes that meeting the cost-benefit test does not require society's winners to compensate the losers:

> Those who die because society rejects inefficient lifesaving programs will not be around to benefit from the bigger pie. Does this fact require condemnation of any policy that stops short of maximum effort to prevent deaths? No. It is inevitable that public policy will create losers who are beyond the reach of compensation. But this fact should spur thinking about who the losers are and how we feel about their plight.[3]

The widows and orphans of workers whose deaths could have been prevented at a cost somewhat greater than the economist's optimal expenditure will no doubt take great comfort in the fact that their loss will stimulate scholars to think more about how society should feel about their plight.

Though it may be "inevitable" that public policy will create losers who are beyond the reach of compensation, it is *not* inevitable that the number of such victims has to be as great as that mandated by cost-benefit analysis. In a world in which workers are seldom fully compensated for occupational illness, the merit of a technology-based approach is that, to a much larger degree than the cost-benefit approach, it reduces the need for after-the-fact compensation. Under the cost-benefit-based approach, significant financial burdens fall on individual undercompensated workers and their families. By comparison, the additional costs imposed by a technology-based standard are passed on to consumers or absorbed by stockholders. The individual impact on any one consumer or stockholder is insignificant compared with the burden on uncompensated workers and their families. Protecting workers with technology-based standards may be more costly to society than compensating them after the fact. But since no realistic mechanism exists to ensure adequate compensation, fairness demands that workers should be protected instead.

Mendeloff, however, argues that stringent regulation is unfair if the poor ultimately pay the additional costs.[4] To the extent that cost savings from less stringent regulations are passed on to consumers, and not to shareholders and bond owners, there may be some truth to this observation. But the economic analysis necessary to show that the poor are the primary beneficiaries of unsafe workplaces has yet to be undertaken. Since the poor tend disproportionately to gravitate toward the riskiest jobs, the hypothesis seems inherently implausible.

Technology-based standards also reduce the number of workers requiring compensation by focusing the agency's attention on real risk-reduction technologies, rather than embroiling the agency in intense but ultimately unresolvable debates over the degree of risk posed by varying degrees of exposure to a hazardous substance. A cost-benefit test would inevitably tend to drive the agency toward unenforceable work practice standards and ineffective personal protective devices, rather than toward the installation of new technologies to protect worker health. While technology-based standards are not very likely to induce highly innovative changes in health and safety technologies,[5] they do have the capacity to nudge technology beyond the addition of personal protective devices to preexisting protections.

Public Versus Private Values

As Chapter 18 discussed, many economists simply assume that when individuals make public policy choices, they are guided by the same values that motivate them in making purchasing decisions in private markets. Since no rational consumer would pay $25 in a private market for something that was worth only $20, the economist assumes that voters intend their representatives to reject policies whose costs exceed their economic benefits. "The average individual," write Buchanan and Tullock, "acts on the same basis of the same overall value scale when he participates in market activity and in political activity."[6] In other words, says Tullock, "Voters and customers are essentially the same people. Mr. Smith buys and votes; he is the same man in the supermarket and in the voting booth."[7]

In Chapter 18, we discussed an alternative view that social policy choices provide an opportunity for citizens to value certain things more highly than they do when they go to the store. Individuals are willing to assign different values in public decisions because they offer an opportunity to confirm noneconomic principles of importance to them. As consumers, we may dislike paying more for manufactured products because of the costs of protecting workers, but as citizens we can rationally vote for extremely costly and, by the economist's "willingness to pay" measure, irrational goals. We vote in favor of such costly goals because they permit us to reaffirm to ourselves that occupational disease is not merely inefficient—it kills people. In other words, the goals we set as voters constantly remind us as we assume our roles as consumers that there are things more important than the pursuit of material wealth.[8]

Some economists are skeptical that people will behave in such an altruistic fashion, because in the economic paradigm individuals behave only in a "self-interested" manner. With such a cramped view of human nature, it is no wonder that economics has been labeled "the dismal science." While self-interest is undeniably an important human motivation, it is not the *sole* determinant of human behavior. We may act out of greed, but we also extend love, charity, care, and sympathy to others.[9] Everyday perception bears this out. So does psychological experimentation.[10] The wellsprings of empathy are uncertain. They may be biological,[11] psychological,[12] or even self-interested.[13] Whatever their source, it is abundantly clear that all judgments and preferences cannot be reduced to a unidimensional quantitative form.[14]

Public policy-making provides us an opportunity to express our empathy with those who are less fortunate. It is an opportunity for those of us with sufficient wealth to purchase our way out of the danger of occupational disease to choose to protect those who do not have that option. When we reject cost-benefit analysis as a guide to public policy, we not only better protect workers, we ennoble ourselves.

SHIFTING THE BURDEN OF PROOF

The solution to OSHA's seeming inability to promulgate standards at a reasonable pace is not to capitulate to the extortionate threat of industry resistance by promulgating mild standards that provide few additional protections to workers. Mendeloff himself notes, though somewhat disapprovingly, that the OSH Act places a high priority on worker safety and health.[15] As the Supreme Court noted in the *Cotton Dust* case, this salutary goal cannot be accomplished if OSHA routinely subjects its health standards to a cost-benefit test. The solution lies in reducing OSHA's burden of proof.

One frequently employed burden-shifting divide is a permit requirement. Congress has used this technique in regulatory areas ranging from radio licensing to drug regulation. The fundamental premise behind the permit requirement is that no one has a right to engage in a specified activity without permission. To obtain a permit, the applicant must make specified showings sufficient to persuade the permit-issuing authority that the applicant meets the statutory criteria. Although the agency may not arbitrarily deny a permit to an applicant who meets the criteria or take a permit away from a holder who has not engaged in proscribed conduct, the burden of demonstrating that the criteria are in fact met lies on the applicant and on the permit holder at permit renewal time. Although it is unlikely (and indeed undesirable) that Congress would require all employers to obtain a permit from OSHA prior to employing workers, the permit device may have a role to play in especially hazardous workplaces.

A less intrusive burden-shifting device would take advantage of a congressionally mandated a priori classification and place the burden on employers to demonstrate that they deserved a different classification. Much of the resistance to OSHA's current feasibility-based standard-setting process is the perception that it requires OSHA to require standards so stringent as to threaten the viability of the entire industry. There is language in an early District of Columbia Circuit opinion suggesting that Congress intended feasibility-based standards to push the regulated industry to the breaking point.[16] In a brief to the Supreme Court, OSHA stated that a standard would be feasible if "the industry will maintain long-term profitability and competitiveness."[17] Although OSHA has never pressed an industry to such extreme lengths, many of its critics have used the possibility of draconian requirements to attack the feasibility-based approach.

If the problem with OSHA standards is the fear of outrageous feasibility-based standards, then one possible solution is to give OSHA the flexibility to promulgate less stringent technology-based standards in some cases. Rather than press the industry to the point of economic disaster, Congress could amend the OSH Act to require that industries install the "best available technology," a term that could be defined to require "top of the line" technologies but not the development of new technologies. EPA's experiences in regulating water and air pollution suggest how Congress might reform the OSH Act to accomplish this shift in emphasis.

EPA REFORM

When it became apparent that EPA could not regulate water and air pollution effectively under its original mandate, Congress amended the Federal Water Pollution Control Act[18] (FWPCA) and the Clean Air Act (CAA)[19] to change EPA's burden of proof. As originally enacted, the FWPCA required EPA to identify toxic water pollutants and to establish limitations on their discharge sufficient to protect the public with "an ample margin of safety."[20] After EPA's standard-setting process got bogged down in complicated and acrimonious hearings, Congress amended the FWPCA to require EPA to use a technology-based approach, unless that approach would not adequately protect water quality.[21] Under its new powers, EPA was authorized to regulate toxic pollutants by requiring, on an industry-by-industry basis, the application of the "best available technology economically achievable" (BAT).[22]

The technology-based approach allowed the agency to avoid the enormous difficulties it had previously encountered in attempting to determine "safe" levels for toxic pollutants and "ample" margins of safety. To establish BAT, EPA had to survey the relevant industry and other industries with similar effluents and identify the best technologies available that would work in the industry. While this was not a trivial task, it was usually less resource-intensive and controversial than promulgating media-quality-based standards. If sufficient evidence existed to show that a more stringent standard was required by media quality considerations, the agency could still promulgate such a standard. Using its BAT mandate, EPA has promulgated standards for the electroplating, aluminum forming, and petrochemical industries and successfully survived judicial review of those standards with remands on only a few relatively unimportant issues.[23]

Congress adopted a similar approach toward shifting EPA's burden of proof for establishing air pollution standards for "clean air" areas. Prior to 1977, the statute provided no clear way to meet the statutory goal of "prevention of significant deterioration" of air quality in areas that met the media-quality-based ambient air quality standards. After the courts held that the agency had to protect clean air areas, the agency devised a program (which Congress later adopted in the 1977 CAA amendments) in which major new stationary sources were required to install the "best available technology," whether or not it would have a demonstrable effect on media quality.[24] EPA was thereby relieved of any burden of proving that visibility or other aesthetic values would be disturbed prior to requiring the installation of cleanup technologies.

Air quality considerations were incorporated into the new program through a "zoning" scheme under which states were required to designate clean areas into one of three classes, each of which had a specified increment of allowable pollution. Once that increment was used up, no more sources of that pollutant would be allowed unless the state changed the classification.[25] In addition to specifying the increments, Congress made initial classifications for all clean air areas in the United States. Most areas were placed in the middle category, and the states were given the power in most cases to upgrade the classification or downgrade it.

Had Mendeloff been asked how best to deal with EPA's problems in the mid-1970s he might well have prescribed a reduction in the stringency of the media-quality-based standards. Since industry challenges were making it very difficult for the agency to write water-quality-based effluent limitations for toxic chemicals that would be capable of providing an "ample margin of safety," Mendeloff would probably have urged Congress to require EPA to match the stringency of those standards to his cost-benefit test. Instead, Congress adopted a flexible but stringent technology-based approach. Rather than requiring EPA to make individualized cost-benefit assessments for each of the toxic substances it proposed to regulate, Congress allowed EPA to regulate entire industries and to divide the country into broad classes. Congress attempted to remove some of the roadblocks to regulation that EPA faced by allowing it to focus on technologies rather than debate endlessly about media quality impacts.

A NEW MANDATE

Drawing on its experience with EPA, Congress could adopt a regulatory scheme that requires OSHA to establish a list of chemicals and other harmful physical agents that "could reasonably be anticipated to cause a material impairment of health or functional capacity." These words would signal Congress's intent to mandate a threshold lower than "significant risk" for including a substance or hazard on the list. The list would be compiled without regard to actual workplace exposures, thus precluding the need for costly risk assessments. The focus would be upon the capacity of the chemical to do harm at any realistic exposure level.

Congress could ensure that politics played a lesser role in developing the list by delegating the list-writing task to NIOSH rather than OSHA. Delegating that function to the National Institute of Occupational Safety and Health (NIOSH) may avoid OSHA's writing the list in a way that avoids regulating intransigent or politically favored industries. If Congress thinks that NIOSH would not be an appropriate agency for this function, it could specify that the list contain at

Table 20–1
OSHA Reform

CLASS	DEFINITION	REGULATORY LEVEL
I	Regulation as Class II presents a significant risk of material impairment	Extent permitted as feasible
II	Any hazard on list presumed to be in this class unless redesignated	Extent permitted by Best Available Technology
III	Regulation as Class II unnecessary to prevent a reasonable anticipation of material impairment	Extent permitted by nongovernmental consensus standard

least those chemicals considered to be carcinogens or suspected carcinogens by outside expert bodies, such as the National Cancer Institute.

The scheme envisioned here would establish three broad categories of industries as indicated in Table 20–1. Any industrial category in which an employee was exposed to any substance on the list would initially fall into Class II and would retain that classification until redesignated by OSHA. All industrial categories in Class II would be required to install the "best available workplace risk reduction technology" (BAT) by a specified deadline. OSHA would be required to promulgate generic standards defining BAT on an industrywide basis prior to a statutory deadline designed to give regulatees sufficient lead time to install the required technologies.

As with EPA's statutes, the term "best available risk reduction technology" would be defined by reference to the best technology actually being used within the relevant industry, technologies that could relatively easily be transferred from industries presenting similar hazards, and pilot plant technologies that OSHA could demonstrate were available for use in new and existing workplaces. To avoid protracted battles over the degree of protection afforded by the identified technology in practice, OSHA could take the position that if the prescribed technology did not meet OSHA's predicted permissible exposure limit (PEL) in a particular workplace after having been properly installed, a variance would be available under which the PEL would be based on the level that the technology did consistently reach in the workplace. OSHA would be authorized to require medical monitoring and medical removal protection, but it would also have the option not to require such protection. Hazard identification and training requirements would be the same as those established under the current hazard identification standard.

The statute would specify that personal protective devices could not be considered in determining the best available technology, and employers would not be allowed to meet the standard through personal protective devices. For example, if OSHA established the standard for an industry as a set of PELs for all listed substances found in that industry, ambient concentrations of the listed substances could not exceed the PELs in any place where employees might be exposed for more than a very brief period of time. Variances would be available for Class II industries on a case-by-case basis if the individual company requesting the variance demonstrated that meeting the standard was technologically infeasible or if the costs per worker of meeting the standard for that company greatly exceeded the per worker costs of the other companies in the industry.

OSHA would redesignate a chemical or substance if it would be inappropriate to treat it as a Class II hazard as indicated in Table 20–1. OSHA would be required to redesignate the hazard to the more stringently regulated category (Class I) if regulation under Class II would leave workers exposed to a "significant risk of material impairment to health or functional capacity." For Class I hazards, OSHA would require employers to reduce exposure to the extent "feasible." This would require the installation of the best technology foreseeable on the horizon, including pilot plant technologies and technologies in use in similar industrial contexts in other countries. Personal protective devices would be allowed to the extent necessary to reduce the risk to a level of insignificance, but they would be phased out as engineering controls were installed. So long as personal protective devices were necessary to reduce the risk, the companies would be required to engage in engineering research relevant to the risk at issue with the goal of developing additional engineering controls. Thus, the ultimate goal would be to reduce the risk to a level of insignificance without reliance on respirators. Medical monitoring and medical removal protection would be mandated by statute for all Class I industries.

Hazard identification requirements would be the same, except that training would include training in the proper use of personal protective devices and that employers could not claim trade secrecy status for any information relevant to health of any substance that posed a significant risk. To facilitate training and communication, employers in Class I would be required to establish a workplace health committee composed of elected employee representatives and designated employer representatives with the power to investigate employee complaints and monitor the progress of risk-reduction technologies. The statute would state explicitly that industries in Class I were "pervasively regulated" so as to avoid any constitutional objections to unannounced OSHA inspections for the purpose of enforcing the health-related requirements, and it would mandate at least annual inspections of all Class I companies.

Finally, OSHA would be empowered to identify high-risk operations in Category I industries for which a permit would be required. To secure a permit, an individual company in the category would be required to submit to OSHA (or perhaps a delegated state official) a health protection plan showing how any personal protective device requirements would be enforced, how medical monitoring and removal would be implemented, and specifying the additional efforts that the company was undertaking to identify and implement new engineering controls. The permit would have to be renewed on a yearly basis, at which time OSHA could monitor the company's progress. The permit would substantially facilitate enforcement.

Variances would be available from Class I standards, but not from the other Class I requirements, only on the ground of technological infeasibility, a showing that should be very difficult to make, given the option of relying upon personal protective devices. If a company could not afford to meet the standard with its existing resources, it would have to go out of business rather than continue to expose workers to a significant health risk.

A regulated entity or trade association could petition OSHA to redesignate an industry into the least stringently regulated category (Class III) if it could demonstrate on the basis of well-established scientific studies and exposure analyses that employees in the industry "could not reasonably be anticipated to suffer material impairment of health or functional capacity" under any realistic exposure scenarios. Industries in Class III would be required to reduce employee exposure to the extent permitted by applicable standards promulgated by nongovernmental entities such as ACGIH. Medical surveillance and medical removal protections would not be required.

Unlike Mendeloff's proposal, this suggested regulatory approach is addressed more to the problem of underregulation than overregulation, because it is far from clear that overregulation is the serious problem that Mendeloff perceives it to be. Yet the scheme does allow for less burdensome regulation in cases in which OSHA lacks sufficient information to support a "significant risk" determination. In such cases, OSHA could not rely upon speculative technologies, and economic feasibility could play a role in granting variances. By relieving OSHA of some, but not all, of the burdens that it now faces, the solution suggested here should increase OSHA's regulatory output, even if industry and union opposition continues unabated. At the same time, even the least stringent designation (Class III) would update the consensus standards automatically, rather than forcing the Agency to undertake a massive PEL generic rulemaking as it did during the Pendergrass years.

The proposal, however, does not ignore entirely the relationship of costs and benefits. In any case where OSHA has a lower burden of proof, it has regulatory authority only to impose regulatory requirements that are likely to be less costly. If there is only a reasonable anticipation of harm, OSHA can require the reduction of exposure only to the level of BAT, and not the level of feasibility. Moreover, an individual company has an opportunity to obtain a variance upon a showing that its per worker costs would greatly exceed the costs of its competitors.

As with Mendeloff's proposal, workers can object that the proposal weakens the substantive principle established by the existing statute that workers are entitled to be protected to the extent "feasible." Under the proposed regime, any given worker faces a somewhat higher chance of receiving less protection than his peer who is one of the fortunate few to be subject to an OSHA standard under the existing regime, but the new approach should protect many more workers than the current scheme does. Moreover, unlike Mendeloff's idea, the proposal retains strict regulation of a substance when it poses a significant risk. Thus, workers are entitled to more protection when the evidence warrants it.

EMPOWERING OSHA WITH MORE RESOURCES

A large part of the explanation for OSHA's failure to maintain a reasonable standard-setting pace is its chronic lack of rulemaking resources. Even major changes in the statutory scheme will go for naught if OSHA does not have the resources necessary to accomplish its task. OSHA will still need to assess the risks posed by workplace hazards, and it will need to undertake expensive engineering surveys to determine the economic and technological feasibility of risk-reduction technologies. Even if the courts are willing to accept much less in the way of support for OSHA regulations, the agency will have to assemble a substantial body of information for each rulemaking effort merely to satisfy minimal standards of rationality. In addition, OSHA must prepare cost and financial analyses to circulate to OMB as part of the regulatory impact assessment process, and it must ordinarily prepare an environmental impact statement to comply with the National Environmental Policy Act. All of these functions require expertise and resources, both of which OSHA currently possesses only in minimal amounts.

OSHA's rulemaking failures can to some degree be laid at Congress's doorstep. Congress has charged OSHA with the awesome responsibility of ensuring that workers are protected, but at the same time it has declined to provide OSHA with the funds necessary to accomplish this task. In recent years, however, the greater portion of the blame must go to the Reagan administration, which systematically carved away at OSHA's budget, and the Bush administration, which has not asked Congress to replenish the agency's resources after the lean Reagan years. Although Congress has never been especially liberal in its funding for OSHA, it has been in the awkward position since the early 1980s of appropriating for OSHA more money than the agency requested.

Even with a substantially reduced burden of justification, OSHA will need at least to double its standard-setting staff in the Health Standards Directorate if it is to have any hope of increasing its production rate for health standards. If the OSH Act is not to remain an empty promise, Congress must put its money where its mouth is and empower OSHA with greater resources. If Congress is unwilling to find resources for OSHA in the normal budget process, it could examine alternative ways to fill OSHA's coffers. For example, Congress could let OSHA keep the fines that it levies, rather than return them to the U.S. Treasury. A few mega-fines per year could support a much larger health standards staff, and the proposal would give the agency a greater incentive to discover violations. Another possibility is to prescribe an injury tax for employers that sets out a schedule of payments due OSHA for various workplace injuries. This would give employers an incentive to improve workplace safety at the same time that it was increasing OSHA's resources. While all of these off-budget revenue-enhancing devices have drawbacks (the ability to keep fines will no doubt affect OSHA's enforcement discretion, and an injury tax may induce employers to underreport injuries), some such technique may be essential in an age in which "taxation" is a dirty word.

CONCLUSIONS

Virtually all observers agree that OSHA encounters enormous obstacles when it writes health standards, but there is less agreement about what should be done to overcome those obstacles. Like a professional football team, OSHA can achieve success in at least two ways. It can, as Mendeloff suggests, lower its expectations and play only college teams or (better still) high school teams. That tactic will no doubt substantially increase its victory margin, but it will not have accomplished very much at the end of the season. Alternatively, OSHA can beef up its line and seek out tactical advantages over the other teams. It may not win as many games this way, but it will have accomplished something. If one team still appears to have insurmountable advantages, it may be necessary to change the rules of the game to put the teams on a more equal footing. The changes suggested in this chapter are of this latter variety. It may be that the entity with the power to change the rules (Congress) will not be persuaded that a change is necessary, but it is better to try to change the rules than to lower the quality of the play.

NOTES

1. *American Textile Mfrs. Inst.* v. *Donovan*, 452 U.S. 490, 519–20 (1981).
2. John Mendeloff, *The Dilemma of Toxic Substance Regulation: How Overregulation Causes Underregulation at OSHA* (Cambridge, Mass.: MIT Press, 1988), 172.
3. Ibid., 33.
4. Ibid., 31.

5. D. Bruce La Pierre, "Technology Forcing and Federal Environmental Protection Statutes," *Iowa Law Review* 62 (1977): 825–26, notes 324, 325.

6. James Buchanan and Gordon Tullock, *The Calculus of Consent* (Ann Arbor: University of Michigan Press, 1962), 138.

7. Gordon Tullock, *The Vote Motive* (London: Institute for Economic Affairs, 1976), 5.

8. Thomas O. McGarity, "Media Quality, Technology and Cost-Benefit Balancing Strategies for Health and Environmental Regulation," *Law and Contemporary Problems* 46 (Summer 1983): 194–95.

9. Steven Kelman, *Making Public Policy: A Hopeful View of American Government* (New York: Basic Books, 1987), 240.

10. Ervin Staub, *Positive Social Behavior and Morality: Social and Personal Influences*, vol. 1 (New York: Academic Press, 1978) 2–5, 58–69.

11. Roger Masters, *The Nature of Politics* (New Haven: Yale University Press, 1989): Edward O. Wilson, *Sociobiology, the New Synthesis* (Cambridge, Mass.: Harvard University Press, 1975), ch. 5.

12. Sharon Brehm and Saul M. Kassin, *Social Psychology* (Boston: Houghton Mifflin, 1990), 302–06, 471–83.

13. Robert Frank, *Passions Within Reason: The Strategic Role of the Emotions* (New York: Norton, 1988).

14. Charles Taylor, "The Diversity of Goods," in *Utilitarianism and Beyond*, ed. Amartya Sen and Bernard Williams (New York: Cambridge University Press, 1982), 129.

15. Mendeloff, *Dilemma*, 104.

16. *Industrial Union, AFL-CIO* v. *Hodgson*, 499 F.2d 467, 478 (D.C. Cir. 1974).

17. *American Textile Mfrs. Inst.* v. *Donovan*, 452 U.C. 490, 520 (1981).

18. 33 U.S.C. §§ 1251–1376 (1988).

19. 42 U.S.C.A. §§ 7401–7642 (West Supp. 1991).

20. 33 U.S.C. § 1317(a) (1988).

21. McGarity, "Media Quality," 202.

22. 33 U.S.C. § 1311(b)(2)(A) (1988).

23. In 1990, Congress amended sec. 112 of the CAA (the section addressing hazardous air pollutants) in an almost identical fashion. Congress told EPA to write technology-based standards reflecting the "maximum available control technology" for categories of sources emitting listed hazardous air pollutants. If residual risks are still unacceptable, EPA must demand even greater reductions in hazardous emissions.

24. 42 U.S.C.A. § 7475(a)(4) (West Supp. 1991).

25. 42 U.S.C.A. § 7472 (West Supp. 1991).

Part VI

EXTERNAL REFORMS: EMPOWERING WORKERS

21

Lighting a Fire: When OSHA Is a Reluctant Regulator

In February 1987, Judge Patricia Wald bestowed upon OSHA the record for regulatory delay when 14 years after farm workers' representatives petitioned the agency for a field sanitation standard, it still had not acted.[1] Judge Wald's opinion quoted from the previous recordholder, a case concerning National Highway Traffic Safety Agency (NHTSA), where the court had observed, "In the context of a thirteen year gap between law and enforcement," it is "hard to imagine a more sorry performance of a congressional mandate than that carried out by NHTSA and its predecessors." Judge Wald lamented that "[u]nfortunately, truth is often stranger than fantasy. In this case, for 14 years farmworkers have been unsuccessfully petitioning the Department of Labor to provide sanitation standards equivalent to those which the federal government under the OSH Act has guaranteed to all other workers in its jurisdiction."[2] She aptly characterized the field sanitation saga as the Bleak House of administrative law:

The rulemaking record demonstrates beyond dispute that lack of drinking water and toilets causes the spread of contagion, bladder disease, and heat-prostration among farmworkers. Yet resistance to issuing the standard . . . has been intractable. An arsenal of administrative law doctrines has provided the justification for ricocheting the case between the agency and the courts for over a decade: a decade in which field workers have gone without benefit of drinking water or the most rudimentary sanitary facilities.

The court ordered OSHA to promulgate the standard within 30 days in order to "bring an end to this disgraceful chapter of legal neglect."[3]

The field sanitation standard demonstrates both that the courts can hold OSHA accountable when it fails to protect workers and that they are usually very reluctant to do so. The role of the judiciary in forcing OSHA to regulate is an important aspect of workplace health and safety regulation. Chapters 12 and 13 suggested a variety of actions that OSHA can take to increase its effectiveness. But the agency's history indicates that its leaders may sometimes be hostile to its mission. Certainly, Thorne Auchter and Robert Rowland did little to protect workers during the five years they headed the agency. Even when its leaders are not opposed to regulating, outside pressures from the Office of Management and Budget (OMB), Congress, or industry trade associations can sap OSHA of its will to fulfill its regulating obligations. When OSHA is a reluctant regulator, workers have turned to the courts and to Congress for assistance. This chapter explores the role of judicial and political review when OSHA refuses to act.

THE AGENCY-FORCING LAWSUIT

The Administrative Procedure Act (APA) requires OSHA and other administrative agencies to give "interested persons" the right to petition an agency to promulgate a regulation. It also requires the agencies to conclude matters presented to them "within a reasonable time" and to give "[p]rompt notice" of the denial of a petition.[4] To ensure compliance, the federal courts are authorized to compel agency action that is "unreasonably delayed."[5] If a court finds that an agency has been too slow in responding to a petition, it will issue an order, called a writ of mandamus, that requires the agency to make a decision within a specified time period. Legal action to require an agency to respond to a petition is commonly known as an agency-forcing lawsuit.

During the Reagan administration, the agency-forcing lawsuit was the strategy of choice for workers seeking to hold OSHA accountable for its failure to act. From 1981 to 1988, OSHA promulgated a total of four health standards for ethylene oxide, asbestos, benzene, and formaldehyde. For all but the asbestos standard, OSHA acted only in response to a lawsuit alleging that it had unreasonably delayed a decision.[6] The courts were also responsible for pressuring OSHA to promulgate the field sanitation standard and to extend the hazard communication standard to all industries.[7] Since these six standards constitute about half of all of the health and safety standards promulgated during the Reagan administration, and almost all of the important standards, the courts clearly played an important role in forcing OSHA to regulate during that time.

The Delay in Combating Delay

Although agency-forcing lawsuits have stimulated OSHA action, success has come only after considerable delay. For example, workers started suing OSHA concerning the field sanitation standard in 1977 and were not successful until 1986. During that period, the District of Columbia Court of Appeals ruled on their lawsuit three separate times.[8] An agency-forcing lawsuit is time-consuming for two reasons. First, workers sue OSHA only after it is clear that a decision on a petition will not be forthcoming. Second, the courts are unwilling to order

OSHA to expedite its decision making without compelling evidence it is acting in bad faith.

The typical case starts when a new scientific study indicating that a common workplace substance may be hazardous is reported in the press. An OSHA official will state that the agency is concerned and is looking into the matter, but months (or even years) pass without a formal response. Eventually a union or public interest group petitions the agency (usually with great fanfare) to promulgate a standard. Upon receipt of the petition, OSHA agrees to consider the matter by a certain date, then typically misses its deadline. At that point, the petitioner (again with much fanfare) files suit demanding that the agency respond to the petition within a reasonable time. By this point, several years will have passed since the scientific report was first published.

Despite the delay, a court usually will not order OSHA to expedite its decision making unless workers have overwhelming evidence that OSHA is acting in bad faith.[9] One reason for this deference is that judges are conscious of the fact that under our constitutional arrangement of government, the executive branch has the primary responsibility for implementing the laws that Congress enacts. The courts also defer to OSHA out of a belief that the agency is in a better position to analyze whether the technical complexity of an issue requires it to delay a decision until additional information can be accumulated. Finally, judges fear that an order requiring OSHA to expedite decision making will inadvertently cause a diversion of scarce resources from other, more important topics.

When OSHA Is Sued

The judicial reluctance to order expedited decisionmaking is evident in the cases brought against OSHA during the Reagan administration. As mentioned earlier, the District of Columbia Circuit ordered OSHA to promulgate its field sanitation standard only after the workers had sued the agency for a third time. OSHA's response to the Supreme Court's benzene remand also illustrates how judges are reluctant to order OSHA to go faster.[10] In July 1983, OSHA had promised to complete the benzene standard by June 1984. OSHA not only missed that deadline, but at the time it was sued by the United Steelworkers Union in late 1984, it had not yet issued a notice of proposed rulemaking, which is the first step in the rulemaking process. The union asked the court to compel OSHA to complete the standard within eight months. Although the court was aware of "the seriousness of the health risks posed by benzene and the consequent need for prompt agency action," it accepted OSHA's new proposed completion date of February 1987 for several reasons. First, "[i]n reaching its determination, the agency must, of necessity, deal with a host of complex scientific and technical issues." Second, "OSHA obviously cannot know at present how many comments it will receive or the nature of those comments." This was important because the Administrative Protection Act requires OSHA to read and answer the comments it receives concerning a proposed rule. Third, "judicial imposition of an overly hasty timetable at this stage will ill serve the public interest. The rule promulgated by the agency, not to mention the agency's rationale for the rule, must be constructed carefully and thoroughly if the agency's action is to pass judicial [review].'' The court did warn, however, that its doors were open to the union if OSHA "failed to act with appropriate diligence in following the estimates it has tendered to this court."[11]

Judges are willing to force OSHA to move more rapidly than its own timetable only in the rare case, like the field sanitation standard, where the agency's bad faith is obvious. Even so, the agency-forcing lawsuit is of benefit to workers, because the availability of judicial review forces OSHA to pay attention to the petitions it receives. Many beneficiary groups believe that if it were not for the threat of a lawsuit, OSHA would never take up difficult and controversial projects.[12] A surprising number of professionals in the Health Standards Directorate agree with this assessment. Moreover, judicial review undoubtedly results in speedier decisions. Although courts tend to accept whatever timetable OSHA submits, they are less tolerant of further delays when OSHA does not adhere to its own schedule. Moreover, when OSHA submits a completely unrealistic timetable, as it did in the field sanitation case, the court will probably reject it.

Statutory Deadlines for Avoiding Delay

Workers would be in a better position when they sued OSHA for unreasonable delay if OSHA had to meet a statutory deadline for responding to petitions for new rules. When an agency has missed a statutory deadline, the courts are less likely to accept its excuses for delay and are more likely to order it to speed up its decision-making process.[13] When a statutory deadline exists, a court is no longer in the awkward position of second-guessing how the agency should use its resources. Congress has determined that question, and the judiciary's role is to enforce the legislature's will.

The Environmental Protection Agency's (EPA) experience with statutory deadlines, however, suggests that the concept is quite controversial. Congress has established dozens of deadlines for EPA rulemaking, and some critics have argued that those deadlines have done more harm than good. For example, the deadlines that require EPA to regulate hazardous air pollutants have been described as "ludicrous."[14] In some cases, statutory deadlines do not demonstrate adequate sensitivity to agency resource constraints and priority conflicts. In other cases, Congress no doubt fails to appreciate that proceedings of different degrees of complexity require different deadlines.[15] When Congress sets unrealistic deadlines, agencies are more likely to take regulatory action that is hasty, without adequate evidentiary support, and thus subject to judicial reversal, or to divert its resources to litigation in an effort to justify its failure to meet the deadlines.[16] Moreover, unrealistic deadlines can contribute to public distrust of the agency. Former EPA administrator William Ruckelshaus, an opponent of statutory deadlines, charges that unrealistically short deadlines have "undermined confidence in EPA managers, caused the public to measure them against unrealistic goals, and to think we've failed and obscure the successes we've made. Deadlines reinforce the sense that we (EPA) are not getting anywhere, to the detriment of public sense of confidence in government."[17]

The OSH Act imposes some deadlines on OSHA. First, if OSHA appoints a rulemaking advisory committee, there is a 270-day deadline for the completion of the committee's work and a 60-day deadline for OSHA's response to the committee's recommendations. Second, OSHA must make a decision whether to promulgate a proposed standard within 60 days after completion of any hearing held on it. Third, if OSHA promulgates an emergency standard, it must promulgate a permanent standard "no later than six months after publication of the emergency standard."[18] In a study for the Administrative Conference of the United States (ACUS), Edward Tomlinson concluded that "OSHA has found the statutory deadlines difficult to meet and has not normally met them," that the deadlines have "undermined OSHA's efforts to determine its own priorities by forcing it to concentrate its resources on rulemaking proceedings that are subject to statutory deadlines," and that the deadlines do not apply to the stages of the rulemaking process that are the most important causes of delay.[19]

While deadline critics would like to eliminate statutory deadlines altogether, they ignore the fact that deadlines are an important tool for holding agencies accountable. As OSHA's experience has demonstrated, without a legislative deadline, the courts have been reluctant to overrule an agency's proposed timetable, even when it appeared to be dilatory. Moreover, even if statutory deadlines do not result in strict compliance, they permit a court to insist on more timely compliance than it might feel comfortable enforcing without them. Perhaps most important, deadlines give beneficiaries leverage to ensure that a lethargic or reluctant agency does not attempt to avoid its sometimes controversial rulemaking responsibilities by placing tough issues on the back burner.

The few deadlines in OSHA's current statute are probably inappropriate. They are generally too strict, and they are applicable to the wrong activities. Indeed, as explained in Chapter 12, the deadlines for advisory committees have probably played a large role in OSHA's virtual abandonment of that process. The fact that deadlines are inappropriate for some purposes does not imply, however, that they will not enhance OSHA decision making in other contexts. The goal should not be to eliminate deadlines but to create realistic ones that, as one judge put it, are tailored not to "overstimulate the organism."[20]

One solution is for Congress to require OSHA to set its own rulemaking deadlines and adhere to them. The ACUS agrees that the problems caused by unreasonable deadlines would be mitigated if an agency sets its own timetable.[21] Congress could further assure accountability by providing that agency-set deadlines could be extended only for good cause and only for congressionally determined intervals (e.g., 90 days). Finally, courts should be given authority to enforce OSHA's deadlines when the agency misses them.

Without deadlines, OSHA has the option of delaying its response to citizen petitions for years. With deadlines, workers would have a means of prodding OSHA to regulate more quickly. By permitting OSHA to set its own schedule, most of the disadvantages of statutory deadlines can be successfully minimized. If agency-forcing lawsuits nevertheless caused some diversion of OSHA's resources to inappropriate initiatives, the result should be considered a necessary cost of holding the agency accountable. Finally, if OSHA establishes an effective priority-setting process, as recommended in Chapter 12, it should be better able to cope with deadlines and the resulting litigation.

Statutory Hammers

In addition to setting deadlines for agency action, Congress might consider the use of another legislative tool it has employed to hold EPA more accountable. In a series of statutory provisions metaphorically dubbed "hammers," Congress has, in addition to specifying a deadline for EPA action, provided that if EPA misses the deadline, the "hammer" falls and a regulatory result prescribed by the statute automatically goes into effect.[22] Since the hammer is designed to have a drastic impact on the regulated industry, regulatees have an interest in moving the rulemaking along. Congress could establish a "hammer" for OSHA by providing that if OSHA did not write a standard for a listed chemical before a deadline, the legally applicable PEL would automatically be the most stringent of a national consensus standard, a NIOSH recommendation for the chemical, or the most stringent PEL required by any state. The "hammer" technique allows Congress to press the regulated industry, but it also gives the agency an opportunity to write its own standard. In this manner, Congress can ensure both that a controversy is resolved and that it is resolved in an expeditious fashion. If the agency does not act, the legislative decision will take effect. If the agency does act, Congress will have forced the agency to resolve the matter expeditiously.

THE AGENCY-FORCING CONGRESSIONAL HEARING

Workers also turn to Congress for assistance when OSHA is a reluctant regulator. Members of Congress sympathetic to the plight of workers can attempt to prod OSHA through political pressure, or they can attempt to pass legislation to remedy the workers' problem. Of course, those who oppose OSHA's actions can also petition members of Congress friendly to their cause. At the behest of both groups, Congress has often intervened to influence OSHA to change its direction. A longtime OSHA observer reports that "[t]hrough its broad oversight authority and its power of the purse—backed, of course, by legislative power—Congress has consistently and insistently influenced the agency in its implementation of the statute. This influence has been exercised, like the power of court review, sometimes to goad the agency, sometimes to restrain the agency, and, on occasion, to do both."[23]

Congress has at its disposal a variety of techniques to influence OSHA and other regulatory agencies. The most typical forum for exerting political pressure is the legislative hearing in which committee members publicly criticize an agency's actions and attempt to obtain its commitment to change. Congressional committees can also bring political pressure to bear on agencies through committee reports, hearings on presidential nominations, and direct communications with administrators. Legislative solutions include appropriations designed to punish and reward agencies or to place restrictions on their activities, and direct legislation that overrules an agency decision or makes a decision the agency refuses to make.[24]

Congress has relied on several of these techniques in its oversight of OSHA.[25] Early in OSHA's history, for example, a House committee held a hearing to examine OSHA's delay in issuing a pesticide standard. Committee members pressed Assistant Secretary Guenther to explain why OSHA had not acted to protect farm workers from exposure to toxic pesticides.[26] OSHA soon after issued an emergency pesticide standard (that was later vacated after judicial review).[27] In the mid-1970s, Congress used an appropriation rider to stop OSHA's efforts to establish a field sanitation standard. The standard, which was proposed in 1976, resulted in a storm of criticism during a debate on an OSHA appropriation bill.[28] Congress then enacted a rider prohibiting the expenditure of funds to inspect and enforce OSHA standards on farms that employ ten or fewer workers. Soon thereafter, OSHA discontinued its efforts to write a field sanitation standard. According to one insider, "the timing [made] it clear that Congressional pressure was the major cause for the abandonment."[29] In 1989, seven OSHA appropriations riders were in effect, including the farm exemption rider originally enacted in 1976.[30]

In the 1980s, Congress made active use of hearings and other oversight techniques. At a 1981 hearing, Assistant Secretary Auchter was sharply questioned concerning changes he had proposed early in his administration.[31] Two years later, members of a House committee criticized OSHA for the manner in which it was developing the ethylene oxide standard, including the agency's off-the-record contacts with employer representatives.[32] During this period, House committees also investigated OMB's involvement in OSHA's rulemaking several times.[33] Congress, however, did not stop at holding hearings. It also passed legislation that ordered OSHA to promulgate a regulation protecting workers employed at hazardous work sites.[34]

Congressional Oversight and EDB

While Congress has sometimes influenced the direction that OSHA has taken, the agency has been able to ignore legislative pressure on other occasions. The congressional hearings that addressed OSHA's delay in regulating ethylene dibromide (EDB) illustrate the limits of the agency-forcing hearing. EDB, a fumigant for grains, fruits, and vegetables, is used to control insect infestations.

Studies indicating that EDB caused cancer in laboratory animals had been around for years when state officials began to detect EDB residues in food. Although these residues were not directly relevant to worker health, investigations soon revealed that some workers were being exposed to significantly higher levels of EDB than were consumers of food. Reacting to these studies, several unions, including the International Brotherhood of Teamsters, which represented workers who transported EDB-treated grain and fruit, petitioned OSHA in September 1981 to reduce workers' exposure to the chemical. OSHA promised the union "expedited treatment," but no action was forthcoming during the next two years. In September 1983, the Subcommittee on Labor Standards of the House Committee on Education and Labor held a widely publicized hearing concerning OSHA's delay.[35] The leadoff witness at the hearing was Thorne Auchter, who promised the committee that "[a] proposed rule revising OSHA's EDB standard will be completed shortly."[36] Auchter explained that the cause of the two-year delay was the necessity of hiring consultants to collect the data necessary to propose a regulation. Nevertheless, some committee members, including Representative George Miller, were openly critical of Auchter:

Mr. Miller: . . . So now we are 2 years later, and we still have workers covered by a standard that everybody accepts as inadequate.

Mr. Auchter: Is that a question?

Mr. Miller: No; that is the bottom line, Mr. Auchter.

Mr. Auchter: No; it is not.

Mr. Miller: Yes; it is. That is the bottom line.

Mr. Auchter: The bottom line is to have a responsible, enforceable, legal regulation. . . .

Mr. Miller: . . . [N]othing has happened. That is the bottom line. . . .[37]

Other committee members, however, defended the agency. Representative Ronald C. Packard stated, "It would appear to me, Mr. Chairman, that there has been more done in the last 2 years to move in the direction of a position than there had been in the previous 4 years."[38]

The hearing probably had the effect of prompting OSHA to issue a notice of proposed rulemaking in November 1983. Once again, however, the agency bogged down. In May 1984, the Subcommittee on Health and Safety of the House Committee on Education and Labor held a short hearing concerning the delay of the EDB standard. The only witness was Suzanne Kossan, an industrial hygienist for the Teamsters Union. The chairman of the committee, Representative Joseph M. Gaydos, indicated this sympathy and involvement: "I certainly agree with your concerns, you know, on the delays in OSHA standards setting procedure, and we have been complaining bitterly about it."[39] The second hearing had no lasting effect on OSHA. Moving much more rapidly than OSHA, EPA virtually mooted the question in 1984 by canceling most registrations of

EDB for use as a pesticide.[40] Although the 1983 hearings caused OSHA to issue a proposed rule, Congress was unable to sustain a level of political pressure sufficient to force the agency to promulgate a final rule in a timely manner.

The Limits of Legislative Oversight

Administrative agencies possess considerable freedom to ignore congressional attempts to control their action. They will generally succumb to congressional pressure only if there is insufficient countervailing political pressure to resist congressional control.[41] The outcome reflects an "interior process of policy-making" in which interest groups, members of Congress, the agency, and representatives of the president bargain over regulatory issues.[42] In OSHA's case, attempts to force the agency to be a more active regulator have engendered considerable opposition. What workers favor, employers will usually oppose. In the past, Congress has often been stymied by these disagreements. Moreover, congressional efforts to pressure OSHA are often resisted by the White House. Indeed, as Part II detailed, OSHA's go-slow approach during most of the Reagan administration came in response to White House directives. Because oversight normally yields few political advantages to committee members, it usually occurs as an ad hoc response to a highly publicized crisis. When oversight does occur, it is often an uncoordinated effort of several different committees.[43] One scholar found that "[m]ost administrative agencies must answer to at least six committees, three in the Senate, and three in the House."[44]

The EDB episode illustrates many of these limitations on legislative oversight. The first oversight hearings came in response to the extensive publicity concerning the dangers of EDB to consumers, and they were well covered by the press. Spurred by this attention, OSHA came to the hearings with a promise to start the rulemaking process within six months. At the hearing, OSHA was criticized by some committee members and unions, but it was defended by other members. Although a different committee revisited the matter one year later, there was no systematic follow-up by either committee, probably because committee members had moved on to other matters. Once congressional attention was diverted elsewhere, OSHA felt free to give EDB a low priority and to turn its attention to matters that it considered more pressing.

Congress's capacity for oversight of OSHA would be enhanced if it enacted statutory deadlines for the agency of the type recommended earlier in this chapter. If OSHA were required to set a deadline for each of its rulemaking initiatives, the deadlines would help put OSHA's productivity on the legislative agenda, increase congressional attention to protecting workers, and improve legislative oversight. If deadlines were not met, Congress could require the agency's management to explain what problems were impeding their progress. Deadlines would also assist OSHA in seeking an appropriate level of resources. In oversight and appropriation hearings, it would have the opportunity to demonstrate the level of resources necessary to meet applicable deadlines. Moreover, even if

OMB did not allow OSHA to seek additional resources, deadlines would be useful. If OSHA missed the deadlines and did not request additional resources, Congress would be alerted to the possibility that OMB budget oversight resulted in underfunding the agency.

The Future of Oversight

Workers will continue to seek judicial and congressional oversight of OSHA but, based on past experience, they can expect only limited success in forcing OSHA to regulate. Workers have had some success with agency-forcing lawsuits in pressuring OSHA to regulate, but only after substantial delays. They have had less success with the agency-forcing congressional hearings. The difference may be explained by the fact that the courts have the legal authority to order OSHA to expedite its decision-making process, and there is at least a threat that they will actually do so. By comparison, congressional committees must rely primarily on political pressure to persuade the agency to act. OSHA can resist these pressures as long as it can generate its own political support.

NOTES

1. *Farmworker Justice Fund, Inc.* v. *Brock*, 811 F.2d 613 (D.C. Cir. 1986).

2. 811 F.2d at 633.

3. 811 F.2d at 614.

4. 5 U.S.C. §§553(b), 555(e) (1988).

5. 5 U.S.C. § 706(1) (1988); *Sierra Club* v. *Thomas*, 828 F.2d 783, 795–96 (D.C. Cir. 1987).

6. In *United Steelworkers of America* v. *Rubber Manufacturers Association*, 783 F.2d 1117 (D.C. Cir. 1986), the court accepted an OSHA-proposed schedule to expedite the agency's decision on benzene. Similarly, in *International Union, UAW* v. *Donovan*, 756 F.2d 162 (D.C. Cir. 1985), the court ordered OSHA to conform to a timetable submitted by the agency to the court concerning formaldehyde. And in *Public Citizen Health Research Group* v. *Auchter*, 702 F.2d 1150 (D.C. Cir. 1983), the court ordered OSHA to promulgate a rule for ethylene oxide on an "expedited basis" and "as promptly as possible."

7. In *Farmworker Justice Fund, Inc.* v. *Brock*, 811 F.2d 613 (D.C. Cir. 1987), the court ordered OSHA to promulgate the field sanitation standard within 30 days. See also *National Congress of Hispanic Citizens* v. *Marshall*, 626 F.2d 882 (D.C. Cir. 1979); *National Congress of Hispanic Citizens* v. *Usery*, 554 F.2d 1196 (D.C. Cir. 1977). In *United Steelworkers of America* v. *Pendergrass*, 855 F.2d 108 (3rd Cir. 1988), the court ordered OSHA to promulgate a hazard communication standard for all industries immediately.

8. *Farmworker Justice Fund, Inc.* v. *Brock*, 811 F.2d 613 (D.C. Cir. 1987); *National Congress of Hispanic Citizens* v. *Marshall*, 626 F.2d 882 (D.C. Cir. 1979); *National Congress of Hispanic Citizens* v. *Usery*, 554 F.2d 1196 (D.C. Cir. 1977).

9. Sidney Shapiro and Robert Glicksman, "Congress, the Supreme Court, and the Quiet Revolution in Administrative Law," *Duke Law Journal*, 1988, 832.

10. *United Steelworkers of America* v. *Rubber Manufacturers Ass'n*, 783 F.2d 1117 (D.C. Cir. 1986).

11. 783 F.2d at 1120.

12. Margaret Seminario, Department of Occupational Safety, Health, and Social Security, AFL-CIO, telephone interview, 4 Nov. 1986.

13. Shapiro and Glicksman, "Congress," 839.

14. John Graham, "The Failure of Agency-Forcing: The Regulation of Airborne Carcinogens Under Section 112 of the Clean Air Act," *Duke Law Journal*, 1985, 123.

15. U.S. Congress, Senate Committee on Governmental Affairs, *Study on Federal Regulations—Delay in the Regulatory Process*, 95th Cong., 1st sess., S. Doc. 95–72, 1977, 147; Edward Tomlinson, "Report on the Experience of Various Agencies with Statutory Time Limits Applicable to Licensing or Clearance Functions and to Rulemaking," Administrative Conference of the United States, *Recommendations and Reports* (Washington, D.C.: United States Government Printing Office, 1978), 122; Alden Abbott, "The Case Against Federal Statutory and Judicial Deadlines: A Cost-Benefit Appraisal," *Administrative Law Review* 39 (1987): 182.

16. Shapiro and Glicksman, "Congress," 835–36.

17. Environmental and Energy Study Institute, *Statutory Deadlines in Environmental Legislation: Necessary but Need Improvement* (Washington, D.C.: The Institute, 1985), 48.

18. 29 U.S.C. § 655B(b)(1)-(2), 655(c), 655(c)(3) (1988).

19. Tomlinson, "Experience of Various Agencies," 201–02.

20. *National Resources Defense Council* v. *Train*, 510 F.2d 696, 712 (D.C. Cir. 1975).

21. ACUS Recommendation no. 78–3, "Time Limits on Agency Action," 1 C.F.R. 305.78–3 (1990).

22. Shapiro and Glicksman, "Congress," 839.

23. Benjamin Mintz, "Disorder and Early Sorrow in the OSHA Program," *American Industrial Hygiene Association Journal* 30 (1989): 99.

24. Richard Pierce and Sidney Shapiro, "Political and Judicial Review of Agency Action," *Texas Law Review* 59 (1981): 1198–99.

25. Mintz, "Disorder," A–99.

26. U.S. Congress, House Committee on Education and Labor, Subcommittee on Agricultural Labor, *Hearings on Farmworker Occupational Safety and Health*, 92nd Cong., 2d sess., 1972, 15–20.

27. 41 *Fed. Reg.* 15,576 (1976).

28. *Congressional Record*, 94th Cong., 2d sess., 1976, 122: 20,366–78.

29. Mintz, "Disorder," A–99.

30. Ibid., A–107, no. 95.

31. U.S. Congress, Senate Committee on Labor and Human Resources, Subcommittee on Investigations and General Oversight and Subcommittee on Labor, *Hearings on Oversight on the Administration of the Occupational Safety and Health Act*, 97th Cong., 1st sess., 1981, 79–82.

32. U.S. Congress, House Committee on Education and Labor, Subcommittee on Labor Standards, *Hearing on Use and Control of Ethylene Oxide*, 98th Cong., 1st sess., 1983, 222–64.

33. U.S. Congress, House Committee on Government Operations, *Office of Management and Budget Control of OSHA Rulemaking: Hearings*, 97th Cong., 2d sess., 1982;

House Committee on Government Operations, *Hearings on OMB Interference with OSHA Rulemaking*, 98th Cong., 1st sess., 1983.

34. 51 *Fed. Reg.* 45,654 (1986).

35. U.S. Congress, House Committee on Education and Labor, Subcommittee on Labor Standards, *Hearing on Use and Control of Fumigant Ethylene Dibromide*, 98th Cong., 1st sess., 1983.

36. Ibid., 8.

37. Ibid., 41.

38. Ibid., 42.

39. U.S. Congress, House Committee on Education and Labor, Subcommittee on Health and Safety, *Hearings on OSHA: General Oversight*, 98th Cong., 2d sess., 1984, 9.

40. 49 *Fed. Reg.* 17,144 (1984) (cancellation of EDB pesticide registration for grain); 49 *Fed. Reg.* 17,148 (1984) (ban on use of EDB in processed foods); 49 *Fed. Reg.* 14,182 (1984) (cancellation of EDB registration for citrus fruits and papaya for domestic consumption).

41. Pierce and Shapiro, "Political," 1200.

42. Theodore Lowi, *The End of Liberalism: Ideology, Policy and the Crisis of Public Authority*, 2d ed. (New York: Norton, 1979), 106.

43. Pierce and Shapiro, "Political," 1201–02.

44. James Freedman, *Crisis and Legitimacy: The Administrative Process and American Government* (Cambridge: Cambridge University Press, 1978), 67.

22

Empowering Workers: Enforcing the OSH Act

On October 23, 1989, several explosions rocked a Phillips Petroleum Co. plastics plant in Pasdena, Texas, leaving 23 workers dead and more than 100 injured. The blasts occurred when gas that was released during the polyethylene manufacturing process somehow ignited. OSHA had not conducted a comprehensive or "wall to wall" inspection of the plant since 1975, although the agency had cited Phillips for four "serious" safety violations at the plant after 1984.[1] A later OSHA investigation discovered that a number of internal audits conducted by Phillips's own safety personnel and by outside consultants had identified unsafe conditions, but these audits "had been largely ignored."[2]

OSHA and union officials had different versions of how OSHA had failed to prevent the Phillips tragedy. OSHA officials explained that the agency had targeted those industries with the highest injury rates for full-blown inspections and that, using those criteria, the chemical industry's accident rate was well below those of other industries. These officials maintained that the agency needed more resources to do a better job of discovering dangerous situations like those at the Phillips plant.[3] Union officials countered that increasing OSHA's budget alone cannot adequately guarantee effective enforcement of the agency's standards. A representative of the textile workers union noted, "When federal OSHA does all of 15 textile inspections in the state of Alabama in 1988, I wouldn't say that a 10 percent increase in their budget is going to make a helluva difference."[4]

The Phillips accident illustrates that empowering workers to force OSHA to promulgate regulations in a more timely manner will have little impact if OSHA is unwilling to enforce those standards. Indeed, weak enforcement was a hallmark of most of the Reagan years. But the Phillips accident also demonstrates that lack of enforcement is not entirely a matter of OSHA's weak will. As Chapter

14 discussed, OSHA's enforcement staff will never be large enough to inspect more than a fraction of the country's workplaces every year. As a result, an employer's chances of being inspected remain relatively low.

In the final analysis, worker participation is necessary to keep alive the OSH Act's promise of safe employment and places of employment.[5] This chapter considers how workers can be empowered to assist in enforcing OSHA's regulations. It considers both situations where OSHA is a reluctant cop and situations where OSHA lacks the resources to be an aggressive cop. Workers can play a role in improving the enforcement of health and safety standards in both circumstances if they are entitled to walk-around pay, to participate in OSHA's settlement negotiations, and to enforce the OSH Act through a private enforcement action.

WALK-AROUND PAY

The OSH Act allows employees to participate in OSHA enforcement by accompanying the inspector as he walks around the employer's plant searching for possible violations, but it does not require employers to compensate employees for the time during which they exercise this "walk-around" right.[6] In 1975, a court affirmed OSHA's initial position that walk-around time was not compensable, because the employer derived no benefit from the employee's "services."[7] One of Assistant Secretary Bingham's first official acts, however, was to reverse the walk-around policy by holding that an employer's refusal to pay employees for walk-around time constituted discrimination under Section 11(c) of the OSH Act. When the U.S. Chamber of Commerce challenged this policy change, the District of Columbia Circuit in 1980 held that OSHA could not effect it without engaging in notice and comment rulemaking under the Administrative Procedure Act.[8] OSHA responded to the remand in one of the "midnight regulations" that President Reagan suspended, and the agency never revived it. Since the old policy remains in effect, workers who exercise their right to observe OSHA inspections are subject to pay reductions.

Not surprisingly, few workers are willing to take a cut in pay just to make sure that the OSHA inspector is doing the job right. Congress could easily empower workers to play this very limited role in OSHA enforcement by amending the OSH Act to clarify the right of workers to walk-around pay. Otherwise the right to participate in OSHA inspections is little more than an empty gesture.

EMPLOYEE PARTICIPATION IN OSHA SETTLEMENTS

When an OSHA inspector issues a citation against an employer, OSHA procedures allow the employer to attend an informal "settlement conference" with the inspector's supervisor or another regional official to discuss the citation and the terms and conditions under which OSHA would be willing to withdraw the citation prior to the employer's filing a notice of contest.[9] After a notice of contest is filed, attorneys from the Solicitor of Labor's Office may meet informally with the employer and attempt to reach a settlement agreement.[10] Employees fear that if they cannot participate in these informal settlement conferences, upper-level OSHA officials will "give away the store."[11] The OSH Act is silent on this question, but it does give employees the limited right to contest a citation if they believe that "the period of time fixed in the citation for the abatement of the violation" is unreasonable.[12] Otherwise, the secretary's discretion to withdraw a citation as a result of settlement negotiations is unreviewable.[13]

As Chapter 10 pointed out, informal settlements are highly desirable from the agency's point of view. According to former Assistant Secretary Pendergrass:

Settlement of cases saves the agency time, money, and other resources that would otherwise be consumed in litigation. Those resources can be redirected to preventative, rather than remedial, activities. Of equal, if not greater importance, is that settlements avoid the delays and uncertainties of litigation and thus bring about more quickly and more surely the abatement of workplace hazards. Simply stated, the accomplishment of OSHA's mission depends in large part on the existence and utilization of an efficient settlement mechanism.[14]

Pendergrass cited the fact that fewer than 5 percent of all OSHA citations were appealed to the Occupational Safety and Health Review Commission (OSHRC) during the Reagan administration as proof that the agency's settlement policy was working, but it could just as easily be cited as evidence that OSHA's leadership was giving away the store.

OSHA recognizes that employees have a legitimate interest in the outcome of settlement negotiations, and it believes that they can often contribute useful information and insights to the settlement process.[15] OSHA's settlement regulations therefore allow employees and their representatives to participate in informal settlement negotiations, but leave the matter entirely to the discretion of the OSHA official or Solicitor's Office attorney conducting the negotiations.[16]

None of the strong arguments favoring settlements are diminished in the least by a general rule allowing employee representatives to attend settlement negotiations. Excluding employee representatives gives the strong impression that the agency has something to hide. If, as Pendergrass maintained, the settlement conferences are ultimately in the best interest of workers because they result in more rapid correction of serious health and safety problems, then it is hard to understand why the beneficiaries should be excluded. As Justice Brandeis observed, "Sunshine is the best disinfectant."[17] Congress should amend the OSH Act to give employees and their representatives the unqualified right to observe settlement negotiations.[18]

Congress could empower workers still further if it gave them genuine participatory rights. While the right to observe settlement conferences should prevent fraud and corruption, and should ensure that OSHA has good reasons for withdrawing citations, giving the employees and their representatives full partici-patory rights would help ensure that settlements are not too lenient. The fact that OSHA settles 95 percent of its cases (as opposed to 70 percent during the Bingham years) may suggest that it is being too generous with employers who threaten to litigate. The only way to provide employees with full participatory rights is to allow them to object to the terms of the settlement. For example, employees could be given the power to persuade an administrative law judge (ALJ) that the settlement terms were too lenient and to secure an order that the enforcement proceedings must continue.

Employes will no doubt respond that enforcement of governmental standards is properly a governmental function, and outsiders should not be allowed to direct the use of scarce governmental resources.[19] Under the approach suggested here, however, the employees would not have an absolute veto power over settlements; they would still have to persuade a neutral governmental official (the ALJ) that the case warranted prosecution. The power would exist only in instances in which the agency had already determined initially that the case was worth prosecuting.

OSHA knows that it cannot possibly litigate every citation (or even a substantial number of citations) "to the hilt." The employers know this, and they can use the threat to fight a citation "tooth and nail" to exact large concessions. Giving employees the power to object to settlements empowers them to exert necessary leverage in the opposite direction. This could make employers less willing to participate in the settlement process, and it would no doubt result in more contested cases going to trial. This in turn could mean that hazardous conditions are not as rapidly corrected and that fewer fines are ultimately issued. Employees are aware of this, and to the extent that objecting is not in their own best interests, they presumably will decline to do so.

As with all of the worker empowerment vehicles addressed in this and Chapter 23, there is a risk that employees or their representatives will abuse the power to contest settlements to achieve goals (such as increased wages or greater leverage in collective bargaining negotiations) unrelated to health and safety. But that risk is considerably reduced by the fact that an independent entity (the ALJ) has the final say after a "paper hearing" on whether the settlement should be accepted. Thus, it will be very difficult for employees to abuse this relatively modest power.

DEPUTIZING WORKERS

By universal agreement, OSHA's inspectorate is pitifully small when measured against the task of inspecting all of the workplaces subject to OSHA's jurisdiction. With today's staff, a typical employer can expect to be the subject of an OSHA inspection only extremely rarely in the absence of a complaint or serious accident. Moreover, when the OSHA inspector finally shows up at the door, the employer can refuse him or her entrance unless he or she has an administrative warrant issued pursuant to some "neutral" selection process,[20] and, unless there is an obviously dangerous situation at the workplace, such as an accident, the employer can usually delay the inspection by a few days if it objects to the warrant. Horror stories from the meat-packing and construction industries during the late 1980s attest to the inadequacy of OSHA's current enforcement efforts. Although it is clear that substantial resources should be infused into OSHA's enforcement effort, the ultimate solution to the problem of spotty and superficial enforcement may be to empower workers to enforce the law without OSHA's help.

In the early 1970s, Congress recognized that the Environmental Protection Agency's inspectorate would never be up to the task of enforcing the environmental laws for the hundreds of thousands of sources of air and water pollution. It therefore included "citizen enforcement" provisions in all but one of the major environmental statutes.[21] These provisions generally allow any affected citizen to sue in a federal district court to enforce environmental permits and emissions limitations.[22] The citizen must provide 60 days' advance notice to give the agency an opportunity to assume the burden of the enforcement litigation, but if the government does not act within that time period, the citizen may control the litigation. Some citizen suit provisions allow private citizens to ask the court for an injunction requiring the source to come into compliance by a date certain, and others allow citizens to sue for monetary penalties. All such provisions allow successful citizens to recover their attorney fees and other litigation costs.[23]

Although the citizen enforcement provisions were little used in EPA's early days, they came dramatically to life during the Reagan administration when EPA began to dismantle its enforcement apparatus. Companies that believed they were immune from EPA prosecution soon found themselves targets of citizen suits demanding millions of dollars in fines. The courts have been receptive to these suits, often ordering major changes in polluting operations and assessing heavy penalties.

Congress could easily draw upon the environmental model to empower workers to enforce OSHA standards in court if OSHA fails to do so. Congress could amend the OSH Act to provide that any worker could enforce occupational safety and health standards and/or the General Duty Clause, in OSHRC (as is now required of OSHA) or directly in a federal court. Congress could require a 60-day notice to give OSHA an opportunity to bring and diligently prosecute the action, in which case the employee would be entitled to intervene as a matter of right. Employees could be allowed to sue for statutory penalties and injunctive relief requiring that continuing hazards be reduced or eliminated.

Amending the OSH Act to allow workers to enforce OSHA standards has several advantages. First, it gives workers some control over their own destinies. They will no longer be forced to rely upon the limited resources and commitment of the federal bureaucracy for protection. Although there is little empirical evidence addressing the efficacy of citizen enforcement,[24] it is likely that workers would be in a better position to assess the need for enforcement than the OSHA inspectorate, particularly in the realm of safety standards, where noncompliance is easily disguised.

Second, the threat of worker enforcement may give OSHA the incentive it needs to pursue especially important or precedent-setting cases, an option that it would have during the 60-day notice period.[25] OSHA already operatès on the assumption that enforcement of conditions identified by employee complaints has a high priority. The 60-day notice filings would identify for OSHA those alleged violations that are of most concern to the primary beneficiaries of its standards.

Third, worker enforcement has the potential to supplement substantially the limited resources that state and federal governments devote to OSHA enforcement activities. "Privatizing" OSHA enforcement by empowering workers to enforce the OSH Act can help close the "gap between promise and performance."[26] This function may be especially important in times in which federal resources are dwindling and the beneficiaries of regulation are unconvinced of OSHA's commitment to enforcing the statute.

Finally, deputizing workers may be the only way to avoid agency "captivity" at the local level. Like the right to challenge settlements, worker enforcement may be a necessary counterweight to the substantial leverage that the threat to litigate gives to employers.[27] Assuming that OSHA standards do in fact protect workers from significant risks and are feasible, there should be no legitimate reason for an employer to be in violation of an OSHA standard. The added likelihood of detection and prosecution of violations should give employers an added incentive to comply with the law.[28]

Empowering workers to enforce OSHA standards poses several significant implementation problems, but careful efforts to weave employee enforcement into the existing system should overcome the most serious disadvantages. One obvious disadvantage is the potential for overburdening OSHRC and the courts with trivial cases that do not warrant judicial attention. To some extent this potential is reduced by the natural incentive that employees and their representatives will have to save their own limited resources for really important violations.[29] The experience under the environmental statutes demonstrates that the expense of bringing an enforcement action deters frivolous actions, even by "ideological plaintiffs," and the advent of substantial citizen enforcement litigation in the early 1980s did not put a noticeable strain on the judicial system.

Worker enforcement could be counterproductive to the extent that it provoked resentment among OSHA inspectors who viewed it as an invasion of their bureaucratic turf.[30] Some inspectors might resent the unspoken implication that they were not performing adequately. Most OSHA inspectors are sufficiently committed to the concept of a safe workplace, however, that they are not likely to let such petty considerations keep them from doing their jobs. The agency would always have the power to intervene in an ongoing suit or, if it acted within 60 days, to seize control of any worker enforcement initiative. In the environmental area, at least, "the agency still retains a dominant position in defining and implementing enforcement policy."[31] No doubt the agency will remain dominant in the workplace context as well. In any event, if citizen suits do in fact reduce OSHA morale, that may be the price that has to be paid to achieve a more universal enforcement effort.

Work enforcement is built upon the assumption that all OSHA standards are necessary to reduce risks and are feasible in every workplace to which they apply. This assumption was undoubtedly false in the case of many OSHA "consensus" standards that were never tested by notice and comment rulemaking. As Chapter 3 discussed, OSHA was brutalized in the press during the early 1970s when a few overly meticulous inspectors prosecuted violations of some absurd consensus standards. Although the agency launched an ambitious project during the Bingham years to get rid of these "nitpicking" standards, it is very difficult to write a standard with sufficient detail and nuance to be applicable to every conceivable workplace. Empowering workers to enforce OSHA standards to some extent robs the agency of the enforcement discretion that is sometimes critical to the successful implementation of a generic standard.

Nevertheless, a number of vehicles exist for reintroducing discretion into the enforcement picture. The 60-day notice provision gives the agency the unqualified right to regain control over the litigation while allowing workers to persuade the judge that the agency has abused its enforcement discretion. Even when the agency does not take over the litigation, it can intervene and make its views known to the judge. The judges themselves have the power to adjust the severity of any penalty to the magnitude of the risk actually posed by the employer's conduct. Finally, to eliminate the possibility of irrational attempts to enforce the unexamined consensus standards, Congress could limit worker enforcement actions to health and safety standards promulgated through full notice and comment procedures. This measure, however, would preclude worker attempts to enforce the General Duty Clause.

Even with these limitations, a worker enforcement provision will probably make the agency even more careful about writing precise standards that could not be misinterpreted or abused by overzealous workers or worker representatives. Ironically, this might have the effect of slowing OSHA's rulemaking pace, an obviously undesirable result. Yet there is surprisingly little evidence that the threat of citizen enforcement actions by overly enthusiastic environmental groups has had a negative impact on EPA's standard-setting pace, although it may have had some effect on the specificity with which permitters write conditions in EPA-required permits. Employees, in any event, should be aware of this detrimental impact of abusive enforcement efforts and should avoid bringing nit-picking actions that will have no real effect on workplace safety and health.

When enforcement is managed by a single agency, the agency can attempt to ensure consistency in the application of policies. Worker enforcement actions can disrupt this consistency and lead to unfairness in enforcement results.[32] The potential for inconsistency and unfairness can be reduced by OSHA's liberal use

of the 60-day notice requirement to intervene or take over worker-initiated litigation. Yet this response is limited by OSHA's general lack of enforcement
resources. To the extent that the agency is using its resources to monitor em-
ployee-filed cases, it cannot use them to file its own actions.[33] The solution also
rests on the ambitious assumption that OSHA headquarters has the ability to
identify the important issues in a worker enforcement action, communicate its
national policy to its regional offices, and initiate its own action within 60 days.[34]

As might be predicted, coordination between EPA and citizen suits has been
difficult to achieve in the environmental area. Boyer and Miedinger observe,
"As a practical matter [the 60-day notice] provisions have been largely ineffectual
in coordinating public and private enforcement. They have instead provided a
context within which a variety of informal coordination mechanisms and activities
have evolved."[35] Boyer and Miedinger suggest that one solution to the inconsistency problem is for the agency to promulgate or codify an enforcement policy
and require private enforcers to follow that policy.[36] But enforcement policies
are subject to the same rigidities that afflict generic standards, and they have the
perverse effect of revealing to potential violators the kinds of conduct that the
agency regards as of lesser importance, thereby undermining the deterrent effect
of the threat of prosecution.

While the difficulties of coordination should not be ignored, the potential for
inconsistency is present, in any event, in OSHA's decentralized enforcement
system, in which most states have been delegated primary enforcement authority.
The added potential for inconsistency resulting from worker enforcement suits
is not likely to be great. Moreover, the Administrative Conference of the United
States has made recommendations for achieving better coordination between
citizens and agency enforcement that, if followed by OSHA, should minimize
coordination difficulties.[37]

Another disadvantage of worker enforcement actions is their potential to disrupt stable relationships between the government and regulatees.[38] This should
not be an insurmountable problem in the workplace context, however, because
workers and employers also come into the arrangement with a preexisting stable
relationship. Moreover, to the extent that the relationship between employers
and OSHA has had the effect of reducing compliance with OSHA standards,
the relationship (which might border on captivity) probably *should* be
destabilized.

Finally, deputizing workers bears the potential for abuse. Unscrupulous workers or unions could use the threat of bringing an enforcement action to extract
concessions unrelated to workplace safety from employers. If violations of OSHA
standards are putting workers at risk, agreeing to waive enforcement for some
other concession would constitute a gross abuse of trust on the part of a union,
but the possibility cannot be ignored. There are, however, several possible
answers to this serious objection to worker enforcement. First, although the same
potential exists in the environmental area, there is little evidence that "bounty
hunters" are extorting concessions out of companies who violate permit limitations. Second, the OSHRC and the courts can effectively shield against abuse

by rejecting actions that allege trivial violations that do not involve serious health risks. In the environmental area, "courts have generally been able to control innovative litigants' attempts to use citizen suits for purposes not intended by Congress . . ."[39] Finally, Congress could address the problem directly by enacting sanctions against the threat of using a worker enforcement action for purposes unrelated to worker health or safety.

The concept of worker enforcement has been forcefully resisted by employers and their trade associations. They challenge the legitimacy of turning an uneducated worker into an instant "cop with a mission." Privatizing enforcement, employers argue, allows worker enforcers to "bypass the existing structures of limited authority and political accountability that confine the powers of the regulatory state."[40] Many employers already question the legitimacy of OSHA's existing intrusions into what they regard as the proper realm of employer autonomy, and the thought of empowering workers to seek judicial orders and fines is deeply antithetical to the authoritarian vision of the employment relationship that is shared by most employers in the United States and underlies the "employment at will" doctrine that is still putatively in effect in most states.[41]

The citizen suit idea has achieved a degree of legitimacy in the area of environmental enforcement that suggests its staying power. But in that context, the illegitimacy of polluting another's property had long been established and protected (albeit ineffectively) by the common law of nuisance. On the other hand, the notion of empowering a worker to tell an employer how to arrange the workplace runs against the grain of a capitalist culture with a common law tradition of placing the blame for workplace disease and injury on the workers. Giving workers the right to enforce OSHA standards will reflect a fundamental shift in public attitudes toward work in modern America. It will require a rather thoroughgoing rejection of the concept of the boss as a master and an acceptance of the concept of the workplace as a field of common endeavor where both employer and employee have rights and responsibilities.

We may not yet have achieved that degree of consensus necessary to secure the enactment of legislation empowering workers to enforce the OSH Act. If not, it may be adequate merely to beef up OSHA and state enforcement efforts and, as Chapter 23 relates, protect workers who file complaints. But the time may be ripe to test the political waters. The principle that no one (not even the boss) is above the law is a powerful one in this society. When the human toll of inadequate OSHA enforcement becomes immediately visible on nightly television, it may be difficult for employers and their representatives to argue that all is well in the workplace. Worker enforcement actions can never become a complete substitute for effective state and federal enforcement, but they can be an important adjunct to OSHA's own efforts.

NOTES

1. Kirk Victor, "OSHA's Turnabout," *National Journal* 21 (25 Nov. 1989): 2892.
2. *BNA Occupational Safety and Health Reporter* 19 (4 May 1990): 150, 151.

3. Ibid.

4. Ibid.

5. Charles Noble, *Liberalism at Work: The Rise and Fall of OSHA* (Philadelphia: Temple University Press, 1986).

6. Occupational Safety and Health Act § 8(e), 29 U.S.C. § 657(e) (1988); Mark Rothstein, *Occupational Safety and Health Law*, 3rd ed. (St. Paul, Minn.: West Publishing, 1990), §§ 241–42.

7. *Leone* v. *Mobil Oil Corp.*, 523 F.2d 1153 (D.C. Cir. 1975).

8. *Chamber of Commerce of the U.S.* v. *OSHA* 636 F.2d 464 (D.C. Cir. 1980); Benjamin W. Mintz, "Occupational Safety and Health: The Federal Regulatory Program—A History," *Fundamentals of Industrial Hygiene*, 3rd ed., ed. Barbara A. Plog (Washington, D.C.: National Safety Council 1988), 697, 711.

9. 29 C.F.R. § 1903.19 (1991).

10. U.S. Congress, House Committee on Education and Labor, Subcommittee on Health and Safety, *OSHA Oversight: Hearings on Fire Brigade Standard and Employer/Employee Roles in Settlement Conferences*. 100th Cong., 2d sess., Serial no. 100–82, 1988, 207 (hereafter cited as House, *OSHA Oversight on Settlement Conferences*) (testimony of John Pendergrass, assistant secretary for occupational safety and health).

11. Thomas E. Quigley, "Employee Involvement in the OSHA Settlement Process," *Detroit College of Law Review* 3 (1990): 579.

12. Occupational Safety and Health Act § 10(c), 29 U.S.C. § 659(c) (1988).

13. *Cuyahoga Valley Ry. Co.* v. *United Transportation Union*, 476 U.S. 3 (1985).

14. House, *OSHA Oversight on Settlement Conferences*, 206.

15. Ibid., 208.

16. 29 C.F.R. § 1903.19 (1991).

17. See *United States* v. *Hubbard*, 650 F.2d 293, 330 (1980).

18. See Sy Holzmann, "The Occupational Safety and Health Act: Is It Time for Change?" *Northern Kentucky Law Review* 17 (1989): 177, 188.

19. U.S. Congress, House Committee on Education and Labor, Subcommittee on Labor-Management Relations, *Hearings on H.R. 3368, Whistleblower Protection Act*, 101st Cong., 1st Sess., 1989, 172.

20. *Marshall* v. *Barlow's, Inc.*, 436 U.S. 307 (1978).

21. Jeannette L. Austin, "The Rise of Citizen-Suit Enforcement in Environmental Law: Reconciling Private and Public Attorneys General," *Northwestern University Law Review* 81 (1987): 227, no. 47.

22. Clean Air Act § 304, 42 U.S.C.A. § 7604 (West. Supp. 1991); Clean Water Act § 505, 33 U.S.C. § 1365 (1988).

23. 42 U.S.C.A. § 7604(d) (West Supp. 1991); 33 U.S.C. § 1365(d) (1988).

24. Barry Boyer and Errol Miedinger, "Privatizing Regulatory Enforcement . . . ," *Buffalo Law Review* 34 (1985): 833.

25. Ibid., 843.

26. Ibid., 838.

27. Ibid., 843.

28. Austin, "Rise," 247.

29. Ibid., 256.

30. Boyer and Miedinger, "Privatizing," 841.

31. Ibid., 958.

32. Austin, "Rise," 236; Boyer and Miedinger, "Privatizing," 896.

33. Austin, "Rise," 236.

34. Boyer and Miedinger, "Privatizing," 897–98.

35. Ibid.

36. Ibid., 896.

37. Administrative Conference of the United States," Coordination of Public and Private Enforcement of Environmental Laws," Recommendation no. 85–3 (1985), 1 C.F.R. § 305.85–3 (1991).

38. Boyer and Miedinger, "Privatizing," 893–94; Austin, "Rise," 258–59.

39. Boyer and Miedinger, "Privatizing," 838–40.

40. Ibid., 842.

41. Ray Marshall, *Unheard Voices: Labor and Economic Policy in a Competitive World* (New York: Basic Books, 1987), 94.

23

Empowering Workers: Rethinking Employment Relationships

It's not surprising that the poultry industry doesn't want anyone to know what is happening at the slaughter plants. That is because their only law on the job is to keep the line moving as fast as possible. Nothing else is tolerated. . . . The women in the plants describe the conditions as modern slavery. You do what you're told. . . . When the workers can't work anymore, they are simply told that they're fired. The usual explanation is you're not needed anymore. There's not corrective action for the dangerous conditions that cause these injuries. It's only to throw away the workers once they're used up. . . . It's natural to ask why they would take this kind of abuse. . . . It's because there is no other choice. There aren't other jobs that are available. For almost all workers, the result is that they keep their mouth shut and do what they're told.[1]

Donna Bazemore, who gave the above testimony, has recognized an industrial fact of life: the employment relationship defines workers' capacity to act in their own behalf. Since most employees may be fired for any reason, or no reason at all, a worker who brings a citizen's suit, or otherwise engages in activities to spur OSHA enforcement, can expect a swift pink slip. Thus, it is not enough to arm workers with the right to petition for new standards and to sue to enforce those standards if they are not protected from employer retaliation. Likewise, providing greater information to workers through the hazard communication standard, a renewed New Directions program, and even the enactment of the proposed High Risk Occupational Disease Notification Act[2]—will have little practical impact if workers' right to know is not accompanied by a correlative right to act. An effective program of empowering workers requires rethinking the traditional legal arrangements that define how employment works in this country.

This chapter considers two ways in which the relationship of workers and management can be restructured to establish rights through which workers can protect themselves. First, we propose that the "right to act" protection under the OSH Act should be extended and strengthened to prevent employers from firing workers who contact OSHA or otherwise seek the benefits of the protections of the OSH Act. Second, we propose that Congress mandate the use of joint labor-management committees empowered to make decisions concerning workplace safety and health. These committees allow workers to become part of the decision-making process that affects their health and safety. Both reforms would substantially alter the current labor market. Although workers may currently lack sufficient political power to implement these proposals, they suggest a future direction that could make the right to a healthful and safe workplace a reality.

EMPLOYMENT AT WILL AND THE NATIONAL LABOR RELATIONS ACT

The starting point for any discussion of the right to act is the "employment at will" doctrine that has dominated the American workplace since the nineteenth century.[3] This doctrine recognizes the right of one person to employ another for an agreed-upon wage and the right of the employee to terminate that arrangement pursuant to the terms and conditions of the agreement, but it recognizes no further rights on the part of the employee. The employer may terminate the employment relationship for any reason not forbidden by the employment contract. The doctrine has had remarkable staying power despite changes in social and technological conditions that have rendered most of its philosophical underpinnings obsolete.

The "employment at will" doctrine is now riddled with legislative exceptions, the most prominent of which are the National Labor Relations Act, which establishes numerous employee rights related to collective bargaining, and Title VII of the Civil Rights Act of 1964, which prohibits unfair employment practices based on race, sex, religion, or national origin. Beginning in the 1940s, state common law courts also began to whittle away at the doctrine, and the Constitution now entitles some public employees to due process before being fired.[4] Drawing upon the public employee cases, some state courts are beginning to find that private employees with satisfactory records have an implied right not to be terminated without a good reason.[5] Yet the fact that approximately 80 percent of the work force in 1990 lacked the right to demand that employers have "just cause" to terminate the employment relationship makes the United States "the last major industrial democracy that has not heeded the call of the International Labor Organization for unjust dismissal legislation."[6]

Worker representatives reasonably maintain that an employee should have a right to refuse unduly dangerous work assignments without fear of retaliation. Employees currently have a limited right to act under the National Labor Relations Act (NLRA) and the Labor Management Relations Act (LMRA).[7] The NLRA gives employees the right to engage in "concerted" work refusals to protest unsafe workplaces or work practices.[8] The refusal, however, must be in good faith, and it may not be unreasonable.[9] Moreover, a collective bargaining agreement may by its own terms protect workers who leave the job for safety related reasons.[10] But such contractual provisions are the exception rather than the rule, and they are in force only in unionized workplaces. Since only about 19 percent of the work force is unionized,[11] Section 7 of the NLRA affords only a very limited right to act.

Perhaps the most significant limitation of the NLRA is its requirement that the exercise of the right to act be done collectively. For example, in *Myers Industry Inc.*,[12] a truck driver discovered that his truck did not meet state safety requirements when he was involved in a wreck in Tennessee. After his employer told him to drive the truck back to Michigan anyway, he refused and notified the Tennessee police. The police issued a citation and ordered the truck impounded until it was fixed (it was later sold for scrap). When the employee returned home, he was fired for informing the police. The National Labor Relations Board held that since the employee acted on his own and since there was no collective bargaining agreement, he was not engaged in "concerted activity" and therefore was not subject to the protections of the NLRA. The Board rejected the "presumed consent doctrine," under which it would be presumed that other employees would consent to a single employee's efforts to provide a safer workplace.[13]

Section 502 of the LMRA provides that the "quitting of labor by an employee . . . in good faith because of abnormally dangerous conditions . . . [shall not] be deemed a strike."[14] Although the matter is still unsettled, this provision appears to protect a single employee not acting in concert when there is a no-strike obligation in his or her collective bargaining contract.[15] It offers no protection whatsoever to a nonunionized employee. Moreover, under a 1974 Supreme Court holding, the unionized employee must present "ascertainable objective evidence supporting its conclusion that abnormally dangerous conditions exist."[16] The use of the word "abnormal" makes this test very difficult to meet. Even severe conditions that violate OSHA standards may arguably be "normal" for the job.[17]

THE RIGHT TO ACT UNDER THE OSH ACT

The OSH Act does not specifically address the question of whether an employee has a right to refuse unsafe employment, but (as we shall discuss in more detail later in this chapter) Section 11(c) of the Act prohibits an employer from taking any adverse action against an employee for exercising any rights provided by the statute. In 1973, OSHA promulgated a regulation that gives an employee the right to refuse work assignments involving dangerous conditions that pose a serious risk of death or injury.[18] The Supreme Court upheld the regulation in *Whirlpool Corp.* v. *Marshall*,[19] a case in which employees were required to climb out on a suspended wire-mesh screen that was subject to tearing. After one man died from a fall through the screen, OSHA inspected the facility and issued an order forbidding employees to step on the screen. When two maintenance workers refused a direct order to work on the screen, they were officially reprimanded. The Court held that OSHA was authorized to file a complaint under Section 11(c) for the violation of the "right to act" regulation. The Court noted that even though the OSH Act provided a specific remedy (an employee-requested OSHA inspection), there could be times when an employee justifiably believed that this process would not be sufficiently protective. This would occur when (1) the employee reasonably believed the working conditions posed an imminent danger of death or serious bodily injury, and (2) the employee believed there was insufficient time or opportunity to seek redress from the employer or to inform OSHA.

If limited to *Whirlpool*-like situations, the OSH Act's right to act could be a very narrow one. The safety risk at issue in that case was obvious and substantial; a fellow employee had recently died. OSHA had already been to the plant, and the employer's orders to the complaining employees constituted a blatant violation of a direct order from OSHA. The employees could easily have concluded that an OSHA complaint would not reduce the risk posed by the insubstantial wire screen. Surprisingly few cases have been decided after *Whirlpool*, a fact that is probably attributable in part to the Reagan administration's reluctance to sue employers on behalf of discharged workers. Thus, it is not at all clear, for example, that an employee may refuse work that involves chronic exposure to a carcinogenic chemical that is not acutely toxic.[20] Presumably, the time available to deal with the problem through normal enforcement channels would deprive the employees of any legitimate reason immediately to walk off the job. If employers are able to confine the OSHA "right to act" regulation to situations where a recalcitrant employer in blatant violation of an OSHA directive orders employees to work under extremely risky conditions and there is no opportunity to seek alternative relief, then few employees will be willing to take the risk of losing their jobs in the hope of prevailing in an action under the regulation.

Expanding the Right to Act

There are many good reasons for expanding the right to act beyond its current narrow confines. Giving workers the right to refuse hazardous work without retaliation would in a fundamental way empower them to take control over their own lives in the essential area of safety and health. It would also adjust the bargaining positions of the parties to a more equitable level. The overall result should be workplaces that are considerably safer than in the past.

Most employers are predictably opposed to expanding the right to act.[21] At the same time that it empowers workers, it takes power away from the boss. Mark D. Cowan, deputy assistant secretary of labor for OSHA during the Auchter years, predicted that full implementation of the right to act would bring about a "fundamental rearranging of our entire American business."[22] The critical question is whether such a reordering is necessarily a bad thing. It would admittedly represent a rejection of the authoritarian premises underlying the "employment at will'' doctrine, but that may be necessary for a properly functioning twenty-first-century workplace.

Like empowering workers to enforce OSHA standards, the right to act bears the potential for abuse. A critically situated employee could refuse to work for arbitrary reasons unrelated to health and safety, and thereby disrupt the entire workplace. Wildcat strikes could be justified after the fact as concerted refusals to do hazardous work. Yet the employees who currently possess a limited right to act apparently are not disruptive. More important, employers are not powerless to persuade the court (or administrative decision maker) that the right is being abused in particular cases.

A Modest Proposal

The highly fragmented existing statutory regime for protecting the employee's right to act places the burden of justification on the employee. Just as the burden of demonstrating the existence of a ''significant risk'' has hampered OSHA's efforts to write standards, it is difficult for workers to prove that a work situation was ''abnormally dangerous'' and that they were ''reasonable'' in concluding that the hazards were real and substantial. The solution again lies in a burden-shifting device. The employee should have an initial burden of demonstrating that adverse employment action was taken as a result of a position that the employee took with respect to workplace conditions that either violated an OSHA standard or gave rise to a reasonable apprehension of serious injury. The employee should also have the burden of showing that he or she gave the employer a reasonable opportunity to correct the problem or reasonably believed that the employer would not correct the problem even if informed. The test for whether the employee's position was justified should be an objective one, but the burden should be on the employer to demonstrate that the employee's conduct was ''unreasonable in the circumstances'' or that the primary motivating factor behind the employee's action was not a reasonable belief that the workplace conditions were unsafe. This last requirement appears to exist under current interpretations of Section 11(c).[23] But if the employee demonstrates that the workplace condition violated an OSHA standard, the fact that the employee knew about the condition at the time of employment or that the employee willingly encountered the risk in the past should not be a defense.

PROTECTING WORKERS FROM RETALIATION

All of the foregoing worker rights, in addition to the essential right to lodge a complaint with OSHA, critically depend upon the effectiveness of the protections afforded against employer retaliation. Without immunity from employer discrimination based on the exercise of protected rights, employees who value their jobs will ''keep their mouths shut and do what they are told,'' and occupational safety and health will thereby suffer. It is, unfortunately, virtually impossible to detect and rectify all of the subtle retributive techniques that can, as a practical matter, make the employment relationship difficult or even impossible for the worker. But it is possible at least to award back pay to the worker who is fired or less overtly eased out of a job. Section 11(c) of the OSH Act prohibits an employer from discriminating against any employee because that employee exercised any right afforded by the Act.[24] Congress regarded Section 11(c) as an essential inducement for employees to participate in the enforcement of OSHA standards and in the general maintenance of a safe workplace.

Unfortunately, the promise of Section 11(c) is rarely realized in practice. To a large extent, its failure is OSHA's failure. During the Reagan years, the agency was not a diligent protector of employee whistle-blowers. Since OSHA did not go to any special effort to inform employees of their Section 11(c) rights, many fired employees did not know that the OSH Act provided a remedy. In a General Accounting Office survey of OSHA inspectors, almost 80 percent said that fewer than half of all workers are knowledgeable about their rights.[25] Thus, the Government Accountability Project concluded that ''[m]ost [protected workers] are not even aware of their rights before the thirty day statute of limitations passes.''[26] If anything, OSHA investigators often seem more interested in the motives of complaining employees than in the subject matter of the complaints.

By far the most serious drawback of Section 11(c) from the employee's perspective is the fact that only OSHA may sue to challenge an adverse employment action. Section 11(c) establishes a procedure under which the employee must file a complaint with OSHA within 30 days after the alleged discrimination and OSHA must notify the employee of its determination within 90 days.[27] If OSHA decides to pursue the matter, it first attempts to reach a settlement with the employer. If this is unavailing, OSHA may ask a district court for relief, including an injunction or an order reinstating the employee with back pay.[28] The Act, however, does not require automatic reinstatement, and it does not specify a time limit within which OSHA must seek judicial relief.[29] Section 11(c) does not allow the employee to sue the employer if the agency does not take action within the prescribed time period or if the employee is dissatisfied with the action that the agency does take. The courts have uniformly held that the OSH Act does not give rise to an implied private right of action on the part of employees for damages or other relief.[30] Worst of all, some courts have held that the OSH Act's antidiscrimination process preempts any action for relief that an employee might seek under state common law.[31]

The courageous worker who files a Section 11(c) complaint faces a number of hurdles. In most cases the employee does not file the complaint until after the employment relationship has ended and he or she is out of work. Since there is no provision in the OSH Act for immediate reinstatement pending OSHA's investigation of the complaint, all delay works to the advantage of the employer.

Since there are no deadlines for bringing the case to trial, once OSHA has decided that a claim is meritorious,[32] the employee may well be out of a job for years while the case is being litigated.

Moreover, the probability that OSHA will take the case is quite low. According to a General Accounting Office breakdown of the 3,600 complaints filed in fiscal year 1989, 31 percent were dismissed by OSHA out of hand, 38 percent failed initial screening, 15 percent were withdrawn by the complainant, and only 16 percent were determined to be meritorious.[33] Employee representatives believe that OSHA often unjustifiably terminates its investigation after only cursory attempts to obtain the facts. A 1987 investigation of 249 OSHA case files obtained from OSHA under the Freedom of Information Act by the Wisconsin Council on Occupational Safety and Health tends to bear this out. The report found "overwhelming evidence that OSHA not only fails to take worker discrimination complaints seriously, it seems to do everything possible to discourage and deter workers from pursuing such complaints at all."[34] The report found little evidence that OSHA was willing to spend time tracking down witnesses or otherwise investigating the facts underlying the complaint, preferring instead to rely upon the complaining employee to come up with the necessary evidence to support the claim. The report concluded that some OSHA investigators "appeared to view their role as that of protector of the status quo, and view[ed] workers concerned about on-the-job hazards as nuisances or troublemakers."[35] Finding that workers received reinstatement and back pay in only 6 percent of the cases it examined, the report concluded that the key factors in the successful cases "were a strong union and an intense personal determination not to give up."[36]

In some cases, OSHA finds itself in an institutional conflict of interest. OSHA may terminate an investigation because the information that the complaining employee uncovered cast doubt on the quality of previous OSHA inspections. For example, when a neurosurgical nurse complained to OSHA that she believed her twin infants died because of her long-term exposure to nitrous oxide in the hospital's operating room, the agency initially botched the investigation by showing up unprepared to take air samples. When the investigator returned the next day with sampling equipment, the hospital staff had spent the previous night attempting to patch up the leaking equipment. A later inspection found that waste gas levels were ten times higher than those recommended by the National Institute of Occupational Health and Safety (NIOSH). After the complaining nurse was forced to take a leave of absence for "dress code violations," the OSHA investigator assigned to the case concluded that the nurse had been the victim of unlawful discrimination. The head of the OSHA regional office, however, decided that the matter should not be referred to the regional solicitor for litigation. An attorney in the regional solicitor's office who had been assigned to review the case later testified that he had concluded that the forced leave was "only a pretext to rid the hospital of its most active safety and health advocate" and that he thought the case was worth pursuing. The attorney believed that the regional

OSHA had decided not to pursue the 11(c) complaint because it might bring to public attention OSHA's incompetent handling of the initial investigation.[37]

The rare employee who pursues the process to completion is entitled to injunctive relief and reinstatement with back pay. Injunctive relief will seldom make the employee whole. Employers can find many subtle ways to ensure that "disloyal" employees suffer, including harassment on the job, lower job evaluations, and blackballing employees who apply for promotions or for jobs with other employers.[38] Even reinstatement with back pay does not offer complete relief for the emotional trauma that necessarily accompanies the loss of a job, the loss of health insurance and pension benefits, and the sometimes humiliating attempts to overcome the "disloyalty" stigma that employers often attach to one who has filed a Section 11(c) complaint. The OSH Act does not explicitly allow for consequential damages, such as pain and suffering, even though such damages are typically available in common law contexts in which one person has wronged another.[39]

Under OSHA's regulations, protected activity need not be the sole reason for taking action against the employer. As long as it was a "substantial reason" for the employer's action, or if the action would not have taken place "but for" the protected activity, Section 11(c)(1) provides a remedy.[40] The burden of proof, however, remains on OSHA to make these showings. OSHA also has the burden of demonstrating that the employee's action was taken in "good faith."[41] Once OSHA has made these prima facie showings, the employer may still prevail if it demonstrates to the satisfaction of the court that "it would have reached the same decision even in the absence of the protected conduct."[42]

In the final analysis, a strong antiretaliation program is critical if OSHA is to have any significant impact in the real world. The Supreme Court has held that OSHA may not normally inspect a plant without a warrant based on "administrative probable cause" or issued pursuant to a neutral selection process.[43] Without brave employees who are willing to bring violations to OSHA's attention, the agency's enforcement efforts would be seriously jeopardized.[44]

On April 10, 1989, President Bush signed the Whistleblower Protection Act of 1989, which makes universal antiretaliation protections available to federal employees who blow the whistle on waste and fraud in the federal government.[45] Although the administration did not support similar legislation to protect private-sector whistle-blowers,[46] the need for greater protections is becoming increasingly apparent. For example, 26 percent of the OSHA inspectors questioned in a recent General Accounting Office survey said that workers receive little or no protection when they report violations to OSHA.[47] Sensing the message that Section 11(c)'s protective shield is not effectively available to them, workers are beginning to complain less about unsafe workplaces. As the states become increasingly active in the area of private-sector whistle-blower protection, however, employers may begin to press the federal government to enact omnibus legislation preempting local laws.

The most significant disadvantage of the current arrangement, from the employee's perspective, is that OSHA is in complete control of the process. If OSHA declines to prosecute a case, the employee is without a remedy, because there is no private right of action for wrongful termination or discrimination under the OSH Act. The employee's fate should not rest entirely in the hands of overworked bureaucrats in the Department of Labor, nor should it hinge on the judgment of an OSHA official who may indirectly be responsible (through negligence or neglect) for the condition about which the employee has complained.

Congress could make the OSH Act's antiretaliation protections considerably stronger by empowering employees to sue in court to enforce Section 11(c)'s nondiscrimination commands. Congress could require that the employee exhaust administrative remedies within the Department of Labor before filing suit, but the employee should have the autonomy to enforce Section 11(c) if OSHA determines that the claim is not worth pursuing. Congress has given civil service employees the power to bring their own claims in court under the Whistleblower Protection Act of 1989.[48] There is no good reason why employees in the private sector should not have the same protection. In addition, Congress could add to existing protections by allowing the courts in proper cases to provide full relief to discharged employees, including immediate reinstatement and consequential damages for emotional suffering. Congress has not seen fit to criminalize employer retaliation against employees who exercise their statutory rights, despite the fact that this is clearly antisocial conduct that should be punished. Allowing employees to recover consequential damages should provide an added incentive for employers to comply with the OSH Act's antiretaliation requirements. Allowing employees to recover punitive damages in cases of egregious employer conduct could provide an even stronger incentive.

Employers have objected that these changes will allow employees to hassle employers with frivolous suits and to abuse the process for unrelated purposes.[49] If Congress finds this to be a serious problem, it could empower the courts to order sanctions, such as paying court costs and attorney fees, against employees (and their attorneys) who brought frivolous suits. Congress should probably allow the system to work for a time before implementing this potentially unnecessary remedy, however, because it would no doubt have a chilling effect on employees' exercise of their rights.

LABOR-MANAGEMENT COMMITTEES

Many labor leaders and employers have become convinced that workplace health and safety could be substantially improved in a somewhat less adversarial fashion by creating labor-management committees for individual facilities and empowering the committees to make decisions about safety and health in the workplace. The idea of joint labor-management health and safety committees is not especially new. Many plants have had such committees for decades, and there are a wide variety of institutional options among the committees that already exist. Under the right conditions, joint health and safety committees have a great potential to enhance workers health and safety, but they must first overcome some critical hurdles.

The joint committee idea arose out of the collective bargaining process in unionized plants. In 1951 approximately 15 percent of the collective bargaining agreements in the manufacturing sector and 11 percent of the agreements in the nonmanufacturing sector provided for joint health and safety committees. The proportions were roughly the same in 1971. But by 1986, 62 percent in the manufacturing sector and 27 percent in the nonmanufacturing sector provided for joint committees.[50] In mid-1988, OSHA published an advance notice of proposed rulemaking soliciting comments on whether it should develop guidelines on joint programs in all workplaces,[51] but nothing came of the effort.

Most labor-management committees limit their functions to reviewing, commenting, and making recommendations,[52] and they play no role in investigating accidents and resolving disputes.[53] Very few have the power to hire and fire the company's safety personnel, although most can make their opinions known to management.[54] Still fewer committees have the power to shut down machinery or unsafe processes. An in-depth 1989 study of joint health and safety committees by the Department of Labor's Bureau of Labor-Management Relations and Co-operative Programs concluded that joint committees "are more often forums for discussion and mechanisms to promote understanding and attitude change than mechanisms for actual change."[55]

By contrast, in Sweden, "joint consultation has evolved into joint decision-making, with a true redistribution of workplace power."[56] In that country, the committee model obtains in most workplaces, and workers on the committees must be trained at the expense of a fund financed by a 0.1 percent payroll tax on all employers.[57] Labor-management committees in Sweden generally have the power to do the following:

1. Veto any plans for new machines, materials, or work processes for health and safety reasons;

2. Decide how to spend the company health and safety budget, which is generally negotiated through local bargaining;

3. Approve the selection and direct the work of the company doctor, nurse, safety engineer, or industrial hygienist;

4. Review all corporate medical records, monitoring results, and other information on hazards;

5. Shut down dangerous operations until the hazards can be corrected. Individual workers also have that right; and

6. Decide how much time they need to do their safety committee work, all of which must be paid for by the company.[58]

Although the joint committees address most workplace health and safety issues, worker training in Sweden is conducted by the unions, using the materials that they have developed.[59]

The Swedish model has evolved in the context of a legal regime in which all workers "have a clear, unencumbered right to refuse unsafe work."[60] Since workers in the United States have no similar right, there are only a few examples of successful implementation of the joint committee model in this country. One example is the contract between the Electronic and Electric Workers and General Electric. It establishes a safety and health committee, and worker representatives receive full pay for the one day per week that they devote to committee matters. The parties attempted to divorce the committee from union-management politics by prohibiting stewards and members of the union's executive committee from becoming committee members. The committee may investigate an allegedly hazardous work site immediately and call for a meeting with management within 24 hours. Although there is no specific language empowering the committee to shut down an unsafe operation, the company will generally do so at the committee's recommendation. The employee who is the committee's chairman believes that "GE has grown to respect us probably because of our continuity and because our safety and health committee only handles safety and health."[61]

The joint committee approach has enormous potential for effectively dealing with workplace safety problems.[62] Joint committees facilitate vital safety-related communication between workers and management.[63] Joint committees in individual plants can address safety hazards at the point of production much more effectively than intermittent OSHA inspections performed by an overworked inspectorate.[64] Since the workplace safety problem stems to some extent from the fact that workplaces are inadequately designed to facilitate the interaction between the worker and the production technology, worker input in workplace design decisions through joint committees could be especially useful.[65] A study conducted by the American Center for the Quality of Work concluded that in instances where a committee was working effectively, "dramatic improvements" in safety and health were seen over a two-to-three-year period.[66]

Despite these considerable advantages, joint committees do have several drawbacks, not all of which are easily remedied. The joint committee's potential for addressing health issues is probably quite limited, because individual committees are unlikely to have the expertise necessary to evaluate the hazards posed by exposure to toxic chemicals. A joint committee with real power represents a threat to "traditional management prerogatives,"[67] and some managers are dubious about the ability of workers to make worthwhile contributions to workplace safety.[68] Few companies are likely to give joint committees the power to mandate the installation of expensive engineering controls.[69] It may also be true for practical reasons that the joint committee approach is not well suited to some employment contexts, such as construction sites at which there may be multiple employers and unions.

One obvious problem with the joint committee idea is that the management representatives on the committee will generally possess a great deal more formal education and expertise in health and safety matters than the employee representatives. For example, the typical laborer or production line employee is not likely to have the expertise required to evaluate technical literature.[70] The line employees do, however, have a great deal of expertise about how things work in the real world, and this may more than offset their lack of formal education. To the extent that education is a necessity, employees can receive training at numerous OSHA- and NIOSH-sponsored training courses, if the resources are available to support such training.[71] Employers should be willing to pay for training and to compensate employees during the training process.[72]

Some skeptical union representatives have argued that joint committees are "paper tigers" that merely provide another vehicle for employers to impose their will upon employees.[73] This skepticism turned to cynicism in the early 1980s when the Reagan OSHA offered employers reduced general schedule inspections as a quid pro quo for establishing joint committees and maintaining good safety records.[74] Many union officials are opposed in principle to nonadversarial institutional entities with the power to make decisions affecting the workplace.[75] While it is undoubtedly true that employer representatives have tended to dominate joint committees in the past,[76] fears of employer dominance of joint committee deliberations can be alleviated to a limited degree by giving labor and management equal representation on the committee and rotating the chairmanship.[77]

Some commentators have even suggested that the joint committee movement has a strongly antidemocratic strain and is really part of a "neocorporatist" approach to addressing workplace safety and health.[78] One commentator argues that "the team concept has become a metaphor for the union's philosophy that says we are moving toward a classless society in which the interests of the working class and those of big business are becoming similar lately."[79] It is difficult to see, however, how empowering workers to have a say in workplace health and safety is antidemocratic, unless the process of choosing employee representatives to the committee is not participatory. It is also difficult to square with this position the fact that rank-and-file workers often exert pressure on union leaders to enter into such cooperative arrangements.[80]

Another serious union concern about joint committees is the fact that participation may expose the unions to liability for employee injuries.[81] Because workers' compensation is notoriously inadequate for injured workers, they and their attorneys are always on the lookout for potential defendants in workplace accidents. Several employees have sued their unions for negligence in failing to use their power on joint committees to remedy workplace conditions that lead to injuries.[82] In at least one case, however, a court of appeals has held that such suits are preempted by the LMRA.[83] In some cases, management requires the union's agreement to accept a share of liability as a precondition to its participation.[84] So long as the committees possess the discretion that is necessary to their proper operation, members of the committees and the entities that sponsor them must face the possibility of liability for negligence.[85] Yet if the labor representatives assume a docile advisory role, the committee will lose its capacity to effect real change in the workplace.

The antidote to union fears about tort liability for decisions made by joint committees is legislation freeing members of the committees from individual liability for discretionary decisions made by the committees. This might still leave the unions themselves vulnerable, insofar as their officers participated on the committees. Yet it may be better for the committees if union officers were discouraged from participating on the committees. The committees are likely to be more successful if they are removed from the adversarial collective bargaining process.

As with other worker empowerment proposals, joint committees could be abused to seek ends unrelated to safety and health. Some managers express concern that unions will use the process to strengthen their position in collective bargaining negotiations.[86] Interestingly, some union representatives are afraid that the process will be abused by management to weaken the position of unions with the workers or to keep unions out of nonunionized workplaces.[87]

The question of whether joint committees should be mandated by law is a close one. The Department of Labor report noted that joint health and safety committees ''are fragile political entities that fail as often as they succeed,'' and they are likely to succeed ''only when they have the full support and commitment of top management, union leaders, and rank and file workers.''[88] Perhaps the most important institutional barrier to joint committees is the traditional adversarial relationship between labor and management in this country.[89] Without a sense of mutual trust and the shared goal of improving workplace health and safety, the committee cannot function. Both sides must leave their traditional antagonisms outside the committee room. The joint committee is not the place for hidden agendas and jockeying for position in other battles. Worker health and safety are far too serious for this sort of strategic behavior. For this reason, the joint committee must be divorced entirely from the collective bargaining process in unionized workplaces.[90]

Although labor-management committees of an advisory nature can be useful in increasing employee consciousness about health and safety and in enhancing employer sensitivity to employee health and safety concerns, they are likely to have little real impact on safety and health if they do not have real power. Joint committees should have the authority to resolve health and safety disputes in nonunionized workplaces. In unionized workplaces, employees should be required to seek relief from the committee before proceeding with the grievance process specified in the collective bargaining agreement. Joint committees should also have the unreviewable power to shut down production lines upon determining that they present an imminent threat to the health or safety of workers.[91] In addition, joint committees will function most effectively if they are composed of equal numbers of labor and management representatives, if labor representatives receive health and safety training and are compensated for their time in training and in meetings, if the committees have the power to hire outside consultants when necessary, if all committee members have full access to all relevant corporate information, and if the committees are allowed fully to investigate all accidents and safety complaints.[92]

CONCLUSION

Two broad approaches are available for empowering workers to play a larger role in maintaining safety and health in the workplace. The adversarial approach empowers workers by giving them rights and protecting them from retaliation for the exercise of those rights. The focus is on the worker activities, such as lodging an OSHA complaint, filing a citizen enforcement action, or refusing to work, that can force employers to do something about unsafe workplaces. The cooperative approach empowers workers by allowing their representatives to sit and vote on health and safety committees with the power to address health and safety problems and to shut down operations if the problems are not adequately addressed. Both approaches require management to surrender some of its jealously protected prerogatives, and both approaches require employees to take health and safety matters seriously.

The cooperative approach has much to recommend it, because it is much less disruptive when employees and employer representatives are able to develop a spirit of mutual trust and cooperation. Yet although the cooperative approach has been successfully implemented in Sweden and in some American workplaces, health and safety committees with real power are very rare in the United States. Indeed, in order to provide management with sufficient incentives to acquiesce in the cooperative approach, it may ultimately be necessary to implement a fairly vigorous version of the adversarial approach.

NOTES

1. U.S. Congress, House Committee on Education and Labor, Subcommittee on Labor-Management Relations, *Hearings on H.R. 3368, Whistleblower Protection Act*, 101st Cong., 1st sess., 1989, 43 (testimony of Donna Bazemore, worker at a North Carolina poultry plant). (Hereafter cited as House, *Hearings on H.R. 3368*).

2. H.R. 1309, 99th Cong., 1st sess., 1985.

3. Sar A. Levitan, Peter E. Carlson, and Isaac Shapiro, *Protecting American Workers: An Assessment of Government Programs* (Washington, D.C.: Bureau of National Affairs, 1986), 226.

4. *Perry* v. *Sindermann*, 408 U.S. 593 (1972).

5. Levitan et al., *Protecting Workers*, 228.

6. Ibid., 232.

7. National Labor Relations Act § 8(a)(1), 29 U.S.C. § 158(a)(1) (1988); *National Labor Relations Board* v. *Washington Aluminum Co.*, 370 U.S. 9 (1962). See generally Mark Rothstein, *Occupational Safety and Health Law*, 3rd ed. (St. Paul, Minn.: West Publishing, 1990), 468–69. James C. Robinson, *Toil and Toxics: Workplace Struggles*

and Political Strategies for Occupational Health (Berkeley: University of California Press, 1991): 47–51; Cynthia L. Estlund, "What Do Workers Want? Employee Interests, Public Interests, and Freedom of Expression Under the National Labor Relations Act," *University of Pennsylvania Law Review* 140 (1991): 921.

8. Rothstein, *Occupational Safety*, 468–69.

9. Ibid.

10. Nicholas A. Ashford and Chistina Ayers, "Changes and Opportunities in the Environment for Technology Bargaining," *Notre Dame Law Review* 62 (1987): 810; Larry C. Backer, "Refusals of Hazardous Work Assignments: A Proposal for a Uniform Standard," *Columbia Law Review* 81 (1981): 550.

11. Bureau of the Census, *Statistical Abstract of the United States 1991* (Washington, D.C.: United States Government Printing Office, 1991), 425, table 697.

12. *Meyers Industries*, 268 N.L.R.B. 493 (1984), *remanded sub nom. Prill* v. *NLRB*, 755 F.2d 941 (D.C. Cir. 1985), *reaffirmed* 281 N.L.R.B. 882, *enf'd sub nom. Prill* v. *NLRB*, 835 F.2d 1481 (D.C. Cir. 1987), 86.

13. Zachary Fasman, "Labor Board Adopts Conservative View on Employee Rights," *Legal Times*, 10 Nov. 1986, 12.

14. Labor Management Relations Act of 1974, § 502, 29 U.S.C. § 143 (1988).

15. Backer, "Refusals," 553–54.

16. *Gateway Coal Co.* v. *United Mineworkers*, 414 U.S. 368, 387 (1974); Rothstein, *Occupational Safety*, 485.

17. Rothstein, *Occupational Safety*, 485; Backer, "Refusals," 556–57.

18. 29 C.F.R. 1977.12(b)(2) (1991).

19. 445 U.S. 1 (1980).

20. Benjamin Mintz, "Occupational Safety and Health: The Federal Regulatory Program—A History," in *Fundamentals of Industrial Hygiene*, 3rd ed., ed. Barbara A. Plog (Washington, D.C.: National Safety Council, 1988), 712.

21. House, *Hearings on H.R. 3368*, 295.

22. *BNA Occupational Safety and Health Reporter* 18 (31 May 1989): 2131.

23. Backer, "Refusals," 566.

24. 29 U.S.C. § 660(c)(1) (1988).

25. House, *Hearings on H.R. 3368*, 122.

26. Ibid., 225–26.

27. 29 C.F.R. 1977.15(d)(3) (1991); *Donovan* v. *Square D. Company*, 709 F.2d 335 (5th Cir. 1983); Rothstein, *Occupational Safety*, 243.

28. 29 U.S.C. § 660(c)(2) (1988). See Rothstein, *Occupational Safety*, 244.

29. *Marshall* v. *Intermountain Electric Co., Inc.*, 614 F.2d 260 (10th Cir. 1980); Rothstein, *Occupational Safety*, 209.

30. *George* v. *Aztec Rental Center, Inc.*, 763 F.2d 184 (5th Cir. 1985); *Taylor* v. *Brighton*, 616 F.2d 256 (65h Cir. 1980); Rothstein, *Occupational Safety*, 244–45; Mintz, "A History," 712.

31. *Braun* v. *Kelsey-Hayes Co.*, 635 F. Supp. 75 (E.D. Pa. 1986); cf. *Rayner* v. *Smirl*, 873 F.2d 60 (4th Cir. 1989) (state whistle-blower protection statute preempted by the Federal Railroad Safety Act).

32. Ibid.

33. House, *Hearings on H.R. 3368*, 124.

34. Joan M. McManus, "The Deadly Dilemma When OSHA Fails to Protect the Workers' Right to a Workplace Free of Health and Safety Hazards," in U.S. Congress,

Senate Committee on Labor and Human Resources, *Hearings on Oversight of the Occupational Safety and Health Administration*, 100th Cong., 2d sess., S. Hrg. 100–719, 1988, 624 (hereafter cited as Senate, *Oversight Hearings of 1988*).

35. Ibid.

36. Ibid.

37. *BNA Occupational Safety and Health Reporter* 13 (17 Nov. 1983): 664.

38. House, *Hearings on H.R. 3368*, 223–24.

39. *Prosser and Keeton on the Law of Torts*, 5th ed., ed. W. Page Keeton, Dan B. Dobbs, Robert E. Keeton, and David G. Owen (St. Paul, Minn.: West, 1984), 348, 359; Loraine M. deJong, "Awards for Future Noneconomic Damages Such as Pain and Suffering Should Not Be Reduced to Reflect Their Present Value," *Rutgers Law Journal* 18 (Summer 1988): 1119.

40. Rothstein, *Occupational Safety*, 237–40.

41. Ibid.

42. Ibid.; *Donovan* v. *Diplomat Envelope Corp.*, 587 F. Supp. 1417 (E.D.N.Y. 1984), *aff'd*, 760 F.2d 253 (2nd Cir. 1985).

43. *Marshall* v. *Barlow's, Inc.*, 436 U.S. 307 (1977).

44. House, *Hearings on H.R. 3368*, 225–26.

45. Whistleblower Protection Act of 1989, 5 U.S.C.A. §§ 1201, 1211–22, 3352, 7701 (West Supp. 1991).

46. House, *Hearings on H.R. 3368*, 66.

47. Ibid.

48. Whistleblower Protection Act of 1989, 5 U.S.C.A. § 1221 (h)(1) (West Supp. 1991).

49. House, *Hearings on H.R. 3368*, 14–15, 154, 297–98.

50. Department of Labor, Bureau of Labor-Management Relations and Cooperative Programs, *The Role of Labor-Management Committees in Safeguarding Worker Safety and Health*, BLMR 121 (Washington, D.C.: United States Government Printing Office, 1989), 3, table 1.

51. 53 *Fed. Reg.* 26,790 (1988).

52. Department of Labor, *Labor-Management Committees*, 29.

53. Ibid., 11, 30.

54. Ibid., 29.

55. Ibid., 30. See also Robinson, *Toil and Toxics*, 56–58.

56. Department of Labor, *Labor-Management Committees*, 32; Steven Kelman, *Regulating America, Regulating Sweden: A Comparative Study of Occupational Safety and Health Policy* (Cambridge, Mass.: MIT Press, 1981).

57. Department of Labor, *Labor-Management Committees*, 32.

58. Ibid.

59. Ibid., 38.

60. Ibid., 32; American Labor Education Center, "Labor-Management Health and Safety Committees in Sweden, West Germany, Austria, and Saskatchewan, Canada," draft prepared for OSHA, June 1980, 4.

61. *BNA Occupational Safety and Health Reporter* 17 (11 May 1988): 1824.

62. Robinson, *Toil and Toxics*, ch. 8.

63. Department of Labor, *Labor-Management Committees*, 29.

64. *BNA Occupational Safety and Health Reporter* 18 (23 May 1989): 2131.

65. Ibid. (8 June 1988): 30.

66. Ibid. 14 (7 June 1984): 8.

67. Ibid., 29.

68. Ibid., 35.

69. Department of Labor, *Labor-Management Committees*, 38.

70. Senate, *Oversight Hearings of 1988*, 491 (statement of Dr. Imogen Sevin Rodgers, Office of Risk Assessment, Health Standards Program, OSHA).

71. Ibid., 492.

72. *BNA Occupational Safety and Health Reporter* 14 (7 June 1984): 8; ibid. 18 (23 May 1989): 2131.

73. Department of Labor, *Labor-Management Committees*, 1.

74. Ibid., 31.

75. Ray Marshall, *Unheard Voices: Labor and Economic Policy in a Competitive World* (New York: Basic Books, 1987), 165.

76. Department of Labor, *Labor-Management Committees*, 5.

77. Ibid., 35–36.

78. Charles Noble, *Liberalism at Work: The Rise and Fall of OSHA* (Philadelphia: Temple University Press, 1986), 224–29.

79. Eric Mann, "Business Forum: Reorganizing the Factory; Work Teams Muffle Labor's Voice," *New York Times*, 11 June 1989, F2, col. 2.

80. Marshall, *Unheard Voices*, 167.

81. Department of Labor, *Labor-Management Committees*, 29.

82. *Occupational Safety and Health Reporter* 11 (4 Feb. 1982): 725.

83. *Clarke* v. *Laborers' International Union of North America, AFL-CIO*, 916 F.2d 1539 (11th Cir. 1990).

84. Department of Labor, *Labor-Management Committees*, 35.

85. *BNA Occupational Safety and Health Reporter* 14 (7 June 1984): 8; memorandum to IUD Executive Council from Howard Samuel, dated 22 Jan. 1982, in ibid. 11 (4 Feb. 1982): 726.

86. Department of Labor, *Labor-Management Committees*, 35.

87. Ibid.

88. Ibid., 1.

89. Ibid., 35.

90. Ibid., 36.

91. Ibid., 11.

92. Ibid., 6–7, 9–10.

Selected Bibliography

BOOKS AND REPORTS

Ashford, Nicholas. *Crisis in the Workplace*. Cambridge, Mass.: MIT Press, 1976.

Bacow, Lawrence. *Bargaining for Job Safety and Health*. Cambridge, Mass.: MIT Press, 1980.

Barth, Peter. *Workers Compensation and Work-Related Injuries*. Cambridge, Mass.: MIT Press, 1980.

Berman, Daniel. M. *Death on the Job: Occupational Health and Safety Struggles in the United States*. New York: Monthly Review Press, 1978.

Bollier, David, and Joan Claybrook. *Freedom from Harm: The Civilizing Influence of Health, Safety, and Environmental Regulation*. Washington, D.C.: Public Citizen, 1986.

Claybrook, Joan. *Retreat from Safety: Reagan's Attack on America's Health*. New York: Pantheon, 1984.

Greenwood, Ted. *Knowledge and Discretion in Government Regulation*. New York: Praeger, 1984.

Hadden, Susan. *Read the Label: Reducing Risk by Providing Information*. Boulder, Colo.: Westview Press, 1986.

Hensler, Deborah, et al. *Compensation for Accidental Injuries in the United States*. Santa Monica, Calif.: Rand Institute, 1991.

Judkins, Bennett. *We Offer Ourselves as Evidence: Toward Workers' Control of Occupational Health*. Westport, Conn.: Greenwood Press, 1986.

Kelman, Steven. *Making Public Policy: A Hopeful View of American Government*. New York: Basic Books, 1987.

Levitan, Sar, Peter Carlson, and Isaac Shapiro. *Protecting American Workers: An Assessment of Government Programs*. Washington, D.C.: Bureau of National Affairs, 1986.

Marshall, Ray. *Unheard Voices: Labor and Economic Policy in a Competitive World*. New York: Basic Books, 1987.

McGarity, Thomas O. *Reinventing Rationality: The Role of Regulatory Analysis in the Federal Bureaucracy.* Cambridge: Cambridge University Press, 1991.

Mendeloff, John. *Regulating Safety: An Economic and Political Analysis of Occupational Safety and Health Policy.* Cambridge, Mass.: MIT Press, 1979.

Mintz, Benjamin W. *OSHA: History, Law, and Policy.* Washington, D.C.: Bureau of National Affairs, 1984.

Moore, Michael, and W. Kip Viscusi. *Compensation Mechanisms for Job Risks: Wages, Workers Compensation, and Product Liability.* Princeton: Princeton University Press, 1990.

National Academy of Sciences, National Research Council. *Counting Illnesses and Injuries in the Workplace: Proposals for a Better System.* Washington, D.C.: National Academy of Sciences Press, 1987.

National Cancer Institute, National Institute of Environmental Health Sciences, and National Institute for Occupational Safety and Health. *Estimates of the Fraction of Cancer in the United States Related to Occupational Factors.* Washington, D.C.: United States Government Printing Office, 1978.

National Safe Workplace Institute. *Basic Information on Workplace Safety & Health in the United States.* Chicago: The Institute, n.d.

————. *Beyond Neglect: The Problem of Occupational Disease in the U.S.—Labor Day '90 Report.* Chicago: The Institute, 1990.

————. *Failed Opportunities: The Decline—U.S. Job Safety in the 1980s.* Chicago: The Institute, 1988.

————. *The Rising Wave: Death and Injury Among High Risk Workers in the 1980s.* Chicago: The Institute, 1987.

————. *Safer Work: Job Safety and Health Challenges for the Next President and Congress.* Chicago: The Institute, 1988.

Nelkin, Dorothy, and Michael Brown. *Workers at Risk: Voices from the Workplace.* Chicago: University of Chicago Press, 1984.

Noble, Charles. *Liberalism at Work: The Rise and Fall of OSHA.* Philadelphia: Temple University Press, 1986.

Page, Joseph O., and Mary-Win O'Brien. *Bitter Wages: Ralph Nader's Study Group Report on Disease and Injury on the Job.* New York: Grossman, 1973.

The President's Report on Occupational Safety and Health. Washington, D.C.: United States Government Printing Office, 1980.

Robinson, James C. *Toil and Toxics: Workplace Struggles and Political Strategies for Occupational Health.* Berkeley: University of California Press, 1991.

Rosner, David, and Gerald Markowitz. *Dying for Work: Workers' Safety and Health in Twentieth-Century America.* Bloomington: Indiana University Press, 1987.

Rothstein, Mark. *Occupational Safety and Health Law,* 3rd ed. St. Paul, Minn.: West Publishing, 1990.

Sierra Club. *Poisons on the Job: The Reagan Administration and American Workers.* San Francisco: Sierra Club Books, 1982.

Smith, Robert. *The Occupational Safety and Health Act: Its Goals and Achievements.* Washington, D.C.: American Enterprise Institute, 1976.

Sunstein, Cass. *After the Rights Revolution: Reconceiving the Regulatory State.* Cambridge, Mass.: Harvard University Press, 1990.

Triano, Christine, and Nancy Watzman. *All the Vice President's Men: How the Quayle Council on Competitiveness Secretly Undermines Health, Safety, and Environ-*

mental Regulation. Washington, D.C.: Public Citizen Congress Watch and OMB Watch, 1991.

U.S. Congress, House Committee on Government Operations, Subcommittee on Manpower and Housing, *Occupational Illness Data Collection: Fragmented, Unreliable, and Seventy Years Behind: Communicable Disease Surveillance*. 98th Cong., 2d sess., 1984, H.Rep. no. 98–1144.

U.S. Congress, Office of Technology Assessment, *Identifying and Regulating Carcinogens*. Washington, D.C.: United States Government Printing Office, 1987.

————. *Occupational Safety and Health: Assuring Accuracy in Employer Injury and Illness Records*. Washington, D.C.: United States Government Printing Office, 1988.

————. *Preventing Illnesses and Injury in the Workplace*. Washington, D.C.: United States Government Printing Office, 1985.

U.S. Congress, Senate Committee on Labor and Human Resources. *Hearings on Oversight of the Occupational Safety and Health Administration*. 100th Congress, 2d sess., S.Hrg. 100–719, 1988.

Viscusi, W. Kip. *Employment Hazards: An Investigation of Market Performance*. Cambridge, Mass.: Harvard University Press, 1979.

————. *Risk by Choice: Regulating Health and Safety in the Workplace*. Cambridge, Mass: Harvard University Press, 1983.

Wilson, Graham K. *The Politics of Safety and Health: Occupational Safety and Health in the United States and Britain*. Oxford: Clarendon Press, 1985.

Worrall, John. *Safety and the Workforce: Incentives and Disincentives in Workers Compensation*. Ithaca, N.Y.: ILR Press, 1985.

ARTICLES

Ashford, Nicholas, A. "The Role of Advisory Committees in Resolving Regulatory Issues Involving Science and Technology: Experience from OSHA and EPA." In *Law and Science in Collaboration: Resolving Regulatory Issues of Science and Technology*, ed. J. Daniel Nyhart and Milton M. Carrow. Lexington, Mass.: Lexington Books, 1983.

Bartel, Ann, and Lacy Thomas. "Direct and Indirect Effects of Regulation: A New Look at OSHA's Impact." *Journal of Law and Economics* 28 (1985): 1.

Boyer, Barry, and Erroll Miedinger. "Privatizing Regulatory Enforcement: A Preliminary Assessment of Citizen Suits Under Federal Environmental Laws." *Buffalo Law Review* 34 (1985): 833.

Bruff, Harold. "Presidential Power and Administrative Rulemaking." *Yale Law Review* 88 (1979): 451.

DeMuth, Christopher, and Douglas Ginsberg. "White House Review of Agency Rulemaking." *Harvard Law Review* 99 (1986): 1075.

Gaines, Sanford E. "Science, Politics, and the Management of Toxic Risks Through Law." *Jurimetrics Journal* 30 (1990): 271.

Graham, John D., and James W. Vaupel. "The Value of a Life: What Difference Does It Make?" In *What Role for Government? Lessons from Policy Research*, ed. Richard J. Zeckhauser and Derek Leebart. Durham, N.C.: Duke University Press, 1983.

Gray, Boyden. "Presidential Involvement in Informal Rulemaking." *Tulane Law Review* 56 (1982): 863.

Houck, Oliver. "President X and the New (Approved) Decisionmaking." *American University Law Review* 36 (1987): 535.

Kelman, Steven. "Cost Benefit Analysis and Environmental, Safety, and Health Regulation: Ethical and Philosophical Considerations." In *Cost-Benefit Analysis and Environmental Regulations: Politics, Ethics, and Methods*. ed. Daniel Swartzman, Richard A. Liroff, and Kevin G. Crooke. Washington, D.C.: Conservation Foundation, 1982.

———. "Occupational Safety and Health Administration." In *The Politics of Regulation* ed. James Q. Wilson. New York: Basic Books, 1980.

Landrigan, Phillip. "The Recognition and Control of Occupational Disease." *Journal of the American Medical Association 266* (Aug. 1991): 676.

Latin, Howard A. "The 'Significance' of Toxic Health Risks: An Essay on Legal Decisionmaking Under Uncertainty." *Ecology Law Quarterly* 10 (1982): 339.

Levin, Michael. "Politics and Polarity: The Limits of OSHA Reform." *Regulation* 3 (Nov./Dec. 1979): 33.

McCaffery, David. "An Assessment of OSHA's Recent Effects on Injury Rates." *Journal of Human Resources* 18 (1983): 144.

McGarity, Thomas O. "Media Quality, Technology and Cost-Benefit Balancing Strategies for Health and Environmental Regulation." *Law and Contemporary Problems* 46 (Summer 1983): 159.

———. "OSHA's Generic Carcinogen Policy: Rulemaking Under Scientific and Legal Uncertainty." In *Law and Science in Collaboration: Resolving Regulatory Issues of Science and Technology*, ed. J. Daniel Nyhart and Milton M. Carrow. Lexington, Mass.: Lexington Books, 1983.

———. "Regulatory Analysis and Regulatory Reform." *Texas Law Review* 65 (1987): 1243.

———. "Substantive and Procedural Discretion in Administrative Resolution of Science Policy Questions: Regulating Carcinogens in EPA and OSHA." *Georgetown Law Journal* 67 (1979): 729.

McGarity, Thomas O., and Sidney Shapiro. "The Trade Secret Status of Health and Safety Testing Information: Reforming Agency Disclosure Policies." *Harvard Law Review* 93 (1980): 837.

Mintz, Benjamin W. "Disorder and Early Sorrow in the OSHA Program." *American Industrial Hygiene Association Journal* 40 (1989): 99.

———. "Occupational Safety and Health: The Federal Regulatory Program—A History." In *Fundamentals of Industrial Hygiene*, 3rd ed., ed. Barbara A. Plog. Washington, D.C.: National Safety Council, 1988.

Morrison, Alan. "OMB Interference with Agency Rulemaking: The Wrong Way to Write a Regulation." *Harvard Law Review* 99 (1986): 1059.

Nichols, Albert, and Richard Zeckhauser. "OSHA After a Decade: A Time for Reason." In *Case Studies in Regulation: Revolution and Reform*, ed. Leonard Weiss and Michael Klass. Boston: Little, Brown, 1981.

Olson, Eric D. "The Quiet Shift of Power: Office of Management and Budget Supervision of Environmental Protection Agency Rulemaking Under Executive Order 12291." *Virginia Journal of Natural Resource Law* 4 (1984): 1.

Percival, Robert A. "Checks Without Balance: Executive Oversight of the Environmental Protection Agency." *Law and Contemporary Problems* 54 (Autumn 1991): 127.

Pierce, Richard. "The Role of Constitutional and Political Theory in Administrative Law." *Texas Law Review* 64 (1985): 469.

Pierce, Richard, and Sidney Shapiro. "Political and Judicial Review of Agency Action." *Texas Law Review* 59 (1981): 1175.

Robinson, James C., and Dalton G. Paxman. "OSHA's Four Inconsistent Carcinogen Policies." *American Journal of Public Health* 81 (June 1991): 775.

———. "Technological, Economic, and Political Feasibility in OSHA's Air Contaminants Standard." *Journal of Health Politics, Policy and Law* 16 (1991): 1.

Robinson, James C., Dalton G. Paxman, and Stephen M. Rappaport. "Implications of OSHA's Reliance on TLVs in Developing the Air Contaminants Standard." *American Journal of Industrial Medicine* 19 (1991): 3.

Rothstein, Mark. "OSHA After Ten Years: A Review and Some Proposed Reforms." *Vanderbilt Law Review* 34 (1981): 71.

———. "Substantive and Procedural Obstacles to OSHA Rulemaking: Reproductive Hazards as an Example." *Boston College Environmental Affairs Law Review* 12 (1985): 627.

Schroeder, Elinor, and Sidney Shapiro. "Responses to Occupational Disease: The Role of Markets, Regulation, and Information." *Georgetown Law Journal* 72 (1984): 1231.

Shapiro, Sidney A., and Robert Glicksman. "Congress, the Supreme Court, and the Quiet Revolution in Administrative Law." *Duke Law Journal*, 1988, 819.

Shapiro, Sidney A., and Richard Levy. "Heightened Scrutiny of the Fourth Branch: Separation of Powers and the Requirement of Adequate Reasons for Agency Decisions." *Duke Law Journal*, 1987, 387.

Shapiro, Sidney A., and Thomas O. McGarity. "Reorienting OSHA: Regulatory Alternatives and Legislative Reform." *Yale Journal on Regulation* 6 (Winter 1989): 1.

Strauss, Peter, and Cass Sunstein. "The Role of the President and OMB in Informal Rulemaking." *Administrative Law Review* 38 (1986): 181.

Viscusi, W. Kip. "The Structure and Enforcement of Job Safety Regulations." *Law and Contemporary Problems* 49 (1986): 127.

Index

ABOUT THE AUTHORS

THOMAS O. McGARITY is Farish Professor of Law at the University of Texas in Austin. He is the author of *Reinventing Rationality* (1991).

SIDNEY A. SHAPIRO is Rounds Professor of Law at the University of Kansas in Lawrence. He is the author (with Joseph Tomain) of *Regulatory Law and Policy* (1992).

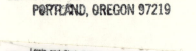